Media and Revolt

Protest, Culture and Society

General editors:

Kathrin Fahlenbrach, Institute for Media and Communication, University of Hamburg.

Martin Klimke, New York University Abu Dhabi.

Joachim Scharloth, Technische Universität Dresden, Germany.

Protest movements have been recognized as significant contributors to processes of political partici-pation and transformations of culture and value systems, as well as to the development of both a national and transnational civil society.

This series brings together the various innovative approaches to phenomena of social change, protest and dissent which have emerged in recent years, from an interdisciplinary perspective. It contextualizes social protest and cultures of dissent in larger political processes and socio-cultural transformations by examining the influence of historical trajectories and the response of various segments of society, political and legal institutions on a national and international level. In doing so, the series offers a more comprehensive and multi-dimensional view of historical and cultural change in the twentieth and twenty-first century.

Media and Revolt

Strategies and Performances from the 1960s to the Present

Edited by

Kathrin Fahlenbrach, Erling Sivertsen,
and Rolf Werenskjold

berghahn
NEW YORK · OXFORD
www.berghahnbooks.com

First published in 2014 by
Berghahn Books
www.berghahnbooks.com

Library of Congress Cataloging-in-Publication Data

Media and revolt : strategies and performances from the 1960s to the present /
edited by Kathrin Fahlenbrach, Erling Sivertsen, and Rolf Werenskjold.
        pages cm. — (Protest, culture and society ; v. 11)
    Includes bibliographical references and index.
    ISBN 978-0-85745-998-5 (hardback) — ISBN 978-1-78533-042-1
    (paperback) — ISBN 978-0-85745-999-2 (ebook)
    1. Radicalism in mass media. 2. Protest movements in mass media. 3. Mass
media—Political aspects—Europe—History—20th century. 4. Mass media—
Political aspects—Europe—History—21st century. 5. Mass media—Political
aspects—United States—History—20th century. 6. Mass media—Political
aspects—United States—History—21st century. I. Fahlenbrach, Kathrin
editor of compilation. II. Sivertsen, Erling editor of compilation.
III. Werenskjold, Rolf editor of compilation.
    P96.R322E87 2013
    659.2'93224—dc23
                                                              2013022203

British Library Cataloguing in Publication Data

A catalogue record for this book is available from the British Library

ISBN: 978-0-85745-998-5 hardback
ISBN: 978-1-78533-042-1 paperback
ISBN: 978-0-85745-999-2 ebook

Contents

Illustrations

Figures

Tables

Acknowledgments

We thank all the contributors for their collaboration on this book. A special thanks goes to Dean Sverre Liestøl, Lindsey Stokes, and Ramona Bäuml for supporting the editorial process.

We would like to dedicate this book to the memory of Stuart Hilwig, a wonderful scholar, colleague, and dear friend, from whose knowledge and expertise we all benefited enormously. He will be greatly missed.

Kathrin Fahlenbrach, Erling Sivertsen, and Rolf Werenskjold
Hamburg/Volda, December 2013

Introduction

Media and Protest Movements

Kathrin Fahlenbrach, Erling Sivertsen,
and Rolf Werenskjold

In his famous protest song "The Revolution Will Not Be Televised" (1969/70), Gil Scott-Heron made a strong contrast between the mass media and revolution: on the one hand, a passive consumerist culture that is dominated by television; on the other, protest and revolution on the streets of those who are marginalized in society and will never become visible in television culture. Like many other protesters around 1968, Scott-Heron proclaimed a general change of society, a revolution, as the only way of providing emancipation and equal rights for marginalized social groups. Television, being part and instrument of the preestablished order and affirming its rules and values, would not be interested in such a change and would be the wrong place for fighting for a new social order.

Ironically enough, it was around 1968 that the mass media, and especially television, discovered the attractiveness of protest events. Since then, the strong opposition between the mass media and protest and its actors, on both sides, has lessened. In addition, a complex interrelation between them evolved. As this volume demonstrates from a multidisciplinary perspective, Western societies even saw a growth in the close interrelation between the mass media and protesters.

Social movements of the nineteenth century, such as the labor movement or the women's movement, expressed their protests in the streets and in oppositional journals or magazines. These alternative media predominantly addressed their own participants and their sympathizers. Since social movements in this period had only a limited access to the mass media, they needed prominent alliance partners within the media and the political system to give them public legitimacy. They concentrated their engagements both on protest in the streets and by building institutional organizations as parties or trade unions.[1]

The development of the mass media after 1945 radically changed the preconditions of political discourses. In particular, the rise of television as a leading mass medium in the 1960s marks a turning point in Western democracies. Because public attention via television became a relevant currency of political power, political representatives have since had to adapt to its criteria of news coverage.[2] This implies that public discourses, dominated by television, became more open to different actors, groups, and organizations:[3] according to the criteria of media selection, they have to concur today not only in terms of political programs and goals, but also in terms of media adequacy.[4]

In the 1960s, the Western mass media discovered the news value of protest events, so, at least for moderate movements, it is easier today to access the mass media sphere. The reasons are manifold. Two of the most relevant are: protest actions attracting the attention of the viewers because of their dramatic character; and the polarization between protesters and addressees visualizing huge and often diffuse social groups, institutions, or governments. By covering protest events, the Western mass media, especially television, may act as a "social center" of democratic societies (cf. Couldry 2003; Gitlin [1980] 2003). Nevertheless, the interrelation between social movements and the mass media is highly complex and often paradoxical, as Gitlin ([1980] 2003) showed in his canonical study. Although both sides might follow up on different or even divergent motifs and frames, there is a structural bind between them that is first of all based on the common need for public attention. Often, both aim to attract public attention by the use of dramatic and symbolic pictures.

Since this era, the mass media has switched from being a "bystander," observing conflicts between protesters and their addressees, to being a "player," actively participating in the conflict (Gamson 2006). As Gamson argues, participation begins with their use of pictures and the way they represent the different players within the public "arena." While they follow up on specific journalistic and economic interests, they have their own selective criteria when covering protest visually. When protests are represented by pictures, this implies different processes of framing: the actions are framed by a camera and its apparatus; by the journalists and their interpretational frames; and, finally, by the editing process and the layout.[5]

During the twentieth century, social movements gained a remarkable influence in Western societies as social and political actors through their public presence. Especially the moderate ones, such as the peace movement, the women's movement, or the environmental movement, were successful in influencing not only common sense culture, norms, and values, but also laws and politics.[6] Despite being marginalized at the beginning, they articulated a need for change that generally fit into the worldviews and attitudes of journalists and other media representatives—and of the established culture.[7] As Dieter Rucht (2004) argues, moderate movements do not intend to change society as a whole, but present themselves as "early-warning-systems," touching on the relevant crises and problems of Western societies, and have the potential to attract the interest of mass media actors.

Today, social media on the internet is another important sector of the public mobilization and self-organization of social movements.[8] On the one hand, social media might be used to attract mass media attention, for example, by addressing prototypical news values in the dissemination of information and pictures on blogs or on YouTube.[9] Given the possibilities of interactive digital media and the internet, protest actors gained, on the other hand, greater autonomy from the mass media. Since the end of the first decade of the twenty-first century, we may observe a growing relevance of web-based social media. They allow social movements like the global justice movement, the Occupy movement, or the Arab revolutionaries to communicate transnationally and build networks beyond national borders (della Porta 2007; Gitlin 2012; Schiffrin and Kircher-Allen 2012; Eltantawy and Wiest 2011). Recently, we witnessed the instruments that social media offered people in North Africa to organize protests and revolutions against their authoritarian and totalitarian regimes. As these revolts demonstrate, social media sites are especially efficient in mobilizing huge groups of supporters and active protesters, addressing them personally as "friends."

By addressing a broad spectrum of media, ranging from the press to television and film to the internet, this volume seeks to fundamentally analyze the role of the mass media and online media in protest. Presenting systematic approaches and specific case studies, especially focusing on Europe and the United States, the volume deals with the questions of how social movements use the mass media to gain public attention as a primary source of political mobilization, how the mass media reacts to protest performances and frames protest issues specifically, and which specific forms of interaction social movements and the mass media have developed since the 1960s.

Systematic Approaches to Media and Protest

This volume presents current studies reflecting the complex interrelation between media and protest from different disciplinary perspectives: sociology, social psychology, history, and media studies. While the analysis of media and protest has for a long time been isolated in single disciplinary discourses, we aim to foster interdisciplinary exchange between multiple discourses. This is all the more important because the connection of insights and methods from different scholarly perspectives is necessary to comprehensively scrutinize the many political, social, and cultural dimensions in the interactions between media and protest actors.

During the last decade, framing theory has obtained an increasingly predominant position within media studies.[10] In relation to research on social movements, politics, journalism, and public opinion, it is regarded by some authors as more relevant than the agenda and cultivation theory that dominated media studies from the end of the 1960s until the beginning of the 1990s.[11] In the history of media research, the concept of framing is widely established. Walter Lippmann used a similar term as early as the 1920s. He emphasized that journalists had a tendency to make generalizations through "the pictures in their heads," based on distinct notions or framings (Lippmann 1922). The term has its starting point in gestalt and cognitive psychology (Bartlett 1932) and social anthropology (Bateson 1972). It gradually became part of sociology (Goffman 1974), economy (Kahneman and Tversky 1979), linguistics (Tannen 1979: 137–81), studies of social movements (Snow and Benford 1988),[12] political science (Schön and Rein 1994), media research (Tuchmann 1978; Gitlin [1980] 2003), and public relations research (Hallahan 1999).

Similarly, as with Lippmann, interpretative sociology investigates how one experiences and understands reality on the basis of cognitive frames. Relevant representatives of this line of research are Alfred Schütz and Erving Goffman. Schütz (1962) argued that one purposely produces social sense out of one's daily experiences, where single actions simultaneously construct and reproduce culture. Both our self-image and our image of others are linked more to interpretations of the world than to the world itself. Goffman (1974) used framings to explain the principles of organization that govern collective actions and their participation by individuals.

Frames are the guiding cognitive schemata that increase the understanding of actions and compartmentalize our impressions—in order to make sense of the world. In recent framing theory within the fields of media and communication research, the works of S. D. Reese (Reese et al. 2001; Reese 2007: 119–41) and Entman (2003, 2007: 163–73) have been central in their explanation of how social phenomena are constructed by the media, subsequently affecting the audience's interpretation. Entman argued that all framings will contribute to: (1) a definition and a limitation of the problem, (2) an identification of the cause of the problem, (3) a basis for moral judgment, and (4) a suggestion of solutions and remedial actions. What is framed and stressed can change framings in the news item (1993: 51–59). The historian Gitlin proposed the following definition of the framing concept: "Frames make the world beyond direct experience look natural. … Frames bring order to events by making them something that can be told about; they have power because they make the world make sense ([1980] 2003: 6)."

The interdisciplinary and long-running use of the framing concept in different fields of the social sciences indicates its relevance for research on social processes, including protest communication. The original meaning has therefore undergone many changes and differentiations (see also Johnston and Noakes 2005). This volume presents several studies using framing theory to understand social movements and to interpret the media representation of protest.

Apart from studies using framing theory in specific case studies,[13] three chapters deal with it from a more theoretical point of view. Bert Klandermans's contribution gives an outline of relevant sociopsychological studies treating the basic relations between protest movements and the mass media on the level of cognitive framing. He argues that media make a relevant contribution in motivating people to protest by providing them with frames and interpretations of a social or political situation. "They [the media] engage in the processes of interpretation and definition of the situation directly by delivering interpretations or indirectly by transmitting other party's interpretations; they take part in the formation of shared definitions of the situation" (Klandermans, this volume). The framing of protest goals, motifs, and actions matters in many ways. As Klandermans shows, it is especially relevant for the mobilization and commitment of members within a social movement. Furthermore, protest actors might develop framing strategies in order to address the mass media, touching on guiding values, norms, and ideals of certain journalistic scenes, groups, and generations. Finally, it has to be considered that the framing of protest within the mass media discourses can only be partly influenced by the activist themselves.

The framing strategies of protest actors are considered more intensively in Baldwin Van Gorp's contribution. He deals with the way social movements develop framing strategies in order to influence agenda setting and the media's interpretation of their protest issues. He presents an inductive analysis examining frames or frame packets used by the mass media to cover protests against the establishing of an asylum seekers' center in Belgium.

Another relevant aspect of media framing of protest is covered by Sigurd Allern. He discusses journalists' motifs in framing news stories. He develops an approach that aims to better understand the communicative exchange between activists and journalists on the basis of framing processes. He also presents some case studies to assess the relations between the framing concept and other familiar concepts of journalism, such as "news angles" and "hooks".

Contentious Pictures of Protest in the Mass Media

Most studies of protest and the media's ability to influence a mass audience are focused on the analysis of text and verbal messages. As Barret and Barrington have shown, however, media also contains visual images that may have significant impact, either alone or as a reinforcement and emphasis of the editorial policy in relation to matters that are expressed in the text (2005).

A number of analyses of politics, election campaigns, and opinion studies have shown that visual frames have a strong influence on public attitudes in relation to individuals, events, and issues. These studies have shown that voters often base their opinions on political candidates on impressions from press photographs or television images of them (Barret and Barrington 2005; Coleman and Banning 2006). Studies have also shown that the sizes of the photos used in the press are important in attracting public attention (Wanta 1988). Visual images may play an important role in the framing process. Messaris and Abraham's 2001 study of Afro-Americans in the news has demonstrated that visual communication differs from both oral and written communication. Visual framing is easier to take for granted and may contain opinions that would have been far more controversial and met with more arguments if the same message had been put forward in words.

Fox and Pasternak (2011) have shown that visual representation of conflict in general contributes to the shaping of collective memory. Despite the relevant role of contentious imagery for the public image and for the success of social movements, it has barely been investigated. This volume presents several studies using both quantitative and qualitative methods to analyze contentious imagery in the interaction between protest actors and the mass media.

Press photos in print news on the student movement stand at the core of Stuart Hilwig's contribution. In several earlier studies, he has shown how the conservative Italian media framed the protest movement in 1968: the *Sessantotto* was mainly framed negatively in the major Italian newspapers. In his current study, Hilwig analyzes the use of images in the Italian press. In a close reading of selected press photos, he documents how the negative discourse was supported by a corresponding negative framing utilizing photos.

Rolf Werenskjold and Erling Sivertsen studied all the photos in three major Norwegian newspapers to examine the frames used in the coverage of protest events in 1968. Based on empirical studies, they have developed a set of frame categories that are used to analyze the framing of protest by the published photos. The analysis shows that the most conservative and largest newspaper had the most complex photographic material with respect to framing variation, while the other two newspapers provided more biased photo coverage of the protesters in various countries.

Antigoni Memou's chapter examines the photographic material published in the student press in France during May 1968. She argues that to a large extent, photos in the student press supported and strengthened the demands of the student movement. Memou's study clearly shows major differences between student and mainstream newspapers. She focuses on how they portrayed the police, the protesting students, and the alliance between students and workers in this turbulent month of 1968.

Apart from print media, public imagery of protest is dominated today by fictional and nonfictional images in film and television. Therefore, this volume presents three studies investigating the aesthetics and politics of contentious imagery in audiovisual media.

Starting from a historian's perspective, Stefan Eichinger aims to create a new kind of typology to classify political films from the 1960s and 1970s. His typology is related to three dimensions: the first deals with the characteristics of political films, the second with the format, and the third with the institutional context in which they were made available to the public. Eichinger's typology aims to increase the understanding of political films with relevance to the protests of the period studied.

Two more studies investigate the close interaction between protest actors and television, both taking the student movement in the 1960s as a historic threshold in the development of interrelation. Todd Michael Goehle's analysis is based on a survey study of the public's reactions to media coverage of the protests in West Germany in 1968. He demonstrates that the formation of public opinion was based on the coverage of the student uprising, which took place within a dynamic media system. This system included television personalities, the media elite, activists, and the audience. Goehle discusses his material in a dialogue with earlier studies of television and protest. All the various power groups involved made their own efforts to achieve a broad spectrum of political, economic, and social objectives.

In her contribution, Kathrin Fahlenbrach also puts a special focus on the beginning of a new era of public protest actions in the 1960s, when television became a leading mass medium. Furthermore, she offers an outlook on different forms of professional interaction between protest actors and television, taking a closer look at different media strategies of protest activists, especially in television.

The Mass Media and Protest: The Beginning of a New Era in 1968

As the previous section already indicates, the book presents several studies analyzing the end of the 1960s in Western societies as a turning point in the interrelation of the mass media and social movements and the beginning of a new era of mass media–based protest performances. Across different chapters, the volume argues that the close and even symbiotic relation between social movements and the mass media has its historical roots in particular in the late 1960s (cf. Fahlenbrach 2002; Werenskjold 2008, 2012). The student movements in Europe and the United States were the first social movements that not only used the street and alternative media to express their protest in public, but also used the mass media strategically for achieving their goals. In this specific situation in media history, when television grew into a leading mass medium, protest movements and the media started to develop common principles of political expression: news values and criteria of media coverage, such as the personalization or symbolization of news, were considered by the protest actors in their public actions and self-representations (Preston 2009; O'Neill and Harcup 2009); at the same time, the mass media, especially television, discovered the event character and dramaturgical power of public protest.

As well as the contributions mentioned above, other authors in the volume discuss the historic era of the late 1960s in their articles, representing a fundamental change of protest. Naoko Koda focuses on the dissident newspaper the *Guardian* as a mouthpiece for the anti-Vietnam movement in the United States. The newspaper was published in New York and played a vital role in the critical debate about the American war in Vietnam. Over a period of twenty years, it became one of the most important publications of the antiwar movement in the United States by bringing alternative news about the Vietnam War to the public's attention. Koda shows how the newspaper played a vital role for left-wing groups nationwide.

David Carter deals with the media coverage of the civil rights demonstrations in the United States in the 1960s. The chapter provides a vivid overview and discussion of the changes that occurred in the media coverage of the black freedom struggle both in the press and in television from 1964 to 1968. Carter discusses how the media shaped public opinion and contributed to securing the Civil Rights Act in the 1960s.

Another study presented in this book focuses on the media strategies of the civil rights movement. Craig Peariso starts his discussion of the Black Panther Party with the observation that it is relatively well-known how the party used the mass media to convey their messages. In his chapter, he therefore deals with the lesser-known angle of how revolutionary organizations such as the Black Panther Party were able to use their leaders' appeal to catch the attention of reporters and photographers.

While the "mythological" value of 1968 in the collective memory of most Western societies and its effects, especially in terms of cultural change, is intrinsically tied to the mass media, the student movement was, at the same time, the first movement that at some given moment lost control of its public image. In the end, and even today, the media dominated the public understanding of their goals, their motives, and even their collective identities (cf. Fahlenbrach 2002). Thus, 1968 first demonstrated the nonintended and paradoxical effects that social movements in Western societies encountered in their communication with the mass media.

Professional Media Strategies and Media Actors

Since the Student Movement, social movements have professionalized their public communication strategies. By directly targeting the selective criteria of media coverage, they not only aim to be recognized by them but also aim to control their public framing. Successful movements such as the ecologist movement or the human rights movement therefore plan their public communication with the help of professional institutions, such as nongovernmental organizations (NGOs) and public relations agencies. This volume presents three case studies that demonstrate this professionalization by using the example of the global justice movement (Teune; Doerr and Mattoni) and Greenpeace (Riese).

An early and specific case of professionalized media strategies is discussed by Hanno Balz. In his study of the Red Army Faction (RAF), Balz explores the problematic relationship between the mass media and terrorism. He examines how the RAF interpreted the mass media, and how this understanding influenced their actions both ideologically and physically. He specifically explores the strategies of the RAF to gain media attention and thus makes the point that both terrorists and journalists are mutually dependent on each other when aiming to gain public attention. As a result, as Balz points out, terrorism is partly created through media discourses.

As mentioned before, social movements in the first decade of the twenty-first century developed more pragmatic and multifaceted strategies to use and guide public attention. This implies the use of web-based social media and the addressing of the mass media by adapting to their selective news criteria and production rules.

In his contribution, Simon Teune has developed a theoretical framework for examining various events organized by social movements, in which the mass media played a role both as an important actor and as a partner. He reconstructs the public agendas and political contexts that shaped the media coverage of four meetings of the European Social Forum, documenting and discussing its rise and fall in public attention. The fate of the forum is explained by the lack of resonance in the major mass media outlets, resulting from missing links to dominant public agendas and media frames at these times.

The contribution of Juliane Riese shows how the Greenpeace campaign against Norwegian whaling in the 1990s can be understood as another example of a failed media strategy. Riese documents how their framing strategies, which were previously successful, this time failed to mobilize a public opposition against the whalers in Norway. Indeed, Riese argues that the Greenpeace campaign even resulted in increased support for whalers in the Norwegian mass media.

Both studies provide insight into the development and realization of professional strategies aimed at media attention, while also demonstrating their risks and pitfalls for social movements. Furthermore, such strategies may produce nonintended effects within a movement. The reason is that this development conflicts with the mostly antihierarchical ideas of social movements and the emphasis on their grassroots basis. NGOs such as Greenpeace or Attac are suspected by protest actors as only making their decisions and actions according to the pragmatic rationale of the political and media establishment. The base of the ecologist movement or the global justice movement, for example, no longer widely accepts them as their representatives.[14]

Grassroots Protest in the Digital Age

Today, the internet offers new possibilities, especially for internal grassroots communication. It enables movements to effectively build global networks of protest. Furthermore, it offers new possibilities to realize the old dream of an "antihierarchical," egalitarian form of communication that confronts the public with all the information that mainstream media excludes and ignores. This dream of a participative alternative medium, first formulated by Berthold Brecht (1927/2002) in his "radio theory," is partly realized when the internal communication of protest movements are considered. But these new networks have their limits when it comes to externally communicating protest topics and goals to a wider public: they still need the mass media in order to be recognized beyond the borders of their networks and to use this public attention as a resource of power.

The relevant role of the internet is another focus in this book. The studies presented here include research on the use of the internet in single movements and the way protest is covered in online mass media journalism.

In a metatheoretical perspective (in part I), Ralph Negrine offers a broad outline of media research in the 1970s, which provides a critical perspective on demonstrations, protests, and the mass media. He emphasizes that the mass media is not only a passive spectator, but also an active participant, especially if protest actions and events are part of the mass media news. He argues that in contrast to the 1970s, the role of the internet has changed the role of media technology in protest communication. Negrine discusses how the internet changed news coverage and the public image of protest, which are communicated to more people than ever before.

The effects of the internet on the mass media are most obvious in the establishment of online journals and web outlets of print media and television. Øystein Pedersen Dahlen asks in his chapter whether these online media differ in their coverage of protest issues from print media. More specifically, he explores how protest actions against the World Trade Organization were presented and framed by some leading British and Norwegian online newspapers during its Hong Kong meeting in December 2005. Based on an empirical framing analysis, he discusses the role of the protestors by examining the way their arguments were covered differently in the journals.

A relevant effect of the internet on protest communication and mobilization today lies in the transgression of national public spheres. As Nicole Doerr and Alice Mattoni show in this volume, social media and other forms of online communication have established transnational public spaces. This enlargement of public spheres also results in the genesis of transnational collective identities, as Doerr and Mattoni demonstrate for the EuroMayDay Parade. In their case study, they discuss how globalization, European integration, and the increased use of the internet by activists have changed national public arenas.

The internet also stands at the core of Roy Krøvel's contribution, making the case for an early example of online mobilization, the Mexican Zapatistas. Krøvel argues that they were successful in using the internet for their guerrilla actions even without having any decisive media strategy. In reconstructing the frames in media discourse, especially influenced by prominent writers and intellectuals, he shows that the Zapatistas were received publicly as the first digital guerrilla actors, becoming for several prominent supporters "mythical" heroes of the new online era of protest.

Luca Rossi and Giovanni Boccia Artieri's chapter focuses more specifically on how protest can be organized in the digital age. According to these authors, social media (such as blogs, Facebook, and Twitter) redefine the way protest movements communicate both internally and externally. Thus, in order to understand protest movements today, it is necessary to frame them in the wider picture of how the relationship between media and society has changed during the digital age. Every aspect of the way in which protest movements act today can be regarded as an opportunity offered by the new media scene where protests take place.

The North African revolutions in Tunisia, Egypt, or Libya, taking place at the beginning of 2011, gave impressive proof of this fundamental change.

They demonstrated that social media sites transgress the limits of rigorously controlled public spheres, even in authoritarian and totalitarian regimes, and offer social movements new ways to mobilize huge groups of protesters.

But internet and social media also matter for more culturally driven movements, especially in oppositional subcultures. In his chapter, Hendrik Spilker analyzes how the internet and other digital technologies have been adopted in the Norwegian punk movement to produce and distribute alternative music. Spilker investigates the way these technologies have been integrated in the cultural and political expression of punk as an international "counterculture." Spilker's case study is based on interviews with current Norwegian punk activists and former punks who were active in the 1980s at a youth center in Trondheim. He underlines and creates a close connection between punks and hackers in Norway.

Conclusion

As this introduction indicates, the volume presents many interdisciplinary and international perspectives on media-based protest performances. Both the mass media and the interactive digital media are shown as being elementary parts of contentious communication. While the mass media directly interprets and guides the public framing and interpretation of protest, it is analyzed not only as a "bystander" but also as active "player" (Gamson 2006) in the arena of protest. The rather symbiotic interrelation between social movements and the mass media, both aiming for public attention, is rooted historically in the late 1960s, an era where both "players" discover each other and develop new rules of interaction, which are professionalized later on. For this reason, "1968" is treated extensively here as a historic landmark in several aspects: regarding the general "visual turn" in the mass media and in performing protest, when pictures are discovered as powerful economic and political resources by journalists and by activists; regarding the development of mass media strategies by activists; and finally, regarding the symbiotic relation between these two "players."

Since the late 1960s, both the mass media and protest activists have therefore been interrelating public actors that guide the collective interpretation of a given crisis by providing the public with interpretations and cognitive frames that allow people to cope with a problematic situation. As several chapters in this book demonstrate, it is first of all a discursive struggle (including pictures) concerning dominant frames, definitions, and interpretations that still dominate contentious communication even today. Looking at the current use of social media in democratic and nondemocratic societies, we learn that the public arenas are about to expand even more. They enable people, even in authoritarian and totalitarian states, to articulate their discontent and anger publicly, transgressing institutionalized censorship and repression.

We are currently standing at the crossroads of a new era of web-based protest communication. At this time, it seems more than necessary to reconsider the historic roots and developments of protest, carried out according to the rules of the mass media and interactive digital media from a scholarly point of view.

Notes

1. This especially concerns the workers' movement, which built social democrat and communist parties in diverse countries.
2. Consequently, politics became a "largely mediated experience," as Carpini and Williams state (2001: 161): "political attitudes and actions result from the interpretation of new information through the lenses of previously held assumptions and beliefs."
3. Carpini and Williams (2001: 167) stress this opening of the public sphere for marginalized groups, especially for the current network of television and new media: "What is clear that this new media environment presents a clear challenge to the authority of elites … who served as gatekeepers under the old system. … there is evidence that new or marginalized groups, along with new or formerly non-political media, are playing a more central role in setting and framing the public agenda."
4. The interrelation between media and protest movements are closely analyzed (see, e.g., Gitlin 2003; Fahlenbrach 2002; Koopmans 2004; Gamson 2006; Werenskjold 2008, 2012).
5. The influence of Gamson's writings on protests is explained concisely and developed in Johnston and Noakes (2005).
6. For example, laws on equal rights for women in Germany and other European countries or laws concerning the protection of the environment. In many European countries, the development of ecological parties is one of the most manifest effects of the environmental movement on the political system.
7. Following the framing approach of Gamson, one could argue that such movements have "a natural advantage because their ideas and language resonate with the broader culture" (2006: 254).
8. Van de Donk et al. (2004) present comprehensive research on the role of new media for the internal and external communication and organization of social movements (cf. also Bennett 2003).
9. A prominent example is the picture of the Iranian protester Neda, who was beaten to death by Iranian policemen, which gained global media attention.
10. See summary articles on the status of international studies on framing in the *Journal of Communication,* especially Van Gorp (2007). See also Weaver (2007).
11. See the summary of media studies in Werenskjold (2008).
12. For an extensive summary of the status of studies of social movements, see Snow, Soule, and Kriesi (2004).

13. See the chapters by Hilwig, Werenskjold and Sivertsen, Dahlen, Teune, and Krøvel.
14. Gamson (2006) characterizes this problem as a recurrent dilemma of movement actors that get a "media standing." While pragmatically adapting to the discursive rules of the mass media public sphere, they lose acceptance within the movement.

Bibliography

Barret, A. W. and L. W. Barrington. 2005. "Bias in Newspaper Photograph Selection." *Political Research Quarterly* 58(4): 609–18.

Bartlett, F. C. 1932. *Remembering. A Study of Experimental and Social Psychology.* Cambridge: Cambridge University Press.

Bateson, G. 1972. *Steps to an Ecology of Mind.* New York: Ballantine Books.

Bennett, W. L. 2003. "New Media Power: The Internet and Global Activism." In *Contesting Media Power: Alternative Media in a Networked World,* ed. N. Couldry and J. Curran. Lanham, MD: Rowman & Littlefield.

Brecht, B. 1927/2002. "Radiotheorie". In *Texte zur Medientheorie,* ed. G. Helmes and W. Köster. Stuttgart: Reclam.

Coleman, R., and S. Banning. 2006. "Network TV News' Affective Framing of the Presidential Candidates: Evidence for a Second-level Agenda-setting Effect through Visual Framing." *Journalism & Mass Communication Quarterly* 83, no. 2: 313–28.

Couldry, N. 2003. *Media Rituals: A Critical Approach.* London: Routledge.

della Porta, D. 2007. *The Global Justice Movement: Cross-National and Transnational Perspectives.* Boulder, CO: Paradigm.

Eltantawy, N., and J. B. Wiest. 2011. "Social Media in the Egyptian Revolution: Reconsidering Resource Mobilization Theory." *International Journal of Communication* 5: 1207–24.

Entman, R. M. 1993. "Framing: Towards Clarification of a Fractured Paradigm." *Journal of Communication* 43, no. 4 (December): 51–59.

———. 2003. *Projections of Power: Framing News, Public Opinion, and U.S. Foreign Policy.* Chicago: University of Chicago Press.

———. 2007. "Framing Bias: Media in the Distribution of Power." *Journal of Communication* 57, no. 1 (March): 163–73.

Fahlenbrach, K. 2002. *Protestinszenierungen: Visuelle Kommunikation und kollektive Identitäten in Protestbewegungen.* Wiesbaden, Germany: Westdeutscher Verlag.

Fox, P., and G. Pasternak. 2011. *Visual Conflicts: On the Formation of Political Memory in the History of Art and Visual Cultures.* Newcastle upon Tyne, UK: Cambridge Scholars.

Gamson, W. 2006. "Bystanders, Public Opinion, and the Media." In *The Blackwell Companion to Social Movements,* ed. D. Snow, S. A. Soule, and H. Kriesi. Malden: Blackwell.

Gitlin, T. (1980) 2003. *The Whole World Is Watching: Mass Media and the Making and Unmaking of the New Left.* Berkeley: University of California Press.

———. 2012. *Occupy Nation: The Roots, the Spirit, and the Promise of the Occupy Wall Street.* New York: Itbooks.

Goffman, E. 1974. *Frame Analysis: An Essay on The Organization of Experience.* New York: Harper & Row.

Hallahan, K. 1999. "Seven Models of Framing: Implications for Public Relations." *Journal of Public Relations Research* 11, no. 3: 205–42.

Johnston, H., and J. Noakes, eds. 2005. *Frames of Protest: Social Movements and the Framing Perspective.* Lanham, MD: Rowman & Littlefield.

Kahneman, D., and A. Tversky. 1979. "Prospect Theory: An Analysis of Decision under Risk." *Econometrica* 47, no. 2 (March): 263–91.

Koopmans, R. 2004. "Movements and Media: Selection Processes and Evolutionary Dynamics in the Public Sphere." *Theory and Society* 33, nos. 3–4 (June): 367–91.

Lippmann, W. 1922. *Public Opinion.* New York: Harcourt, Brace.

Messaris, P., and L. Abraham. 2001. "The Role of Images in Framing News Stories." In *Framing Public Life: Perspectives on Media and Our Understanding of the Social World,* ed. S. D. Reese, O. H. Gandy, and A. E. Grant. Mahwah, NJ: Lawrence Erlbaum Associates.

O'Neill, D., and T. Harcup. 2009. "News Values and Selectivity." In *The Handbook of Journalism Studies,* ed. T. Hanitzsch, K. Wahl-Jorgensen, and the International Communication Association. New York: Routledge.

Preston, P. 2009. *Making the News: Journalism and News Cultures in Europe.* London: Routledge.

Reese, S. D. 2007. "The Framing Project: A Bridging Model for Media Research Revisited." *Journal of Communication* 57, no. 1 (March): 119–41.

Reese, S. D., O. H. Gandy, and A. E. Grant. 2001. *Framing Public Life: Perspectives on Media and Our Understanding of the Social World.* Mahwah, NJ: Lawrence Erlbaum Associates.

Rucht, D. 2004. "The Quadruple 'A': Media Strategies of Protest Movements since the 1960s." In *Cyber Protest: New Media, Citizens and Social Movements,* ed. W. Van de Donk, B. D. Loader, P. G. Nixon, and D. Rucht. London: Routledge.

Schiffrin, A., and E. Kircher-Allen. 2012. *From Cairo to Wall Street: Voices from the Global Spring.* New York: New Press.

Schön, D. A., and M. Rein. 1994. *Frame Reflection: Toward the Resolution of Intractable Policy Controversies.* New York: Basic Books.

Schütz, A. 1962. *Collected Papers: The Problem of Social Reality.* The Hague: Nijhoff.

Snow, D. A., and R. D. Benford. 1988. "Ideology, Frame Resonance, and Participant Mobilization." *International Social Movement Research* 1: 197–217.

Snow, D. A., S. A. Soule, and H. Kriesi. 2004. *The Blackwell Companion to Social Movements.* Malden, MA: Blackwell.

Tannen, D. 1979. "What's in a Frame? Surface Evidence for Underlying Expectations." In *New Directions in Discourse Processing,* ed. R. O. Freedle. Norwood, NJ: Ablex.

Tuchman, G. 1978. *Making News a Study in the Construction of Reality.* New York: Free Press.

Van de Donk, W., B. D. Loader, P. G. Nixon, and D. Rucht, eds. 2004. *Cyber Protest: New Media, Citizens and Social Movements.* London: Routledge.

Van Gorp, B. 2007. "The Constructionist Approach to Framing: Bringing Culture Back In." *Journal of Communication* 57, no. 1 (March): 60–78.

Wanta, W. 1988. "The Effects of Dominant Photographs: An Agenda-Setting Experiment." *Journalism Quarterly* 65, no. 1: 107–11.

Weaver, D. H. 2007. "Thoughts on Agenda Setting, Framing, and Priming." *Journal of Communication* 57, no. 1 (March): 142–47.

Werenskjold, R. 2008. "The Dailies in Revolt: The Global 1968 Revolts in Major Norwegian Newspapers." *Scandinavian Journal of History* 33, no. 4 (December): 417–40.

———. 2012. *That's the Way It Is? Medienes rolle i proteståret 1968.* Oslo: Det humanistiske fakultet, Universitetet i Oslo.

Williams, B. A., and M. X. Delli Carpini. 2011. *After Broadcast News. Media Regimes, Democracy, and the New Information Environment.* Cambridge: Cambridge UP.

Part I

Systematic Approaches
to Protest and Media

Chapter 1

Changes of Protest Groups' Media Strategies from a Long-Term Perspective

Dieter Rucht

This chapter explores the relationship between protest groups and the mass media with a special but not exclusive emphasis on progressive leftist groups in West Germany. It aims at answering two questions: What are the basic shifts of leftist (or progressive) groups' media strategies from the 1950s to the present? What factors, both exogenous and endogenous, have influenced these strategic shifts?

Conceptually, the analysis will rely on a distinction between four ways in which protest groups can deal with media. It is argued that in different periods, protest groups put different emphasis on one or several of these media-related strategies. Given the broad scope of this analysis, the chapter will mainly rely on secondary analysis.

The Conceptual Framework

Basic Characteristics of the Modern System of Mass Media

Modern mass media, in particular newspapers/journals, radio, television, and the internet, represent a complex and partly interrelated system that serves entertainment, information, education, the expression of interests and opinions, deliberation, and mobilization. As far as political communication and mobilization is concerned, the mass media are a crucial link between the citizenry and the political decision makers (Bennett and Entman 2001). They are both a forum and an actor. Not only do they show (in a highly selective way) what is going on in politics, but based on their selection criteria, biases and opinions, they are also shaping people's minds, including those of the political decision makers.

While the mass media generally compete with each other for the attention (and money) of the mass publics, this competition mostly occurs within vaguely defined market segments. These segments are oriented toward certain social milieus, characterized by similar social and educational backgrounds, age cohorts, territorial spaces, political leanings, lifestyles, etc. Most newspapers, for example, represent a rough political-ideological tendency (in German, *redaktionelle Linie*) so that they can be located on the Left-Right axis. Accordingly, they have differential positions vis-à-vis different political subjects. While there are some players and some kinds of political events that are covered, though not necessarily positively, almost obligatorily (e.g., the results of a presidential election), other actors and events have to struggle to get media coverage.

On the input side, the mass media are constantly bombarded with an abundance of offers: reports by news agencies, press releases, press conferences, speeches, commentaries, and invitations to watch and cover various kinds of events. Not only because of their limited carrying capacity, but also because of their own selection criteria, most of this input goes into the wastebasket. On the output side, individual media and journalists are keen to be the first—and hopefully exclusive—source for offering what they deem to be spectacular, newsworthy or at least interesting. Therefore, they actively seek stories, news, pictures, commentaries, interviews, etc. This search is highly strategic and selective, so that political actors cannot hope to be approached more or less automatically in order to respond to the media's requests. The likelihood of actors and events being covered in the mass media depends on a number of factors, of which, besides issue attention cycles (Downs 1972), the news values of actors and events are crucial (Staab 1990). Such values, for example, conflict, damage, prominence, credibility and proximity to the audience, are partly endogenous "objective" properties of the actors/events but partly also ascribed and socially constructed attributes. News values are also crucial for social movements and protest groups trying to gain mass media coverage (Hocke 2002).

The Relationship between Social Movements/ Protest Groups and Media

In scholarly literature, the relationship[1] between mass media and social movements is sometimes characterized as symbiotic (Wolfsfeld 1984; Imhof 1996). This view is based on a simplistic assumption: on the one hand, the mass media are keen to cover spectacular conflict, possibly with the occurrence of aggression and physical violence. This is something protest groups may potentially offer. On the other hand, protest groups, in order for their voices and claims to be heard, actively seek media coverage and sometimes even engage in spectacles or aggressive acts to secure that coverage. In other words, protest groups and the mass media are said to need, and profit from, each other. While such a symbiotic relationship may occur in certain instances, most other cases are characterized by a fundamental asymmetry. Protest groups, to the extent that they seek a mass audience to become known and attain support, desperately need the mass media, while the media, facing the daily avalanche of inputs, are hardly dependent on protest groups. To be sure, there is a general expectation that the media should not ignore large and/or very disruptive protests. Indeed, the mass media tend to cover such events to a high degree (Smith et al. 2001). But this pattern does not apply to the great bulk of protest mobilization, which only takes place on a small or medium-sized scale and does not comprise disruptive action, let alone violence. Consider that in cities such as Berlin and Paris more than three thousand protests take place every year. As a result, most of these groups, who are unable to mobilize the masses or are unwilling to resort to severe disruption, are either doomed to be ignored by the mass media (usually with the exception of local newspapers) or seek to compensate for their unattractiveness by other means. This brings me to a typology of the strategies that protest groups can choose with regard to media.

Media Strategies of Protest Groups

In an earlier publication, I typified and exemplified four kinds of strategies that social movements/protest groups can choose. These strategies, named the "quadruple A" (Rucht 2004), are:

> *Abstention:* No effort is made to access media, usually because of frustrating and unsuccessful attempts in the past.
> *Attack:* Protest groups actively criticize the structure, mechanisms, and biases of the mass media, appealing to certain general normative standards (openness, plurality, truthfulness) and professional rules (balance between different views, verification, separation between facts and opinion, etc.), and hoping that this will result in a reduction of selection and description biases.
> *Adaptation:* Protest groups try to discover and instrumentally use the mechanisms and rules of the mass media in playing the latter's game, for instance, by staging media-savvy protest events, offering adequate quotation and sound bites, and establishing personal contacts with journalists. In terms of their publicly visible actions, apart from serving the media's hunger for big numbers or disruptiveness (Shoemaker et al. 1987), pro-

test groups can rely on two other tactics that also imply news values: First, they may seek prominent, credible or politically relevant supporters and allies. These options range from a movie star to an established political party. Second, they may engage in creative and innovative actions that, by their very form, are attractive to media. This is why protest groups sometimes engage in performative action like street theater or risky stunts.

Alternative: Protest groups can rely on self-controlled or self-produced media such as flyers, posters, newsletters, brochures, books, radios, video groups, and, more recently, the various tools offered by the internet (emails, websites, chat rooms, Facebook, Twitter, etc.).

Of course, these four kinds of attitudes toward media are not mutually exclusive. While this is obvious for the last three, it is also possible that one and the same group moves over time from abstention to one or several of the three other patterns, or vice versa.

While it is relatively easy to investigate which media-related strategies are generally applied by which kinds of groups (after all, this is public or semipublic information), it remains a theoretical and empirical challenge to identify both the structural and situational factors that make groups choose a certain strategy or a combination of different strategies. To my knowledge, only a few theoretical thoughts are available on this causal question. Nevertheless, common sense would lead us to formulate some plausible hypotheses. For example, when protest groups encounter the mass media that are not only open but also generally supportive to their claims, these groups would have few reasons to attack the media or to agonize on how to improve their adaptation and/or alternative strategies. While more such ad hoc hypotheses could be formulated, it might be wiser to first consider a number of empirical cases of interaction between media and protest groups. This may allow us to produce better-informed hypotheses, move toward some tentative conclusions, and, based on further and broader empirical investigations far beyond the scope of this chapter, ultimately formulate a theory about the interrelationship between protest groups and the mass media. Before addressing and presenting a few empirical cases, I first wish to provide a brief historical background on that relationship in Germany.

A Brief Historical Background

Up until the nineteenth century, social movements and protest groups in Central and Western Europe were embedded in fairly distinct social milieus (Lepsius 1966). Communication and mobilization was mainly based on networks of people who were physically close to each other and met face-to-face in their neighborhoods, market places, factories, churches, pubs, voluntary associations, clubs, etc. With the partial erosion of such milieus and the shift from parochial and local to nationwide contention (Tilly 1978), mediated communication, in particular via newspapers, became an increasingly important instrument of political communication. In the early decades of the twentieth century, the major social milieus were to a large extent still congruent with basic ideological tendencies. The social milieus relied on their own media, which, in part, served as the mouthpiece of and catalyst for milieu-specific political activism. Therefore, for particular groups, access to their ideologically similar media was relatively easy while attempts to gain (positive) coverage in ideologically distant media were doomed to failure.

In Germany, up to the point when the Nazi movement seized power, a plethora of ideologically bound media existed, each occupying their own specific position in a highly segmented media market (Wilke and Noelle-Neumann 1994: 439). This changed dramatically when the Nazis began to streamline and rigidly control all forms of mass media so that these served as a platform and an agent for strong but also sophisticated political propaganda and mobilization. In addition to newspapers and other more traditional tools such as posters and flyers, radio became a primary source for political mobilization "from above."

After the defeat of the Nazi regime, a new era of mass communication began. With both the help and pressure of the Allied forces, a fairly pluralistic system of mass media, especially newspapers, was established along with democratic political institutions in West Germany. However, in contrast to the era of the Weimar Republic, this system of mass media was hardly segmented along the lines of the former or existing traditional social milieus (and corresponding political parties), which were rapidly decaying. This does not mean that the major media, especially the newspapers, could no longer be located on the Left-Right axis. However, their positioning was less obvious and more flexible because most media tried to secure some sort of internal pluralism and, probably more important, most media tried to comply with standards of professional journalism. These standards required a more detached and balanced way of reporting, and a separation between news and the opinions of journalists and other actors. Thus, from the 1950s onward, West German protest groups of all types and political leanings faced a system of mass media that, by and large, was similar to that of other Western liberal democracies (Voltmer 1993). Obviously, a strikingly different situation existed in the communist bloc countries where, to various degrees and with some changes over time, the mass media were centrally controlled and inaccessible to opposition groups.

A Chronological Look at Selected Protest Campaigns

From the end of the Second World War, a plethora of different types of social movements, political campaigns, and protest groups were revitalized or came into existence. These phenomena have been studied from various angles. Apart from numerous cases studies, there is also a large amount of quantitative data on protest events from 1950 onward that allows us to identify the occurrence and characteristics of all kinds of protest (Rucht 2003). Moreover, several broader studies on sets of movements, in particular the so-called new social movements, have been written. Furthermore, a comprehensive handbook on social movements in Germany from 1945 to the present has been published (Roth and Rucht 2008).

Yet very little research has been carried out on the media strategies of protest groups. Some scholars have written more generally about attempts to establish a counterpublic (for Germany, see, e.g., Stamm 1988; Oy 2001; more generally, see Warner 2002). Others have studied particular aspects, such as the development of underground or alternative press in certain periods (Peck 1991; McMillian 2011), or the media strategies of groups like Greenpeace (Dale 1996). However, no detailed study is available that would compare the use of different media strategies over time and across groups or issues. The following presentation of selected protest campaigns and their usage of media is nothing more than a first step toward such a comparison, which, however, would deserve a much broader and deeper investigation in order to attain more solidly grounded findings and conclusions.

I chose large and memorable campaigns, not necessarily because of their coverage in the mass media but rather because of their investment in terms of mobilization efforts. In addition, I focus on cases for which primary literature is available and/or that I know from my long-standing study of social movements and political protest in Germany. I excluded the situation in East Germany where, with the remarkable exceptions of June 1953[2] and the peaceful revolution of 1989, it was only possible to engage in small and relatively modest forms of protest. Such protests were mainly based on face-to-face mobilization that, to some extent, was flanked by a samizdat-like underground press (e.g., the newsletter *Grenzfall*). These media, however, had a very low circulation and could not be distributed in public.

The 1950s

Contrary to common assumptions, the 1950s were not a quiet time in terms of political protest in Germany. This period was marked by occasional unrest, such as strikes and the mobilization of groups that had suffered in the war and were now asking for state subsidies. However, these issues were not remarkable in terms of the groups' media strategies. Protest was staged by conventional organizations usually based on formal membership. These organizations tended to rely on their own means of communication and mobilization, such as flyers, posters, and newsletters. Large protests were covered by the mass media as part of an almost obligatory news reporting. The organizers made few efforts to influence this media coverage.

Yet the picture was more differentiated for the two major waves of peace protests: the first directed against the reestablishment of an army in the early 1950s, the second against nuclear weapons under control of West Germany some years later. On the one hand, given the disastrous experience of the Second World War, large numbers of West Germans sympathized with the protest against rearmament. Support was widespread among social democrats and trade unionists but also among "progressive" groups within the Protestant Church. No wonder that segments of the mass media were relatively open to these groups' activities against rearmament, at least in the early years of the campaign. On the other hand, the coexistence of West Germany alongside a communist state in East Germany as part of the Soviet bloc and the general climate of the Cold War fostered strong anticommunist attitudes in major parts of the population and among almost all political elites. Protests for peace and against rearmament fell under the suspicion of serving the interests of, or even being steered by, Moscow. In response to the protesters' critique of West German institutions and politics, people uttered, "If you don't like it here, just walk over to the other side." With the intensification of the Cold War and the ever-stronger embedding of West Germany in the Western alliance, the groups protesting against the reestablishment of a regular army faced more and more difficulties in accessing the mass media. For example, two nationwide and "illegal" collections of signatures, presented as "referenda" against rearmament in 1951/52 and 1955, were discredited as communist enterprises and met with much suspicion by the mainstream media.

Anticommunist attitudes were also a background factor during the second wave of protests (around 1957/58), which were directed against atomic weapons in the hands of the West German army. The situation, however, changed significantly with one single incident on 12 April 1957: the publication of an open letter signed by a few renowned physicians, among them several Nobel Prize winners. The group sharply rejected atomic weapons in the hands of the West German army while at the same time promoting, in accordance with an earlier initiative of the US government, the idea of "atoms for peace," that is, the civil use of nuclear power for energy production. This initiative was widely covered and for the most part favorably discussed in the mass media. Together with subsequent mass protest, peaking in 1958, this initiative constituted a breakthrough. Atomic weapons for the West German army were no longer promoted, while the mass publics tended to accept the civil use of nuclear power, for which preparatory steps had already been made a few years earlier.

Whereas the movement against the reestablishment of an army in West Germany failed because of an increasingly unfavorable public opinion and a related defection of the leadership of the social democrats and the trade unions, the movement against nuclear weapons for the German military was successful, though not so much because of its inherent strength, but thanks to the somewhat unexpected support from scientists. One public letter was enough to turn the tide.

The 1960s

In terms of the frequency and size of protests, the first half of the 1960s was a very calm period. Also, with regard to protesters' media strategies, no significant new developments can be observed, albeit with the remarkable exception of the Easter marches. These marches, inspired by the British Aldermaston march initiated by the Campaign for Nuclear Disarmament in 1958, were first staged in West Germany in 1960 on a small scale with around one thousand participants, most of them religiously motivated pacifists. Gradually, though less in the form of marches and more in that of rallies, the event attracted more and more people, with an overall turnout of around three hundred thousand participants in 1968. The marches and rallies were coordinated by a central committee (*Zentralausschuss*) that was keen not to be identified with the communist Left. In their first years, the marches received little media coverage. In some places, they were even physically restrained by the public authorities who, for example, requested the demonstrators march in orderly rows outside the city centers. With their spread across West German cities and their increasing size, the marches also received more mass coverage. Interestingly, the coordination committee was very much concerned with providing appropriate coverage. Prior to and after the marches, the committee began to discuss the shape of the protests with regard to coverage in newspapers. Based on a comprehensive collection of newspaper reports about the protests, the organizers evaluated what was good and what had gone wrong, which slogans to use and which to avoid, how to deal with communist supporters who might undermine the credibility of the noncommunist groups in the eyes of the mass media, etc. To my knowledge, this was the first significant and systematic effort of West German protest groups to develop a strategy of adaptation. This strong orientation toward the mass media also became apparent when the organizers of the Easter marches, at the height of their quantitative success in 1968, decided to no longer continue the annual protests. The main reason for this was the heavy influx of leftist political groups who were using the Easter marches as a stage for articulating issues beyond peace and disarmament. The core organizers of the Easter marches were afraid of losing control over the event and therefore being discredited in the eyes of the mass publics, which, in 1968, definitely feared the increasing radicalism of the so-called extraparliamentary opposition.

This opposition was crucial in shaping the image of protest during the second half of the 1960s. Upon closer examination, it was a loose composite of more specific conglomerates, in particular the peace movement, the movement against the emergency laws, and the intellectual New Left, which largely overlapped with the student movement. In its early phase, the movement against the emergency laws was strongly supported, and also organizationally sustained, by large parts of the Social Democratic Party and the trade unions. In this period, the issue was widely covered and debated in the mass media. When, however, the social democrats and the trade unions gradually changed their mind and to a large extent withdrew from the movement, the latter found itself not only with almost no resources but also with very limited access to the mainstream media, especially because the movement was now identified with the radical, and partly communist, Left. After the *Bundestag* passed the emergency law in May 1968, this was no longer a relevant issue in the public. To the dismay of its organizers, the struggle was over and lost. What instead had moved to the foreground was the rebellion of the student movement, something that, regarding media strategies, is of tremendous interest for scholarly observers.

Before the summer of 1967, students had already begun to create or further develop their own media, clubs, and leftist associations. Also, they had staged several protest actions that, due to their symbolic radicalism, did receive some media coverage. From 2 June 1967, however, the situation began to escalate. One factor was the inaction of the police when counterdemonstrators physically attacked students protesting against the Persian shah visiting Berlin. The other and more important factor was the severe overreaction of the police on the evening of the same day. The shooting of a demonstrator lying helpless on the ground by a police officer in civilian clothes created a public outcry, particularly when it became clear that, contrary to early statements of the authorities, the victim was completely innocent. From this event onward, the protests began to radicalize. Due to a series of provocative and sometimes violent protests, the revolt became a hot topic in all of the mass media. The interest in covering the revolt was further spurred by similar protests occurring in many other countries. The conservative press and, in particular, the yellow press commented on the rebellious students in an extremely negative, if not openly hateful, way, characterizing the students, for example, as "lazy," "dirty" or "long-haired apes." In addition to newspapers, television became an extremely important forum for documenting and commenting on the students' protest activities. This was indeed the first revolution to be televised (Gitlin 1980).

Parts of the movement and the media engaged in an uneasy interaction. The student activists, on the one hand, were well aware of their attractiveness to the media. To some extent, they designed their activities so that media coverage was secured. On the other hand, most student activists could see and read on an almost daily basis that the way they were portrayed by the mass media was beyond their control. Large parts of the media were strongly biased against the students. Some journalists tended to distort facts. Many commented more on the form of protest and the outfit of the protesters than on their motives and arguments.

Because of the prevalence of a highly selective and negative reporting, the student activists resorted to two media strategies. First, they engaged in attacking the mass media in various ways, ranging from a verbal critique on how the media operate to physical attacks on the property of the infamous Springer press house. These latter kinds of actions were spurred on by the almost fatal shooting of Rudi Dutschke, the most prominent movement leader, who was stigmatized by the Springer press. The students reacted with the blockade and destruction of facilities, in particular delivery trucks, as part of the so-called Expropriate Springer Campaign (*Enteignet Springer-Kampagne*) around Easter 1968. This inspired a similar campaign in Italy directed against the newspaper *La Stampa,* with the slogan "La Stampa = Springer" (see Hilwig 1998).

Second, the student activists promoted the idea of "creating a counter-public" (*Gegenöffentlichkeit schaffen*) by trying to establish and expand their own media, organizing their own congresses, clubs, discussion circles, teach-ins, and university courses. They even propagated the creation of a "critical university" as an alternative to the existing universities, which they considered to be hierarchical, rigid, antidemocratic and outdated.

This double strategy of attack and alternative also resonated among certain pockets in the established media. Some liberal and left-oriented journalists sympathetic to the students' critique of mainstream media tried to implement some reforms at their places of work and, in a few cases, were able to achieve institutional changes. One of the most significant results of these efforts was the modification of the bylaws and property rights of the leading political magazine *Der Spiegel,* giving journalists more say and more control over the publishing house. It is also worth mentioning that Rudolf Augstein, the founder of the magazine, and Gerd Bucerius, the co-owner and editor of the liberal weekly *Die Zeit,* donated money to student organizations on several occasions for the purpose of documenting incidents of supposed unjustified policy repression, paid lawyers defending students in court, and strengthened attempts to counter the propaganda of the Springer press (*Die Zeit* 10 June 2009: 43–44; *Die Zeit* 18 June 2009: 52–53). With this money, some activists set up a so-called Institute for Counterpublics (*Institut für Gegenöffentlichkeit*) in Berlin, which, however, only published one report and was dissolved soon afterward.

In these years the students also put forward the idea of creating an alternative nationwide newspaper—an idea that, although it seemed utopian, did eventually materialize as *die tageszeitung,* a left-alternative newspaper established in 1978/79 (see Flieger 1992). Though no longer maintaining its initial alternative structure, consisting of equal pay and no bosses, the paper continues to exist today.

The 1970s and 1980s

By the late 1960s, the extraparliamentary opposition had already become fragmented and dissolved into different strands and tendencies, ranging from left-wing terrorism to a variety of communist/Maoist sects to engagement within the Social Democratic Party (SPD) and the liberal Free Democratic Party (FDP). Most important, however, was the impact of the extraparliamentary opposition on the gradually emerging new social movements, among these groups of feminists, environmentalists, antinuclearists, and activists focusing on urban restructuring, social and identity issues, Third World problems, etc. Unlike the claims of the previous student movement, those of the new social movements gradually resonated in major segments of the overall population, in particular the well-educated people in the human service sector. Because most parts of the new social movements were ideologically less radical and socially less distinct than the student activists, relevant parts of the mainstream population were sympathetic to or even openly supportive of them. Also helpful was the fact that scientific experts, some of the social democrats, and, regarding some issues, local down-to-earth people such as farmers, vine growers and fishermen were in favor of the new movements.

Evidently, this change of the overall political climate also had consequences for the media strategies of these movements. The strategy of attack, which was so prevalent for the student movement of the 1960s, was no longer central, especially when it became clear that major parts of the media were ready to cover the movements, or at least their moderate parts, in a favorable light. Some media researchers even argued that left-liberal journalists were instrumental in spearheading the movements by shaping ordinary people's minds in favor of their own idiosyncratic worldviews (Kepplinger 1989). While this seems to be exaggerated, it still holds that major sections of the mass media were not opposed to the new social movements. Only groups at their radical fringe continued to complain about the mass media because they felt themselves to be either ignored or misrepresented.

In the first half of the 1970s, the issues of abortion and nuclear power were particularly conducive in reducing the tensions between challenger movements and the mass media. A well-orchestrated public campaign to liberalize abortion, starting with the "self-accusation" of partly prominent women to have undergone an abortion, was launched in a 1971 issue of *stern,* the most popular weekly magazine at that time. This action, modeled on the French example and initiated by a feminist journalist who had witnessed the French campaign, found a stunning and mostly positive resonance in other media and the broader populace.

The second issue that was instrumental in creating bridges between challenger groups and mainstream media was the protection of the environment and the struggle against nuclear power. In these cases, reputable scientists, a minority of leading politicians, and supportive local people helped to shed a differentiated and sometimes decidedly positive light on the protesters, who could no longer be characterized as crazy outsiders.

While most conservative media, particularly in the early phase of the new social movements, kept its distance from or flatly criticized these groups, the latter gradually found themselves in a kind of downhill struggle, especially when compared to the situation of the extraparliamentary opposition in the late 1960s. Given such a situation, there was no strong incentive to invest much energy into both adaptation and building an alternative strategy. Nevertheless, the media-related activities of new social movements became more conscious, targeted, and professionalized due to these groups' growing life span, increase in resources and experiences in dealing with mass media. This development is best epitomized by Greenpeace, an organization whose very rationale was to stage spectacular actions designed to get a maximum of supportive media coverage (for Germany, see Rossmann 1993; Krüger and Müller-Henning 2000). While almost no other social movement went as far as Greenpeace, these other organizations still became more routinized and sophisticated in dealing with the mass media. Even the more radical groups, such as the squatters that, apart from earlier struggles in Frankfurt, had their heyday in the early 1980s, were quite aware of the need to gain media coverage that was as favorable as possible. While the mostly young and politically radical squatters were not well prepared to directly interact with established media, there was a group of more established supporters, among them some university professors, who, on the one hand, sought to explain the reasons for squatting to the wider audience and, on the other hand, tried to provide a symbolic shield for squatters by occasionally spending a night in squatted houses that were threatened with evacuation by more or less repressive police.

By the late 1970s and early 1980s, there were indications that in West Germany a kind of overarching "alternative movement" was in the making. In part this was wishful thinking because, at a closer glance, no such ideologically, thematically and socially coherent movement existed. Still, these years were marked by the mushrooming of groups and projects that in some areas, especially in the big cities, evoked the image of an emerging "second culture" (Hoffmann-Axthelm 1978). While many groups were thematically specialized, one could also observe the evolution of a broader and more general movement infrastructure. Important components of this infrastructure were local papers, brochures, radios, presses, book stores, and, last but not least, the daily *tageszeitung* mentioned above. The mushrooming of groups and initiatives even triggered the production of so-called *Stattbücher,* a kind of local directory or guide that listed and described the plethora of groups existing in a particular city. In West Berlin, for example, the first *Stattbuch* was published in 1978 and was followed by another five editions in subsequent years, eventually listing thousands of groups that could not all be reasonably attributed to the "alternative" sector. In my view, the creation of these media or media-related groups in this period was not essentially the result of a desperate political need to circumvent (unfavorable reporting by) mainstream media but rather a byproduct of a quickly growing alternative milieu that, to some extent, became increasingly self-centered so that critiques warned of the possibility of drifting into self-inflicted ghetto situation (Kraushaar 1978).

The various groups and movements that seemed to converge for a while in an encompassing alternative milieu basically maintained their specificities and autonomy, so that they continued to be centered on specific issues (environment, antinuclear, women, gay, etc.) or ideological tendencies (autonomous groups, communists, anarchists, nondogmatic socialists, etc.). At the same time, they shared some basic values and had some overlaps, so that parts of them were able to conduct joint campaigns, for example, against the NATO double-track decision, large-scale nuclear facilities, and the plan to implement a national census, which, because of widespread resistance, was cancelled.

The radical groups among the new social movements, for better or worse, had to rely on their own internal media (in the case of some communist groups, with the financial support of the East German regime). The more moderate groups as well the bigger social movement organizations tended to combine a strategy of adaptation with one of alternativeness. One form of adaptation was the use of press conferences, which were organized more frequently in the 1980s (as well as the 1990s) than in the decades before, as protest event data on Germany shows.

From the 1990s to the Present

While many observers commented on the gradual decline and/or institutionalization of the new social movements in the 1990s, a closer look reveals that, by and large, the actual level of activity did not decrease. What changed was the perception of protest. To some extent, the existence, claims and protests of the new social movements were gradually perceived as part of normal political activity and were therefore met with less excitement by the mass media than in earlier periods (Rucht 2007). As for newspapers, new social movement protests were not generally ignored, but simply received less space. The coverage of many protests tended to resemble more a weather report than a criminal story, so that the activities were often overlooked by the average reader.

To be sure, there are exceptions from this picture of the normalization and trivialization of protest. One is the countermobilization against the rapid rise of right-wing extremist and xenophobic groups starting in the early 1990s. Almost all established media were highly critical of right-wing extremism and therefore not only had an attentive eye on these groups, but also on the countermobilization. There were even a few demonstrations where leading politicians marched along with left-wing antifascists to express their opposition to the right-wingers. It is also worth mentioning that in 1992/93 the initiative to launch mass demonstrations against xenophobia did not only come from social movements, but also from freestanding journalists. Some of them, based on their direct access to "their" media, were able to organize mass demonstrations within a few days, especially the so-called light chains, which attracted several hundreds of thousands of people. In these evening events, the participants silently carried candles to express their dismay with right-wing extremism and xenophobia. No wonder that such peaceful events for promoting a human cause organized by journalists found the unconditional applause of all established media (while being criticized by some left-wing groups as a shallow and merely symbolic activity that would neither challenge the right-wing extremists nor really help their victims).

A second remarkable exception from the overall pattern of new social movements' relations with media are the so-called autonomous groups, who tended to appear as the "black block" in some demonstrations and occasionally engaged in skirmishes and street fights with the police. These groups were well aware that their activities would almost automatically guarantee media coverage, albeit an exclusively negative one. Nevertheless, they thought that this kind of activity was worthwhile because it signaled the existence of anti-systemic groups who might otherwise be simply ignored.

A third case that differs from the movements' prevailing interaction with the mass media are the groups that tried to block the transport of used nuclear fuel to intermediary deposits (Kolb 1997). The burned fuel from nuclear reactors was reprocessed in France and then transported back to Germany to be taken temporarily to a particular site near Gorleben before eventually being buried at a nuclear waste dump, which was still to be legalized and constructed. Resistance against these mostly annual transportations continues today. It is specific in at least three respects: (a) the activists adhere to the idea of civil disobedience, which implies disruptive and partly illegal, but strictly nonviolent action; (b) they are very creative in varying their tactics; though unable to stop the nuclear transports, they managed to delay the transportation, even with the presence of up to sixteen thousand policemen, relying on impressive technical equipment; and (c) the groups actively seek contact with the mass media and, in part, design their activities to secure the interest and occasionally even the admiration of the media. The protesters successfully play the game of David vs. Goliath, which, at least in this case, is attractive to the media. Also, some of the larger antinuclear groups have their quasi-official speakers, known to the press. These speakers are experienced in dealing with the press, knowing exactly how to write a press release, organize a press conference, and give an interview. The same could be also said for the groups that, in the same spirit of civil disobedience, fight the introduction of genetically modified crops by destroying plants. These groups, both in Germany and abroad (especially in France), are very aware of the advantages and pitfalls in getting mass media coverage.

With the rise of the so-called global justice movements, a reorientation of existing, as well as the introduction of new media strategies can be observed, beginning roughly in the mid-1990s. One important element of these movements is to profit from the occasion of official international meetings and summits to stage countersummits accompanied by more or less disruptive protest activities. The very presence of thousands of journalists at the official meetings almost guarantees attention for the challenger groups. These groups' activities tend to be far more exciting and colorful for the media when compared to the negotiations at the conference table and the dry press declarations at the end of official meetings. Another new element is the (World) Social Forums, which, initiated as a counterpart to the elitist World Economic Forum, were first held in 2001 in Brazil. Over time, the Social Forums became an institution in their own right on the global, continental, national, and even local level. In more recent years, the World Social Forums have attracted thousands of journalists, though not triggering an ever-increasing media coverage. A comparison of the European Social Forums even indicates a decline in public attention for these kinds of events over time (Teune 2009).

Another noteworthy phenomenon with regard to media strategies is the global justice movements' turn toward an alternative strategy, which greatly, but not exclusively, relies on the internet. Apart from those groups that use the internet to promote a specific policy or claim, a number of internet-based media groups have also come into existence. Most prominent among these groups is Indymedia, created on the occasion of the World Trade Organization (WTO) conference in Seattle in late 1999. In the meantime, the network of Indymedia groups has considerably expanded and currently comprises around 160 groups all over the globe. The internet, however, is not the sole platform of communication and mobilization among global justice movement groups. As an analysis of the media strategies of the groups protesting against the 2007 G8 meeting in Heiligendamm has shown, the activists rely on a broad and quite elaborate spectrum of media-related techniques (Rucht and Teune 2008). They launch press releases and hold press conferences to address the established media; they use radio and even television; they rely on more conventional tools such as newsletters, brochures, posters, flyers, etc.; and they profit from direct contacts with sympathetic or at least open-minded journalists in dailies like the left-alternative *tageszeitung,* Left weeklies and liberal papers. For example, Attac Germany, in its early phase of existence and on the occasion of the protests against the G8 summit in Genoa in 2001, implemented a clever media strategy that resembled the concept of "embedded journalism." Along with activists, they brought journalists to Genoa and supplied them with information about the ongoing events (see Kolb 2005).

These and other examples suggest that the global justice movements focus strongly on the adaptation and, especially, alternative strategies. But one should not completely forget that to a minor extent, attack strategies also come into play. In Heiligendamm, for example, the protesters criticized several media sources for spreading biased information, inventing stories that never happened, relying too much on (biased) police reports, etc. On one occasion, the so-called Clown Army disrupted an official live television broadcast, urging for an "objective press."

At least with regard to the global justice movements, it appears that the usage of different media and channels of communication has become quite diversified, sophisticated and professionalized. Whether the same can also be said for other contemporary groups, such as those of the extreme Right, would deserve an inspection it its own right, but is beyond the scope of this chapter.

Discussion and Conclusions

As can be seen from this rough overview, progressive movements and protest groups in (West) Germany emphasized different strategies over time. The strategy of attack, for example, played an important role for the student movement of the 1960s but was relatively marginal in earlier and later periods. The alternative strategy was dominant in the movement of the 1950s and became important again, though resting increasingly on new technologies, in the global justice movements of recent years.

More generally, it seems that during the last six decades, challenger groups have become increasingly aware of the crucial role of the mass media for raising recognition and making a political impact. To the extent that the scope of mobilization grows and transcends national borders, the mass media become more and more indispensable for protesters. It is no wonder that manuals and guides have been written to instruct challenger groups on how to use the media (see, e.g., Ryan 1990; Salzman 2003). The groups tend to combine different media strategies and gradually broaden their arsenal of media tools. Also, they make use of these possibilities in an increasingly elaborate and professional way. Knowledge about dealing with media is by no means a privilege of large protest organizations with rich resources. Small and informal groups also tend to use different media in a carefully reflected and, relative to their moderate means, effective way. One might assume that the internet has become a key tool for small groups to improve their information and mobilization capacities. Also, one could stress the role of new internet-based groups such as MoveOn.org in the United States and Campact. de in Germany. Nevertheless, I have some doubts about whether all this will make a big difference.[3] At this point in time, the offline media remain crucial as agenda setters and in shaping the political information and attitudes of the broader populace, including the decision makers.

What are the factors that make protest groups choose certain media-related strategies and account for general shifts of strategic patterns over time? Broadly speaking, we can differentiate between endogenous and exogenous sets of factors. In the former category, one might consider the basic ideology, thematic cause, and amount and kind of resources of the protest group. Such factors can be important in particular cases. For example, when protest groups take a politically radical stance and remain small, they are likely to be ignored by the mass media. When these groups, for the sake of getting coverage, resort to highly disruptive action, media coverage is guaranteed. Yet the group and its actions are portrayed in an extremely negative way (Rucht 1995a). Therefore, these kinds of groups have to rely on their own, self-produced media to mobilize and spread the word. Another example illustrating the role of endogenous factors is a group's reliance on a distinct tactic, such as civil disobedience. The resonance of this tactic is largely dependent on an attentive public, and thus the mass media, which are expected not to misrepresent the characteristics, motives and reasons of the protesters. Civil disobedience is an appeal to the judgment of a reasonable public, particularly because the illegal action as such risks being condemned when there is no chance to explain the underlying reasons. It is also clear that a well-staffed social movement organization can invest more resources in creating or using their own media and, at the same time, pursue a strategy of adaptation to the expectations and mechanisms of the established media.

On the whole, however, I would speculate that exogenous factors are far more important than endogenous ones in influencing media-related strategies. Probably the most crucial exogenous factor is a society's degree of openness to the demands of the protest groups as reflected in more general political and cultural factors, as well as "discursive opportunities" (e.g., the plurality of the media system and the prevailing orientations of journalists; see Ferree et al. 2002; Koopmans and Statham 1999: 228; see also Koopmans 2004; Koopmans and Olzak 2004). When protest groups can access the established media and even receive positive coverage, there is no reason for the strategy of attack and, in addition, there is hardly an incentive to invest in alternative strategies. By contrast, when protest groups are ignored or misrepresented by mainstream media in spite of attempts to play the adaptation card, they are driven toward attacking and/or alternative strategies. The strategy of attack, however, is not very promising for small and radical groups because the mass media, even in cases of violations of their own standards, tend to be unresponsive to a critique articulated by the radical fringe. In Germany, this applies not only to the radical Left but even more so to the radical Right.

Another important exogenous factor is the availability of prominent, credible and/or politically relevant allies and supporters. While a demonstration of several dozens of animal rights protesters in Brussels is very likely to be ignored by the mass media in Belgium and other countries, the presence of a celebrity like Brigitte Bardot secures media coverage. By the same token, a major political player such as the German trade union federation DGB supporting a protest campaign makes that campaign appear "serious" and thus opens the door to the mass media.

Looking back over more than half a century, it is questionable whether the average chances of protest groups to be heard by a mass public have really improved. On the one hand, chances for reaching the mass publics have increased due to the diversification of the mass media system, the stronger adherence to professional journalistic norms by the mass media, the professionalization of the adaptation strategy, and, last but not least, the availability of new technologies. On the other hand, the number of issues raised by protest groups also seems to have increased. As a consequence, competition for scarce attention on the side of the mass publics has become stronger. In sum, gaining visibility and eventually support by mass publics remains a constant challenge for which no simple solutions are at hand.

Notes

1. On this relationship, see, for example, Turner (1969); Halloran and Murdock (1970); Altheide and Gilmore (1972); Molotch (1979); Mazur (1980); Wolfsfeld (1984, 1991); Kielbowicz and Scherer (1986); Schmitt-Beck (1990); Gamson and Wolfsfeld (1993); Gamson and Modigliani (1989); Neidhardt (1994); van Zoonen (1996); Baringhorst (1998); Neveu (1999); Fahlenbrach (2002); and Koopmans (2004).

2. A remarkable exception from this pattern was the revolt on 17 June 1953. This was a rather spontaneous uprising initiated by East Berlin construction workers in the first instance, but, given the repressive political control, it was not preceded or accompanied by a media-oriented strategy.

3. Generally speaking, and leaving aside a few success stories and considering not the potential but the actual uses of the internet, it serves to quickly and effectively spread information among those who are already part of an existing network or know what they are looking for. I contend that the internet is not a great tool for mobilizing (Rucht 2005b). Interestingly, groups such as MoveOn.org in the United States and Campact.de in Germany, who originally engaged only in internet-based forms of protest, are increasingly combining online protests, such as electronic collection of signatures, with offline protests, such as rallies.

Bibliography

Altheide, D. L., and R. P. Gilmore. 1972. "The Credibility of Protest." *American Sociological Review* 37, no. 1 (February): 99–108.

Baringhorst, S. 1998. "Zur Mediatisierung des politischen Protests: Von der Institutionen- zur 'Greenpeace-Demokratie'?" In *Politikvermittlung und Demokratie in der Mediengesellschaft*, ed. U. Sarcinelli. Opladen, Germany: Westdeutscher Verlag.

Bennett, W. L., and R. M. Entman, eds. 2001. *Mediated Politics: Communication in the Future of Democracy.* Cambridge: Cambridge University Press.

Dale, S. 1996. *McLuhan's Children: The Greenpeace Message and the Media.* Toronto: Between the Lines.

Downs, A. 1972. "Up and Down with Ecology: 'The Issue Attention Cycle'." *Public Interest* 8, no. 28: 38–50.

Fahlenbrach, K. 2002. *Protest-Inszenierungen: Visuelle Kommunikation und kollektive Identitäten in Protestbewegungen.* Wiesbaden, Germany: Westdeutscher Verlag.

Ferree, M. M., W. A. Gamson, J. Gerhards, and D. Rucht. 2002. *Shaping Abortion Discourse: Democracy and the Public Sphere in Germany and the United States.* Cambridge: Cambridge University Press.

Flieger, W. 1992. *Die TAZ: Vom Alternativblatt zur linken Tageszeitung.* Munich: Ölschläger.

Gamson, W. A., and A. Modigliani. 1989. "Media Discourse and Public Opinion on Nuclear Power: A Constructionist Approach." *American Journal of Sociology* 95, no. 1 (July): 1–37.

Gamson, W. A., and G. Wolfsfeld. 1993. "Movements and Media As Interacting Systems." In "Citizens, Protest, and Democracy," ed. R. J. Dalton, special issue, *The Annals of the American Academy of Political and Social Science* 529 (July): 114–25.

Gitlin, T. 1980. *The Whole World Is Watching: Mass Media in the Making and Unmaking of the New Left.* Berkeley: University of California Press.

Halloran, J. D., P. Elliot, and G. Murdock. 1970. *Demonstrations and Communication: A Case Study.* Hammondsworth, UK: Penguin Books.

Hilwig, S. 1998. "The Revolt Against the Establishment: Students Versus the Press in West Germany and Italy." In *1968: The World Transformed,* ed. C. Fink, P. Gassert, and D. Junker. Cambridge: Cambridge University Press.

Hocke, P. 2002. *Massenmedien und lokaler Protest: Eine empirische Fallstudie zur Medienselektivität in einer westdeutschen Bewegungshochburg.* Wiesbaden, Germany: Westdeutscher Verlag.

Hoffmann-Axthelm, D., ed. 1978. *Zwei Kulturen? Tunix, Mescalero und die Folgen.* Berlin: Verlag Ästhetik und Kommunikation.

Imhof, K. 1996. "Eine Symbiose: Soziale Bewegungen und Medien." In *Politisches Raisonnement in der Informationsgesellschaft,* ed. K. Imhof and P. Schulz. Zurich: Seismo.

Kepplinger, H.-M. 1989. "Voluntaristische Grundlagen der Politikberichterstattung." In *Medienmacht und Politik: Mediatisierte Politik und politischer Wertewandel,* ed. F. E. Böckelmann. Berlin: Volker Spiess.

Kielbowicz, R. B., and C. Scherer. 1986. "The Role of the Press in the Dynamics of Social Movements." In *Research in Social Movements, Conflict and Change,* vol. 9, ed. L. Kriesberg. Greenwich, CT: JAI Press.

Kolb, F. 1997. "Der Castor-Konflikt: Das Comeback der Anti-AKW-Bewegung." *Forschungsjournal Neue Soziale Bewegungen* 10, no. 3 (September): 16–29.

———. 2005. "The Impact of Transnational Protest on Social Movement Organizations: Mass Media and the Making of ATTAC Germany." In *Transnational Protest and Global Activism,* ed. D. della Porta and S. Tarrow. Lanham, MD: Rowman & Littlefield Publishers.

Koopmans, R. 2004. "Movements and Media: Selection Processes and Evolutionary Dynamics in the Public Sphere." *Theory and Society* 33, nos. 3–4 (June): 367–91.

Koopmans, R., and S. Olzak. 2004. "Discursive Opportunities and the Evolution of Right-Wing Violence in Germany." *American Journal of Sociology* 110, no. 1 (July): 198–230.

Koopmans, R., and P. Statham. 1999. "Ethnic and Civic Conceptions of Nationhood and the Differential Success of the Extreme Right in Germany and Italy." In *How*

Social Movements Matter, ed. M. Giugni, D. McAdam, and C. Tilly. Minneapolis: University of Minnesota Press.

Kraushaar, W., ed. 1978. *Autonomie oder Getto? Kontroversen über die Alternativbewegung.* Frankfurt: Neue Kritik.

Krüger, C., and M. Müller-Henning. 2000. *Greenpeace auf dem Wahrnehmungsmarkt.* Münster, Germany: Lit.

Lepsius, R. 1966. "Parteiensystem und Sozialstruktur: Zum Problem der Demokratisierung der deutschen Gesellschaft." In *Wirtschaft, Geschichte und Wirtschaftsgeschichte: Festschrift zum 65. Geburtstag von F. Lütge,* ed. W. Abel, K. Borchardt, H. Kellenbenz, and W. Zorn. Stuttgart: G. Fischer.

Mazur, A. 1980. "The Rise and Fall of Public Opposition in Specific Social Movements." *Social Studies of Science* 10, no. 3 (August): 259–84.

McMillian, J. 2011. *Smoking Typewriters: The Sixties Underground Press and the Rise of Alternative Media in America.* New York: Oxford University Press 2011.

Molotch, H. 1979. "Media and Movements." In *The Dynamics of Social Movements,* ed. M. N. Zald and J. D. McCarthy. Cambridge, MA: Winthrop.

Neidhardt, F. 1994. "Öffentlichkeit, öffentliche Meinung, soziale Bewegungen." In *Öffentlichkeit, öffentliche Meinung, soziale Bewegungen,* ed. F. Neidhardt. Kölner Zeitschrift für Soziologie und Sozialpsychologie 34. Opladen, Germany: Westdeutscher Verlag.

Neveu, E., ed. 1999. *Médias et mouvements sociaux: Reseaux.* Paris: Hermes Science.

Oy, G. 2001. *Die Gemeinschaft der Lüge: Medien- und Öffentlichkeitskritik sozialer Bewegungen in der Bundesrepublik.* Münster, Germany: Westfälisches Dampfboot.

Peck, A. 1991. *Uncovering the Sixties: The Life and Times of the Underground Press.* New York: Citadel.

Rossmann, T. 1993. "Öffentlichkeitsarbeit und ihr Einfluß auf die Medien: Das Beispiel Greenpeace." *Media Perspektiven,* no. 2: 85–94.

Roth, R. and D. Rucht, eds. 2008. *Handbuch Soziale Bewegungen in Deutschland seit 1949.* Frankfurt: Campus.

Rucht, D. 2003. "Bürgerschaftliches Engagement in sozialen Bewegungen und politischen Kampagnen." In *Bürgerschaftliches Engagement in Parteien und Bewegungen,* ed. Deutscher Bundestag. Enquete-Kommission "Zukunft des Bürgerschaftlichen Engagements". Opladen, Germany: Leske + Budrich.

———. 2004. "The Quadruple 'A': Media Strategies of Protest Movements since the 1960s." In *Cyber Protest: New Media, Citizens and Social Movements,* ed. W. van de Donk, B. D. Loader, P. G. Nixon, and D. Rucht. London: Routledge.

———. 2005a. "Appeal, Threat, and Press Resonance: Comparing Mayday Protests in London and Berlin." *Mobilization* 10, no. 1 (February): 163–81.

———. 2005b. "The Internet as a New Opportunity for Transnational Protest Groups." In *Economic and Political Contention in Comparative Perspective,* ed. M. Kousis and C. Tilly. Boulder, CO: Paradigm Publishers.

———. 2007. "The Spread of Protest Politics." In *The Oxford Handbook of Political Behavior,* ed. R. J. Dalton and H.-D. Klingemann. Oxford: Oxford University Press.

Rucht, D., and S. Teune, eds. 2008. *Nur Clowns und Chaoten? Die G8-Proteste in Heiligendamm im Spiegel der Massenmedien.* Frankfurt: Campus.

Ryan, C. 1990. *Prime Time Activism: Media Strategies for Organizers.* Boston: South End Press.

Salzman, J. 2003. *Making the News: A Guide for Activists and Nonprofits.* Boulder, CO: Westview Press.

Schmitt-Beck, R. 1990. "Über die Bedeutung von Massenmedien für Soziale Bewegungen." *Kölner Zeitschrift für Soziologie und Sozialpsychologie* 42: 642–62.

Shoemaker, P. J., T.-K. Chang, and N. Brendlinger. 1987. "Deviance As a Predictor of Newsworthiness." In *Communication Yearbook 10,* ed. M. L. McLaughlin. Newbury Park, CA: Sage.

Smith, J., J. D. McCarthy, C. McPhail, and B. Augustyn. 2001. "From Protest to Agenda Building: Description Bias in Media Coverage of Protest Events in Washington, D.C." *Social Forces* 79, no. 4 (June): 1397–423.

Staab, J. F. 1990. "The Role of News Factors in News Selection: A Theoretical Reconsideration." *European Journal of Communication* 5, no. 4 (December): 423–43.

Stamm, K.-H. 1988. *Alternative Öffentlichkeit: Die Erfahrungsproduktion neuer sozialer Bewegungen.* Frankfurt: Campus.

Teune, S. 2009. "The Limits to Transnational Attention. Rise and Fall in the European Social Forums' Media Resonance." Paper presented at the conference Shaping Europe in a Globalized World? Protest Movements and the Rise of a Transnational Civil Society, Zurich, 23–26 June 2009.

Tilly, C. 1978. *From Mobilization to Revolution.* Reading, MA: Addison-Wesley.

Turner, R. H. 1969. "The Public Perception of Protest." *American Sociological Review* 34, no. 6 (December): 815–31.

Van Zoonen, L. 1996. "A Dance of Death: New Social Movements and Mass Media." In *Political Communication in Action,* ed. D. L. Paletz. Cress Hill, NJ: Hampton Press.

Voltmer, K. 1993. *Mass Media: Political Independence of Press and Broadcasting Systems.* Wissenschaftszentrum Berlin. Working Paper FS III 93-205.

Warner, M. 2002. *Publics and Counterpublics.* New York: Zone Books.

Wilke, J., and E. Noelle-Neumann. 1994. "Pressegeschichte." In *Fischer Lexikon Publizistik Massenkommunikation,* ed. E. Noelle-Neumann, W. Schulz, and J. Wilke. Frankfurt: Fischer Taschenbuch Verlag.

Wolfsfeld, G. 1984. "Symbiosis of Press and Protest: An Exchange Analysis." *Journalism Quarterly* 61, no. 3 (September): 550–55.

———. 1991. "Media, Protest, and Political Violence: A Transactional Analysis." *Journalism Monographs,* no. 127 (June): 1–61.

Chapter 2

Framing Collective Action

Bert Klandermans

While I am writing this chapter, my newspaper is commemorating the revolution in Romania. We all remember the pictures of Ceausescu standing on a balcony overlooking a crowd mobilized in his support. Unexpectedly, the crowd begins to hiss and shout. Disbelief and confusion strike Ceausescu's face. He turns around and disappears inside the building. As the event was orchestrated to boost Ceausescu's popularity, it was broadcast around the country. A few days later Ceausescu had fallen. For once, the revolution *was* televised.

Of course, the actual Romanian revolution had already been imminent for much longer, in an unobtrusive manner—as evidenced by a chain of brutally repressed protest events, which were concealed from the public at large by strict censorship—until the balcony scene broke the pluralistic ignorance. Suddenly, the weakness of the dictator became clear to the people. The unthinkable fall of the dictator became thinkable. The events illustrate in a powerful manner the crucial role of the media for protest movements: on the one hand, by showing that effective control of the media can prevent protest events in one part of a country from spreading to other parts or even prevent people from becoming aware that protest is taking place in another part of the country, and on the other hand, by showing that the media play an important role in the diffusion of protest throughout the nation if circumstances allow it.

The contributions in this volume elaborate on the role of the media for protest movements. This chapter takes us back a step and offers a guided tour along the social psychological study of protest. This is relevant because many of the factors involved in the social psychology of protest are affected by the media. The reasons protest movements evolve and people take part in collective action staged by such movements cannot be taken for granted, and result from processes of defining and interpreting the situation, such that participation in collective action appears an appropriate thing to do. Framing collective action concerns the processes of consensus mobilization needed for people to decide to take part in collective action. The media are at the heart of the mechanisms implied in such processes of interpretation and dissemination. In the following pages I will first explain how social psychology approaches collective action and will then discuss the key elements of the framing process. I conclude with remarks on the role of the media.

The Social Psychological Approach

Three features characterize the social psychological approach to social movements. The *first* is that social psychology takes the individual as its unit of analysis. It does not provide answers to questions such as why a social movement develops at a given moment, why movements grow bigger or disappear, or why movements succeed or fail, since this is the realm of sociology, political science, and history. A social psychology of protest tries to understand the dilemmas individuals face and the choices they must make when confronted with the opportunity to take part in collective action. What makes them choose to engage or defect, to take part or quit? The *second* aspect of a social psychological approach to social movements is the acknowledgment that people live in a perceived reality. As perceptions are steered by mental frameworks such as cognitive schemata, attitudes, ideologies, and frames, reality as perceived is not a fixed entity. Therefore, it is open for debate and attempts at persuasion. The resulting perceptions may not be real, but they are real in their consequences; that is, they impact on people's behavior. A *third* element concerns the fact that we are dealing with *collective* action. Collective action presupposes shared definitions of the situation—shared grievances, shared cognitions, shared objectives—and involves specific motivational dynamics.

The answer most people would offer as to why they take part in protest is: "Because I am aggrieved." Indeed, illegitimate inequality, suddenly imposed grievances, and violated principles have all featured as reasons for why people take to the streets (Klandermans 1997). Yet this is far from the big picture. Undoubtedly, people protesting are aggrieved, but many aggrieved people never take part in protests and many grievances in a society never generate protest movements. Obviously, the story is more complicated, and the matter to explain is not so much that people who protest are aggrieved, but that people who are aggrieved protest.

The media play an important role in all these aspects. They communicate and comment on the existence of social movements and the stage for collective action. They engage in the processes of interpreting and defining the situation, both directly by delivering interpretations or indirectly by transmitting another party's interpretations; they take part in the formation of shared definitions of the situation. Media play an important role in the development of movements over time. Movements develop in cyclical patterns, and it is the media that not only document but also help shape the cycle. As the media report on a movement, gradually more people come to know about it and more and more people take part. Influenced by media coverage, people may also change their minds and behavior over time.

Movement Participation

Movement participation is among the key concepts of a social psychology of social movements. But what *is* movement participation? The concept of movement participation is much fuzzier than one is inclined to believe. Participation refers to a whole array of different behaviors, ranging from signing petitions to sit-ins, consumer boycotts to rallies, marches, demonstrations, vigils, violence, self-mutilation, donating money, and many more. The social psychological dynamics of different forms of participation diverge. We cannot conclude that someone is willing to take part in a rally or wants to donate money from the fact that he or she is willing to sign a petition. Each form of participation has its own motivational dynamics that may lead someone to be willing to participate in one behavior but not in another. In figure 2.1, I present a typology of forms of participation.

The typology is built on two dimensions: effort and duration. Some activities require little effort, others a lot; some are limited in time while others are unlimited. In order to illustrate that the social psychological dynamics vary, let me tell the story of thresholds and free riders. Activities in the low effort/limited duration square typically require large numbers to make any impression on policy makers at all. It does not make much sense to have a

DURATION

		limited	*unlimited*
E **F** **F** **O** **R** **T**	*low*	I: giving money signing petition peaceful dem.	III: membership two nights a month manning the telephone
	high	II: Sit-in unauthorized dem. strike	IV: committee member voluntary worker

Figure 2.1. The Process of Participation

petition with only ten signatures; you need thousands if not hundreds of thousands. People know this, and thus, for them to be motivated it is important to know that some threshold level will be reached. Therefore, an important element of the persuasion strategy must be how to make people believe that enough other people will participate. Activities in the high effort/unlimited duration square, on the other hand, must solve the free rider dilemma. For these activities it usually suffices to have only a few participants who are willing to make an effort. As a consequence, many people can afford to take a free ride. Willingness to participate in this type of activity thus implies readiness to give 90 percent or more of the supporters that free ride.

In the remainder of this chapter I will discuss the dynamics of participation, the framing processes that play an important role in this participation, and the way media feature in processes of framing.

The Dynamics of Participation

Figure 2.2 provides the seven key concepts of the social psychological framework for the explanation of movement participation that I will elaborate in the pages to come.

The first three concepts—demand, supply, and mobilization—refer to the context of participation. The demand side of protest refers to the proportion of the population in a society that is sympathizing with the cause. The supply side of protest refers to the opportunities of protest offered to people. If there is no supply of protest, the demand might be high but nothing will happen. If, on the other hand, there is no demand there is no point in offering opportunities to protest. Mobilization is the marketing mechanism of social movements. Somehow, demand and supply must be brought together. It must be communicated to people who want to protest that there will be opportunities to protest. Without mobilization, a high demand and a strong supply would get nowhere.

The next three concepts—instrumentality, identity, and ideology—concern the motivation to participate. They form the core of the social psychological approach. They are

- **DEMAND**

- **SUPPLY**

- **MOBILIZATION**

- **INSTRUMENTALITY**

- **IDENTITY**

- **IDEOLOGY**

- **EMOTIONS**

Figure 2.2. Dynamics of Participation

the three fundamental motives that drive people who participate in protest. People participate in protest because they believe that participation helps to change their situation, because they identify with the other participants, or because their norms and values are violated. As the three motives work in an additive manner, they can compensate one another.

Emotions—finally—are the most recent addition to the framework. It would come as a surprise to nobody that emotions play an important role in the social psychological dynamics of movement participation. Yet, it was only recently that emotions were taken into account. Emotions have long been seen as irrational. Social movement literature, however, began moving toward a conceptualization of movement participation as rational behavior, after having been perceived as irrational for a long time. In addition, emotions are complicated phenomena, both theoretically and empirically. As a consequence, it has never been easy to measure emotions.

Demand and Supply

The demand side of participation requires studies of processes such as socialization, grievance formation, causal attribution, and the formation of collective identity. In reference to the example I started this chapter with—the people of Romania—one could think of issues such as having an oppositional background or not being socialized in a city or a rural area. As for grievance formation, it is, for example, important to know about the citizens' personal experiences with communist rule. Causal attribution relates to the question of who to blame for the adverse situation—Ceausescu, the government, communism? As for collective identity, it obviously makes a difference whether someone identifies with the Communist Party or the opposition.

The supply side of participation concerns matters such as action repertoires, the effectiveness of social movements, the ideologies movements stand for, and the constituents of identification they offer. Was the opposition in Romanian society organized? What kind of activities were being organized and were those activities effective in one way or another? Are churches involved in the oppositional movement, or any other societal organization? What is the ideological position of these organizations? Do organizations have charismatic leaders people can identify with?

Mobilization

Much social movement research concerns the mobilization process, which is understandable, given that mobilization is the mechanism that brings demand and supply together. Without mobilization there would be no action, even in circumstances of high demand and high supply. The study of mobilization concerns matters such as the effectiveness of persuasive communication, the influence of social networks, and the perceived costs and benefits of participation. As for the effectiveness of communication, organizers must solve a crucial problem, namely, who are the people demanding protest and how can they be reached? Sometimes this problem is easy to solve if, for example, it concerns the inhabitants of a neighborhood or the workers in a company, but most of the time there are no easy solutions to the problem. Under stark repression, as was the case in Romania, mobilization is extremely difficult and indeed dangerous. Censorship makes newspapers, radio, and television unusable, while organizers and movement activists run the risk of being imprisoned or worse. In a way, Romanian society was a perfect example of a people high on demand but low on supply of protest and failing at mobilization. Once the protest movement appeared in the open and mobilization could no longer be oppressed, the system quickly collapsed.

Social networks are part of the solution to the problem of how to reach and mobilize potential participants. People are involved in all kinds of organizations and social networks: labor unions and neighborhood organizations, churches, sports clubs, and so on. In addition to such formal organizations they are also embedded in interpersonal networks: friendship networks and networks of relatives, family, and others. Such networks are of crucial significance in mobilization campaigns. They serve as a communication network and fuel the motivators of participation by controlling some of the costs and benefits of participation. Participation in collective action can be costly but also rewarding, and the balance of costs and benefits influence people's motivation to participate. I will come back to this in the discussion of instrumental motivation.

Consensus Mobilization versus Action Mobilization

Mobilization can be divided into the processes of convincing and activating. I call a movement's attempts to convince people consensus mobilization. These attempts embrace grievance interpretation, causal attribution, possible measures to be taken, protest activities to be staged, and so on. Consensus mobilization is a long-term enterprise. It takes time—sometimes years—to convince people of the plausibility of a movement's points of view. However, the possible success in activating people is limited by the degree of success of consensus mobilization. Action mobilization concerns the transformation of consensus into action. Indeed, it is difficult enough activating sympathizers; turning people into sympathizers is even harder. Therefore, action mobilization campaigns tend to concentrate on transforming sympathizers into participants.

Steps toward Participation

Action mobilization is a process that evolves in various steps, each having its own explanation (see figure 2.3).

As action mobilization concerns the transformation of sympathizers into participants, the process as it is conceived of in figure 2.3 starts with that part of the population that sympathizes with the movement's cause, which in social movement literature is often depicted as the mobilization potential of a social movement. As mentioned, the size of the mobilization potential reflects the success or failure of the consensus mobilization efforts. The first problem to solve is targeting the sympathizers. This step seems obvious but its significance is often overlooked, both by organizers and researchers. Formal and informal networks, strong and weak ties to movement organizations, and all kinds of communication channels are important vehicles of mobilization at this stage.

The next step involves motivating people to participate. I will elaborate on the motivational dynamics of participation in more detail in the next section on motivational dynamics. Here it suffices to reiterate that someone sympathizing with the cause of a movement does not guarantee that he or she is prepared to participate. Moreover, being motivated for one activity—let's say signing a petition—does not necessarily mean being motivated for another activity—for instance, joining a site occupation. Motivation is specifically the motivation to take part in the specific activity that one has been mobilized for. In the final step, those who have been motivated to participate must actually be persuaded to take part. This is still a significant step to take. For example, in a study we conducted of the mobilization campaign

Figure 2.3. Action Mobilization

for a demonstration, 60 percent of those who said that they were prepared to take part in the demonstration the next day did not go (Klandermans and Oegema 1987). Indeed, this is a complicated step for organizers. What is an organizer to do? People have been targeted; their motivation has been aroused; what more can an organizer do to make sure that someone participates? At this final stage, it is the strength of the motivation, the height of remaining barriers, *and* the influence of friends that make the difference. It is your friends that make you live up to your promises. This is understandable. If two friends decide to take part in an event, each of them will make sure that the other does not pull out.

Motivation

Instrumentality, identity, and ideology are the three fundamental motives that drive people to participate in collective action. This is not to say that each motive should necessarily be active, or that it should be equally strong. For some people one specific motive can be more important than the other, and the same holds for some movements. One might imagine that in the case of the Romanian people instrumentality, that is, aiming for a better government, was most important. Identity motives, on the other hand, might be more important for the gay and lesbian movement, while ideological motives may have been more important for participants in the demonstrations against the Iraq War.

These three motives reflect a development in the social psychological theorizing on movement participation. It began with models emphasizing the instrumentality of movement participation (Klandermans 1984; Opp 1989). Following resource mobilization theory, movements were seen as politics with other means. It was supposed that people participate in social movements because they feel that participation can help to reach some external goals at affordable costs. As time went by it became clear that instrumentality was not the only factor. Simon and his collaborators began to argue that in addition to the calculative instrumentality motive there is also a less calculative identity motive that generates a perceived inner social obligation to participate (Simon et al. 1998), and recently, van Stekelenburg proposed that ideological motives are responsible for a perceived inner moral obligation to participate (van Stekelenburg 2006; van Stekelenburg and Klandermans 2007).

Perceived Costs and Benefits

The instrumental motive to participate in collective action conceives of action participation as controlled by the perceived costs and benefits of participation. Figure 2.4 presents my expectancy-value model as it was published in the *American Sociological Review* in 1984. The model holds willingness to participate dependent on collective benefits and selective incentives. The selective incentives are the expected outcomes of participation multiplied by the value of those outcomes. Between values and expectancies, a multiplicative relationship exists that implies that each factor must be higher than zero. If an expected outcome is not valued it does not make a difference; and if a valued outcome is not expected, it does not make any difference either. Some outcomes are called selective incentives because they are contingent upon participation. Others are characterized by jointness of supply, that is, once they are realized, everybody benefits, including those who did not take part in their realization. Therefore, they are called collective benefits. This makes collective action vulnerable to free rider behavior, that is, nonparticipation under the assumption that one will reap the collective benefits anyway. The key factor of this part of the model is the expectations: expectations about the behavior of others, expectations that the goal will be reached, and expectations about the contribution of one's own behavior.

Inner Social Obligation

The drive originating from identification with other participants is the perceived inner social obligation to act on behalf of the collective. Stürmer and his collaborators demonstrate that the motivating force behind collective identity is such a perceived inner obligation (Stürmer et al. 2003). In so-

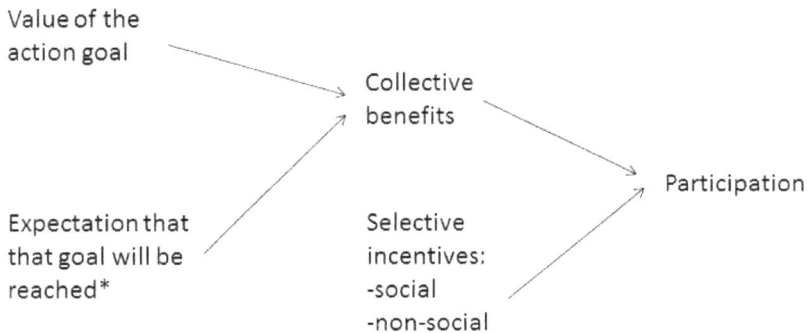

*the expectation that goal will be reached
- expectations aboat the behaviors of others
- the expectations that action goal will be reached if any others participate
- the expectation that own participation will increase likelihood of success

Figure 2.4. The Motivation to Participate

cial psychological and motivational terms, a perceived inner obligation to participate is important because it is impossible to take a free ride on such an obligation. An inner obligation to participate can only be met by acting upon it, that is, by participating.

Inner Moral Obligation

Ideology as a motivating force results in an inner obligation as well, but this time a perceived moral obligation (van Stekelenburg and Klandermans 2007). Norms and values are violated, such as equality or protecting the weak, and in order to maintain their moral integrity people choose to participate in collective action. And again, one cannot take a free ride on a perceived inner obligation.

An Additive Model

Instrumental, identity, and ideological motives presumably combine in an additive manner. That is, each motive adds to the other two in explaining why people participate in collective action, although the relative contribution need not be equal on all occasions. This implies also that the three motives can compensate one another. Indeed, someone can participate in a protest event while not being convinced that it will have much impact on politics, but still identifying with the other participants, and this is what makes this person participate. Alternatively, someone can feel so upset about the violation of some core value, for example, animal rights, that he wants to express his indignation irrespective of the expected political outcomes. Van Stekelenburg (2006) was the first to demonstrate that depending on the organizer or the issue, the relative weight of the motives varied. She proposed and tested the theory that movements might have different action orientations that appeal differentially to the three key motives. Borrowing Turner and Killian's (1987) distinction between power-oriented, participation-oriented, and value-oriented movements, she argued that power-oriented movements appeal more to instrumental motives, and value-oriented movements more to ideological motives. Her study results supported this hypothesis.

Emotions

Politics—and especially politics of protest—are full of emotions. People are *fearful* about terrorism, *angry* about proposed budget cuts, *shocked* about senseless violence, and *proud* of their group's identity. Clearly, there is an emotional component in how people react to their social and political environment. Yet, amazingly little is known about where exactly emotions fit in to the context of movement participation. In collective action research, emotions are a novice with a long history. In the first half of the previous century, emotions were at the center of collective action studies. Collective action was seen as an irrational response to discontent and emotions were equated with irrationality. As a reaction to these approaches, the dominant academic discourse on collective action participation shifted to rational, structural, and organizational explanations. As a result, emotions as they accompany protest were neglected altogether. The rational trend has now been reversed, and we see emotions back on the research agenda of students of collective action (Jasper et al. 2004; Jasper 1997; van Zomeren et al. 2004). Emotions permeate protest at all stages: recruitment, sustained participation, and disengagement (Jasper 2007). Goodwin, Jasper, and Polletta (2001: 13) argue that emotions are socially constructed, but that "some emotions are more [socially, B.K.] constructed than others, involving more cognitive processing." In their view, emotions that are politically relevant are more at the social construction end of the scale than other emotions. For these emotions, cultural and historical factors play an important role in the interpretation (i.e., perception) of the state of affairs by which they are generated. Emotions, these authors hold, are important in the growth and unfolding of social movement and political protest. Obviously, emotions can be manipulated. Activists work hard to create moral outrage and anger and to provide a target against which these can be vented. They must weave together a moral, cognitive, and emotional package of attitudes.

Emotions can be classified in terms of the approach and avoidance tendencies they provoke. Van Stekelenburg and Klandermans (2007) discuss various theories that elaborate on that distinction. Fear is typically an avoidance-oriented emotion that generates inactivity; anger, on the other hand, is approach-oriented and associated with participation in collective action. The factor that moderates whether people react with fear or anger to an infringement of their rights or status seems to be control. If someone feels they have some control of a situation, anger is the most likely response; if someone does not feel in control, fear is the most likely response. In social psychological approaches to emotions, anger is seen as *the* prototypical protest emotion. For those of us who have been part of protest events or watched reports on protest events in the news media, this is hardly surprising. Indeed, it is hard to conceive of protest detached from anger. But other emotions may also be relevant in stimulating protest participation. Indignation is one of these emotions, which "puts fire in the belly and iron in the soul" and, therefore, stimulates protest participation (Gamson 1992).

Research suggests that the same emotion processes (i.e., appraisals, emotions, and action tendencies) operating at the individual level and in interpersonal situations also operate in intergroup situations. People do experience emotions on behalf of their group when the social category is salient *and* they identify with the group at stake (Smith 1993). Since collective action is by definition a group phenomenon and group identification appears to be an important factor in determining collective action, one may assume that group-based emotions impact on protest behavior. Van Zomeren (2006) demonstrated that this is the case. Indeed, group-based anger reinforces protest participation. A question that remains to be answered is whether emotions function as a path to participation separate from instrumentality, identification, and ideology or as an amplifier of these motivations. So far, research by van Zomeren and van Stekelenburg suggests that either process is plausible (van Zomeren 2006; van Stekelenburg 2006).

Collective Action Frames

The beliefs, attitudes, and emotions discussed in the previous section combine into collective action frames. A collective action frame, according to Gamson, is "a set of action oriented beliefs and meanings that inspire and legitimate social movement activities and campaigns" (1992: 7). Collective action frames, in other words, are sets of collective beliefs that serve to create a state of mind in which participation in collective action appears meaningful. The relative success of collective action frames in performing their mobilization functions is partly contingent on how well they attend to the three core framing tasks: diagnostic framing, prognostic framing, and motivational framing (Snow and Benford 1988). The former concerns a diagnosis of some state of affairs as troublesome and the attribution of blame or responsibility for the problematic situation. Prognostic framing involves the articulation of a proposed solution to the problem. Motivational framing provides a rationale for engaging in collective action. For a collective action frame to be generated, evaluations of existing circumstance must be cast as shared grievances, which in turn must be transformed into demands to be presented to the authorities held responsible for the negative circumstances. Finally, people must trust that collective action would be an effective means to produce change. Collective action frames are not just any kind of collective beliefs; they concern conflicts in a society. Controversial issues are debated and themes and counterthemes structure the debate. In this context social actors influence the generation of collective action frames through deliberately designed persuasive campaigns or less controlled news discourses.

Collective beliefs do not reside in the individual but are "out there." From this point of view, individual beliefs are appropriated collective beliefs. Accordingly, in explaining the generation of collective action frames, we must account for two separate processes: the *social construction* of collective beliefs in a collectivity and the *appropriation* of those beliefs by individual members of that collectivity. In an attempt to systematize the discussion on the social construction of collective action frames, I have distinguished three different processes: (a) public discourse, that is, the interface of media discourse and interpersonal interaction; (b) persuasive communication during mobilization campaigns by movement organizations, their opponents, and countermovement organizations; and (c) consciousness-raising during episodes of collective action (Klandermans 1992). Public discourse involves everyone in a society or a particular sector within a society. Persuasive communication affects only those individuals who are targets of persuasion attempts. Consciousness-raising during episodes of collective action primarily concerns participants in the collective action, although bystanders can be affected as well. In each setting the formation and transformation of collective beliefs take place in different ways: in the first setting, through the diffuse networks of meaning construction; in the second setting, through deliberate attempts by social actors to persuade; and in the third setting, through discussions among participants in and bystanders of collective actions.

Interpersonal interaction plays an important role in the appropriation of collective beliefs. Such interaction may involve friends or colleagues, or it may occur during encounters between people in buses, in trains, in pubs, at parties, and in today's world of mobile phones, email, or online social networks (van Stekelenburg and Klandermans 2010). Much of what goes on in such interactions concerns the formation of consensus. People tend to validate information by comparing and discussing their views with those of significant others, especially when the information involved is complex—as is always the case with social and political issues. Social psychological research has shown repeatedly that people prefer to compare their opinions with like-minded individuals (Hewstone et al. 1996). As a rule, the set of individuals interacting in one's social networks—especially friendship networks—is relatively homogeneous and composed of people not too different from oneself. But, however important interpersonal interaction in these networks is for the appropriation of collective beliefs, it does not represent all there is to say on the subject. In *Talking Politics,* Gamson (1992) demonstrates that in their conversations about politics people use any kind of information source available: newspapers, movies, advertisements, novels, rumors, their own and others' experiences, and so on. In the course of these interactions cognitions become shared and some consensual definition of the situation is formed. The extent to which a social movement's collective action frame succeeds in mobilizing people depends on whether it resonates with the targeted audiences, a result that materializes in processes of frame alignment.

Frame Alignment

Frame alignment processes encompass the strategic efforts of social movement actors and organizations to link their interests and goals with those of prospective adherents and resource providers so that they will "buy in" and contribute in some fashion to movement campaigns and activities. Unlike the far more diffuse processes of consensus formation, frame alignment concerns the deliberate attempts to mobilize consensus. Four basic alignment processes have been identified. They include "frame bridging," which involves the linkage of two or more ideologically congruent but structurally disconnected frames regarding a particular issue; "frame amplification," entailing the embellishment, crystallization, and invigoration of existing values and beliefs; "frame extension," which depicts movement interests and framings as extending beyond the movement's initial constituency to include issues thought to be of relevance to bystander groups or potential adherents; and "frame transformation," involving changing prior understandings and perspectives among individuals or collectivities, so that things are seen differently than before, as is commonplace with conversions (Snow et al. 1986).

The Role of the Media

Although frame alignment processes employ any possible means of communication, in the context of this chapter I am especially interested in the role of news media and media discourse. Media discourse does not transmit an actor's views in an unbiased way. In this regard social movements are especially disadvantaged, because they have difficulty fitting into the routines of news media. To be sure, movement organizations do attract media attention, but often these organizations lack experience with the media system. As a consequence, they frequently fall victim to the conventions of news making. Yet, whether they like it or not, social actors have no choice but to rely on news discourse, as the mass media is often the only way for an actor to reach his constituency. Therefore, despite its ambiguities, news discourse is crucial to any actor in a conflict. Kielbowicz and Scherer (1986) mention a variety of practices that allow movement organizations to establish more effective relationships with the media, such as carefully adapting news events to the rhythm and cycles of the media; staging events to draw the attention of the media; establishing relationships with some media or some journalists; and meticulously preparing ready-made documents that journalists can use in the preparation of their news item. Yet, despite all these precautions, there is no guarantee that media coverage will be to the actor's satisfaction. All this assumes that there is freedom of expression, but as the Romanian example illustrates, many a nation restricts news discourse in more or less subtle ways.

News media play an important role in the formation and mobilization of consensus. Three examples may serve to illustrate this argument. In a study of the interplay of real-life events, parliamentary debates, news media content, and anti-immigrant party support, Vliegenthart convincingly shows that Dutch newspapers significantly increased the support for anti-immigrant parties (2007). More media attention led to more party support. The size of the effect is considerable: in the long run, the amount of media attention accounts for 30 percent of the variance in anti-immigrant support.

In a study of the news discourse on a conflict between the Dutch government and the labor unions regarding disability payment, Klandermans and Goslinga (1996) found that the unions had difficulties disseminating their views through newspapers. They registered which elements of press conferences given by the unions made it into newspapers and concluded that one had to read all the newspapers to get the complete picture. In line with the above discussion on news discourse, the newspapers provided a limited narrative of the controversy. It informed the readers about who the actors were rather than what the issues were: about who opposed who, rather than what they disagreed about. In terms of the generation of a collective action frame, this is not necessarily a disadvantage. As long as it is made clear, as in the case of the labor union, that a controversy exists, this may be enough of a signal for dedicated union members that they have to support their union. In a way, the limited role of the news media in the generation of collective action frames should comfort the unions, because their efforts to influence news discourse turned out to be moderately successful. Even carefully prepared press conferences do not guarantee that the union's viewpoints make it into the news discourse. This is not to say that news discourse was irrelevant. Presumably, news discourse provided information on the key elements of the government's plan, which were known by almost everybody. But more importantly, it placed the unions in opposition to the government and thus helped to generate an adversarial frame, just as Gamson (1992) suggested in his treatment of the role of the mass media. After all, the union members *did* develop collective action frames. Whereas in the autumn of 1990 virtually no "hot" feeling could be tapped, a year later people not only had a general idea of what the labor union controversy was about, but more importantly, they had a clear view on where to stand: by their union! When this was combined with an already existing readiness to follow their union if it decided to stage collective action, a collective frame was generated.

Finally, in a study among participants in the demonstrations against the war in Iraq in eight different countries, Walgrave and Klandermans (2010) assessed the mobilizing power of the mass media in comparison to other mobilization channels. They distinguished between more open and closed patterns of mobilization; openness and closedness of mobilization were defined in terms of the communication channels employed and of the prominence of strong ties in the mobilization campaign. Closed patterns of mobilization depend more on strong ties and closed channels of communication; open patterns of mobilization do not depend on strong ties, or on ties at all, and employ open channels of communication, such as mass media or interpersonal networks. The authors demonstrated that the openness or closedness of a mobilization campaign affected aspects of the mobilization process, such as the companionship of participants at the demonstration, the point in time they decided to take part, and the distance they traveled. People who were mobilized in an open rather than a closed manner were accompanied by family or friends rather than colleagues or comembers of organizations, decided to participate later, and traveled shorter distances. Moreover, open versus closed patterns mobilized diverging participants. This held for such demographics as gender and age, political attitudes and behavior, and for someone's attitude toward the war. Walgrave and Klandermans (2010) observed several striking differences between channels and ties in their impact on these participant characteristics and discovered some important or even crucial interactions between the two aspects of openness. As for the effects of the strength of ties, we found that on the whole, participants who were tied to the organizations that staged the demonstrations were more involved in politics and leaned more toward the Left. Interestingly, of all the mobilization channels, only movement organizations had the same effect. The other channels did not tap into politically specific populations. Regarding the interaction of ties and channels, it is interesting to see that the effects of channels only existed among participants without ties or with weak to moderate ties. Among people with strong ties to movement organizations, mobilization channels no longer made a difference. That makes sense; chances are high, of course, that people who have strong ties to movement organizations are indeed mobilized through those organizations. For obvious reasons, people who were tied to movement organizations that were staging a demonstration or who were mobilized directly through those organizations were more opposed to the war and less satisfied with their government's policy. The authors also demonstrated that countries differed in terms of mobilization patterns employed and that these differences were related to a variation in the configuration of demand and supply factors in a given country. Strong demand reinforced open mobilization patterns, as did a contentious social movement sector, whereas a dense social movement sector reinforced closed mobilization patterns.

Conclusions

The Romanian revolution was not the only setting in which media appeared to be extremely important. In the preceding pages, I elaborated more generally on the role of media for social movements. I explained how media engage in the formation of consensus and how people appropriate media content and learn about social reality. As they interpret, communicate, disseminate, and set the agenda, the media help define levels of demand and thus contribute to setting the stage for action mobilization. In addition, the media play a role in consensus mobilization. Organizers attempt to employ media channels to disseminate the movement's view. This is not to say that they always succeed in that respect; quite often they do not. Nonetheless, as we saw, mass media do impact on the formation of collective action frames. Media can also play a role in action mobilization. In societies where high levels of consensus are achieved, newspaper coverage might effectively mobilize for action, as evidenced by the White March in Belgium and by the substantial numbers of participants in the anti–Iraq War demonstrations. Finally, news media report on movement activities. In fact, much of what movement organizers do aim at being covered by the media. After all, movements that do not make it into the media do not exist.

Bibliography

Gamson, W. A. 1992. *Talking Politics.* Cambridge: Cambridge University Press.

Goodwin, J., J. M. Jasper, and F. Polletta. 2001. "Return of the Repressed: The Fall and Rise of Emotions in Social Movement Theory." *Mobilization* 5, no. 1: 65–82.

Hewstone, M., W. Stroebe, and G. Stephenson. 1996. *Introduction to Social Psychology: A European Perspective.* Oxford: Blackwell.

Jasper, J. M. 1997. *The Art of Moral Protest: Culture, Biography, and Creativity in Social Movements.* Chicago: University of Chicago Press.

Jasper, J. M., J. Goodwin, and F. Polletta. 2004. "Emotional Dimensions of Social Movements." In *The Blackwell Companion to Social Movements,* ed. D. A. Snow, S. A. Soule, and H. Kriesi. Oxford: Blackwell.

Kielbowicz, R. B., and C. Scherer. 1986. "The Role of the Press in the Dynamics of Social Movements." *Research in Social Movements, Conflicts and Change* 79: 71–96.

Klandermans, B. 1984. "Mobilization and Participation in a Social Movement: Social Psychological Expansions of Resource Mobilization Theory." *American Sociological Review* 49, no. 5 (October): 583–600.

———. 1992. "The Social Construction of Protest and Multi-organizational Fields." In *Frontiers in Social Movement Theory,* ed. A. Morris and C. Mueller. New Haven, CT: Yale University Press.

———. 1997. *The Social Psychology of Protest.* Oxford: Blackwell.

Klandermans, B., and S. Goslinga. 1996. "Media Discourse, Movement Publicity and the Generation of Collective Action Frames: Theoretical and Empirical Exercises in

Meaning Construction." In *Opportunities, Mobilizing Structures, and Frames: Comparative Applications of Contemporary Movement Theory,* ed. D. McAdam, J. McCarthy, and M. Zald. Cambridge: Cambridge University Press.

Klandermans, B., and D. Oegema. 1987. "Potentials, Networks, Motivations and Barriers: Steps toward Participation in Social Movements." *American Sociological Review* 52, no. 4 (August): 519–31.

Opp, K.-D. 1989. *The Rationality of Political Protest: A Comparative Analysis of Rational Choice Theory.* Boulder, CO: Westview.

Simon, B., M. Loewy, S. Stürmer, U. Weber, C. Kampmeier, P. Freytag, C. Habig, and P. Spahlinger. 1998. "Collective Identity and Social Movement Participation." *Journal of Personality and Social Psychology* 74, no. 4 (March): 646–58.

Smith, E. R. 1993. "Social Identity and Social Emotions: Toward New Conceptualizations of Prejudice." In *Affect, Cognition, and Stereotyping: Interactive Processes in Group Perception,* ed. D. M. Machie and D. L. Hamilton. San Diego, CA: Academic Press.

Snow, D. A., and R. D. Benford. 1988. "Ideology, Frame Resonance, and Participant Mobilization." In "From Structure to Action: Comparing Movement Participation Across Cultures," ed. B. Klandermans, H. Kriesi, and S. Tarrow, special issue, *International Social Movement Research* 1: 197–218.

Snow, D. A., E. B. Rochford Jr., S. K. Worden, and R. D. Benford. 1986. "Frame Alignment Processes, Micro-mobilization and Movement Participation." *American Sociological Review* 51, no. 4 (August): 464–81.

Stürmer, S., B. Simon, M. Loewy, and H. Jörger. 2003. "The Dual-Pathway Model of Social Movement Participation: The Case of the Fat Acceptance Movement." *Social Psychology Quarterly* 66, no. 1 (March): 71–82.

Turner, R. H., and L. M. Killian. 1987. *Collective Behavior.* 3rd ed. Englewood Cliffs, NJ: Prentice Hall.

Van Stekelenburg, J. 2006. "Promoting or Preventing Social Change: Instrumentality, Identity, Ideology and Group-based Anger as Motives of Protest Participation." PhD diss., VU University, Amsterdam.

Van Stekelenburg, J., and B. Klandermans. 2007. "Individuals in Movements: A Social Psychology of Contention." In *Handbook of Social Movements across Disciplines,* ed. B. Klandermans and C. Roggeband. Amsterdam: Springer.

———. 2010. "Uploading Unrest: Do ICTs Change Contentious Politics?" Paper presented at the 105th Annual Meeting of the American Sociological Association Annual Meeting, Atlanta, GA, 17 August 2010.

Van Zomeren, M. 2006. "Social Psychological Paths to Protest: An Integrative Perspective." PhD diss., University of Amsterdam.

Van Zomeren, M., R. Spears, A. H. Fischer, and C. W. Leach. 2004. "Put Your Money Where Your Mouth Is! Explaining Collective Action Tendencies through Group-Based Anger and Group Efficacy." *Journal of Personality and Social Psychology* 87, no. 5 (November): 649–64.

Vliegenthart, R. 2007. "Framing Immigration and Integration: Facts, Parliament, Media and Anti-Immigrant Party Support in the Netherlands." PhD diss., VU University, Amsterdam.

Walgrave, S., and B. Klandermans. 2010. "Open and Closed Mobilization Patterns: The Role of Channels and Ties." In *Protest Politics: Antiwar Mobilization in Advanced Industrial Democracies,* ed. S. Walgrave and D. Rucht. Minneapolis: University of Minnesota Press.

Chapter 3

Demonstrations, Protest, and Communication
Changing Media Landscapes— Changing Media Practices?

Ralph Negrine

The title of this chapter is taken from a well-known British study, *Demonstrations and Communication* (1970), which set out to examine how the anti-Vietnam demonstrations in London in 1968 were covered by the media. The authors—James Halloran, Graham Murdock and Phillip Elliott—set out to understand and explain how journalists in the British print and broadcast media came to construct a particular version of that news event and to disseminate that version to a wider public.

It was a groundbreaking study coming at the beginning of the expansion of communication studies in Britain and at a time when there was a growing concern about how the media dealt with news events, issues of deviance, reporting of social problems, and so on. Published at about the same time as Stan Cohen and Jock Young's *The Manufacture of News* (1973), and Cohen's *Images of Deviance* (1971) and *Folk Devils and Moral Panics* (1972), *Demonstrations and Communication* (1970) could be seen as adding considerable weight to the critical analysis of the media, media work, and media representations. If anything can be said to unite these books and the ideas that they contain, it is the theme that the media are not innocent bystanders, nor mere reflectors of events (the "mirror" analogy), but are seriously implicated in the way events become news and acquire the particular media representation that they do.

This theme is central to this chapter, but it is only part of a more complex argument that I wish to present, namely, that while the essence of the discussion that draws on such studies as *Demonstrations and Communication* is still valid, those who engage in protest activities are no longer passive in the process of news production and have acquired skills that enable them to help shape their representation in the media. But, and this is the final part of the argument, the changing media landscape—the rise of the internet and social media, the troubles of the traditional media, fragmentation of audiences, etc.—has had an impact on the practices of media workers, on protest groups, and on the extent and the nature of disseminated imagery and news protest.

While the consequences of all these changes have yet to be fully understood, several tentative conclusions emerge. The first is that those who protest are still dependent on the mainstream media to obtain publicity; the second is that such publicity may still be framed within a "law and order" frame to the disadvantage of protest movements; the third is that the emergence of "new" media has not necessarily opened up more public spaces for protest movements; the fourth is that the nature, organization, and objectives of protest movements will most likely determine their ability to manage their public representation, their tactics and their media strategies. In this respect, not all movements are the same, so their treatment will also vary. In sum, although things have changed considerably over the last four decades and since the publication of *Demonstrations and Communication,* the conditions have not become any more favorable for *radical* protest movements seeking to make their objectives public.

Before we elaborate on these remarks, it is important to set out the key arguments in *Demonstrations and Communication,* since these frame much of what we now take for granted in our understanding of how the media work and how they construct representations of those who seek radical change in the way societies are governed.

Demonstrations and Communication

Although the right to demonstrate and the right to protest are now taken for granted as fundamental rights of citizens in contemporary societies, few in practice could be classified as "politically active," as in taking part in a campaign (Hansard Society 2010: 81).

But if citizens take for granted that they have the right to protest and to articulate concerns in public, it does not necessarily follow that those who protest will be heard either beyond the sounds of their own (possibly collective) voices or heard equally with others. Or, for that matter, that those who protest will be heard with any degree of favor. As many have observed over the years, those who engage in political protest are dependent on the media for the dissemination of their ideas and objectives, and this dependency is not always benign:

In the late 20th century, political movements feel called upon to rely on large-scale communications in order to *matter*, to say who they are and what they intend to say to publics they want to sway; but in the process they become "newsworthy" only by submitting to the implicit rules of newsmaking, by conforming to journalists notions … of what a "story" is, what an "event" is, what a "protest" is. (Gitlin 1980: 3; emphasis in original)

Thus, what makes the mainstream and traditional mass media most valuable, namely, their ability to disseminate information to large numbers, makes them all the more dangerous because it underlines just how dependent one is on them. The media can highlight issues as well as ignore them; they can embrace them or disown them and disparage them. The media, and those who work within the media, are therefore powerful players in stories about protest, and their selections, biases and framing practices are crucial in the process of transmitting accounts and imagery of protest (see Gitlin 1980: 244–45). Consequently, those who understand the way the media work are therefore in a powerful position, because they can play an active part in shaping news stories rather than simply remaining an object of comment.

There is little in any of these observations that is particularly controversial, and they set out what is commonly understood as the power of the media and the lessons that those who engage in protests should take on if they wish to shape their media profile. It may be possible to argue, though, that the protest movements of the 1960s and 1970s—"*opposition* movements" in Gitlin's words (1980: 244; emphasis added)—were different from other protest movements in that their agendas went beyond specific points of focus such as the Vietnam War. For example, Halloran et al. (1970) place the 27 October 1968 anti-Vietnam protest in London in the context of the general national and international political turmoil of the day. As they point out, not only was there a general disappointment in the effectiveness of parliamentary democracy, but there was also a general dissatisfaction in a range of policies that governments—at home and overseas—were implementing: "by the end of 1966 there was a growing feeling among an increasing number of socialists and radical students that the language of parliamentary politics and the styles of politics pioneered by CND [Campaign for Nuclear Disarmament] … could neither express the need for sweeping changes in the political and social system nor effectively bring them about" (Halloran et al. 1970: 61). Opposition movements of the 1960s and 1970s represented fundamental challenges to the status quo.

In such a charged political climate, any protest on the streets of any major European street in the late 1960s was a newsworthy event. When one adds to this the experiences of violent protests and demonstrations in Paris, Chicago and elsewhere in the same year, it quickly becomes obvious why the media could not ignore such events: the political turmoil (Halloran et al. 1970: 192–93), the violent clashes in other cities abroad, the expected numbers of marchers, the aims and objectives of the marchers, and the general expectation that the protests in London would likely lead to "widespread and violent clashes between marchers and police" (Halloran et al. 1970: 70) propelled the event up the scale of newsworthiness (see Galtung and Ruge 1973).

In such circumstances, the decisions of the organizers about what tactics the protest marchers should adopt became quite crucial. If they were to avoid the confrontations that had characterized marches and protests elsewhere, they had to emphasize their intentions to march peacefully yet still make their points in a strong and unambiguous fashion. According to Graham Murdock, "an estimated 70,000 people marched peacefully along the agreed route. ... The organizer of the breakaway march to (the American Embassy) also rejected the tactics of confrontation but announced their intention of registering their protest by their physical presence ... and by the burning of the American flag" (Murdock 1973: 159).

While the organizers could decide on their tactics and hope that protest marchers would march peacefully, they could not control the extent, or the framing, of the media coverage. The media would cover what, to them, was the most newsworthy aspect of the event. More significantly, the media would cover the event in ways that replayed their prior perceptions and judgments of what the event was about: "the media can create 'news' which is not based on the event itself but on those aspects of it to which they have assigned a particular prominence, i.e. the '*event as news*'" (Halloran et al. 1970: 90). Since "the newspapers defined the event as likely to lead to a violent confrontation" (1970: 90), the media sought to confirm this expectation by focusing on violent incidents rather than on peaceful ones. In this instance, that was not the peaceful demonstrators winding their way through the streets of London but a splinter group of demonstrators clashing with the police in front of the American embassy. On the one hand, then, the expectation of violence, and the violence itself, came to define the nature of the 27 October demonstration and to dominate news coverage; on the other hand, the main march and its peaceful protesters became no more than an ineffective sideshow of little media interest. As Murdock has pointed out, the

> newsworthiness of the event was identified with the expectation that "militant students" led by "foreign agitators" would use the cover of the main march to engage in extensive street fighting with the police

and to attack public buildings. The main march itself was emptied of its radical political content and defined as a performance—bizarre, but essentially within the framework of consensus politics. (1973: 161)

In the conclusion of the *Demonstrations and Communication* study, the authors highlight the ways in which a complex, political event becomes simplified and not only devoid of political meaning but placed within a "law and order" frame of violence and nonviolence:

Because of the way both sections of the march were interpreted, it could be argued that however the demonstrators behaved … they "could not win." Reporting of the peaceful main march suggested disorder and quasi-violence, while the Grosvenor Square demonstrations were reported as unqualified, intentional violence. The point of this account is not to dispute whether or not these were correct impressions to give, granted that the story was to be simplified and presented in news terms. The point is that this process of simplification made the story simply one of violence or non-violence which effectively prevented any communication of alternative perspectives on the demonstration through the television news bulletins. (Halloran et al. 1970: 237)

There can be little doubt that *Demonstrations and Communication* successfully unpacked and dissected some of the key features of media practices, for example, the "news values" that play a part in the construction of the public and political imagery of protest movements. Similar work by Gitlin (1980) and Dan Hallin (1986) pushed the analysis further but essentially played with the same mix of ideas, which explored the ways in which media dealt with movements. What unites them is their focus on events that pitted antiwar protesters and radical groups against the forces of "the state," be they the military, the police or governments more generally. The resulting narratives—of protest and antiestablishment activity, student and mob violence—and imagery—tear gas, scuffles, smoke, stone throwing—fall into what Simon Cottle has called "the dominant law and (dis)order frame, labelling protesters as deviant and de-legitimizing their aims and politics by emphasizing drama, spectacle and violence" (2008: 855).

The question that research about the "dominant law and (dis)order" frame immediately poses, though, is whether this media frame, which emerged strongly in the 1960s and 1970s, is still common today and, therefore, whether contemporary movements are treated in similar ways. One obvious difficulty with answering these sorts of questions lies less in our skills at identifying media frames and more in finding appropriate examples of protests or movements that would be similar enough to the ones that occurred in the 1960s and 1970s so as to provide comparative empirical data. The anti–Iraq War protests in 2002/3 might fall into this category, as might antiglobalization movements, and the findings of studies of their media coverage offer some useful comparisons, as we shall see later in this chapter.

But irrespective of whether the "law and (dis)order frame" remains dominant or not, one thing that has changed very significantly since the 1960s and 1970s is the media landscape. In past decades, the focus was very much on how the mass media covered protests and movements and their role in mediating those voices and actions. In today's fragmented media environment, where the *mass* media are much less dominant and other media proliferate, there is no longer a single dominant voice or screen through which we all share news and information. One consequence of this is that it becomes much more difficult to reach the large numbers of readers and viewers that the mass media used to reach; another is that it becomes much more difficult for protestors and demonstrators, as well as politicians, to decide which media are best for reaching the fragmented public. The media landscape has thus become less friendly to movements that wish to reach very large numbers quickly. Furthermore, as the media are now in an increasingly competitive commercial environment, it is possible that they have become even less friendly to protest movements in their pursuit for survival. These are the themes of the next section.

The Changing Media Landscape

Three different points need to be made when considering how the media landscape has changed and the implications of that change for protest movements. These are:

- The lessening dominance of the traditional mass media.
- The continuing dominance of traditional news values.
- The emergence of the internet and social media.

While these three points are obviously connected, it is worth considering them separately.

The Lessening Dominance of the Traditional Mass Media

In the last four decades, the British media landscape has seen enormous changes in both the structure and reach of the traditional mass media. Other countries have experienced similar trends, so the British experience is not so unusual and it does present interesting problems for protest movements.

Perhaps the most obvious and radical transformation in the British media landscape is in the broadcast (TV) sector. When *Demonstrations and Communication* was published in 1970, Britain had only three national television services—two publicly funded (BBC1 and BBC2) and one commercial (ITV). By 2010, there were five national terrestrial services (BBC1, BBC2, ITV1, Channel 4 and Channel 5) and several hundred generalist and specialist channels available via cable and satellite and, increasingly, via the internet.

The ensuing competition for funding has had obvious effects, and not all media have been able to survive intact. Sometimes, as in the case of local news provision, this has resulted in cutbacks and a reduction of news services. At other times, the absence of funding for news production has forced commercially funded news programs to be moved to less popular time slots or to follow a different, and more populist, news agenda. In general, the more competitive media *and news* environment of today has probably contributed to a reduction in the depth of available news provision, to a more populist news agenda for some news services and to a television landscape in which news is only a small fraction of the total provision. Drawing on their 1999 study of news and current affairs provision in Britain over a period of twenty years, Barnett and Seymour concluded that "the BBC has already become almost the sole repository of serious current affairs on British television" (2000: 17). There is no evidence to suggest that this trend will not continue.

Others would perhaps object to these conclusions, since they derive from studies that define "serious" news in very particular ways and so ignore the range of other forms of information provision that can be seen not as part of a tabloid agenda but "as intelligible and in many respects welcome journalistic responses to changes in the technological, economic and political environments which shape political culture" (McNair 2006: 171). In other words, just because a topic features on daytime chat shows, it does not mean that serious issues are not tackled. On balance, though, the evidence suggests that there has been an overall reduction of news about politics, current affairs, and "serious" topics, for example, on the front pages of newspapers (Negrine 1998), on television (Barnett and Seymour 2000), or in the local press, where it is now unusual for local papers to cover the courts and local council meetings.

Just as there has been a fragmentation in media structures, with more and more outlets competing against one another, there has been a fragmentation in the media audience. In 1968, when protesters were marching against the Vietnam War, the BBC's share of the television audience was nearly 50 percent, with the commercial network having a similar share. By 2010, that share has shrunk and few news programs achieve anything like the numbers of viewers that they once did (see Blair 2007).

The print media—even before the arrival of the internet—was not immune to change either. In 1970, the total circulation of paid-for daily newspapers was in the region of 14.5 million; by 2010 it was down to about 11 million, with both tabloids and "serious" newspapers suffering losses.

The Continuing Dominance of Traditional News Values

In their exploration of the properties of news, Galtung and Ruge concluded that "events become news to the extent that they satisfy the conditions of frequency, threshold, unambiguity, meaningfulness, consonance, unexpectedness, continuity, composition" and references to elite nations, people or negativeness (1973: 69–70). While there is some debate about the way these criteria are applicable in all cases, it is very likely that large-scale political demonstrations score highly on many of these conditions: they involve large numbers ("threshold") and elite people or nations, they include the possibility of disruption and the potential for violence ("negativity"), they are "unambiguous," and so on. From a journalistic point of view, therefore, it is unlikely that such an event would not merit attention, especially if there is a prior expectation of disruption and/or violence. This was certainly the case for the events in London in 1968, but their significance was much greater as their coverage appeared in other countries also. Rolf Werenskjold has shown, for example, that the Norwegian press exercised similar "tendencies in the selection of news" in their coverage of demonstrations, strikes and riots in 1968 and that the Norwegian press "gave priority to events in the northern Western elite countries correspond(ing) with a general pattern for the covering of foreign news in Norwegian newspapers in the 1960s, as also Galtung and Ruge have argued" (2008: 425). So, despite the critical comments that the Galtung and Ruge (1973) study has attracted, for example, with respect to its concentration on foreign news and its overconcentration on news as opposed to other outputs, such as features (Tunstall 1971: 20–22), or its inability to explain why sometimes geographically and culturally proximate events do not make it as news (Werenskjold 2008: 432), it still offers a useful way of exploring why certain events become news and others not.

Yet there continues to be an element of tautology in the news selection process: a story is often news because it is in the news; similarly, "big" news stories are evidently, at least to a journalist, "big" news stories and cannot be ignored. When the "top story" is beyond doubt—and it is beyond doubt if all media have defined it as a "top story"—all media will lead with it. Conversely, when "top news stories" are less apparent and clear-cut, the front pages of newspapers may differ considerably, as do the headlines of broadcast programs. It is unlikely that the selections made by journalists today will be significantly different from those made three or four decades ago. Harcup and O'Neill have argued that "Galtung and Ruge ignored day-to-day coverage of lesser, domestic and bread-and-butter news" and that their "taxonomy of news factors appears to ignore the majority of news stories. ... [however,] news stories do frequently contain the factors identified by Galtung and Ruge, ... [but] many items of news are not reports of events at all, but 'pseudo-events,' free advertising or public relations spin" (2001: 276–77). Their own taxonomy, based on an analysis of front-page news stories in three British national newspapers[1] in 1999, produced a list of (self-explanatory) "requirements" (2001: 269) that do not markedly differ from Galtung and Ruge's (1973). So, for example, stories should involve "the power elite," "celebrity," "entertainment," surprise, "bad news," "good news," be significant in magnitude, be relevant to the audience, follow up on previous stories and fit in with the newspaper agenda.

This should not be taken to mean that news of demonstrations, protests, or movements will not be reported, but only that the chances of being reported today may be lower than in the past given the way that news about entertainment and celebrities has gained prominence in the press. To gain publicity, therefore, events may require that extra element of surprise, disruption, or unusualness, so that celebrities and entertainment, and pseudoevents, are pushed to one side. As protest groups have found out, stunts and the prospect of disruption seem to work: the Camp for Climate Action camped alongside Heathrow Airport (2007); Father4Justice, a group seeking to redress the unfavorable treatment that the group members perceive divorced fathers get in the family courts, regularly organized stunts such as climbing Buckingham Palace's defenses to gain publicity (F4J 2008); and in November 2009, members of Greenpeace lowered banners from the Sagrada Família in Barcelona to draw attention to climate change. Such stunts do get covered, though not necessarily consistently—the Sagrada Família stunt was pictured in the *Guardian* (Vidal 2009) but ignored by other newspapers— and this can highlight questions about their purpose and long-term usefulness. If covered, they remind us of protest, albeit fleetingly, but if ignored by the media, they do not have any visibility.

For most protest movements, there is plainly a balance to be struck between frequently being in the headlines on account of the stunts that they pull, though even here the media might tire of these, and the alternative of not being in the headlines at all. Some groups, such as Greenpeace, are able to negotiate between the two and tend to work in public but also behind the scenes. Such groups have always existed, and have sought to gain publicity simply as a way of advancing their causes further within established political systems and practices. Radical protest movements, as we have seen, face other problems: they may never achieve sufficient space for their voices to be heard and/or the publicity they may gain might be unfavorable and fall within the "law and (dis)order frame" described above.

Research into the coverage of the anti–Iraq War movement marches in London in 2003 tends to suggest that the analysis of the relationship between protest movements and the media is more complex than earlier studies identified but that, nonetheless, some of the earlier findings still apply. For instance, protest movements still do not occupy much space in the media even when there is broad support for the concerns of the movement, as there was with respect to the anti–Iraq War coalition before the actual war started. As Murray et al. (2008: 22) report: "Prior to military action, and for a brief period during the start of the war, coverage of protest activity played more positively than negatively for the anti-war movement. . . . Once the conflict got under way, however, positive attention started to decline." More significantly, they report that "the UK press saw the beginning of hostilities as the end of the debate" (Murray et al. 2008: 23). The authors conclude that "[a]s in previous conflicts, and consistent with the literature highlighting the difficulties that protest movements have in accessing media, the anti-war movement was progressively ignored and/or challenged by newspapers. With respect to mainstream media, protest and opposition during war remains a marginal and difficult task" (Murray et al. 2008: 24–25).

Finally, and perhaps as a contribution to Cottle's suggestion (2008: 855) that the "law and (dis)order frame" may be less common today than in the past, it is also worth exploring briefly the way that the demonstrations in London during the G20 summit of world leaders in April 2009 featured in the British print media. The coverage leading up to the demonstration on 1 April 2009 confirms the existence of the "law and (dis)order frame," with many of the news items highlighting the expectation of disruption and violence. This should not be taken to mean that there are no sympathetic accounts of the demonstrators and their aims and objectives, but only that the overwhelming tone is one of impending disruption and violence. That sense of foreboding can be seen in the following selection of extracts:

> The G20 Meltdown campaign is a loose alliance of organizations that will set off from four locations in London a day earlier and converge on the Bank of England, each marching behind one of the "four horsemen of the apocalypse."

Other action is rumored to be planned to disrupt transport and cause chaos in the City in what many believe could be the biggest protests since the poll tax riots. (*Guardian* 2009a)

Protesters plan to use Google Streetview and the micro-blogging site Twitter to cause mayhem at next week's G20 summit in London. (*Daily Mail* 2009a)

A leading hospital is on alert to treat people injured in disorder expected in the City of London and during the G20 summit next week.

All police leave has been cancelled in London for the two days surrounding the summit, which will be accompanied by demonstrations by anti-war groups, environmentalists, anti-globalisation activists and anarchists. (*Times* 2009)

Yesterday, the Metropolitan police were understood to have contacted a number of protest groups warning that the main day of protest, Wednesday 1 April, would be "very violent," and senior commanders have insisted that they are "up for it, and up to it" should there be any trouble. (*Guardian* 2009b)

Cops arrest 5 in G20 terror plot; Summit security shock fake guns and "explosives" found in flat swoops. (*Sun* 2009)

On Wednesday morning, large areas of the City could become a battleground as at least 3,000 police face tens of thousands of demonstrators under the umbrella group "G20 Meltdown" to try to bring the financial heart of Britain to a standstill. (*Mail on Sunday* 2009)

Old habits, it seems, do die hard, as does the suspicion that the press has gotten uncomfortably close to the forces of "law and order," to the extent that newspapers initially merely reproduced a series of scare stories about chaos, security operations and anarchists. As with the 1968 demonstration in London, the images of confrontations and bloodied heads were available aplenty.

The Emergence of the Internet and Social Media

The changed media landscape discussed above inevitably brings to the fore the ascendancy of new communication technologies and of the internet in particular, and there is no doubt that it has helped reshape the landscape of protest and publicity. The use of Google's Street View, Twitter, and other social networking sites by protesters during the 2009 G20 summit is well known and helped connect those who wished to engage in similar activities. The structure of the internet and its ability to connect individuals and groups has created a different way for movements to communicate, internally and externally, but it has not really resolved the issue of how movements can then communicate with a wider public. To communicate internally and to a self-selected group is to limit the effectiveness of protests, which is why that connection to the "outside" world is so critical.

As Lance Bennett (2003) has argued, the properties of the internet create the potential for movements of different types to come into being. The new technology creates new possibilities and new circumstances that were not possible when other modes of communication were dominant. Movements can now be loosely organized, leaderless, flexible and continually regenerating; they can be local or global; they can change their nature and adapt rapidly to changing circumstances. The global reach and speed of the new information and communication technologies make them useful for rapid, global and easy communication and organization. The websites, Facebook groups and Twitter links created by such movements and by individuals become, in effect, sources and resources of information and action. They become those elements that link individuals to one another and to larger groupings so as to advance, protect or challenge authority. For many contemporary movements, the new technologies are the means of linking up. Often, there is no single center of activity but a range of different centers; no leadership but a range of independently run groupings. Pickerill and Webster employ the phrase "an 'electronic spine' that connects key activists" to describe the process of connecting with others (2006: 418). In the same vein, words such as "polycentric (distributed) communication networks" and "hubs" give further indications of how the internet connects diverse and "ideologically thin" (Bennett 2003: 150) organizations.

The creation of connections across space and time not only enable movements to come into being, but also enable dispersed peoples to unite in their endeavor to come together and redefine their own identities and power. But the effectiveness of that power is probably limited by the reach of a movement: publicity growing out of a disruptive street protest is likely to be less effective and favorably received than a protest by millions engaged in peaceful activities. Movements, in other words, have always had to strike a balance between publicity and effectiveness, being inward looking as opposed to outward looking, connecting with the few or the many, and so on. These issues do not disappear in the age of new technologies but, in fact, can become even more problematic given that the new communication technologies do enable almost instantaneous organization and mobilization for those who are connected and "in the loop."

There are also important similarities in terms of the organization and intentions of those who protested in the past and those who protest in the present: apart from the aim of disseminating messages widely and seeking to gain public support, there is the common intent of bringing pressure on those who can bring about change, such as policy makers. Moreover, there is still the dependency on the mass media for wider distribution of the message, which, as before, is not under the control of those who protest. Hence the similarities in the ways in which movements work and seek to achieve change even in the era of the web: to bring pressure by action means getting people on the streets, it means persuading through publicity, which, in turn, means relying on the media to publicize events.

The benefits of organizing via the web are fairly obvious given the speed and spread of messages; the downside might be that activity on the web reaches a fraction of the public that needs to be persuaded and mobilized to protest, or discussions reach only those who are already predisposed to act. It is entirely possible that this was also the case with the radical protest movements of the 1960s and the 1970s, but there is a lingering feeling that getting people onto the streets, in large numbers, for a political cause might be a more powerful signal of intent than internet conversations that may only lead to small demonstrations. It would also be a more newsworthy story and provide a more powerful message.

Conclusion: Demonstrations, Protest, and Communication

In the introduction, I suggested that:

- Those who protest are still dependent on the mainstream media to obtain publicity.
- Such publicity may still be framed within a "law and order" frame, to the disadvantage of protest movements.
- The emergence of "new" media has not necessarily opened up more public spaces for protest movements.
- The nature, organization, and objectives of protest movements will most likely determine their ability to manage their public representation, their tactics and their media strategies.

These conclusions have been supported by a number of points made through-out this chapter. While it is undoubtedly true that we no longer inhabit a world with clear political divisions between Right and Left and that this has given rise to groups—political parties, movements, civil society organiza-tions—that cannot be easily placed along this continuum, there is nonethe-less some evidence that those who protest still find themselves on the outside, often criticized or pilloried. Whether this is simply a consequence of news values that favor the unambiguous and that highlight disorder more read-ily than ambiguity, complexity and qualifications is difficult to say. Given journalistic practices and the continuing obsession with the "significant" and "important," it could well be that news values will override everything else all the time.

In his article on protest movements and communication, Simon Cottle (2008) raised a number of questions that can inform future research. These include the following:

> How do wider shifts in geo-politics and informing processes of political economy alter the contemporary force-field of interests and identities that contend and contest in the field of demonstra-tions and protests, and with what discursive and symbolic impacts? (861)

> How is media awareness and reflexivity built into the tactics de-ployed by demonstrators and their subsequent interactions with the news media? How have these communication tactics evolved across the contemporary demonstration and protest field and how do jour-nalists respond to these reflexive interventions over time and with what representational consequences? (864)

This chapter contributes some thoughts to these questions, but it is only a small contribution to an area of study that is open to a contemporary reassessment and review of the central findings of *Demonstrations and Communication.*

Notes

1. One criticism of the Galtung and Ruge (1973) study is that they used foreign news stories as the basis of their work. Harcup and O'Neill selected front-page news stories from one tabloid newspaper, a midmarket newspaper and a broadsheet newspaper. This too might have an impact on the categories set out above, perhaps overplaying the celebrity and entertainment categories that are at the heart of the tabloid press.

Bibliography

Barnett, S., and E. Seymour. 2000. *From Callaghan to Kosovo: Changing Trends in British Television News 1975–1999.* http://www.ofcom.org.uk/static/archive/itc/research/callaghan_to_kosovo.pdf.

Bennett, L. W. 2003. "Communicating Global Activism: Strengths and vulnerabilities of networked politics." *Information, Communication & Society* 6, no. 2: 143–68.

Blair, T. 2007. "Prime Minister Tony Blair's Reuters Speech on Public Life." BBC News, 12 June. http://news.bbc.co.uk/1/hi/uk_politics/6744581.stm (accessed 27 October 2008).

Camp for Climate Action. 2007. "Heathrow Eco-Protesters Steal a March on Police." *Guardian.* 13 August. http://www.guardian.co.uk/environment/2007/aug/13/activists.transportintheuk (accessed 15 January 2010).

Cohen, S. 1971. *Images of Deviance.* Pelican series. Harmondsworth. Penguin.

———. 1972. *Folk Devils and Moral Panics: The Creation of the Mods and Rockers.* Sociology and the Modern World. London. MacGibbon and Kee.

Cohen, S., and J. Young, eds. 1973. *The Manufacture of News: Deviance, Social Problems and the Mass Media.* London: Constable.

Cottle, S. 2008. "Reporting Demonstrations: The Changing Media Politics of Dissent." *Media, Culture & Society* 30, no. 6 (November): 853–72.

Daily Mail. 2009. "Google Anarchists Targeting the City." 26 March.

Father4Justice (F4J). "Selected Images of Protest." n.d. http://images.google.co.uk/images?q=fathers+for+justice&oe=utf-8&rls=org.mozilla:en-GB:official&client=firefox-a&um=1&ie=UTF-8&ei=ISH5Sq_-N8f84Ab4642wCw&sa=X&oi=image_result_group&ct=title&resnum=4&ved=0CCwQsAQwAw (accessed 15 November 2009).

Galtung, J., and M. Ruge. 1973. "Structuring and Selecting News." In *The Manufacture of News: Deviance, Social Problems and the Mass Media,* ed. S. Cohen and J. Young. London: Constable.

Gitlin, T. 1980. *The Whole World Is Watching.* London: University of California Press.

Guardian. 2009a. "Banks Are Braced for City Riots during G20 Summit after Attack on Goodwins Home." 26 March.

———. 2009b. "Police Tactics Queried As Met Says G20 Protests Will Be 'Very Violent.'" 28 March.

Hallin, D. 1986. *The Uncensored War.* Berkeley: University of California Press.

Halloran, J., Elliot, P. and G. Murdock. 1970. *Demonstrations and Communication: A Case Study.* London: Penguin Books.

Hansard Society. 2010. *Audit of Political Engagement 7: The 2010 Report.* http://www.hansardsociety.org.uk/blogs/publications/archive/2010/03/03/the-7th-annual-audit-of-political-engagement.aspx (accessed 15 January 2010).

Harcup, T., and D. O'Neill. 2001. "What Is News? Galtung and Ruge Revisited." *Journalism Studies* 2, no. 2: 261–80.

Mail on Sunday. 2009. "No Mobile for Jamie When He Cooks for the Obamas." 29 March.

McNair, B. 2006. *Cultural Chaos: Journalisms, News and Power in a Globalised World.* London: Routledge.

Murdock, G. 1973. "Political Deviance: The Press Presentation of a Militant Mass Demonstration." In *The Manufacture of News: Deviance, Social Problems and the Mass Media,* eds. S. Cohen and J. Young. London: Constable.

Murray, C., K. Parry, P. Robinson, and P. Goddard. 2008. "Reporting Dissent in Wartime: British Press, the Anti-War Movement and the 2003 Iraq War." *European Journal of Communication* 23, no. 1 (March): 7–27.

Negrine, R. 1998. *Parliament and the Media: A Study of Britain, Germany and France.* London: Pinter.

Pickerill, J., and F. Webster. 2006. "The Anti-War/Peace Movement in Britain and the Conditions of Information War." *International Relations* 20, no. 4 (December): 407–23.

Sun. 2009. "Cops Arrest 5 in G20 Terror Plot; Summit Security Shock. Fake Guns and 'Explosives' Found in Flat Swoops." 31 March.

Times. 2009. "Hospital All Set for Victims of G20 Violence; London Is Braced for Riots in City Streets As Protesters Vent Anger." 27 March.

Tunstall, J. 1971. *Journalists At Work.* London: Constable.

Vidal, J. 2009. "Barcelona Diary: Fighting Talk, Russian Roulette and Gaudí's 'Green' Makeover." *Guardian.* 2 November. http://www.guardian.co.uk/environment/blog/2009/nov/02/barcelona-climate-change-talks (accessed 15 January 2010).

Werenskjold, R. 2008. "The Dailies in Revolts." *Scandinavian Journal of History* 33, no. 4: 417–40.

Chapter 4

Culture and Protest in Media Frames

Baldwin Van Gorp

The news media and social movement organizations, including institutionalized interest groups and ad hoc protest groups, form interacting systems. The connections, however, must be characterized as asymmetrical. Gamson and Wolfsfeld (1993) discern three reasons why movements need to generate media attention that fits their own purpose in a positive way: first, to mobilize members and raise funds; second, to legitimize the movement's existence; and third, to broaden public acceptance for its aspirations.

Movements can attract media attention by organizing manifestations, from rallies and sit-ins to wild demonstrations and protest marches. During these "public shows," movements and news media can find each other. After all, reports on demonstrations and related pseudoevents are easily translated into news items. Due to the standard setup and the discordant character of the manifestations, the subject of the protest is clear, as are the opponents and the reasons for them taking place. Furthermore, this type of occasion mostly brings about lively (audio)visual material, supplying both the written and the audiovisual press with sufficient source material to turn the event into news. In sum, a number of news factors that are represented in literature (see, e.g., Eilders 2006) apply in the case of protest: negativism, controversy, and visualization certainly, and possibly also potential damage and emotions.

The main purpose of this chapter is to observe closely and reconstruct the frames used in "mediatized conflict" (Cottle 2006). The focus is on the public communication of movements and on how the news media represent the movements' actions and interests. Both the movements and the institutions to which the protest is directed participate in a reciprocal controversy on meaning construction, whereby the stake is often whether the issue can be defined as problematic or unproblematic. In addition, journalists are caught in the middle of this process of meaning construction. They do not only present a forum where the symbolic contests take place, but also add layers of interpretation of events.

The literature on news framing suggests that the conflict frame and the social responsibility frame are two news formats that dominate news reporting (Semetko and Valkenburg 2000). In the conflict frame the accent lies on the contesting parties and the stake of the conflict, while the social responsibility frame pays attention to the origin of the conflict in question or to those responsible for its solution. Yet the outlined categories of conflict and social responsibility need further exploration. Indeed, a journalist can present a demonstration as a conflict. The journalistic interference, however, can be much more fundamental. For instance, suppose that a journalist reporting on a conflict refers to one of the conflicting parties as a sympathetic underdog who is taking a stand against a superior power. In this case, there is every chance that the public will back up the first party, as this description contains implicit, or often explicit (e.g., Papacharissi and Oliveira 2008: 66), reference to the biblical story of David versus Goliath. In that case, a framing analysis is necessary in order to examine which elements (e.g., "underdog") can trigger a scheme in the heads of the receivers that compares with the cultural frame of David versus Goliath. Therefore, the guiding argument of this contribution is that paying attention to the more subtle ways in which the media and movements interact and how cultural symbols and language guide this interaction are important for gaining insight on the relation between media and protest (cf. Zald 1996).

This chapter also suggests how framing researchers can define culturally embedded frames inductively. There has been a lot of discussion about how to conduct a framing analysis (e.g., D'Angelo and Kuypers 2010). I propose an interpretative methodology that focuses on the identification of cultural phenomena as frames by performing a systematic comparison of manifest textual elements. To illustrate this methodology, a case study on the decision to open a refugee center in a local community will be used. This case goes back to the period 2000/1 but is still of current interest.

Culturally Embedded Frames

The Presentation of Issues in a Public Space

The conceptualization of framing is different for each discipline in which it is used. In this chapter, I rely on Gitlin's definition of frames as "persistent patterns of cognition, interpretation, and presentation, of selection, emphasis, and exclusion, by which symbol-handlers routinely organize discourse, whether verbal or visual" (1980: 7). The main difference to other conceptualizations is that, here, framing is about the empirically observable *pre-*

sentation of issues in a public space. How these frames are tied in with, for instance, the underlying ideology of protest groups is the main concern of other disciplines, such as political science (cf. Snow and Benford 2005: 210). This explains why social movements with diametrically opposed ideologies can apply the same frame. For example, the pro-life movement used the civil rights frame to stress the right of the embryo to live, whereas the pro-choice movement used the same frame to stress the autonomy of the mother (Oliver and Johnston 2000).

Frame Mechanisms

When movements or journalists use frames to present issues and events as meaningful, three features of framing deserve specific attention: selection and salience, simplification, and causal reasoning.

First, the inability to perceive objective reality and the chaotic stream of disjointed impressions in their entirety explains why selection and ordering by the news media is inevitable. An essential point is salience, or the process of emphasizing certain information and making it more significant so that the audience will notice it more easily (Entman 1993).

Second, frames are used in this process as simplifying models. More specifically, both journalists and protesters, as well as their opponents, use the existing culture as a "tool kit" to understand "what is going on" (Hertog and McLeod 2001; Swidler 1986). Cultural phenomena as values and narratives present themselves in almost all types of communications. Journalists for their part use these universally understood codes as frames because they constitute meaning, coherence, and ready explanations for issues. Each association between the issue and a broader, cultural phenomenon offers a new perspective from which reality can be perceived. However, due to their omnipresence, journalists are not always conscious of the fact that they copy a restricted amount of frames from each other, and use and reuse them. In this way, news media implicitly suggest not only how the public can understand the news on protest movements, but also which meaning it can attach to the issue generating the protest.

Third, frames as simplifying models offer a causal chain of reasoning (Entman 1993; Snow and Benford 1988). The main assumption of how framing causes an effect is that the manifest framing devices in a message recall a cognitive schema on the basis of which the receiver fills in this causal chain of reasoning, which does not need to be explicitly incorporated in the message (Van Gorp 2007). This observation implies that frames are not just in the individual's head, but that they also reside in social interaction (Snow and Benford 2005) and at a macro level in cultural structures (cf. Polletta 2004).

The Reconstruction of Frame Packages

Inductive Framing Analysis

The aim of inductive framing analysis is, starting from a series of texts—from news messages, including written text and visuals, to spoken texts—to reconstruct the frames applied therein. Each frame is represented as a *frame package,* consisting of framing devices, reasoning devices, and the central frame. *Framing devices* are manifest components of a text that can activate the frame as an abstract idea in the heads of the receivers. *Reasoning devices* consist of the implicit or explicit reasoning connected to the issue being reported on, the definition of the problem, the indication of its origins and consequences, the presentation of a (policy) solution, and the passing of a moral judgment (Entman 1993). Finally, there is the *organizing theme*—the actual frame—that turns the total frame package into an internally consistent entity. The quality of coherence may result in elements in the text that do not belong to the frame package being selectively dropped out, adapted, or marginalized.

The reconstruction of frame packages requires a systematic approach. Four steps—that can advance in a parallel manner—can be distinguished: the open coding, the axial coding, the construction of a frame matrix, and the evaluation.

Open Coding

To be able to gain insight into the potential frames, it is important to collect a broad variety of texts: news reports, as well as texts originating from different actors, advocates, and opponents. The collection of texts has to be analyzed with an "open mind" in order to list all potential framing devices and reasoning devices. The devices can be categorized under five structural dimensions: the syntactic structure, the script structure, the rhetorical structure, the thematic structure, and the intertextual structure (cf. Pan and Kosicki 1993).

The syntactic structure encompasses the number of words and pictures, the layout of a text, the placement of a news article on a page, and the editing of an audiovisual production. These elements are not considered framing devices, but rather are formatting devices. They are important nevertheless, as they provide cues about how readers and viewers of news perceive the salience and importance of the topic being framed.

News reporting is not a summing up of loose pieces of information without any coherence; it follows a script structure. The power of framing is not found in the traditional inverted pyramid structure, but comes into being because the structure of the news leans on the structure of "the story."

The main components of the story are the plot, the characters, and the standpoint of the narrator. The composition of the classical plot roughly consists of the disturbance of a balance and the attempt to restore it. For framing analysis it is pertinent to work out whose standpoint the respective journalists represent. Possibly, they prefer to cite or interview spokespersons of official institutions and experts instead of the protesters. At other times, they may make an appeal to the "ordinary public."

To produce a convincing story, journalists have access to certain rhetorical means. When carrying out news framing analysis, the research may focus attention on elements in the news report that contain a persuasive character. Gamson's five framing devices belong to this rhetorical structure, namely, metaphors, expressions, examples, descriptions, and visual images (Gamson and Lasch 1983). With regard to the analysis of protest marches and rallies, there are some additional points of interest, such as the selective and evaluative reports on the number of participants, statistical data, and lexical choices, as their nature is evaluative. Cohen's analysis (1976) on the press coverage on Mods and Rockers is in this respect the best-known example.

Pan and Kosicki (1993: 71) argue that the central idea, which we designate as a frame, represents the theme of a message. To them, this theme is not the same as a topic. The theme as such characterizes the topic. The establishment of a refugee center, for example, is the topic, while the choice to elaborate on the consequences for the local community is the theme. Related concepts belonging to the thematic structure of a text are issue and perspective. In the example, the granting of asylum is the issue, while the local community constitutes the perspective, and thus the actor who is focused upon.

Explicit and implicit references to other texts result in the intertextual structure of a message, because 'every message is created against the background of other messages dealing with the same matters or issues. In this way, a news message will be part of a greater news story on the issue as a whole (Bird and Dardenne 1997). However, the intertextual structure also contains aspects that are not semantically related, but are temporally related. This includes, for instance, all items and articles pertaining to the paper or the journal from which the news message originates. In this way, an intertextual web is woven. Its complexity becomes more intricate when it turns out that the public can join an almost endless amount of texts to it. The public is, after all, the most important negotiators in the process of meaning construction.

Axial Coding

The next step of the analysis is to look for patterns of devices by linking them to overarching ideas. Whereas in the first step the inventory of devices is made for each separate text, in the second step similarities and differences between the devices are reduced to dimensions. This is a difficult phase, because it is hardly possible to give guidance. It is important to make an abstraction of the specific news stories. The first attributed codes can still originate directly from the material, but the analyst should classify them under global, more abstract concepts. It is also useful to construct schemes and to search for contrasting pairs (e.g., good vs. evil).

Selective Coding and Compilation of a Frame Matrix

A frame matrix consists of a series of rows, reproducing frame packages, and columns representing the reasoning devices and the principal framing devices. Logical combinations need to be found through all the different columns. Each element in a row of a frame package has to be significant. The final goal is to obtain a restricted amount of frame packages. What is lacking is the idea of the organization of the frame. Here we look for values, narratives, myths, and archetypes that complete the frame package into a logical unity.

Evaluation Criteria

There are three criteria that can be helpful in evaluating the suitability of a frame: the broadness of the frame description; its logical structure; and the applicability of a frame in defining other issues. First, the frame package has to be fully described, with an extensive list of framing and reasoning devices. The broadness of the description is also an indicator for the dominance of the frame. Second, the chain of reasoning devices has to be logically consistent. Some frames, however, have the ability to define an issue as not being problematic and, as a matter of course, to absolve some agents of responsibility. Third, the frame must be applicable to other issues. The main challenge here is to decide upon the appropriate level of abstraction. Each frame has to be sufficiently abstract to be applicable to other issues that lie beyond the scope of the specific research topic.

Case Study: The Location of an Asylum Seekers' Center

Background

In order to illustrate the presented inductive approach, I will now discuss the results of a case study in which I followed the reactions to the decision on the location of a refugee center during a ten-month period, both in the field and in the media. On 15 November 2000 news leaked through the media that on 1 January 2001 an open refugee center with a capacity for six hundred residents would open its doors in the rural Belgian municipality of Arendonk. The announcement of the plans immediately provoked protest from the local population.

From a research perspective, the first question in this debate is formulated as follows: which frames dominated the debate? Subsequently, there is the question of whether the framing was done *by* the media, in which case the media took the initiative to apply the frames, or *through* the media, in which case the media frames were taken over from other participants in the field. The second research question therefore is: which participants used the defined frames and how did they do this?

Method

As explained in the previous paragraphs, an inductive framing analysis was used. In addition to a content analysis of all expressions of communication, I attended and observed in the field the most prominent occurrences: resident meetings, information sessions, two protest marches, a torchlight procession, and a solidarity manifestation. The extramedial data collected was completed with other primary data such as the minutes of the gatherings and meetings, pamphlets of both supporters and opponents, petitions, and open and circular letters by political parties and pressure groups. Finally, I gathered 214 newspaper articles and TV broadcasts connected with the events. These came from both national and regional papers and TV broadcasters as well as from free local papers.

Results: Six Dominant Frames

Table 4.1 presents the six frames that appeared as a result of the analysis: the NIMBY frame; the distrust frame; the intruder frame; the victim frame; the lovely frame; and the donor frame.

The NIMBY Frame

This attitude of both local authorities and local residents has been referred to since the 1980s with the acronym NIMBY: not in my backyard. The actors adopted the Not-in-My-Backyard frame in two different ways. First, it was recognized in the protest of the population. "Let them put the center in the mayor's garden!" screamed one of the local residents. Second, the authorities and some of the media used the frame to define the protest of the local community as "the infamous syndrome that promptly surfaces again" (*De*

Table 4.1. Results: The Six Dominant Frames

| Frame | Reasoning devices | | | | |
	Problem definition	*The asylum seeker center*	*Source of the problem*	*Responsibility*	*Solution*
"Not in my backyard"	The local resistance is just an expression of a syndrome driven by their own interest	... as such is not a problem. Negative reactions are inevitable	Egoism and narrow minded prejudice of the local population	The protest of the local population caused the (temporary) problem	The implementation of a decision taken by one party only
	The authorities want to locate a refugee center on a location that is unfit	... will cause problems as the chosen location is harmful to us	An ill-considered decision	Rests with the authorities	To nullify the decision and to move the refugee center
"Politicians are to be distrusted"	Politicians in Brussels want to harm a small community on purpose	... is a sign of mismanagement	Politicians are led by own interests and corruption	Rests with those who are in power	Voice protest or 'punish' the implicated politicians
"Foreigners are intruders"	People with bad intentions are a threat to local reality	... is a bunch of suspicious and possibly criminal foreigners	The unremitting stream of foreigners that do not belong here	Resigning to the asylum policy	A rigid and severe asylum and repatriation policy
"Innocent victim"	Poor people, forced to leave their home countries, searching for a safe haven	... is a shelter for refugees	Violence, persecution and famine, often in countries without democratic governance	Rests with the rich West	Help to attain a lenient and efficient asylum policy
"Everything in the garden's lovely"	The protest is caused by a lack of solidarity and hospitality	... is a sign of our hospitality	A lack of solidarity and hospitality	Rests with the local community	Relieving the pain in the world by an open attitude
"Donor"	There is no problem at all, the location of the centre creates possibilities	... offers lots of possibilities and chances to the community	There is no problem	Evasion because there definitely is no problem	Grabbing the chances

oral basis	Framing devices (selection)				
	Emotional basis	Cultural motive	Metaphor / stereotype	Lexical choices	Visual image
easoning arting from igher' terest . private terest	Egoism	NIMBY	The back yard	"The infamous syndrome that always surfaces"	Individual residents, pointing at the refugee center in their garden
ot taking wn people to account	The sense of suffering injustice	NIMBY	The own back yard and surround-dings	"We are not against asylum seekers, but…."	Protesting manifestants
buse of wer and atus	Distrust, cynicism, anti-political feelings	Values as honesty	The cheating politician	"It cannot be a coincidence that politicians…"	Politicians and their villas with swimming pools
otect e own pulation	Xenophobia	The archetype of the villain and the stereotype of the barbarian	The barbarian and the Mafiosi	"The degradation of the neigh-borhood, the feeling of insecurity	Scared and anxious residents, black men
e moral ty to help ur needy low men	Compassion, powerlessness	Archetype of the victim	Helpless victim	"Nobody leaves his country for no reason", "You cannot simply send them back"	Women and children
lidarity, spitality, lerance etc.	Feeling of solidarity	Values as tolerance	The characteristic Belgian hospitality	'Woolly' terminology: reach out for each other, homeless but no lesser a man	(Multicul-tural) groups people that sing and laugh and dance together
he vernment donor	Thankfulness for the offered chances	Character 'the donor'	The gift	Concrete and practical matters and agreements	Lively neighborhood

Financieel-Economische Tijd 17 November 2000). The definition is different in both these cases. In the first case, the refugee center in their backyard is the central problem, while in the second case it is not, but the "narrow-minded prejudice" of the local population is. The solution in the second situation is to follow through with the decision to locate the refugee center in Arendonk, and in the first, to move the location of the refugee center.

The Distrust Frame

An additional cause for the application of the NIMBY frame could be the strong distrust of the authorities and the unwillingness to accept whatever the authorities want or say (Wolsink 2000). This is in keeping with the second frame that showed up in the analysis and that can be referred to with the underlying message of "politicians cannot be trusted." The Politicians-Cannot-Be-Trusted frame appeals to the cynical attitude regarding the political system. This frame suggested that politicians, far away in Brussels, knowingly treated a little community unfairly. Many rumors also circulated concerning electoral interests and the role of the local authorities therein.

The Intruder Frame

The Foreigners-Are-Intruders frame refers to two cultural motives, namely, the mythical archetype of the villain and the stereotype of the foreigner as a barbarian. This frame presents the asylum seeker as an active profiteer or even a criminal who acts deliberately, and with evil intention abuses the right to request asylum (see also Van Gorp 2005). Looking at the content of the list of requirements submitted by the pressure group, it was obvious that they thought of the asylum seekers as extremely dangerous. A two-meter-high electric fence had to enclose the area, a curfew was to be imposed, the amount of police patrols needed to be drastically expanded, and the authorities needed to financially support the costs of securing the surrounding houses.

The Victim Frame

Next to the implicit message that asylum seekers are criminals, there is the alternative frame that presents them as innocent victims. This Innocent Victim frame is based on the mythical archetype projecting the weakness of human beings (Silverblatt et al. 1999). It refers to the vulnerable or needy person who succumbs to worldly powers, injustice, or oppression or who yields through self-destruction. Although the victim is pitiable and therefore sometimes sympathetic, there is another side to this portrayal: the victim is also passive, weak, and unable to help himself.

The Lovely Frame

Another frame that was distinguished can be described as the Everything-in-the-Garden's-Lovely frame, meaning that the author of a text selects only framing devices with a positive connotation (cf. Hall 1976: 185). Based on the lovely frame, the definition of the situation reads that offering people shelter in the municipality is not a problem. Everybody just has to take a little responsibility and that is enough to show solidarity and become hospitable, patient, tolerant, understanding, and ready to help. Because this frame makes use of "woolly" devices, all concrete objections and practical problems concerning the location of the center for asylum seekers are ignored. While the victim frame starts from the image of the candidate asylum seeker who comes from a concrete, precarious situation, the lovely frame pushes all this misery into the background.

The Donor Frame

A frame that only succeeded to steer the debate indirectly was the frame that connected to the cultural motive of the donor. Seen from this frame, the location of the asylum shelter provides unexpected possibilities. Reference to the cultural values of hospitality and tolerance in the lovely frame are replaced by concrete, practical arguments that persuade the public of the positive influence of an asylum center on the neighborhood. For instance, local traders would be able to supply the center with provisions, the center would create a whole range of employment opportunities, and the neighborhood would become livelier.

Results: The Use of Frames by Supporters and Opponents

The first communication by the federal authorities on the location of an asylum center included elements of the donor frame. The communication strategy was to stress the positive consequences for the villagers, with special attention on the creation of employment. Moreover, the government used the NIMBY frame to reduce the local protest to an attitude inspired by a lack of empathy. The public communication by the local authorities initially contained devices that I associated with the distrust frame. The federal authorities had supposedly not informed the mayor on the decision in advance, so that he too had to hear the news through the media. Later, they kept away from the debate.

In the initial public debate, mainly negative notes were heard. The intruder frame was predominant in the opponents' rhetoric. In addition, the distrust frame was present in the discourse of the opponents. It was remarkable that the opponents also used the NIMBY frame to disguise their more xenophobic arguments against the location of the refugee center: from a humanitarian point of view, they were in favor of the center, but the location was unfit for several reasons. After the torchlight procession in the village, organized by the Flemish extreme right-wing party het Vlaams Blok (since 2004 renamed Vlaams Belang), the supporters of the asylum center in the village united. They amply fitted the lovely frame into their actions and promotion material (see below).

Results: The Use of Frames in the Media

The First Phase: Emphasis on Conflict

The use of certain frames by the media resulted in a focus on the conflicting elements in the events. Thus, the distrust frame was even more dominantly present in the media than it was in the texts written by the other actors. In other words, this is an example of framing *by* the media.

Both national and regional television broadcasters immediately played the mayor of the municipality and the minister's spokesperson off against each other: had the city council been informed of the decision beforehand or not? The media suggested that one of the political players was lying. Therefore, the professional perspective in journalism to hear both sides of an argument paves the way for the discordant character of the news.

The regional paper *Gazet van Antwerpen* initially played a leading role in the application of the distrust frame. Two days after having published the scoop on the asylum center, the paper calculated the amount of asylum seekers in each Flemish province: "One in every 961 inhabitants is an asylum seeker. The concentration in the Antwerp province is 25 times higher than in the province East Flanders" (17 November 2000: 1). In supplementary articles and in the editorial, the paper suggested that the location of the asylum center in that precise municipality could not be a coincidence, especially since it was out of the range of the electoral home base of the responsible minister.

The focus on conflict also emerged from the adoption of the intruder frame voiced by the inhabitants. This was mainly the case for the regional papers. One of the national tabloidlike papers, *Het Laatste Nieuws,* gathered reactions from the local pub. In the nationally oriented papers the opinions and arguments of the local residents were not explicitly published. These papers labeled the local protest as an expression of the NIMBY syndrome. The coverage hardly paid any attention to the underlying political reasoning. The adopted frames distracted attention from this contextualization and reduced the possibilities for an appropriate story in the limited space of newspaper coverage or a news item.

The Second Phase: Frames that Make Themselves Felt in Time

The primary definition of the situation, as it was described by the intruder frame and the distrust frame, defined which of the following events had news value. Thus, regional-oriented media offered a forum for the residents' association where they could inform the public beforehand about their demands and campaigns, like meetings and gatherings at the town hall and the erecting of Christmas trees with black ribbons in their front yards. News that fitted the distrust frame could count on media attention, and possibly also the public's attention.

The Third Phase: The Torchlight Procession As a Key Event

The dominant position of the distrust frame, the intruder frame, and the NIMBY frame was eventually disrupted by a key event: the torchlight procession organized in the municipality by the right-wing party het Vlaams Blok on 11 December 2002. Hundreds of sympathizers chanted the slogan, "No asylum in our neighborhood." Nevertheless, three local residents dared put up a banner during the procession with the slogan, "Take a step to a tolerant Arendonk." In the light of everything that happened that night, this "one-man crusade" was just one story within the bigger whole, but it received a remarkable amount of media attention.

The national channel VRT and the local broadcaster RTV, the two audiovisual media present, broadcast the emotions visually with fast image shifts and close-ups of the skinheads present, the waving of flags with the Flemish lion, the flickering fire, and the chanting crowds. This time it was not the asylum seekers but the marchers who looked intimidating.

The Fourth Phase: A General Reversal of Roles

The torchlight procession of the het Vlaams Blok provoked an initiative that took place on 23 December 2000: a small group of local residents gathered around the Christmas crib to sing songs and to recite poems. All media were present, even the national TV channels with satellite communications. On 26 December, Boxing Day, the newspaper headlines read "Hospitality Bigger Than Hate" (*Het Nieuwsblad*) and "There Is Place at Our Inn" (*De Standaard*), referring to the Christmas story where there was no place at the inn for Joseph and pregnant Mary. The media thus took over the lovely frame from the initiators; this is an example of framing *through* the media.

The two external events, the torchlight procession and the moment of solidarity, set a new course for the media in the debate. While the media in the first phase mainly brought out the news using the intruder and the distrust frames, the key events brought about a "twist in the story": the victim frame and the lovely frame became dominant. During the period that followed, this change in frames led to a new way of reporting the news. Where in the earlier phases the asylum seekers were unwanted intruders, after the solidarity event, they became the victims. In the first phase the local opponents were the victims of the policy and of the local authorities, who did not take their own population into consideration.

Starting from the key events given above, the focus shifted from the content arguments of the opponents to their actions. For example, when the windows of the mayor's house were smashed, the representative of the opponents let slip the remark that she saw the actions as "a form of freedom of speech." The opposition, which the news media interpreted in the first phase as legitimate, was from this point onward referred to as deviant behavior and was marginalized.

Conclusions

In this contribution, a broader cultural approach of framing was presented, including a method to reconstruct a limited range of observable frame packages using an inductive content analysis. Through the comparison of the range of alternative frames, a framing analysis makes it possible to fathom the course of the construction of social meaning. Each frame package includes a specific line of reasoning, from problem definition to feasible lines of action. In order to answer the question of "what is happening," journalists call upon certain culturally embedded frames that are familiar to everyone. One event could be defined by at least six different frames. The culturally embedded frames transformed the decision in a very complex policy matter into a simple event: an expression of misgovernment, a collection of criminal foreigners, a refugee center for the needy, or a unique stimulus for a neighborhood. The actors applied the frames, in combination with the conflict frame, to support the process or limit it, and each frame always pointed out a different actor responsible. In this respect, the frames are an expansion of the generic frames of conflict and social responsibility.

Furthermore, the case study brought the dynamic character of the framing process to the fore. Every frame has its own sponsors in the field, trying to convince the journalists to take over their frame. If they succeed in this, we speak of framing *through* the media. However, the case study shows that framing *by* the media also takes place. The media take over the presented frames of the sponsors, but also actively select frames and define situations themselves. Next, key events can in fact cause a frame shift. Once a certain frame is dominant, the media prefer to give attention to the events that fit the frame. Problems, responsibilities, and solutions will be defined according to those moments and redefined again in order to keep the news flowing.

A frame shift means the dedication of another role to the stakeholders. An actor who appears first as a victim in the media (i.e., the protesting local population) can later on become the offender, and an actor who was first an intruder (i.e., the asylum seeker) can later become the victim.

The illustrated approach to framing offers some new directions for future research. First, it is still unclear to what extent frame selection and application by journalists and social movement organizations is a consciously evolving process. Social movements that are aware of the benefits of the strategic selection of a frame will likely turn out to be the most successful in mobilizing activities. The best communicators are also the best "framers," although there are many factors that may affect the resonance of the applied frames (Noakes and Johnston 2005: 11–16). A further question is how journalists deal with these framing activities and whether they succeed in "counterframing" the debate, by questioning the central frames or introducing new frames. At the least, the case study suggests that the news media are also active "framers." Because frames can be applied for strategic purposes, they don't necessarily provide insight into the belief system of the social movements involved. There may be a discrepancy between the frames applied in public communication and ideology. For instance, in the case study some protesters publically used the NIMBY frame as a motive for why they were against the refugee center, whereas in private communication more racist motivations seemed to prevail. Therefore, it would be interesting to find out how the use of certain frames tie in with ideological positions in a debate.

Bibliography

Bird, E. E., and R. W. Dardenne. 1997. "Myth, Chronicle and Story: Exploring the Narrative Qualities of News." In *Social Meanings of News: A Text Reader,* ed. D. Berkowitz. Thousand Oaks, CA: Sage.

Cohen, S. 1976. "Mods and Rockers: The Inventory as Manufactured News." In *The Manufacture of News: Social Problems, Deviance and the Mass Media,* ed. S. Cohen and J. Young. Thousand Oaks, CA: Sage.

Cottle, S. 2006. *Mediatized Conflict.* Maidenhead, UK: Open University Press.

D'Angelo, P., and J. A. Kuypers. 2010. *Doing News Framing Analysis: Empirical and Theoretical Perspectives.* New York: Routledge.

Eilders, C. 2006. "News Factors and News Decisions: Theoretical and Methodological Advances in Germany." *Communications: The European Journal of Communication Research* 31, no. 1 (April): 5–24.

Entman, R. M. 1993. "Framing: Towards Clarification of a Fractured Paradigm." *Journal of Communication* 43, no. 4 (December): 51–58.

Gamson, W. A., and K. E. Lasch. 1983. "The Political Culture of Social Welfare Policy." In *Evaluating the Welfare State: Social and Political Perspectives,* ed. S. E. Spiro and E. Yuchtman-Yaar. New York: Academic Press.

Gamson, W. A., and G. Wolfsfeld. 1993. "Movements and Media as Interacting Structures." *The Annals of the American Academy of Political and Social Science* 528 (July): 114–25.

Gitlin, T. 1980. *The Whole World Is Watching: Mass Media in the Making and Unmaking of the New Left.* Berkeley, CA: University of California Press.

Hall, S. 1976. "The Determination of News Photographs." In *The Manufacture of News: Social Problems, Deviance and the Mass Media,* ed. S. Cohen and J. Young. Thousand Oaks, CA: Sage.

Hertog, J. K., and D. M. McLeod. 2001. "A Multiperspectival Approach to Framing Analysis: A Field Guide." In *Framing Public Life: Perspectives on Media and Our Understanding of the Social World,* ed. S. D. Reese, O. H. Gandy, and A. E. Grant. Mahwah, NJ: Lawrence Erlbaum.

Noakes, J. A., and H. Johnston. 2005. "Frames of Protest: A Road Map to a Perspective." In *Frames of Protest: Social Movements and the Framing Perspective,* ed. H. Johnston and J. A. Noakes. Lanham, MD: Rowman & Littlefield.

Oliver, P. E., and H. Johnston. 2000. "What a Good Idea! Ideologies and Frames in Social Movement Research." *Mobilization: An International Quarterly* 5, no. 1: 37–54.

Pan, Z., and G. M. Kosicki. 1993. "Framing Analysis: An Approach to News Discourse." *Political Communication* 10, no. 1: 55–75.

Papacharissi, Z., and M. de Fatima Oliveira. 2008. "News Frames Terrorism: A Comparative Analysis of Frames Employed in Terrorism Coverage in U.S. and U.K. Newspapers." *The International Journal of Press/Politics* 13, no. 1 (January): 52–47.

Polletta, F. 2004. "Culture Is Not Just in Your Head." In *Rethinking Social Movements: Structure, Meaning, and Emotion,* ed. J. Goodwin and J. M. Jasper. Lanham, MD: Rowman & Littlefield.

Semetko, H. A., and P. M. Valkenburg. 2000. "Framing European Politics: A Content Analysis of Press and Television News." *Journal of Communication* 50, no. 2 (June): 93–109.

Silverblatt, A., J. Ferry, and B. Finan. 1999. *Approaches to Media Literacy: A Handbook.* Armonk, NY: M. E. Sharpe.

Snow, D. A., and R. D. Benford. 1988. "Ideology, Frame Resonance, and Participant Mobilization." *International Social Movement Research* 1: 197–218.

———. 2005. "Clarifying the Relationship Between Framing and Ideology." In *Frames of Protest: Social Movements and the Framing Perspective,* ed. H. Johnston and J. A. Noakes. Lanham, MD: Rowman & Littlefield.

Swidler, A. 1986. "Culture in Action: Symbols and Strategies." *American Sociological Review* 51, no. 2 (April): 273–86.

Van Gorp, B. 2005. "Where Is the Frame? Victims and Intruders in the Belgian Press Coverage of the Asylum Issue." *European Journal of Communication* 20, no. 4 (December): 484–507.

———. 2007. "The Constructionist Approach to Framing: Bringing Culture Back In." *Journal of Communication* 57, no. 1 (March): 60–78.

Wolsink, M. 2000. "Wind Power and the Nimby-Myth: Institutional Capacity and the Limited Significance of Public Support." *Renewable Energy* 21, no. 1: 49–64.

Zald, M. N. 1996. "Culture, Ideology, and Strategic Framing." In *Comparative Perspectives on Social Movements: Political Opportunities, Mobilizing Structures, and Cultural Framings,* ed. D. McAdam, J. D. McCarthy, and M. N. Zald. Cambridge: Cambridge University Press.

Chapter 5

When Journalists Frame the News

Sigurd Allern

Organizers of social protest movements, demonstrations, and meetings directed against the powers that be often have a strained relationship with the news media. They want media coverage, and are disappointed if the mobilization of thousands or even tens of thousands of people fails to make headlines. On the other hand, they also know from experience that when social protests are treated as "hot news," the coverage may well highlight aspects less favorable for their social and political cause, like clashes between the police and small groups of ski-masked activists. During the wide-ranging demonstrations against the World Trade Organization in Seattle in 1999, "a few Starbucks windows smashed by a hundred 'anarchists' were all the shallower news reports needed to see 'what's the story,' even if tens or hundreds of thousands of demonstrators were marching by playfully, in peace," as Todd Gitlin (2003: xvii) sums it up.

Such experiences with the media are familiar to those who have organized confrontations by globalization reformers at World Bank, International Monetary Fund, or G8 conferences, as well as to opponents of the US-led invasion in Iraq and anti-imperialist solidarity movements. On the other hand, other news reports do present alternative versions of the same realities. A news event can, as media scholars would put it, be *framed* in different ways.

This chapter focuses on analyzing the importance of framing and framing contests in the social construction of news. It first discusses and assesses some of the literature most relevant to the study of social movements and news framing. Later, I will illustrate some important aspects of framing through a case study of news angles and news framing in the media coverage of a Norwegian police action that gave rise to civic engagement and protest actions.

Definitions of Frames and Framing

Today, framing analysis is widely used in a range of academic disciplines, and the concept has multiple meanings. Framing has been called an approach, a theory, a multiparadigmatic research program, and a paradigm.[1] Over the past two decades, research into framing has developed into one of the most influential areas of communications research (Reese et al. 2001; D'Angelo & Kuypers 2010). It has also become an important perspective in studies of social movements (Gitlin 1980; Snow et al. 1986; Gamson 1988, 1992; Gamson and Modigliani 1989; Benford and Snow 2000). This variety of meanings is both a strength and a weakness.

In the social sciences, framing theory is usually traced to the social anthropologist and communication theorist Gregory Bateson (1972). In an essay on play and fantasy, Bateson put forward the concept that when we play, our activity is understood and framed as such, and is thus different from doing the same thing "for real": that is, the distinction between a fight and a play fight. In a discussion of psychological frames, Bateson states that a frame is *metacommunicative:* "Any message, which either explicitly or implicitly defines a frame, *ipso facto* gives the receiver instructions or aids in his attempt to understand the message included in the frame" (1972: 188). Thus, through frames, we categorize messages and their meanings.

The sociologist Erving Goffman was inspired by Bateson. He underlines that in all human communication we are dependent on frames that help to make isolated occurrences intelligible. Frames can be defined as cognitive structures that guide the representation of everyday events (Goffman 1974: 10–11). Frames denote "schemata of interpretation" that enable us "to locate, identify, and label" occurrences in our daily life and the larger world (Goffman 1974: 21). To understand what is going on, we need a frame of reference. Or, in the words of Stephen D. Reese (2001: 11): "Frames are *organizing principles* that are socially *shared* and *persistent* over time, that work *symbolically* to meaningfully structure the social world."

In his pioneering study of the radical American student movement and the protest movement against the war in Vietnam, Todd Gitlin defines media frames as "persistent patterns of cognition, interpretation, and presentation, of selection, emphasis, and exclusion, by which symbol-handlers routinely organize discourse, whether verbal or visual" (1980: 7). Framing is, in a general sense, as unavoidable in journalism as it is in everyday life. Here we should note the difference of perspective when *frame* is used as a noun or as a verb. Most of the "frames" that we use in connection with what exists around us are more or less unconsciously accepted—they are "little tacit theories about what exists, what happens and what matters" (Gitlin 1980: 6). Frames represent interpretive schemata that we need to make sense of the world. However, in both politics and journalism, frames are also actively manufactured, adopted, and contested. Framing here characterizes an active and interactive process, whose keywords are *selection, exclusion,* and *emphasis.*

Frames in news text should not be confused with the *themes* or *issues* of the news; the same topic can be framed in several different ways (Van Gorp 2007). The international media coverage of the Israeli occupation of Palestinian territories is an illustrative example. In a much-cited text, Robert Entman (1993: 52) states: "To frame is to select some aspects of a perceived reality and make them more salient in a communicating text." In their study of how terrorism is covered in the news media, Norris, Kern, and Just (2003: 11) conclude that "the essence of framing is selection to prioritize some facts, images or developments over others, thereby unconsciously promoting one particular interpretation of events." The frame suggests what the controversy is about, the essence of the issue (Gamson and Modigliani 1989). Frames involve implicit information between the lines; they establish a *context* for the interpretation of a news story.

A complicating factor in framing analysis, demonstrated in the vast literature on the subject, lies both in the multiple types of frames and the shifting levels of analysis. One of the dangers (and weaknesses) of framing analysis is the subjective variety of what may be called a "frame," depending on the researcher's own interests and interpretations. We should thus bear in mind Reese's words, cited above, about frames as "organizing principles" that are "socially shared" and "persistent over time" to avoid arbitrary decisions. Through organized and socially shared frames, the news story becomes familiar, recognizable, and therefore easier to interpret. Frames are "prepackaged constructions," writes the criminologist Ray Surette, that "simplify one's dealings with the world by organizing experiences and events into groups and guiding what are seen as the appropriate policies and actions" (2007: 39).

In studies of social movements, the theoretical distinctions and potential similarities between ideology and framing processes have given rise to scholarly debates (see Oliver and Johnston 2000; Snow and Benford 2000; Benford and Snow 2000). One reason for this is that, on the surface, ideologies and broad "master frames" or generic frames (such as frames connected to civil rights or injustice) may appear equivalent. However, the "rights frame" may be used for movements with different ideologies and purposes (Oliver and Johnston 2000: 39). A well-known example is the conflicting and alternative frames concerning abortion. Those who defend a woman's right to make the decision for abortion call themselves pro-choice, whereas their opponents against abortion insist on being framed not as antichoice but as pro-life—retaining the overall rights frame but shifting the focus from the rights of the woman to the rights of the fetus. Words matter.

While "ideology" refers to a wider system of beliefs and values, "frames" and "framing" describe more specific schemata and interpretation processes that in various ways may be *related* to ideologies, as well as to cultural narratives. Through frames, events can be linked to political and institutional discourses in many areas of policy. Ultimately, framing presupposes a standpoint and a perspective; and because frames are negotiated and part of social interaction, they also involve and express power relations between and among classes, groups, and individuals (Entman 2004).

"Collective action frames" are constituted when social movement organizations define their "core framing tasks" and negotiate shared understandings of some problematic condition or situation, discuss and articulate alternatives and solutions, and urge others to act in concert to affect change (Benford and Snow 2000; Snow and Benford 1988). Some of these frames may be of a more general character ("master frames," like rights frames, injustice frames, and choice frames); other collective action frames are more movement specific (Benford & Snow 2000: 619).

News Values, Angles, and Generic Frames

It is often said of news journalism that it *mirrors* reality. But mirrors can be of many shapes, held in different directions—and they may even distort dimensions. A kindred metaphor is the description of journalism as a window on the world. As Gaye Tuchman (1978: 1) points out, the view through a window depends on whether the window is large or small, has many panes or few, whether the glass is opaque or clear, whether the window faces a street or a backyard. The frames will always influence the view. Of course, the window metaphor should not be understood too literally: frames and frameworks both restrict and enable the understanding of meanings.

Sharon Dunwoody (1992: 78) sees professional journalistic frames as akin to scripts and menus that guide selections of issues and constructions of news reports. On the newsroom level, such frames will be linked to common conceptions of news values and standard procedures for evaluating and handling incoming information. Generic news frames concern how journalists and news organizations routinely assign priorities and make sense of information and opinions that can be constructed as news.

In most cases, neither journalists nor standard textbooks on journalism use the concept of "framing."[2] The questions will instead be about what the story is, and especially what the angle is. Some journalists will speak of the importance of identifying a "hook" or "handle" for the news story, that is, finding that important piece of information that will capture the interest of the audience. The reporter (or desk editor) has to choose a perspective and decide what the key elements of the news text will be, formulated through a headline, a lead, and frequently also a picture. These choices involve decisions concerning the selection of the main source(s), composition and dramaturgy, and whether the text should emphasize causes and consequences. Reports about car accidents may, for example, focus on brakes that failed or slippery roads (causes), drunk driving (personal responsibility), or road safety and speed limits (societal perspectives). News angles thus help the journalist to structure information about a central idea, to present what are deemed to be the most interesting or relevant aspects, and thereby also contribute to focus the reader's attention on the selected parts of the topic.

Generic news frames are rooted in journalists' shared perceptions of news values, genre conventions, and audience interests. One study (Semetko and Valkenburg 2000) found five generic news frames often used by media organizations:

> *Conflict frame:* Emphasizing conflict between individuals, organizations, regions, or nations.
> *Human interest frame:* Using a human face or emotional angle to present an event, issue, or problem.
> *Economic consequences frame:* Focusing on economic consequences of an event for individuals, groups, institutions, regions, or countries.
> *Morality frame:* Focusing on moral or religious prescriptions in covering an event, problem, or issue.
> *Responsibility frame:* Presenting an issue or problem in such a way as to attribute responsibility to its cause, or the solution to governments, groups, or individuals.

In his analysis of how TV news frames political issues, Shanto Iyengar (1994) distinguishes between two types of generic frames: "episodic" and "thematic." "Episodic" frames are heavily case-oriented, personalized, and specific, without background information or attempts to contextualize the news. An example could be a television story of a suicide bombing, with little information other than the dramatic pictures and some information about causalities. "Thematic" frames, in contrast, allow more background information and a higher level of abstraction. In practice, however, many news stories will include both episodic and thematic elements, which complicate the empirical analysis.

Culturally embedded news frames are also general in character, and appealing for journalists because they are based on well-known narratives, like that of villain and victim (Van Gorp 2007, 2010: 87). News texts are often implicit moral stories about good and evil, problems and happiness, life and death. In news texts, David repeatedly meets and struggles with Goliath,

heroes are made and villains are punished,[3] sometimes with the benign assistance of journalism in its self-proclaimed role as a watchdog, representing
"the fourth estate." In a study of news coverage of poverty, Van Gorp, Blow,
and van de Velde (2005) found that the news frames were rooted in common
cultural themes, such as the archetypes of villain, victim, and tragic hero, the
stereotype of the vagabond, "and the conviction that each individual has a
pregiven destiny" (quoted in Van Gorp 2010: 86).

Issue-specific frames are those frames typical of and related to the interpretation of social or political issues like minority rights, abortion, environmental problems, or unemployment. However, political frames can also be less
issue specific and of a more strategic and enduring character, like the "Cold
War" frame in the decades after the Second World War and the "war against
terrorism" frame after the events of 11 September 2001.

Framing Contests and Frame Sponsorships

"The relationship between sources and journalists resembles a dance, for
sources seek access to journalists, and journalists seek access to sources,"
writes Herbert Gans (1980: 116). For professional news sources, like government representatives, organizational leaders, politicians, business leaders,
and public relation (PR) practitioners, information subsidies represent a tool
to influence the decisions and priorities of news organizations (Gandy 1982).
Such subsidies may involve exclusive news interviews, access to free information (including visual elements and statistics), polls, and proposals of news
angles. Political parties, lobby groups, and social activist groups may all try
to stage events that fit into an established generic news frame, and give input
that lowers the costs of information gathering. Information subsidies are also
used as a mechanism for enhancing specific frames. Actors strategically culti-
vate their resources and translate them into framing power (Pan and Kosicki
2001)—a process that Gamson (1988) calls "frame sponsorships." The frame
building takes place in continuous interaction between news organizations
and actors outside the media; "the outcomes of the frame-building process
are the frames manifest in the text" (de Vreese 2003).

Such sponsorships also include proactive attempts to influence both issue-specific frames and frames of a more strategic political character. One
strategy in framing contests between claims makers (like social activists,
professional experts, lobbyists, and spokespersons) is *linkage,* an attempt to
associate what is going on with other, previously constructed issues (Surette
2007: 37). Drugs are often linked to other social problems such as crime;
protests against the policies of the World Trade Organization are often linked

to former episodes of violence during demonstrations. But claims of linkage can also be a strategy for social activists, as when police violence is linked to problems concerning racist attitudes in the police, an example discussed in the last part of this chapter.

In his study of the early protest movement against the US war in Vietnam in the 1960s, Gitlin (1980) analyzed various different framing devices used by US media in the coverage of the protests at a moment in history when US political elites, including the pundits of the press and television, actively supported the war effort in Vietnam. News coverage of the early protests against the US war in Vietnam focused generally on certain aspects connected with the demonstrators: their young age, dress, and style (*trivialization*), emphasizing the counterdemonstration (*polarization*), emphasizing *internal dissension,* describing the protesters as deviant and unrepresentative (*marginalization*), underassessing the support (*disparagement by numbers*), and *disparagement of the movement's effectiveness* (Gitlin 2003: 27–28). Such framing devices were typical of the time, and did not change until some of the establishment and the media elites later understood that the United States was going to lose the war, and would have to withdraw its military forces from Indochina.

One recent example of a framing hegemony by authoritative sources, in this case the US government, is the breakthrough for what may be called the *terrorist* frame after the airplane attacks on the World Trade Center in New York on 11 September 2001. The frame concerns not only al-Qaeda, or their hosts, the Taliban movement in Afghanistan; apparently scattered and diverse events are also more generally subsumed and understood within regular patterns: "the terrorist frame can be used to explain the nightclub attack in Bali, the Chechen rebels holding hostages in the Moscow theater, the bombing of Israel tourists in a Mombasa hotel, the suicide bombers in Tel Aviv, or the capture of communist insurgents in the Philippines" (Norris et al. 2003: 11).

Social movement organizations and political activists groups may, however, succeed in influencing public opinion through the introduction of collective action frames that provide a new interpretation of both problems and solutions. Ihlen (2004; Ihlen and Allern 2008) has studied such an example of counterframing in the debate on the building of a new gas-powered plant (GPP) in Norway. The company Naturkraft had, in the mid-1990s, convinced the majority of Norwegian politicians that power from GPPs would replace power from more polluting, coal-fired energy plants in Denmark. This issue-specific "substitution frame" indicated that Norway would increase its own emissions, but *global* emissions would decrease. In 1996 Naturkraft was granted permission to build the plant.

The environmental movement and the group Action against GPPs then decided to focus on what they saw as the basic problem. They formulated a "pollution frame" and started to compare the carbon dioxide emission from GPPs with the emissions from cars ("GPPs pollute as much as 600,000 cars," read one brochure). The main strength of this framing was to make the abstract issue of climate change more concrete. The introduction of the "pollution frame" was combined with plans for demonstrations and civil disobedience, adding a generic news element of conflict and drama to the conflict. This reframing of the GPP issue was a success in the media, and opinion polls came to reflect negative public sentiments toward GPPs. In 1997, the prime minister urged Naturkraft to postpone its construction (Ihlen 2004).

A Death that Sparked a Public Debate

The ways in which the media prioritize, present, and frame news can have political implications and spark debate and public protests. The media coverage of a Norwegian law enforcement action with a deadly outcome serves to illustrate this point. The empirical analysis in this case study is based on Allern and Pollack (2009).

On 7 September 2006, Eugenie Ejike Obiora, a student at the Norwegian University of Science and Technology (NTNU) in Trondheim, lost his life following a law enforcement action. A Norwegian citizen originally from Africa, Obiora had lived in Norway for over twenty years when he died. That day, he visited a social welfare and service office in the city. He was there to appeal against being denied social assistance, but was perceived by the staff as threatening.[4] After what was referred to in media reports as a "scuffle" with four police officers, he was wrestled to the ground on the stairway landing outside the office and handcuffed.

During the arrest, Obiora experienced difficulty breathing and lost consciousness, and, still in handcuffs, was placed in the police car and driven to a hospital. At the hospital, after several attempts at resuscitation, he was pronounced dead. The medical experts' autopsy report stated that it "[was] not possible to determine the exact time of death, but that it must be regarded as most likely that the cessation of circulation had occurred by the time of arrival at the hospital at 14.25, possibly already before transport to hospital took place."[5]

Soon after, the death was interpreted by many, particularly by immigrants and young antiracism activists, as an example of unnecessary force related to Obiora's African origins. This led to public demonstrations, not only in Trondheim, but also in Oslo and elsewhere in Norway. The Norwegian

Bureau for the Investigation of Police Affairs, a separate legal unit under the Ministry of Justice, conducted two investigations into the matter. Just before Christmas 2007, the director general of public prosecutions concluded that no charges would be brought against the police officers involved. At the same time, the director general's conclusion stated: "Even though the action described was not criminal, there is every reason for the police to express regret at the tragic death of Obiora."

The decision prompted new protests. The Obiora case had become a cause célèbre that pointed to widely diverging views on the way the police perform their societal role. In practice, we may speak of two sharply differing and competing mediated discourses on the Obiora case. One discourse was established, constituted, and maintained by police spokespersons, police union representatives, and the legal representative of the police officers involved. The other was established and constituted by Obiora's family and friends, their lawyer, and spokespersons for Norwegian-African organizations and the leadership of the Norwegian Federation of Trade Unions (LO) in Trondheim. Simplifying somewhat, we may speak of a *police discourse,* closely associated with various institutional representatives of the police, and a *racist system discourse,* formulated and maintained by various groups in civil society. Here we will briefly touch on how these discourses became established in the media—and how they were challenged as the case progressed.

The police discourse was premised on the notion of the police doing a vital and difficult job for society, and one in which, unfortunately, the use of force can also be necessary. The work is dangerous, and frontline police officers may risk not only their health but also their lives. Sometimes regrettable mishaps and accidents occur. The death of Obiora is, in this discourse, seen as a consequence of grievous circumstances. The police officers were compelled to intervene, but unfortunately Obiora resisted so violently that when he had to be removed from the social services office, the police officers had to grab him around the neck, force him to the ground, and put him in handcuffs. By contrast, the premise of the racist system discourse is that the death of Obiora was caused by unnecessary police brutality, and that this particularly brutal treatment was due to his African background. The news media's alternative frames related directly to these divergent ways of evaluating the effort and work of the police.

One of the clearest examples of a news frame based on the police discourse is the first mention of the case in the popular tabloid *VG,* then Norway's largest-circulation daily, on 11 September 2006. The headline was "– Fighting for Their Lives." This interpretation of the event was confirmed in the introduction: "The police officers felt they were fighting for their lives when a 48-year-old died during an arrest in Trondheim on Thursday." The primary source for the story was the officers' legal representative, who stated that his clients were acting in self-defense. Obiora had violently resisted the arrest. "He was awfully strong. With a jab of the elbow he managed to fracture three ribs of one of the officers." In other words, according to *VG,* it was the *police officers* who were "fighting for their lives," not Obiora, who actually did die.

In a later phase of the case, the head of the Norwegian Police Federation became a key representative of the police discourse. In interviews and television debates he repeated his main points: Police officers who work on the front line have a difficult and risky job. While the use of force is legitimate, occasionally things may go wrong. In an interview with the newspaper *Klassekampen* on 14 May 2007, he characterized the arrest of Obiora as "good police work." In the climate that the debate around the case had by then created, this was perceived by many as highly offensive, and a short time later the police union leader had to apologize for this statement.

This portrayal of the case stood in clear contrast to *Adresseavisen*'s introductory front-page story on 8 September 2006. "They used a chokehold. The 48-year-old died after being arrested by the police." The sources were two young men who were present at the social welfare and services office during the arrest: "It sounded like he wasn't getting any air, and his legs began to thrash about." The following day, *Adresseavisen* carried a new top story on the case with the headline: "Testifying against the Police." Here, the witness was a teenager (aged seventeen) who declared that he would report to the Norwegian Bureau for the Investigation of Police Affairs to testify that he "saw the deceased 48-year-old being beaten unconscious, while the police held him in an iron grip."

We can note the contrast between the "necessary force" and "needless police brutality" that characterizes the news coverage. On 11 September 2006, *Adresseavisen,* the local newspaper in Trondheim, introduced a new dimension: the suspicion of racist attitudes and that Obiora was handled with extra brutality by the police because he was black. In an interview story, the newspaper reported that immigrants in Trondheim were both grieving and indignant. The persons interviewed said they were not surprised at what had happened. One of *Adresseavisen*'s sources, an immigrant employed as a social worker with the city of Trondheim, told the newspaper that he had himself experienced being put in a choke hold and had had other unpleasant run-ins with the police because of the color of his skin.

The perception that national origin and ethnicity played a role in police conduct was quickly established as a general attitude among the many who protested against the death, especially among young people and other activists involved in efforts to combat racism and discrimination. Antiracist slogans and symbols played a central and highly visible role at all the protest meetings covered in press and television reports. This interpretation, with racism as the keyword, was the counterpart to the police discourse.

Table 5.1 is based on the content analysis of articles in four leading Norwegian newspapers. All stories mentioning the Obiora case and the Norwegian Bureau for the Investigation of Police Affairs in the period after Obiora's death and the subsequent investigation and protest phase (8 September 2006 to 30 September 2008) were analyzed. These four newspapers include the three biggest national dailies, *VG, Aftenposten,* and *Dagbladet,* as well as *Adresseavisen* in Trondheim.

The racism variable concerns whether the articles are framed by a headline or introduction directly linking them to racism or discrimination against immigrants. Coding a "yes" response requires this angle to be explicit. A "no" response includes all other types of reports, most of them straight news about the ongoing investigations without value-oriented statements. As table 5.1 shows, a "racism" frame was openly present in around a quarter of all editorial content (articles weighted by column space), but with a higher percentage present in the two popular tabloids, *Dagbladet* and *VG.* The political protests following the death of Obiora were given especially high priority in these papers. The lower percentage score for the local daily *Adresseavisen* is primarily because that paper had far more extensive coverage of the case than the national dailies. The *number* of stories of this type was at the same level.

The director general of public prosecutions did not issue his conclusive decision—to drop the case against the police—until Christmas 2007. The police officers under investigation told the NRK evening news broadcast *Dagsrevyen* (22 December 2007) that they now felt vindicated and were relieved at the outcome. However, owing to the explosive nature of the case, they were interviewed with their backs to the camera. During the same broadcast, one

Table 5.1. Is the Obiora Case Directly Linked to Racism and/or Discrimination against Immigrants? Percentage of All Articles (weighted by column space) in Which Both the Obiora Case and the Norwegian Bureau for the Investigation of Police Affairs Are Mentioned (8 September 2006 to 30 September 2008), by Newspaper

Racism/Discrimination	Newspaper				
	VG	*Aftenposten*	*Dagbladet*	*Adresseavisen*	All
Yes	34	26	42	14	23
No	66	74	58	86	78
Total	**100**	**100**	**100**	**100**	**101**
N (in 1,000 cm²)	(21.3)	(8.0)	(16.4)	(67.8)	(113.5)

(Cramér's *V:* 0.268)

of Obiora's friends expressed his outrage against those who had "killed him" and characterized the decision of the director general as cowardly.

Another key factor when interpretive frames are established and tied to mediated discourses is that the specific case in focus may become *linked* to other, similar cases. A case involving police brutality will readily provoke memories of earlier examples of the same. In addition, *new* incidents that attract attention may be tied to the original scandal. This also took place in the Obiora case. Let us look at two such examples.

The first important and specific "linkage" was established early on. It was the subject of stories in many newspapers; *Adresseavisen* in Trondheim published the first on 12 September 2006. The policeman who allegedly used a choke hold on Obiora "had been involved in the Baidoo case," a news story from 1999 that had attracted considerable attention. Sophia Baidoo, originally from Ghana, was a cleaner who had inadvertently set off the alarm at a bank in Trondheim where she was supposed to clean. When the police arrived, she could not identify herself and was asked to sit on a chair. When she did not comply or did not understand the request, according to *Adresseavisen,* a "scuffle" ensued. She was placed in a security cell, and later claimed that the police officer had called her "faens svarting" (a bloody nigger). The police officer replied that he had said "svarte faen" (bloody hell) and that she had bitten him. He was initially fined NOK 3,000 for his language, but was later acquitted in court and the fine was annulled. In an interview with *Dagbladet* (13 September 2006), Ms. Baidoo said, "if it is the same police officer who is involved in this incident, I am not surprised."

The other "linkage" tied to the Obiora case involved an arrest in Oslo several years earlier with a fatal outcome. The death, in October 2004, concerned a Swedish citizen, Robert Michael Aconcha-Kohn (aged forty-four), of Swedish-Colombian background. On 12 June 2007, *Dagsavisen* in Oslo reported that he had been strangled when, during an arrest at an Oslo hotel, the police wound an anorak hood around his head while his feet were shackled. Investigators did not find any fault with the way the police acted and decided not to proceed. After a complaint by the parents of Aconcha-Kohn and an intervention by a Swedish lawyer, the director general of public prosecutions reopened the case. The result was that the Oslo police were fined NOK 50,000, but no one informed the victim's family of this decision.

Dagsavisen's story was picked up by other news organizations. In an editorial, *Dagbladet* wrote:

> We have gradually seen numerous examples of how certain police holds are dangerous for arrestees. In the wake of the Obiora case, tests have shown that prone restraint is such a dangerous hold.

Chokeholds are another. The Swedish man arrested in 2004 also had an anorak hood over his face, preventing police officers from seeing that the man's face had changed color and that he was no longer breathing. (13 June 2007)

The new revelation of an "old" case not only caused a stir among the public—and renewed criticism from those already skeptical toward police methods—but also shocked many politicians. In *Dagbladet* (14 June 2007), the minister of justice, Knut Storberget (Labor), expressed worry about public trust in the police, and the newspaper reported that he had summoned the "heads of the Norwegian justice and law-enforcement community" to an emergency meeting to discuss various measures. Storberget had previously indicated his intention to evaluate the Norwegian Bureau for the Investigation of Police Affairs. Now he added that he "also wanted a discussion of both training and instructions in the methods and holds the police use in making arrests." In the article, the *Dagbladet* journalist reminded readers that a few weeks earlier several thousand people had taken part in antipolice demonstrations in several Norwegian cities after the Obiora case was dropped.

There can be no doubt that, taken together, these "linkages" to previous and contemporary cases helped to cement the racist system discourse in public opinion. When one particular interpretive framework becomes influential, news media coverage will also attach greater importance to testimony and information that act to confirm the angle and frame chosen. Because of the public critique and debate connected with the Obiora case, the minister of justice appointed a committee with the mandate to evaluate the control mechanisms concerning complaints against the police (NOU 2009: 12).

Conclusion

The case study presented here highlights the importance and potency of frames when sources and journalists are actively involved in co-constructing news frames. The influence and penetration of different frames is also dependent on the market power of the medium that launches them. An important factor here is that a chosen frame colors and influences the remaining coverage, turning specific news episodes into a more enduring news narrative. Potential news stories that do not fit in are easily dropped as being less newsworthy. However, if different political and social actors present alternative stories and interpretations, as in the case study of the press coverage after the death of Obiora, this increases the chances for more varied coverage and alternative perspectives.

The literature on the subject also indicates that actors improve their chances of achieving impact for their chosen issue-specific frames if they can exploit generic news frames and familiar narratives. Media organizations compete for survival in the marketplace—and frames fused with personal conflicts, moral dramas, and individual responsibilities represent, in most cases, "an offer you can't resist."

Notes

1. See D'Angelo and Kuypers (2010) for an overview.
2. One exception is Wahl-Jorgensen and Hanitzsch (2009), which includes a chapter about framing effects.
3. A parallel example in literature studies could be Vladimir Propp's ([1927] 1968) *Morphology of the Folk Tale*.
4. The facts as presented in these introductory paragraphs are from the Office of the Director General of Public Prosecution's petition in the Obiora case, 21 December 2007.
5. Cited in a report from the Norwegian Bureau for the Investigation of Police affairs, 4 May 2007.

Bibliography

Allern, S., and E. Pollack. 2009. "Mediebilder av politikritikk." *Norges offentlige utredninger*, no. 12 (May): 247–70.

Bateson, G. 1972. *Steps to an Ecology of Mind: Collected Essays in Anthropology, Psychiatry, Evolution and Epistemology.* London: Intertext Books.

Benford, R. D., and D. A. Snow. 2000. "Framing Processes and Social Movements: An Overview and Assessment." *Annual Review of Sociology* 26, no. 1: 611–39.

D'Angelo, P., and J. A. Kuypers. 2010. *Doing Frame Analysis: Empirical and Theoretical Perspectives.* New York: Routledge.

Dunwoody, S. 1992. "The Media and Public Perceptions of Risk: How Journalists Frame Risk Stories." In *The Social Response to Environmental Risk: Policy Formulation in an Age of Uncertainty*, ed. D. W. Bromley and K. Segerson. Boston, MA: Kluwer.

Entman, R. 1993. "Framing: Toward Clarification of a Fractured Paradigm." *Journal of Communication* 43, no. 4 (December): 51–58.

———. 2004. *Projections of Power.* Chicago: University of Chicago Press.

Gamson, W. A. 1988. "A Constructionist Approach to Mass Media and Public Opinion." *Symbolic Interaction* 11, no. 2: 161–74.

Gamson, W. A. 1992. *Talking Politics.* New York: Cambridge University Press.

Gamson, W. A., and A. Modigliani. 1989. "Media Discourse and Public Opinion on Nuclear Power: A Constructionist Approach." *American Journal of Sociology* 95, no. 1 (July): 1–37.

Gandy, O. T. 1982. *Beyond Agenda Setting: Information Subsidies and Public Policy.* Norwood, NJ: Ablex.

Gans, H. 1980. *Deciding What's News: A Study of CBS Evening News, NBC Nightly News, Newsweek and Time.* New York: Vintage Books.

Gitlin, T. 1980. *The Whole World Is Watching.* Berkeley: University of California Press.

———. 2003. *The Whole World Is Watching.* With a new foreword. Berkeley, CA: University of California Press.

Goffman, E. 1974. *Frame Analysis.* Cambridge, MA: Harvard University Press.

Ihlen, Ø. 2004. *Rhetoric and Resources in Public Relation Strategies: A Rhetorical and Sociological Analysis of Two Conflicts over Energy and the Environment.* PhD diss. Oslo: Unipub forlag.

Ihlen, Ø., and S. Allern. 2008. "This Is the Issue: Framing Contests and Media Coverage." In *Communicating Politics,* ed. J. Strömbäck, M. Ørsten, and T. Aalberg. Gothenburg: Nordicom.

Iyengar, S. 1994. *Is Anyone Responsible? How Television Frames Political Issues.* Chicago: University of Chicago Press.

Norris, P., M. Kern, and M. Just. 2003. *Framing Terrorism.* New York, London: Routledge.

NOU 2009:12 (Official Norwegian Report No 12 2009). *Et ansvarlig politi: Åpenhet, kontroll, læring* [A responsible police: Openess, control, learning]. Oslo: Ministry of Justice and Public Security.

Oliver, P. E., and H. Johnston. 2000. "What a Good Idea! Ideologies and Frames in Social Movement Research." *Mobilization: An International Journal* 5, no. 1: 37–54.

Pan, Z., and G. M. Kosicki. 2001. "Framing As a Strategic Action in Public Deliberation." In *Framing Public Life: Perspectives on Media and Our Understanding of the Social World,* ed. S. D. Reese, O. H. Gandy, and A. E. Grant. Mahwah, NJ: Lawrence Erlbaum.

Propp, V. [1927] 1968. *Morphology of the Folk Tale.* Austin, TX: University of Texas Press.

Reese, S. D. 2001. "Framing Public Life: A Bridging Model for Media Research." In *Framing Public Life: Perspectives on Media and Our Understanding of the Social World,* ed. S. D. Reese, O. H. Gandy, and A. E. Grant. Mahwah, NJ: Lawrence Erlbaum.

Reese, S. D., O. H. Gandy, and A. E. Grant, eds. 2001. *Framing Public Life: Perspectives on Media and Our Understanding of the Social World.* Mahwah, NJ: Lawrence Erlbaum.

Semetko, H. A., and P. M. Valkenburg. 2000. "Framing European Politics: A Content Analysis of Press and Television News." *Journal of Communication* 50, no. 2 (June): 93–109.

Snow, D. A., and R. D. Benford. 1988. "Ideology, Frame Resonance, and Participant Mobilization." In *International Social Movement Research: From Structure to Action,* ed. B. Klandermans, H. Kriesi, and S. Tarrow. Greenwich, CT: Jai Press.

———. 2000. "Clarifying the Relationship between Framing and Ideology in the Study of Social Movements: A Comment on Oliver and Johnston." *Mobilization* 5, no. 1: 55–60.

Snow, D. A., E. B. Rochford, S. K. Worden, and R. D. Benford. 1986. "Frame Alignment Processes, Micromobilization, and Movement Participation." *American Sociological Review* 51, no. 4 (August): 464–81.

Surette, R. 2007. *Media, Crime and Criminal Justice.* Belmont, CA: Thompson Wadsworth.

Tuchman, G. 1978. *Making News: A Study of the Construction of Reality.* New York: Free Press.

Van Gorp, B. 2007. "The Constructionist Approach to Framing: Bringing the Culture Back." *Journal of Communication* 57, no. 1 (March): 6078.

———. 2010. "Strategies to Take Subjectivity Out of Framing Analysis." In *Doing Frame Analysis: Empirical and Theoretical Perspectives,* ed. P. D'Angelo and J. A. Kuypers. New York: Routledge.

Van Gorp, B., H. Blow, and M. van de Velde. May 2005. *Representation of Poverty in TV Reports in Belgium: Who Is to Blame?* Paper presented at the annual meeting of the International Communication Association, New York, 26–30 May 2005.

de Vreese, C. H. 2003. *Framing Europe: Television News and European Integration.* Amsterdam: Aksant.

Wahl-Jorgensen, K., and T. Hanitzsch, eds. 2009. *The Handbook of Journalism Studies.* New York: Routledge.

Part II

Protest in the Mass Media around 1968

Print, Film, and Television

Chapter 6

Constructing a Media Image of the *Sessantotto*

The Framing of the Italian Protest Movement in 1968

Stuart Hilwig

The student uprisings that swept the world in the late 1960s quickly achieved widespread notoriety, due in large part to the power of the media to disseminate words and create images that kindled strong emotions among the general population. Perhaps at no time in modern history had scattered protest groups received the attention of so many forms of media, so quickly, and with such widespread circulation. Though the live imagery of televised student battles with police leaps to mind, for many observers of the 1968 student revolt, dramatic news photographs and provocative headlines were equally important in constructing an image of youth rebellion in the late 1960s. Journalists and news photographers, unlike television broadcasters, had the time and editorial selectivity to frame student actions in accordance with their editors' views. Tangled in a love-hate relationship, the student activists bemoaned the mainstream presses' typically negative representations of their goals and actions but also recognized the importance of the press in publicizing their movement.

In Italy, the majority of the newspapers with national circulations took a strong antistudent line, constructing an image of the *Sessantotto* (1968) that was almost wholly negative.[1] From liberal and conservative dailies such as *La Stampa, Corriere della Sera,* and the Vatican's *L'Osservatore Romano,* student protesters were portrayed as either figures of ridicule or dangerous threats to public order and morality. Only the Communist Party's *l'Unità* sought to depict student activists as thoughtful young people peacefully struggling for university reform and political change. These images, positive or negative, have become the visual artifacts that are inevitably recalled when one mentions the student revolts of the 1960s.[2]

It should be noted that the importance of press photographs in the Italian media may derive from the fact that literacy rates in Italy have historically lagged behind those of their western and northern counterparts, and Italians did not achieve high literacy rates until the 1960s. In fact, a survey from 1956 showed that 65 percent of Italians did not read a daily newspaper (Pugliese 2001: 672–73). By comparison, the large French national daily *Le Monde* had no press photographs, and the West German press under the monopoly of media mogul Axel Springer included both photographs and cartoons of the student activists.[3] Political cartoons did not appear extensively in the Italian press until the emergence of *La Repubblica* in the 1970s.

Framing the *Sessantotto*

This study will draw upon an extensive reading and analysis of press articles and photographs from *La Stampa, Corriere della Sera, L'Osservatore Romano,* and *l'Unità* for the period 1967–68. In analyzing these four news sources, over two thousand editions were surveyed and hundreds of articles covering student unrest were examined. Leading articles, editorial pieces, and readers' letters were studied in an effort to determine both the newspapers' position toward student activism as well as the nonstudents' view of the movement. As such, the articles and photographs used in this study are both typical of the media source in which they were published and the newspapers chosen represent the media with the highest circulations in Italy and are thus most representative of the media that most Italians read during the late 1960s. Although exhaustive in terms of the sheer volume of media examined, any analysis of photographs and rhetoric is necessarily qualitative. As a guide to analyzing the Italian press, this study draws upon Todd Gitlin's study of the US media's portrayal of the student protests, *The Whole World Is Watching* (1980). Following Gitlin's lead, this chapter will use frame analysis to show how the Italian press sought to marginalize and delegitimize the student movement by placing the students' actions into what Gitlin and other media theorists have called a "protest paradigm" (Brasted 2005: 5). Gitlin's work on the media framing of student actions identified eleven framing devices used by the media to construct student protest. For the purposes of our study, we shall make use of five of these devices:

1. *Trivialization:* Making light of the movement's language, dress, style, goals.

2. *Polarization:* Emphasizing counterdemonstrations and balancing the New Left student movement against neofascist groups as equivalent "extremists."
3. *Marginalization:* Showing protesters to be deviant or unrepresentative, emphasizing the student Left's Maoist or other non-Italian-Communist-Party (PCI) elements.
4. *Disparagement:* By numbers or undercounting, by emphasizing internal dissension within the movement, and by questioning the effectiveness of student actions.
5. *Delegitimizing:* By focusing considerable attention on those who opposed the student movement, especially persons of authority and government officials (Gitlin 1980: 27–28).

By applying the concept of media framing to an analysis of centrist and conservative newspapers published in Italy in the late 1960s, it becomes clear that these presses used framing strategies to construct an "Italian protest paradigm." In particular, the Italian protest paradigm emphasized the alleged similarities between the New Left student movement and the fascist movement at the beginning of the twentieth century, played upon class tensions between student activists and industrial workers, and exaggerated the Third World brand of revolutionary Marxism extolled by the student movement. The notable counterpoint to this generally hostile Italian protest paradigm was provided by the Communist Party's *l'Unità,* which essentially inverted the framing strategies of the conservative dailies and portrayed students as serious, nonviolent, democratically committed young people who were dedicated to antifascism and university reform. The communist press, however, controlled a meager 8–10 percent of the total press circulation, so for most Italians who followed the events of 1968 in the pages of the daily press, the image of student protest was almost entirely negative (Ginsborg 2003: 291).

The power of the press to distort and create new meanings for an event captured on its pages has been well documented by social philosopher Pierre Bourdieu, who argued:

Journalists ... show us the world as a series of unrelated flash photos. Given the lack of time, and especially the lack of interest and information, they cannot do what would be necessary to make events really understandable, that is, they cannot reinsert them in a network of relevant relationships ... This vision is at once dehistoricized and dehistoricizing, fragmented and fragmenting. (Bourdieu 1998: 7)

As we shall see, the conservative press not only took the student protests and activities out of their actual historical contexts, but also created new ahistorical contexts for the student demonstrations that anachronistically fused them with Italy's fascist past and Cold War present.

But was it possible to link the generally peaceful sit-ins, marches, and civil disobedience of the Italian university movement with the violence and lawlessness of the fascist era? Could readers of the daily newspapers be convinced that the activists represented an insidious "fifth column" in the struggle against world communism? The answer is yes, chiefly due to the abilities of the conservative and centrist presses to frame student actions within the "protest paradigm," offering a distorted image of the student movement that touched upon emotional rather than rational chords within the reader. The scores of readers' letters and pronouncements of politicians show that the press succeeded in conflating contemporary Cold War angst and troubled memories of the fascist past with the university upheavals of the *Sessantotto*.

The Battle of the Valle Giulia

Two key newspapers that framed the student movement within the protest paradigm, Milan's *Corriere della Sera* and Turin's *La Stampa,* made use of what Kathrin Fahlenbrach has called the "psychophysical semantic" of student-press interactions in the late 1960s. Fahlenbrach argues that as the students came to adopt direct action tactics, reminiscent of the situationists, in an effort to draw attention to their movement, the media quickly adapted its framing or staging of the protesters through the publication of dynamic and action-filled images (Fahlenbrach 2002: 177). As noted earlier, the press focus clearly shifted the reader's attention away from the details found in the text of the article and toward the more emotional and visually stimulating headlines and photographs emphasizing dramatic action.

An excellent example of this emphasis on the psychophysical semantic can be seen in the presses' coverage of the Battle of the Valle Giulia. The infamous street battle that took place in a park outside the University of Rome's Faculty of Architecture pitted police against Roman students and could be considered the Italian version of the Grant Park demonstrations in Chicago or the Parisian students' clashes with the forces of order in the Latin Quarter. The conservative presses' coverage of the Battle of the Valle Giulia in Rome turned the event into a national spectacle. Framing the demonstration as a violent threat to public order, the antistudent press contrasted frightening depictions of the activists with benevolent images of the police, who were portrayed either as victims of student violence or saviors of public order.

Following the protest paradigm model, the conservative presses sought to delegitimize student grievances by quoting the testimonies of police and politicians who condemned the students' actions, and offered no voices from the students, who bore the brunt of the injuries.

Figure 6.1, showing the police battling students inside the Valle Giulia, appeared on the front pages of both *Corriere della Sera* and *La Stampa*. This photograph evokes an image of peasant rebellion, with the students brandishing makeshift clubs, the disorderly mob, and the trees in the background. The picture was cropped to make it appear that the students greatly outnumbered the police, thus heightening the perceived threat to public order. *La Stampa*'s headline read, "Violent Battle in the Center of Rome between Students and the Police: Hundreds Injured" (2 March 1968: 1). *Corriere*'s masthead claimed, "Serious New Disorders in Rome with Two Hundred among the Bruised and Injured" (2 March 1968: 1). The article in *Corriere* also carried pictures of overturned cars that had been ostensibly set on fire by the protesters.

Using selective pieces of evidence, the articles in *La Stampa* and *Corriere della Sera* gave minimal attention to the actual causes of the students' demonstration. As the oral historian Alessandro Portelli has noted in his study of the Valle Giulia demonstrations, this image of the police as dutiful public servants has been completely contradicted by student experiences of

Figure 6.1. "The Battle of the Valle Giulia" (*Corriere della Sera* 2 March 1968: 1)

brutality at the hands of the police. Nevertheless, the conservative dailies did help to swing public opinion to the side of the agents of law and order (for examples, see Portelli 1997: 192–98).

The conservative press, for its part, found that marginalizing the students as violent infidels marauding through Italy's universities and public parks was very effective in spawning newer disorders and even making their offices the targets of student outrage. The students' attacks against press buildings served as affirmation of previous news articles describing student "hooliganism."[4] To heighten readers' fears even more, the press employed words and images drawn from the fascist period to depict the generally nonthreatening student demonstrations as crises of public order. *Corriere della Sera* and *La Stampa* deliberately compared the events of the Valle Giulia in Rome and the June protests in Turin with the early days of fascism, despite the obvious historical and political differences.

The Students as "Left-Wing Fascists"

Added to this misleading historical analogy, the press used the language of the Cold War to increase the public's fear that communist subversion led by deviationists of the New Left was imminent. Though the conservative and centrist presses had never shown much support for the Italian Communist Party (PCI), they did attempt to draw sharp contrasts between the Old and the New Left. Since the end of the war, the PCI had been the second largest political party in Italy, had historic ties to the antifascist resistance, and had made a commitment to democratic processes in the late 1940s, so the antistudent dailies framed the student New Left as dangerous Marxists inspired by violent Third World revolutionaries in comparison to the "safe" Old Left. In particular, the press frequently characterized the student rebels as *filocinesi* (Maoists), doubtlessly playing on xenophobic and anticommunist tendencies. As historian Robert Lumley has pointed out, the term *filocinesi* "conjured up the red menace and the yellow peril all in one" (1990: 73), or as one student newspaper article succinctly quipped, "I see student—I see red" (Centro Studi Piero Gobetti 8 February 1968).

Furthermore, the conservative presses fused two contradictory streams of thought, fascism and New Left communism, into a model of "left-wing fascism." The German social philosopher Jürgen Habermas first mentioned the concept of *Linksfaschismus* or "left-wing fascism" to criticize the radical activists in 1967 who he claimed had emulated fascist tactics of the 1930s. Although he regretted his remarks and apologized shortly thereafter, the popular media in West Germany and Italy made frequent use of the idea.[5] In Italy, this charge of "left-wing fascism" was most often directed against the *filocinesi*.

For readers glancing through the pages of *La Stampa* in March of 1968, photographs of students raising their hands in fascist salutes, even if they were really communist students mocking neofascist intruders, undoubtedly provoked scorn among older citizens. For the left-wing students, opposed to fascism but too young to have remembered the regime, the fascist salute could be given to opponents in a spirit of ridicule and derision. On 3 March, a day after the Battle of the Valle Giulia, *La Stampa* featured a half-page photograph of left-wing students raising their hands in fascist salutes. Looking closer, the viewer sees that the students are depicted as rowdy, but not necessarily violent individuals. They even appear to be having a good time, almost as if they are at a soccer match, not plotting to topple the state. In typical journalistic fashion, the photo was framed in such a way to remove the context of the students' gesture. The caption did not explain that the left-wing students had offered the fascist salute to mock their right-wing rivals, nor did it mention the violence perpetrated by the neofascists.

In March 1968, following the events of the Valle Giulia in Rome, the popular press sought to delegitimize the students' right to protest by paying considerable attention to prominent political figures who condemned the students and praised the police. Turin's *La Stampa,* Milan's *Corriere della Sera,* and the Vatican's *L'Osservatore Romano* all headlined Minister of the Interior Paolo Taviani's declaration, "The police do not defend the position of the government, they defend the legal state. They defend democracy" (see *Corriere della Sera* 2 March 1968: 1; *La Stampa* 2 March 1968: 1; *L'Osservatore Romano* 3 March 1968: 8). Although the more conservative *L'Osservatore* gave less coverage to the remarks by communist and socialist politicians than did *La Stampa,* both newspapers reproduced Taviani's remarks almost entirely, particularly his laudatory depiction of the police and his warning that the weakness of the state had been one of the causes of fascism (*La Stampa* 2 March 1968: 1; *L'Osservatore Romano* 3 March 1968: 8).

As these examples have shown, the selective reporting of the mainstream presses created a distorted image for many Italians. For northerners, the main source of news came from the antistudent *Corriere della Sera* and *La Stampa* (see Giuseppe Mazzoleni's [1992] chapter on the Italian mass media). Readers saw the student demonstrators depicted as violent extremists. Provocative words such as disorder, confusion, and hooliganism were used to describe university unrest. Added to these glimpses of chaos in the Italian universities were the references to the early fascist period. By their strategic use of framing to construct an Italian protest paradigm, the conservative and centrist presses had created a simple formula: student unrest = *filocinesi* = fascist methods.

The Students Play a Game of Revolution

The press also framed the student activists as figures of ridicule in order to trivialize the importance of their movement. The conservative presses alternated frightening images of left-wing fascists with caricatures of naïve middle-class kids who had been bamboozled by a romanticized view of Marxist revolution. To be sure, university students had eagerly bought thousands of cheap paperbacks about the lives of Che Guevara and Fidel Castro from the self-styled Marxist publisher Giangiacomo Feltrinelli (Lumley 1990: 39–40). But the critics of the New Left cynically depicted the student activists as a group of young, bourgeois malcontents who claimed to represent the working class, but who were, in reality, a privileged people in search of excitement, a view adopted by many of the workers of Turin.

The conservative presses' characterization of the student activists as misguided followers of Mao sought to disparage the effectiveness of the New Left in Italy. The official Italian Communist and Socialist Parties, similar to their comrades in France, continued to support the traditional organs of the Left, the trade unions. To older Italian communists, the New Left, inspired by Third World revolutionaries and the German American philosopher Herbert Marcuse, represented a bourgeois deviation from their party. Ultimately, many of these supporters of the Old Left bolstered the view of the professors, politicians, and popular press that the left-wing students were dupes to the "infantilism" of the New Left (for a scathing criticism of the student Left, see Aron [1969]). The students, on the other hand, opposed the communist and socialists' complacency and apparent willingness to collaborate with the Christian Democrats after the war. The problem for the students was that they did not have the authority to challenge the legitimacy of the PCI or its antifascist credentials. As the workers' unrest of 1969 demonstrated (as well as the strikes in France in 1968), the revolutionary proletariat, though perhaps inspired by the students, chose to remain firmly within the established organizations of the Old Left.

Prominent intellectuals also questioned the earnestness of the students' commitment to communist revolution, and the conservative press was eager to reproduce their remarks in Italy's dailies. The poet and filmmaker Pier Paolo Pasolini, who was a member of the Communist Party, lampooned the student rebels who had fought with police during the Battle of the Valle

Giulia in a poem that was published in the weekly newsmagazine *L'Espresso*. In his piece, "The Communist Party to the Young!" Pasolini lambasted the New Left as nothing more than spoiled children of the bourgeoisie who had adopted Marxism out of boredom. He wrote,

> You have the faces of spoiled children.
> Good blood doesn't lie.
> You have the same bad eye.
> You are scared, uncertain, desperate
> (very good!) but you also know how to be
> bullies, blackmailers, and sure of yourselves;
> petit-bourgeois prerogatives, friends.
> When yesterday at Valle Giulia you fought
> with policemen,
> I sympathized with the policemen!
> Because policemen are children of the poor (Pasolini 1980: 150)[6]

In a sort of "plague on both your houses," Pasolini's poem not only mocked the students for believing they could represent the working class but also acknowledged his regret for the Communist Party's lack of a vigorous political opposition to Christian Democracy in the 1950s.

Although it is impossible to gauge the students' true attachment to the New Left, Raymond Aron's (1969) contention that the rebels were performing a poorly rehearsed revival of the revolutions of 1848 and had turned campuses into carnivals had an element of truth. As Fahlenbrach points out, the student protesters of the late 1960s had drawn inspiration for public demonstrations and direct action from the situationists of the earlier half of the decade (2002: 177). Like the situationists, the students consciously understood that the revolution should be "fun" and contain elements of the ludicrous. Political scientist Barbara Myerhoff (1971) has argued that although the students' final aims were serious, the methods to draw attention to their cause demanded that the protests be antic and spontaneous. Fahlenbrach's (2002) work clearly documents the ways that students modified their protest forms to fit with media outlets, and this was true of Italian and American student activists. One of these students told Myerhoff that the zaniness of the demonstrations was deliberate, to draw media attention to their demands: "If we don't provide a good show, we won't get on the air" (Myerhoff 1971: 108–11). This image of the students "playing at revolution" stands in stark contrast to the portrayal of the students as dangerous left-wing fascists and further highlights the Italian press and public's equivocal relationship with the protesters of the late 1960s.

Similar to the presses' attempt to construct an image of student activists as misguided followers of the New Left, the popular press succeeded in framing demonstrators as playing a game of revolution.

Figure 6.2, printed in *La Stampa* in May 1968, captured female students giggling and laughing as they escorted the newly freed Guido Viale from prison (10 May 1968: 2). Dressed informally, these "flower children" seem more like players carrying their hero off the soccer field than dangerous revolutionaries. Such playful imagery suggested that these young people's revolt was not serious, and the photo sought to reassure readers that these incidents would eventually subside.

Corriere and *La Stampa* continued to trivialize the students as disorganized, lethargic rebels pretending to lead a revolution under an assortment of banners, flags, and slogans that originated with their heroes of the Third World. *La Stampa* declared in July that "[t]he student 'rebels' will promote actions in the piazza after summer vacation," mocking those activists who put the revolution on hold until after they returned from the beach (9 July 1968: 3).

Figure 6.2. Italian Flower Children: Rebels or Pranksters? (*La Stampa* 10 May 1968: 2)

One of the most striking visual examples of press ridicule directed against student activists appeared in *La Stampa* on 26 March 1968. On page two of the newspaper, a half-page photograph showed Turin student leaders Laura DeRossi and her fiancé, Luigi Bobbio, meeting with DeRossi's parents after their release from jail. The DeRossis were portrayed as concerned, bourgeois parents, and Laura is depicted as a "daddy's girl" rather than an "extremist" student leader. In the picture, *La Stampa* hinted that many of the activists, like Laura DeRossi, were simply bored, wealthy kids who had been swept up by the demonstrations. Laura's father, a wealthy building contractor and owner of a metalworking business in Turin, was clearly a member of the upper middle class and had provided his daughter with a classical high school education and money for university. His social standing was indicated in the photograph by his overcoat and dress shirt, and his patronizing attitude was exemplified by the gentle expression of patting Laura. The photograph suggested that Signore DeRossi was more concerned than angry that his daughter had been detained in jail for a day (Laura DeRossi, interviewed in Passerini 1996: 24–25).

We have seen how the centrist and conservative presses adopted an Italian protest paradigm to construct a dual image of university demonstrators. One image depicted the activists as dangerous left-wing fascists resorting to tactics reminiscent of the early years of the dictatorship. Such an image provoked fear in the viewers and magnified the tensions between the student protesters and the larger society in the late 1960s. In many ways the vilification of the Italian New Left fit the editorial pattern of the conservative and centrist presses, which had supported the Christian Democrats since the beginning of the republic. Rekindling old and personal memories among many Italians, the characterization of student demonstrations as a new version of *squadrismo* (Italien fascist squads in the 1920's) did much to delegitimize and disparage student calls for genuine university reform.

The other image portrayed student activists as figures of ridicule. In stark contrast to the left-wing fascist image of the *filocinesi,* the student *Maoisti* became humorous caricatures of middle-class kids playing a game of revolution. These faux revolutionaries waved the Vietcong flag and carried posters of Chairman Mao similar to the *tifosi*[7] at a soccer match. The press also represented the activists as spoiled children of the bourgeoisie in order to play upon class tensions within Italian society. From the student Left's perspective, the workers would eventually reap benefits from the initial uprisings in the universities, but from the perspective of the press and the Old Left, the student New Left was no more than a brief period of disobedience among the children of the bourgeoisie.

The Students and Communists Fight Back

The student activists were well aware of the presses' tactics in framing their beliefs and actions in a negative protest paradigm. In fact, one article from the Turin students' *l'Anti-Stampa,* entitled "The Two Pincers of the Claw," compared *La Stampa*'s editorial techniques to the United States' strategy in Vietnam of "pacification" and "search and destroy." The student newspaper clearly shows that the press alternated between a soft, pseudounderstanding approach to their movement and a harsh, repressive tone that varied from article to article (Centro Studi Piero Gobetti 8 February 1968). Unfortunately for the students, with a circulation of a few thousand mimeographed copies, their press could not compete with the large dailies in Italy.[8] However, their position would be defended by the Communist Party's small but influential daily, *l'Unità.*

In the late 1960s, the Italian Communist Party's official news organ, *l'Unità,* was second only to Milan's *Corriere della Sera* in daily circulation (Ginsborg 2003: 291). *L'Unità* consistently depicted student protests as democratic and orderly struggles for university reform. As we shall see, the prostudent coverage of *l'Unità* essentially inverted the negative framing techniques adopted by the conservative newspapers. Where the right-wing presses marginalized student activists as "left-wing fascists," *l'Unità* sought to legitimize the New Left's continuities with the antifascist resistance. Where the right-wing press trivialized student demonstrators as ridiculous actors in a farcical revolution, *l'Unità* offered an encouraging image of student protesters as serious agents of university reform.

Despite the criticisms of some Communist Party officials, *l'Unità* remained consistent in its defense of student actions, often evoking the heroic legacy of the *Resistenza.* The left-wing press therefore offered a completely different historical analogy of the student movement than that of the conservative and centrist presses. Rather than a new form of "left-wing fascism," the student activists were transformed into the second generation of antifascist resistance fighters. Resolutely marching under red banners and carrying placards of communist heroes (even if it was Mao rather than Gramsci), the student demonstrators became *l'Unità*'s new face of the continuing struggle against Italian fascism. On 21 January 1968, the newspaper printed a full-page pictorial article entitled, "From the Resistance to Today." By placing a photo of the students' anti-Vietnam demonstrations next to pictures of the famed antifascist protests in Genoa in 1960 and the marches for land reform in southern Italy during the late 1940s, *l'Unità* implied that the students' recent efforts fell within the continuum of the communists' historic and continual struggle against fascism.

Rather than ridiculous or spoiled rich kids out for a lark, the communist press continued to affirm the legitimacy of the students' commitment to Marxism. Contrary to Pasolini's (1980) and Aron's (1969) claims that the students were playing a game of revolution, *l'Unità* championed the activists as significant leaders in an important political movement. Similar to the conservative presses' use of authority figures to delegitimize the students, *l'Unità* published an editorial by Maurizio Ferrara, one of the PCI's Central Committee members, applauding the students as allies of the Communist Party's struggle for real university reform. Ferrara also criticized the "anti-student montage" found on the pages of *Corriere della Sera* and Rome's *Il Messagero* (*l'Unità* 26 February 1968: 3).

In sharp contrast to *La Stampa*'s image of the university activists as rowdy and anarchic revolutionaries, *l'Unità* consistently depicted the students as orderly and alert members of a democratic movement.

Figure 6.3 shows a peaceful, well-organized demonstration of students held at the University of Trento in November 1967. The students appeared well dressed, attentive, disciplined, and committed to reform. The article's headline read, "An Important Moment of Democratic Action in the University," and reported that the sociology students wanted a profound reform of

Figure 6.3. "An Important Moment of Democratic Action in the University" (*l'Unità* 29 November 1967: 8)

the methods and contents of their courses and that they comprised a new "*avanguardia*" (*l'Unità* 29 November 1967: 8). Such a description also reflected the self-image of the PCI, which had always considered itself a "civil" opposition to the government since the inception of the Italian Republic.

The communist press chose a very different photograph for its article on the release of jailed Turin activists Laura DeRossi and Luigi. Unlike the repentant Laura and sheepish Luigi in *La Stampa*'s version of the event, *l'Unità* captured the two activists in a loving embrace. Their experience in the city jail seemed to have not only strengthened their cause but also their love. Furthermore, the picture emphasizes the support of their student companions, rather than DeRossi's parents, indicating the solidarity of the students rather than *La Stampa*'s reproach for the misbehavior of "daddy's little girl."

An example of *l'Unità*'s critique of the forces of order appears in figure 6.4, illustrating a protest in late February at the University of Rome. The photograph on the left, showing the vulnerability and anguish of two female students, contrasted sharply with the massive, martial show of police force outside the rector's building on the right. This diptych bombards the viewer with a skillful use of space and imagery to evoke sympathy for the students and a simultaneous fear of the forces of order. The photograph on the left reveals the emotion of two victims of a police evacuation; both are female and presumably more vulnerable to violence than male victims. The prone student is in physical pain and clearly needs medical attention. The figure on the left is smaller and cropped vertically, emphasizing the closeness of the two students. On the other hand, the photograph of police on the right is larger and horizontal in orientation, emphasizing the vastness of police powers. The jeeps in the foreground and the line of police standing at attention clearly display the impersonal and potentially bellicose attitude of the forces of order. Even without words, this diptych clearly revealed *l'Unità*'s sympathy with the defenseless students (24 February 1968: 2).

Figure 6.4. The Left's View of the Police (*l'Unità* 24 February 1968: 2)

Conclusion

As we have seen in this chapter, the popular press in Italy offered a variety of images and texts to frame the university protests of the late 1960s. Generally, the photographs and headlines that were printed in the Italian press offered characterizations of the student demonstrators that fit within the newspaper's political and editorial inclinations. The vast majority of Italians read newspapers that had centrist or conservative leanings due to the fact that these publishers dominated the media industry. Thus, for those who received their information on the student movement from the daily newspapers in the late 1960s, the image was overwhelmingly negative. The conservative press depicted the student activists as dangerous "left-wing fascists" by printing a disturbing blend of headlines, articles, photographs, and readers' letters that associated the university reform movement with Italy's fascist past and the Cold War present. The conservative press also preyed upon class antagonisms by characterizing students as spoiled rich kids playing a game of revolution.

Conversely, the left-wing press constructed an image of the student movement that opposed the negative image perpetuated by the centrist and conservative presses by simply inverting the negative frames of protest used by the antistudent presses. The most widely circulating of the leftist presses, *l'Unità*, created an image of the student movement that connected the protesters with the antifascist resistance and showed its readers scenes of thoughtful, orderly young people struggling for necessary reforms. Readers of *l'Unità* and several communist politicians voiced their support of and gratitude to student leaders in the pages of the newspaper. The press also published scathing photographs and testimonials of police violence toward peaceful protesters.

Ultimately, however, the prostudent media voice was drowned by the voices more toward the Right, because *l'Unità* could not compete with the conservative and centrist presses' circulation. Public figures like communist playwright Pier Paolo Pasolini openly criticized the student protesters, further undercutting the left-wing press's faint image of the students as serious antifascists working hard for university and political reform. This negative framing of the student movement not only shaped public attitudes toward the students, but also altered the views of Italy's political leaders at the highest levels.

Future studies of the media's role in the Italian *Sessantotto* will inevitably need to take into account the growing influence of television. In the 1950s, few Italians owned television sets, and watching programs was a collective activity that occurred in cafés and political halls. In 1962, the state-run Radiotelevisione italiana (RAI) added a second channel, and by 1965, 49 percent of Italian families owned a television set (Ginsborg 2003: 240–41; Martinelli et al. 1999: 318–19). Since television in the mid-1960s was still tightly controlled by the government, any future analyses of the media and the *Sessantotto* will need to include a discussion of the televised broadcasts of protests, meetings, and public responses to the student movement. The fact that the percentage of Italian families who owned television sets was far more than the percentage of the population that claimed to read daily newspapers makes clear the necessity to investigate television archives for studies of the 1968 phenomenon in Italy and around the globe (Pugliese 2001: 672–73).

Notes

1. For an interesting counterpoint to the Italian press, see Rolf Werenskjold and Erling Sivertsen's chapter in this volume, "Photos in Frames or Frames in Photos? Framing Photos in Black and White—the Global 1968 Revolts in Three Norwegian Dailies," which uses a unique quantitative approach in assessing the ways that the student movement was depicted. Werenskjold and Sivertsen have found that the conservative Norwegian press did not necessarily frame the student movement in a more negative manner than the more left-leaning dailies.
2. In particular, the stunning photographs of the French '68 by Bruno Barbey, an independent photographer for Magnum, have subsequently been reprinted in many of the books on the student movement. See them at http://www.magnumphotos .com/Archive/C.aspx?VP=XSpecific_MAG.ExhibitionDetail_VPage&pid=2TYR YDKUU22I (accessed 11 February 2008).
3. For an excellent analysis of Axel Springer's media empire, see Müller (1968).
4. The word "hooligan" comes from the violent career of Irishman Patrick Hooligan, a street thug who terrorized residents of Southwark, London, in the late nineteenth century.
5. For a discussion of Jürgen Habermas and the controversy surrounding his remarks at the *Kongress Hochschule und Demokratie* in 1967, see Harold Marcuse (1998: 429 and n38).
6. Originally appeared in *L'Espresso* (16 April 1968), *Nuovi Argomenti* 10 (April–June 1968), and *Corriere della Sera* (12 June 1968: 3).
7. In Italian, *tifosi* refers to crazed soccer fans. The word comes from the Italian word for typhoid, because these fans often act like they have a kind of illness.
8. An archival note attached to a copy of *l'Anti-Stampa* from 14 February 1968 indicated that three thousand copies of the article had been distributed (Centro Studi Piero Gobetti).

Bibliography

Archival Sources

Centro Studi Piero Gobetti, *Fondo Marcello Vitale*: Box 14, Folder II, *l'Anti-Stampa* (February 1968).

Newspapers and Other Media

Corriere della Sera
La Stampa
L'Osservatore Romano
l'Unità

Books and Articles

Aron, R. 1969. *The Elusive Revolution: Anatomy of a Student Revolt.* Trans. G. Clough. New York: Praeger Publishers.

Bourdieu, P. 1998. *On Television.* Trans. P. P. Ferguson. New York: New Press.

Brasted, M. 2005. "Framing Protest: *The Chicago Tribune* and the *New York Times* during the 1968 Democratic Convention." *Atlantic Journal of Communication* 13, no. 1: 1–25.

Fahlenbrach, K. 2002. *Protest-Inszenierungen.* Wiesbaden, Germany: Westdeutscher Verlag.

Ginsborg, P. 2003. *A History of Contemporary Italy.* New York: Palgrave Macmillan.

Gitlin, T. 1980. *The Whole World Is Watching.* Berkeley: University of California Press.

Lumley, R. 1990. *States of Emergency: Cultures of Revolt in Italy, 1968–1978.* London: Verso.

Marcuse, H. 1998. "The Revival of Holocaust Awareness in West Germany, Israel, and the United States." In *1968: The World Transformed,* ed. C. Fink, P. Gassert, and D. Junker. Cambridge: Cambridge University Press.

Martinelli, A., A. M. Chiesi, and S. Stefanizzi. 1999. *Recent Trends in Italy, 1960–1995.* Montreal: McGill-Queen's University Press.

Mazzoleni, G. 1992. "Italy." In *The Media in Western Europe,* ed. B. Stubbe Ostergaard. London, Newbury Park: Sage.

Müller, H. D. 1968. *Der Springer Konzern.* Munich: Piper.

Myerhoff, B. G. 1971. "The Revolution As a Trip: Symbol and Paradox." *The Annals of the American Academy of Political and Social Science* 395, no. 1: 108–11.

Pasolini, P. P. 1980. *Heretical Empiricism.* Trans. B. Lawton and L. K. Barnett, ed. L. K. Barnett. Bloomington: University of Indiana Press.

Passerini, L. 1996. *Autobiography of a Generation.* Hanover, NH: University Press of New England.

Portelli, A. 1997. *The Battle of the Valle Giulia: Oral History and the Art of Dialogue.* Madison: University of Wisconsin Press.

Pugliese, S. G. 2001. "The Italian Press." In *Europe Since 1945: An Encyclopedia, Volume I,* ed. B. A. Cook. London: Garland.

Chapter 7

Photos in Frames or Frames in Photos?

The Global 1968 Revolts in Three Norwegian Dailies

Rolf Werenskjold and Erling Sivertsen

> Pictures … are more imperative than writing; they impose mean-
> ing at one stroke, without analysing or diluting it.
> —Stuart Hall and Tony Jefferson, *Resistance through Rituals*

In 1968, press photographers played an important role in the (re)presentation and interpretation of the many protests. The images could mobilize public sympathy and awareness, but also shock and agitate readers (Becker 2003: 291–308). Press photos have been considered an important social force, able to foster changes in the political system (Ritchin 2003: 62–73).

Based on a quantitative analysis of the total photo coverage in the three largest Norwegian daily newspapers in 1968, this chapter discusses the role such photos played in the coverage of the demonstrations, strikes, and revolts. More specifically, what kind of framing did the photos suggest with regard to the protest? Did some frames have a stronger legitimacy than others? It also discusses whether and how news photography in dailies with different political leanings framed the protests. Did the framing in the Norwegian photo coverage differ from the framing in the international press?

The 1968 Revolt in News Photos

1968 can be seen as the climax of different protest movements that defined the late 1960s and continued in several countries in the first part of the 1970s. Accordingly, these protests converged in 1968, something also reflected in the news media coverage. The protest phenomenon was not restricted to Western Europe and the United States, but also occurred in the communist bloc and in the Third World (Gassert 2003; Klimke 2010; Klimke and Gassert 2009). Contrary to many other Western countries, Norway was not marred by violent clashes between demonstrators and the police in 1968. In Norway, the domestic repercussions of the global 1968 revolt came later and were particularly visible in the early 1970s (Werenskjold 2008a).[1] Consequently, it was mainly foreign news that was the most important source of knowledge about revolts abroad (Werenskjold 2008b: 45–57, 2008c: 417–40, 2011).

Few studies have analyzed the photo coverage of 1968 in the media. Activists were highly critical of the mainstream media. They claimed that its coverage intentionally focused on violence, discrediting the protest movement. Examples of these negative frames have been emphasized in studies of the relationship between the media and protest movements in several countries. Gitlin (1980) has demonstrated how news photos portrayed the police's brutality against African American civil rights activists in the early 1960s and gave these protests greater moral legitimacy and political leverage to advocate for legal reform efforts. As long as protests did not question the political system as such, the demonstrators were positively framed by the dominant media. The framing of the protests changed when the revolts gradually became more violent, thus weakening the protests' legitimacy in the eyes of the public. In Europe, a study of the British television coverage of the great antiwar demonstration in London on 27 October 1968 focused on similar issues (Halloran et al. 1970). Halloran and colleagues illustrated the impact of frames in the media by showing how earlier frames are used to frame future events through preframing and adjustment.

Hilwig is probably the only scholar who has made comparative studies of the relationship between the media and protest movements in several countries. He showed how the mainstream media in West Germany and Italy portrayed both the police and the demonstrators and how, through the use of text, photos and caricatures, the German *Die Welt* and Italian *La Stampa* both provided a positive framing of the police and a negative framing of the student demonstrators (Hilwig 1998: 321–50). Hilwig's study focused primarily on confrontations between the police and the students and their respective visual representation through single photos. Here, we use a different method, including all photos during the year 1968. However, the German and the Italian contexts of 1968 were particular. The radical students viewed the media as representatives of the establishment, and the media became one of the main targets of the student revolts. This was not the case in Norway. There were a few protests against the news coverage in the Norwegian newspapers, but they were a pale echo of the demonstrations against the Springer press in West Germany.[2]

Framing in Press Photos

The 1960s saw an increase in the number of photos and visual representations used in the media. Foreign news reporters became proficient in explaining a complex world using images. The news framings were rooted in the journalists' and audience's experiences. Therefore, news was construed at the same time as both new and recognizable.[3] Press photographers contributed to this framing process. Sivertsen's (2006) analysis of framings in photos of Norwegian politicians showed how photojournalists reflected and established a frame that became dominant for some time. The photographers' frames coincided with and contributed to the general theory of media-dramaturgic frames.[4]

The photographer was only one participant in the framing process. The news desk was responsible for the selection, processing, placement, organization, context, and page layout. All participants in this process added to an editorial framing that shaped the impact of a photo. The specific framing of a photo could indicate both certain values and the ideological stance the newspaper sought to transmit to its readers, which could, at times, stand in conflict with its journalistic integrity.

The relationship between photography and reality has always been complex and dependent upon the contexts of which it is part (Wells 2003). In a journalistic context, press photography is obligated toward reality, but also dependent on general legitimacy. Like documentary photography, the press photo is governed by situation, purpose, setting, and an index sign signaling a direct connection between the photo and the event. Similar to newspapers, press photographers are also subject to a range of political allegiances and economic pressures.

The basic premise of this study is that photos and frames are connected on all these levels. Press photos sent to news desks or to news agencies include the photographer's particular framing. However, the photographer loses control with the submission of the photo, which then undergoes the editorial framing process. In this process, new frames emerge. It is reasonable to argue that the higher the consistency of framing between photo, article, and layout, the higher the effects on the readers (Werenskjold 2012). Conversely, the more ambiguity a framing includes, the more room emerges for negotiations of meaning among the audience (Hall 1973). Understanding the editorial framing processes of photographers, journalists, and editorial staff is central for understanding the representations of the protest movements of 1968 and contextualizing the photos appropriately in their historical context.

Newspapers in 1968 did not display a close connection between photos and surrounding text. Many photos functioned as illustrations rather than a documentation of current news. Published photos were often reused as illustrations in later news. The organization of the editorial desks also influenced the use of photos. None of the analyzed newspapers' foreign correspondents sent photos as part of their news reports. There was a clear division between journalists and photographers on the editorial desks. Most photographic material was passed on to the newspapers by the photo services of international news agencies, or the Norwegian News Agency (NTB). Most photos used by the Norwegian press were separated from the news items when they arrived at the editorial desks. Those accompanying foreign news were chosen exclusively by the foreign news editorial desk.[5] Many photos taken by the newspapers' own photographers were never used, but ended up in their photo archives. Although they never appeared in print at the time, ironically, some of those photos acquired iconic status through later publications, shaping the collective memory of 1968.

Material

Together with Norwegian Broadcasting (NRK) and NTB, the three major Oslo newspapers *Aftenposten, Arbeiderbladet* and *Dagbladet* were the central institutions of Norwegian foreign journalism at the end of the 1960s. Combined, these five institutions have represented the core of the Norwegian foreign news system since 1945 (Werenskjold 2012: 227–58). This chapter focuses on the newspapers, each of them with ties to different political parties. As Norway's largest newspaper, *Aftenposten* was close to the conservative party. *Arbeiderbladet* was connected to the social-democratic party, while *Dagbladet* supported the culturally liberal and politically central party. In 1968, both the conservative and the liberal party were part of the nonsocialist coalition governing Norway.

These three newspapers were dominant within the Norwegian media system in the late 1960s (Hallin and Mancini 2004; Bastiansen 2006). They were mouthpieces of the political establishment, thereby representing a great number of the attitudes toward the protests in 1968. *Aftenposten,* with both a morning and evening edition, had the largest circulation. *Dagbladet* was Norway's second-largest newspaper. The alleged culturally liberal image of the newspaper made it the preferred newspaper among radical students in the late 1960s. The newspaper was critical toward NATO and the American war in Vietnam. *Arbeiderbladet* was the third most important newspaper in Oslo, but as a representative of the political opposition and the former government, its influence was far greater than its circulation suggested (Werenskjold 2008b).

Method

Due to the complex structure of print media, any comprehensive analysis of the framing of the global 1968 revolt in contemporary newspapers needs to go beyond attitudes in editorials and editorial comments and explore the interplay between visual material (e.g., photos, caricatures, illustrations) and news or feature articles, as well as headlines, leads, captions, and other references (Tankard 2003: 95–106, 101). This study is a quantitative analysis of the framing with regard to all 508 published photos from 417 news stories about the global protest events in 1968. The sample photos are divided into six main categories based on the common dramaturgy they express and as a result of an inductive approach to the material. Geographically, the global events have been assigned to the categories "First," "Second," and "Third" World.[6]

The first group comprises images of *elite persons*—people belonging to the establishment. These photos are mainly portraits of officials or politicians from archives. The second group consists of photos related to *situations* after protest actions. These photos show the visible *consequences* of the clashes. The third group of photos shows the *demonstrations*. This group comprises photos of *demonstrators* or *demonstrations in general* without direct confrontations with the police or military and appears primarily as an expression of *power in numbers*. They may also include depictions of individuals or smaller groups of demonstrators. The fourth group includes photos focusing on *individual leaders of protest actions*. The fifth category displays *conflict events* and shows violent clashes between the police/military forces and demonstrators. The sixth category comprises *unspecified* images in the news items, such as maps, drawings, or other illustrations.

The classification of the framing of press photos is methodologically a difficult matter. Since the aim of this study is an analysis of the totality of the photo coverage of a phenomenon that was followed closely in the Norwegian press in 1968, we have chosen few variables and many analysis units. Earlier studies of press photos connected to the 1968 protests have emphasized the impact of single photos, without taking into account their validity and reliability compared to the total coverage (Hilwig 1998: 321–50). Our goal is to examine how the photos were used and interpreted. As a consequence, this analysis focuses on main structures in the material that illuminate how the newspapers focused on and portrayed the establishment or the protests. The categories are made quantifiable; they separate only between a positive, neutral and negative framing. Furthermore, the categories are clear and exclusive: each and every photo receives only one classification. However, a photo of police violence could serve both as an example of a negative framing of the establishment or a negative framing of violent protests. In this analysis, an assessment of who is the main and more active protagonist in the photo has therefore been used as an additional criterion for classification. Theoretically, both headlines and captions are designed to facilitate understanding of the photograph's intention in conjunction with the textual coverage. Our analysis, however, found that this is not a reliable determinant.

The framing of the protest movements was connected to how the newspapers framed the overall response of the establishment to the challenges it was confronted with. However, the authorities' use of force is often viewed in connection to the degree to which it is seen as legitimate and meets a purpose, and to which it contributed to a solution of the original problem. A negative framing of the photos of demonstrators in this context is primarily linked to photos portraying them as disturbing the peace or threatening the public order. The framing of the photos, potentially supported through a particular use of captions and headlines, thus gives us some insight into whether or not the newspaper's editorial desks in 1968 saw the demonstrators' cause as legitimate (Hall 1972: 64). A positive framing of the protests did often appear as a negation to the negative framing, in the form of photographs portraying the protests as peaceful and activists as "apostles of youthful zeal and energy."

Analysis of the Press Photos

In 1968, the various news categories had a fixed placement and volume in the newspapers. News photos therefore competed with the text in terms of priority. The relatively high share of press photos in *Dagbladet* therefore led to less text, which can be understood as an editorial policy. *Arbeiderbladet's* foreign news editorial desk had the opposite policy. There is little knowledge about such policies in other Norwegian newspapers in 1968. The same applies to the usage of the press photography in international newspapers. Corresponding analyses on the use of news photography have not yet been conducted.

On average, news items that had at least one photo made up 22 percent of all news items on the global protest events in the three newspapers. *Aftenposten* had a share somewhat below this number, while *Dagbladet* was well above average. Many of the photos were purely illustrations, without any independent newsworthiness.

As table 7.1 shows, *Aftenposten* had a total of 167 news items with one or more photographs in 1968. The news items with photos made up 16 percent of all news items on demonstrations, strikes or riots. Even though *Aften-*

Table 7.1. *Aftenposten, Arbeiderbladet,* and *Dagbladet* in 1968: News about Protests Including Photographs

Total	*Aftenposten* (*N* = 1061)		*Arbeiderbladet* (*N* = 610)		*Dagbladet* (*N* = 428)	
	Number	Percent	Number	Percent	Number	Percent
News Items with Photos	167	16%	117	19%	133	31%

posten had the largest relative news coverage of the analyzed newspapers, it had the lowest share of photos in relative terms. *Arbeiderbladet,* with 19 percent, had a larger share of news photos than *Aftenposten. Dagbladet* had the fewest news items on the phenomenon under investigation, but, at 31 percent, had almost twice the amount of news items with one or more photographs than *Aftenposten.*[7]

As in the general news coverage of the global revolts in 1968, the photo coverage of Norwegian newspapers also focused on the most industrialized countries in northwestern Europe and the United States (the First World). Those countries with the most comprehensive coverage of the phenomenon also had the most extensive photo coverage, both with regard to the total number of photos and the variation of the different kinds of photos used in the articles.

As tables 7.1 and 7.2 illustrate, in *Aftenposten,* 70 percent (117 of 167) of all news items with photos came from the so-called First World. In *Arbeiderbladet,* the numbers were 77 percent (90 of 117), and in *Dagbladet* 79 percent (105 of 133). *Dagbladet* had far more news items with photos than the other newspapers compared to the total percentage of news items from the First World. The major newspapers also covered other countries in the region. The figures may therefore not always be comparable for each country on a detailed level. The main bulk of photos were from Europe, with the main emphasis on France, West Germany, Great Britain, and Italy. In addition, there was photo coverage of the United States. A significant number of news items with photos came from Norway, where the coverage of local demonstrations against the Soviet invasion in Czechoslovakia in August 1968 increased these numbers. News with photos from Sweden and Denmark made up only a small proportion of the total. The marginal photo coverage of events in other Scandinavian countries coincided with the general lack of news coverage of the protest phenomenon in these neighboring countries (Werenskjold 2008b: 417–40).

As table 7.2 demonstrates, news containing photos from the so-called Second World made up 20 percent of all news from the region in *Aften-*

Table 7.2. *Aftenposten, Arbeiderbladet,* and *Dagbladet* in 1968: News about Protests in the First, Second, and Third World Including Photographs

Total	First World			Second World			Third World		
	Aftenposten N = 700	*Arbeiderbladet* N = 407	*Dagbladet* N = 332	*Aftenposten* N = 194	*Arbeiderbladet* N = 116	*Dagbladet* N = 49	*Aftenposten* N = 167	*Arbeiderbladet* N = 87	*Dagbladet* N = 47
Number of News Items with at Least One Photo	117	90	105	39	20	14	11	7	14
Percent of News Item with at Least one Photo	17%	22%	32%	20%	17%	29%	7%	8%	30%

posten. The photo coverage centered around two countries, Czechoslovakia and Poland, emphasizing the former. *Arbeiderbladet* had far fewer reports with photos from this region, but the photo coverage was 17 percent of all news items. News with photos from four countries was published in *Arbeiderbladet:* Czechoslovakia, Poland, Yugoslavia, and the Soviet Union. The photo coverage from Czechoslovakia also dominated this region's coverage in *Arbeiderbladet. Dagbladet* had the fewest photos from the Second World, but in relation to the total number of news items, at 29 percent the photo coverage was a much higher share of the total news items in the newspaper.

The same tendencies were replicated in the coverage of the Third World. As table 7.2 makes clear, *Aftenposten* had the most news items on protests from the region, but the share of the news items containing a photo was relatively low. *Arbeiderbladet* did not give much priority to photos from the Third World. Even though *Dagbladet* had the poorest news coverage of the Third World, it still had the highest share of news with photos.

Categories of Photos in the News

All three Norwegian newspapers used news photos in all categories. All the newspapers emphasized news photos featuring officials, cultural representatives, protests, and demonstrations, as well as clashes between the police and demonstrators. Due to their subscription to the same international agencies, the three newspapers had, in principle, the same access to the material, but their different selections highlight different priorities.

Dagbladet and *Arbeiderbladet* had more news photos of figures that could be regarded as officials and cultural representatives than *Aftenposten,* as figure 7.1 shows. In contrast, *Aftenposten* had the most photos of protests and demonstrations compared to *Dagbladet* and *Arbeiderbladet. Arbeiderbladet,* on the other hand, had the largest share of photos of violent clashes between the police, soldiers, and demonstrators. *Dagbladet's* news items with photos emphasized the violent clashes the least. Although all newspapers used photos of persons that could be defined as protest leaders, *Dagbladet* had the largest share, followed by *Arbeiderbladet* and *Aftenposten.* With regard to the consequences of street demonstrations in their news items, *Aftenposten* and *Dagbladet* focused on this the most, while *Arbeiderbladet* emphasized this aspect the least. *Dagbladet* had the largest share of unspecified photos, a category that was present in the two other newspapers to a lesser extent.

As table 7.3 demonstrates, events in the First World enjoyed the highest priority for all newspapers, featuring the most geographically diverse photos and the most varied use of photos in terms of assigned categories. *Aftenposten* had the most varied coverage in all three regions, while *Dagbladet* had the

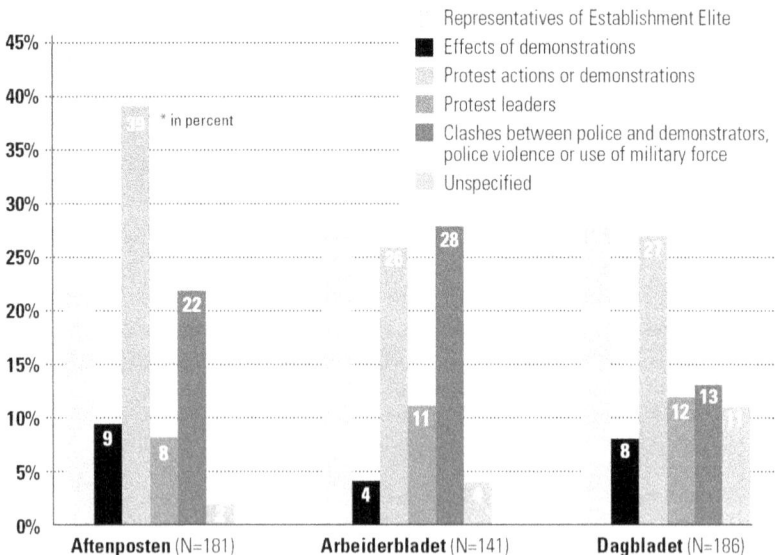

Figure 7.1. *Aftenposten, Arbeiderbladet,* and *Dagbladet:* Categories of Topics in News Photos of Protest (Percentage)

Table 7.3. *Aftenposten, Arbeiderbladet,* and *Dagbladet:* Categories of News Photos of Protests in the First, Second, and Third World in 1968 (Percentage)

Total	First World			Second World			Third World		
	Aftenposten N = 126	*Arbeiderbladet* N = 113	*Dagbladet* N = 144	*Aftenposten* N = 44	*Arbeiderbladet* N = 21	*Dagbladet* N = 21	*Aftenposten* N = 11	*Arbeiderbladet* N = 7	*Dagbladet* N = 21
Representatives of the Elite	25%	9%	27%	27%	14%	71%	25%	24%	57%
Effects of Demonstrations	9%	5%	9%	4%	—	—	10%	—	—
Demonstrations	35%	55%	27%	26%	38%	—	27%	33%	19%
Protest Leaders	11%	—	—	13%	5%	—	13%	10%	5%
Conflict	20%	23%	36%	26%	43%	29%	13%	24%	10%
Unspecified	1%	9%	—	4%	—	—	12%	10%	10%

most photos from the Third World. The main bulk of *Dagbladet*'s photos from the Third World still consisted of photos of officials taken from the newspaper's own photo archive, which functioned mostly as illustrations of the news text. In percentage points, *Dagbladet* had far fewer photos of demonstrations, protest leaders, and clashes between the police and demonstrators from the Third World than the other newspapers. Conversely, it had the largest share of photos of confrontations between the police and demonstrators in the First World. The case of *Arbeiderbladet* is special in this context, since it had the largest share of photos from demonstrations in all geographical regions, with a particularly large share from the First and the Second World. Likewise, the newspaper had the largest share of photos from confrontations between police and demonstrators in both the Second and the Third World, and the second largest share of overall photos from the First World.

The Framing of Photos in the News

Both Roland Barthes (1991: 53) and Stuart Hall (1972: 53–87) have argued that news photography contributes to new dimensions of meaning. As Hall and Jefferson have argued: "Pictures … are more imperative than writing;

they impose meaning at one stroke, without analysing or diluting it" (Hall and Jefferson 1976: 53). Photos are therefore crucial in presenting an additional layer of meaning about an issue or a complicated matter. According to Hall (1973), they can be read in a nuanced way, making a distinction between the preferred and dominant reading (positive), the negotiated reading (neutral), and the oppositional reading (critical). What distinguishes our approach from Hall is that our focus is on the sending rather than on the receiving end. Our questions are therefore: What kind of framing can we extrapolate from the photos used in the news items in the newspapers under consideration? Did these photos give an unambiguous framing of both the establishment and the protests? Was there any difference in how the various newspapers framed the events through their use of photos?

As figure 7.2 exemplifies, the newspapers utilized a complex framing of the protest events in 1968. None of the newspapers had any comprehensive positive framing of the officials or cultural representatives tied to the protest phenomenon in the analyzed photos. Arguably, this is connected to the fact that most photos in this category were mainly neutral portraits based

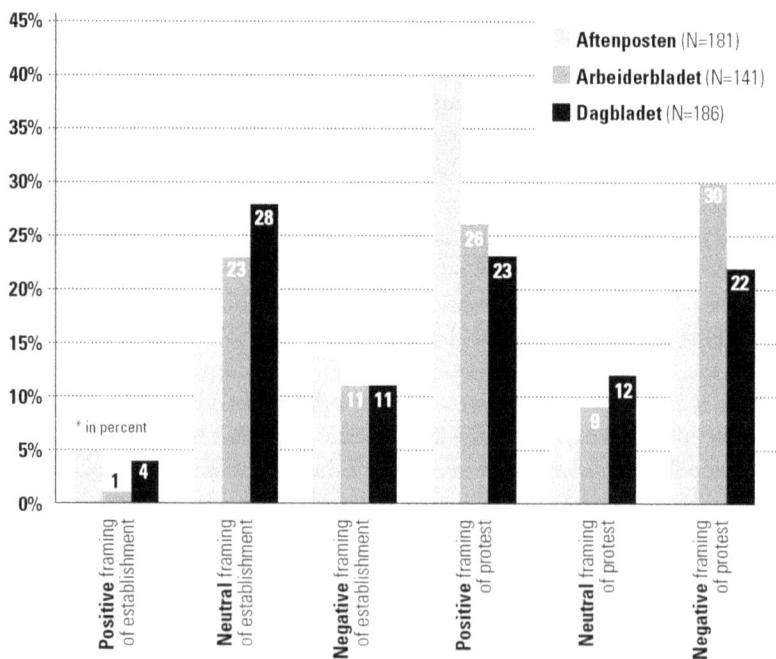

Figure 7.2. *Aftenposten, Arbeiderbladet,* and *Dagbladet:* Framing in News Photographs of Protests in 1968 (Percentage)

on archival material and used for illustrative purposes. *Dagbladet* had the highest number of photos with such a framing compared to the other two newspapers.

Surprisingly, the politically conservative newspaper *Aftenposten* had the largest share of photos with a negative framing of the establishment's (police and military) response to the global protest events of 1968, as table 7.4 reveals. This framing category comprises photos showing police violence or could be interpreted as exaggerated use of force, as figures 7.3 and 7.4 show.

Figure 7.3. A Negative Framing of Police Violence during a Demonstration in Rome, Winter 1968. (The photo was used as an illustration in May. *Aftenposten* 16 May 1968: 10; Photo: AP)

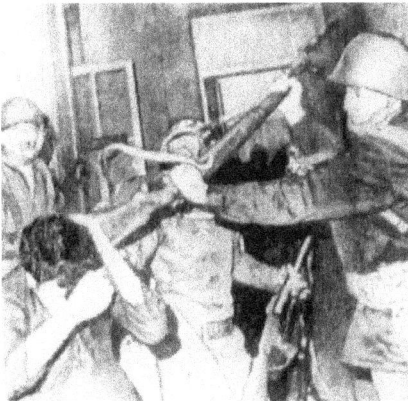

Figure 7.4. A Negative Framing of Police Violence during the Student Riots in Mexico City (*Aftenposten Aftenutgave* [evening edition] 31 July 1968: 1; Photo: AP)

With a far higher comparable share than *Arbeiderbladet* and *Dagbladet,* *Aftenposten* also displayed the most news photos framing the protest events in a positive way. All three newspapers had a certain share of photos framing the protests in a neutral way. This implies that the demonstrators were not regarded as a threat to the public order or the status quo, as figure 7.5. shows. *Dagbladet* had the most photos from this category, while *Aftenposten* had the least.

Arbeiderbladet's photos contained the most negative framing of the protests. This category was smaller in *Dagbladet,* and fewest in *Aftenposten.* This framing by *Arbeiderbladet* separated it from the two other newspapers in this category.

Common to the news items containing photos from the events in the First World in all newspapers were competitive framings, different photos giving a positive or a negative impression of the establishment and of the protests. Figure 7.6 and 7.7 show an example of contradictory frames of the race riots in the United States. All newspapers used photos showing the police abusing their power and photos portraying the police force in a negative way. None of the framings was without competition, apart from the framing of the photos showing the Norwegian protests against the Soviet invasion of Czechoslovakia.

Figure 7.5. A Positive Framing of French Student Leader Daniel Cohn-Bendit. He is strolling peaceful in front of the police. The photo is used as an illustration. (*Aftenposten* 9 May 1968: 19; Photo: AP)

Figure 7.6. A Positive Framing of the Civil Rights Leader Ralph Abernathy and the Poor People's March on Washington (*Aftenposten* 8 May 1968: 6; Photo: AP).

As table 7.4 shows, *Aftenposten* had the highest share of positive framings from protest events in the First World, but the newspaper also had an equally large share of negative framings. *Aftenposten* also had the largest portion of negative framings of the establishment in the selection of newspapers—that is, photos that, among other things, depicted the use of force or police violence, or portrayed officials or the police force in a negative light. The newspaper exhibited a high number of positive as well as negative framings of the protests in France, the United States, Norway and West Germany. Still, the dominant category varied from country to country. Pictures from France, the United States and Italy had the largest proportion of negative framings of the establishment.

Figure 7.7. A Negative Framing of an African American Stealing a Shirt during a Race Riot (*Aftenposten* 1 June 1968: 13; Photo: AP).

Table 7.4. *Aftenposten, Arbeiderbladet,* and *Dagbladet:* Categories of Framing in Photos of Protests in the First, Second, and Third World in 1968 (Percentage)

Total	First World			Second World			Third World		
	Aftenposten N = 126	*Arbeiderbladet* N = 113	*Dagbladet* N = 144	*Aftenposten* N = 44	*Arbeiderbladet* N = 21	*Dagbladet* N = 21	*Aftenposten* N = 11	*Arbeiderbladet* N = 7	*Dagbladet* N = 21
Positive Framing of Establishment	6%	1%	6%	2%	5%	—	—	—	—
Neutral Framing of Establishment	15%	23%	24%	14%	5%	24%	18%	57%	62%
Negative Framing of Establishment	13%	8%	12%	9%	14%	5%	45%	43%	14%
Positive Framing of Protest	29%	19%	19%	75%	76%	62%	27%	—	10%
Neutral Framing of Protest	7%	11%	13%	—	—	10%	9%	—	5%
Negative Framing of Protest	29%	38%	27 %	—	—	—	—	—	10%

It was the positive framing of the demonstrations against the Soviet invasion of Czechoslovakia in Norway in particular that contributed to the high positive numbers in table 7.4.

The photos in *Aftenposten* from the Second World were marked by the positive framing of the protests against the Soviet invasion in Czechoslovakia in August and October 1968. None of the photos from the protests in Czechoslovakia had a neutral or a negative framing. Figures 7.8, 7.9 and 7.10 show a positive and very emotional framing of the protests. *Aftenposten's* photos from the Third World showed much more negative framings of the establishment than photos from other regions. In particular, the photos about protest events in Mexico and China put the establishment in an unfavorable light. At the same time, the newspaper had a particularly positive framing of the protests in both Mexico and Vietnam.

Dagbladet had a larger share of negative framings than *Aftenposten* in their photos of protests in the First World, but the newspaper had a far smaller number of positive framings. *Dagbladet* also had a smaller number of

Figures 7.8, 7.9, and 7.10. A Positive and Very Emotional Framing of the Protests in Czechoslovakia against the Soviet Invasion.

Figure 7.8. A Commemoration and Protest at the University Square in Bratislava against the Killing of a 17-Year-Old Girl by Soviet Soldiers. Aftenposten 23 August 1968: 1; J. A. Martinsen, *Aftenposten*.

Figure 7.9. White Paint and Brushes in the Resistance against the Occupiers and as a Macabre Remembrance of the German Invasion in 1939. *Aftenposten Aftenutgave* (evening edition) 26 August 1968: 1.

Figure 7.10. A Young Mother in Prague Killed by the Soviets. *Aftenposten* 31 August 1968: 7.

negative framings of the establishment. Although not as high as *Aftenposten* or *Arbeiderbladet,* positive framings of the protests in the Second World in *Dagbladet* were also considerable. Similar to the other newspapers, the positive framing of the protests in Czechoslovakia proved dominant.

Dagbladet had twice the number of photos from the Third World than the two other newspapers. The largest proportion of photos from the region had a neutral framing of the establishment and relied on the newspaper's use of archival photos of officials. *Dagbladet* had an equal share of positive and negative framings of the protests. *Dagbladet* was the only newspaper with a negative framing of the protests in the Third World, and had a far smaller proportion of negative framings of the establishment in the region. The negative framing of the establishment was due to a preponderance of photos from the revolts in Mexico during the summer and fall of 1968.

In this sample, *Arbeiderbladet* stood out as having the largest share of negative framings of the protests in the First World. The newspaper also had the lowest share of positive framings of the protests and the lowest share of negative framings of the establishment. Characteristically, *Arbeiderbladet* had a larger proportion of negative framings of protests from all countries reported on. The largest share of negative framings included photos from West Germany, France, the United States, Italy, Great Britain, and Japan. These findings can be connected to the kind of photos that were given priority. The newspaper had a larger share of photos showing conflict than the other newspapers. Norway was the only country where the newspaper had a far larger share of photos with a positive framing of the protests rather than a negative one. The positive framings of *Arbeiderbladet* were, as in the other newspapers, mainly due to the demonstrations against the Soviet invasion in Czechoslovakia. *Arbeiderbladet*'s photo coverage from the Second World was both far smaller and from more countries than *Aftenposten*'s. *Arbeiderbladet*'s framing of the photos from the Third World was either neutral toward the establishment or gave a negative impression of how the establishment handled the protests. The photos with a negative framing of the establishment were tied to protest events in Mexico and Panama during the summer and fall of 1968.

Conclusion

We have argued that news photography plays an important role in the local interpretations of the global protests of 1968. Previous studies have established the significance of the global revolt at the end of the 1960s for the Norwegian media (Werenskjold 2008b: 417–40, 2011). Given their leading role in the media system, newspapers still determined the media agenda in Norway. Most media focused on the revolts in the industrialized Western countries. The photos in the analyzed newspapers reinforced this tendency. Both with regard to the total number of news and in news including photos, protest events in the Third World received the least attention. In the newspapers, only about 20 percent of the news stories had one or more photos. Since the protests took place mainly outside Norway, most of the photos were taken by foreign press photographers and made available by international news photo agencies.

One could easily expect that the conservative newspaper *Aftenposten* would portray the protests more negatively, using more negatively framed photos than *Arbeiderbladet* and *Dagbladet,* with their different political and cultural foundations and, hence, different readerships. However, there is little in our analysis to sustain such notions. Rather, the photos in *Aftenposten* exemplify a weakening of party allegiances and ideologically motivated coverage, thereby showing its prominence in the news professionalizing process. *Arbeiderbladet,* in contrast, was the most party-controlled newspaper; the party even selected the newspaper's editor during its annual convention. Politically, it had the most to lose on the political Left as a result of the protest movements with regard to their opposition against Norwegian foreign policies and the NATO membership. This fact helps explain the large share of negative framings in the photos in *Arbeiderbladet.*

This analysis emphasizes six categories of photos. It could be claimed that the dramaturgy in these categories is a rather common way to portray protest narrative, even in current press coverage of demonstrations and protest events. *Aftenposten* is, however, unique, with an equal number of positive and negative framings of the protests, while *Dagbladet* and *Arbeiderbladet* both have more negative than positive framings. As mainstream papers, they had a far more differentiated framing of the protests than those in West Germany and Italy. Arguably, it is not only the protest phenomenon that must be understood from a national context, but also media framing of photos. Likewise, greater attention needs to be paid to the fact that national media systems are historically and culturally defined (Hallin and Mancini 2004). Future studies on media representations of protest must consider national and comparative perspectives.

Dagbladet published, as a percentage, far more pictures than the other newspapers, but had less sophisticated photographic coverage of the protests. Many of the photos were archival material used for illustration rather than documentation. All three newspapers used photos that focused on students and youth far more often than other social groups, thus strengthening the notion of the revolt as a student revolt. Only photos from France, Czechoslovakia, and the United States indicated that there were other social segments involved in protest activities. This may indicate the newspapers' need to play down the significance of the protests.

The majority of photos from Norwegian demonstrations were from the protests against the Soviet invasion of Czechoslovakia in August 1968. In Norway, however, the demonstrations against the Soviet invasion mobilized far more people and received support from a much broader political spectrum than the demonstrations against the Vietnam War in the United States. Only a few photos from the demonstrations against the Vietnam War appeared in the Norwegian press. Instead, all three newspapers, but particularly *Dagbladet,* used a large number of photos of officials. To a certain degree, this can be explained by the newspapers' emphasis on the political consequences of the revolt. Another explanation could be based on economic reasons, since the newspapers saved money by reprinting one photo several times. At that time, the financial situation was best in *Aftenposten* and more difficult in *Dagbladet* and *Arbeiderbladet.*

Photos from Czechoslovakia have a special status in the analyzed sample. They focus more on the individual protest and despair on the one hand, and on the Soviet armed forces' superiority on the other hand, than press photos of the demonstrations in Western countries (Werenskjold 2008c: 45–57). All photos from Czechoslovakia in the three newspapers were unambiguously positive in regard to the protests. The difference between legitimate and illegitimate was important to the newspapers when they reported on protests through photos and texts. In these cases, the photos seemed to function as *"adjective amplifiers,"* that is, photos that could either *"amplify"* the sympathy of the reader or infuriate him/her (Hall and Jefferson 1976: 57–58).

All Norwegian newspapers denounced the use of violence, whether this was due to the demonstrators' or the police's exaggerated use of force. The traditional Norwegian reformism can probably explain this attitude. At the same time, they supported a notion that political power is based on a social contract between the people and the state. If the contract was broken by the state, revolt was regarded as legitimate and just. Photos framing protests in Eastern Europe coincided with this pattern. This was also largely applied to photos from authoritarian dictatorships, both in southern Europe and in the Third World.

The Norwegian newspapers were not so systematically controlled that the editorial desks avoided competitive framings. This was especially the case on topics where editorial comments did signal an ideologically founded opinion. This was also the case with the photos of protest events in northern Europe and the United States. These were marked by competitive framings that simultaneously gave a positive and negative impression of the protests.

An analysis of the framing of photo usage in the press gives a basis for assessing important aspects of the total framing of stories in newspapers. However, a complete framing analysis of the connection between the text, photos, and other news items in 1968 remains the task of future research.

Notes

1. The philosophy students' action week at the University of Oslo in January 1969 and the protests against the educational reforms presented by the Ottesen committee are generally considered the beginning of the Norwegian student protest (see Vold et al. 1969).
2. For example, see the demonstrations against *Adresseavisa* in Trondheim, 19 April 1968 and *Aftenposten* in Oslo, 23 April 1968.
3. For culture in the framing process, see Van Gorp (2007: 60–78).
4. For the development of and changes in framing of press photographs in Norway, see Sivertsen (2006).
5. For the many routine elements in the editorial processes in connection with the processing of photos, see Hall and Jefferson (1976: 61) and Tversky and Kahneman (1981: 453–58).
6. The quantitative analysis of content is rooted in a long international research tradition; see Pool (1959) and Berelson (1971). Although noting its different local variants, this analysis is nonetheless based on the understanding that the protest phenomena in 1968 were not restricted to Western and industrialized countries. The classification into "three worlds" (and their problems) is discussed in Werenskjold (2008b: 424).
7. For a quantitative analysis of the news coverage of the global 1968 revolt in the three Norwegian newspapers, see Werenskjold (2008b).

Bibliography

Barthes, R. 1991. *The Responsibility of Forms: Critical Essays on Music, Art, and Representation.* Berkeley: University of California Press.

Bastiansen, H. G. 2006. "Da avisene møtte TV: Partipressen, politikken og fjernsynet 1960–1972." Oslo: Det humanistiske fakultet, Universitetet i Oslo.

Becker, K. 2003. "Photojournalism and the Tabloid Press." In *The Photograph Reader*, ed. L. Wells. London: Routledge.

Berelson, B. 1971. *Content Analysis in Communication Research.* New York: Hafner.

Gassert, P. 2003. "Atlantic Alliances: Cross-Cultural Communication and the 1960s Student Revolution." In *Culture and International History*, ed. J. C. E. Gienow-Hecht and F. Schumacher. New York: Berghahn Books.

Gitlin, T. 1980. *The Whole World Is Watching: Mass Media in the Making and Unmaking of the New Left.* Berkeley: University of California Press.

Hall, S. 1972. "The Determinations of Newsphotographs: Working Papers." *Cultural Studies* 3: 53–87.

———. 1973. *Encoding and Decoding in the Television Discourse.* Birmingham, UK: Centre for Contemporary Cultural Studies.

Hall, S., and T. Jefferson. 1976. *Resistance through Rituals: Youth Subcultures in Post-War Britain.* London: Hutchinson.

Hallin, D. C., and P. Mancini. 2004. *Comparing Media Systems: Three Models of Media and Politics.* Cambridge: Cambridge University Press.

Halloran, J. D., P. R. C. Elliott, and G. Murdock. 1970. *Demonstrations and Communication: A Case Study.* Harmondsworth, UK: Penguin.

Hilwig, S. J. 1998. "The Revolt Against the Establishment: Students Versus the Press in West Germany and Italy." In *1968 The World Transformed,* ed. C. Fink, P. Gassert, and D. Junker. Washington DC: German Historical Institute; Cambridge: Cambridge University Press.

Klimke, M. 2010. *The Other Alliance: Student Protest in West Germany and the United States in the Global Sixties.* Princeton, NJ: Princeton University Press.

Klimke, M., and P. Gassert, eds. 2009. *1968: Memories and Legacies of a Global Revolt.* Bulletin of the German Historical Institute 6. Washington DC: German Historical Institute.

Pool, I. de S. 1959. *Trends in Content Analysis.* Urbana: University of Illinois Press.

Ritchin, F. 2003. "1968: The Unbearable Relevance of Photography." *Aperture* 171: 62–73.

Sivertsen, E. 2006. "Sceneskifter og linseskifter: Veksten og fallet til en fortolkningssramme for politikerportretter." *Norsk medietidsskrift* 13, no. 4: 340–62.

Tankard, J. W. Jr. 2003. "The Empirical Approach to the Study of Media Framing: Perspectives on Media and our Understanding of the Social World." In *Framing Public Life,* ed. S. D. Reese, O. H. Jr. Gandy, and A. E. Grant. Mahwah, NJ: Lawrence Erlbaum Associates.

Tversky, A., and D. Kahneman. 1981. "The Framing of Decisions and the Psychology of Choice." *Science* 211, no. 4481 (January): 453–58.

Van Gorp, B. 2007. "The Constructionist Approach to Framing: Bringing Culture Back In." *Journal of Communication* 57, no. 1 (March): 60–78.

Vold, H., P. F. Christiansen and Filosofistudentenes arbeidsutvalg. 1969. *Kampen om Universitetet.* Oslo: Pax.

Wells, L. 2003. *The Photography Reader.* London: Routledge.

Werenskjold, R. 2008a. "1968: A Chronology of Protest in Europe." *1968 in Europe: Online Teaching and Research Guide* to Klimke, M. and J. Scharloth. 2008. 1968 in Europe. A History of Protest and Activism, 1965-1977. Palgrave Macmillian Transnational History Series. New York: Palgrave Macmillian. http://1968ineurope.sneakpeek.de/index.php/chronologies/index/37

———. 2008b. "The Dailies in Revolts: The Global 1968 Revolts in Major Norwegian Newspapers." *Scandinavian Journal of History* 33, no. 4: 417–40.

———. 2008c. "Opprør på Dagsorden! Effektene av den norske nyhetsdekningen av de globale protestene i 1968." *Tekniikan Waiheita: Finnish Quarterly for the History of Technology* 26, no. 2: 45–57.

———. 2011. "The Revolution Will Be Televised: The Global 1968 Revolts on Norwegian Television News." In *Between Prague Spring and French May: Opposition and Revolt in Europe, 1960–1980,* ed. M. Klimke, J. Pekelder, and J. Scharloth. New York: Berghahn Books.

———. 2012. *That's the Way It Is? Medienes rolle i proteståret 1968.* Oslo: Det Humanistiske Fakultetet, Universitetet i Oslo.

Chapter 8

Revolt in Photos

The French May '68 in the Student and Mainstream Press

Antigoni Memou

The black-and-white photographs of students demonstrating, occupying universities, constructing barricades, setting fires on street corners, throwing flaming Molotov cocktails, and fighting with the police, taken during the events in Paris in May 1968, stand as quintessential images of a remarkable revolt. Initially published in newspapers, magazines, leaflets, and activist material, the photographs were later reproduced on the internet, in photobooks, in academic books, in institutional displays, and kept in public and private archives. Historians, political theorists, and sociologists have used these photographs to "illustrate" their accounts of the '68 events, disregarding the ability of photography to be a source of historical, political, or sociological research. This chapter regards these photographs not simply as an "exercise in nostalgia"—as Fred Ritchin once put it (Ritchin 2003: 62–73)—but as a path to reexplore, rethink, and discuss the French May 1968.

The chapter focuses on the photographs published in the student and mainstream press during May and June 1968. In particular, the chapter examines the student newspapers that were published during the events, namely, *Action, Barricades, L'Avant Garde Jeunesse, Servir Le Peuple, Le Monde Libertaire,* and *Lutte Socialiste,* and three French dailies published in Paris, *Le Figaro and L'Humanité.* Given that *Le Monde* did not include any photographs in its editorials, it will not be included in this analysis.[1]

The chapter focuses on a selection of distinctive photographic instances from these publications, aiming at shedding light on the real differences that separated the photographs published in the student and mainstream press. In particular, the chapter argues that the differences arose around three broad themes: the representation of the police, the figure of the young protester, and the representation of the alliance between the students and the workers during the events. These instances are not the only pertinent examples, but are, in my view, the important ones, illustrating the role that media played in the ways May '68 was framed by photography. Based on the premise that the photographic meaning depends on some external matrix of conditions and presuppositions, that it is "necessarily context determined" (Sekula 1984: 4), the chapter examines how photographs of May '68 function within these different contexts. In the following, an outline of the movement, the major student and mainstream publications, and their political orientation will be followed by an analysis of the photographic material published in them.

The Movement, its Publications, and the Mainstream Press

The events of May 1968 were initiated as a large-scale student protest. The first protests were documented at the beginning of May, when students closed Nanterre's Faculté de Lettres. The arrest of five hundred students at the Sorbonne after a poorly attended meeting on 3 May was followed by the occupation of the Sorbonne, calls for liberation of the arrested, and the first barricades and clashes between the students and the police (Reader 1993: 10). As is well-known, the government's tactics and the increasing brutality of the police contributed to the explosion of public meetings, organized action committees, and vigorous demonstrations along the boulevards and the narrow streets of the Latin Quarter, widespread occupations that culminated with the highly symbolic "night of the barricades." In the "night of the barricades" on 10 May, students and workers constructed barricades in the Latin Quarter, responding to the established social order and the oppressive power of the police, and creating a space for expressing their demands (Touraine 1971: 176). The violence exhibited between the police and the students and the symbolic value of the barricades—a revival of a technique used in earlier moments of popular uprisings in French history, namely, in 1830, 1848, and in the Paris Commune—mobilized other social groups (Weber, as quoted in Fraser 1988: 185; Reader 1993: 11). A large wave of support for the students was generated as a response to the government's repression (Feenberg and Freedman 2001: 25–26).

The movement was organized by various groups and committees and was lacking formal leadership, hierarchy, and centralized structure. In the university milieu, various revolutionary and sometimes conflicting groups, affiliated with Maoism, Trotskyism, anarchism, and looser forms of revolutionary socialism, filled the void left by the Union Nationale des Étudiants de France (UNEF) (National Union of French Students)and its main component the Union des Étudiants Communistes (UEC) (Union of Communist

Students), the student organization of the orthodox Parti Communiste Français (PCF) (French Communist Party), which had gradually lost its strength after the war in Algeria and failed to attract a great number of the activist student youth (Seidman 2004: 24).[2] At the dawn of the student mobilization in May 1968, the main groups were two Trotskyist groups, Jeunesse Communiste Révolutionnaire (JCR) (Revolutionary Communist Youth) and Fédération des Étudiants Révolutionnaires (FER) (Federation of Revolutionary Students), the Maoist group Union des Jeunesses Communistes Marxistes-Leninistes (UJCML) (Union of Marxist-Leninist Communist Youth), the Fédération Anarchiste (FAF) (Anarchist Federation), and the small socialist group Étudiants Socialistes Unifiés (ESU) (Socialist Students Unitied). The newspapers published by these groups became the most crucial sites of the production and distribution of the movement's ideas during the events. The movement's main paper, *Action,* which represented the UNEF, the SNEsup (Syndicat National de l' Enseignemen Supérieur, National Union of Higher Education), and the 22 March movement, became very popular and was widely disseminated during May (Feenberg and Freedman 2001: 43).[3] It often had a detachable front page that could be used as a street poster, and was notable for the absurdity, eccentricity, and humor of its slogans and cartoons, frequently by Siné, a well-known French political cartoonist famous for his anticolonialism and anticapitalism (Ross 2002: 114–15n123). *Action*'s popularity grew rapidly during May and June and provided daily information about the evolution of the events, especially when other journals and newspapers were paralyzed by the strike. After the decline of the movement, in the second half of 1968, *Action* "was one of the outlawed publications particularly pursued by the government, in part because of its rapid growth from 100,000 printings of each issue to 550,000" (Ross 2002: 114–15n123). *Barricades* was published by the high school student organization Comité d'Action Lycéens (CAL) (High School Action Committees), and was circulated during May. CAL was founded shortly before the May crisis as a combination of Comité Viêtnam de Base (CVB) and Comité Viêtnam National (CVN) (National Committee On Vietnam), both organizations opposing the Vietnam War (Ross 2002: 217). Most of the members of the CAL were "militants of far left youth movements who had broken with young Communists because of the soft attitude of PCF towards the Vietnam War" (Ross 2002: 217).

The Trotskyist part of the movement was represented by the monthly circulated journal *L'Avant Garde Jeunesse,* which became the mouthpiece of the JCR, one of the two Trotskyist groups. The JCR was among the initiators of the 22 March movement and exercised the greatest influence on the movement, as it "proved more open in its theoretical approach, more flexible in its tactics, more aware of the specific problems of the student movement, and as such was to exercise a greater influence during the crisis" (Singer 2002: 58). *L'Avant Garde Jeunesse* stopped being circulated in June 1968, when the JCR was declared illegal by the government. Smaller minorities within the movement were the Maoist (UJCML), anarchist, and "socialist" groups. The UJCML's journal was published by both students and workers and was called *Servir Le Peuple.*[4] The anarchist group, FAF, published a newspaper called the *Le Monde Libertaire,* while the ESU, a small socialist party, and their equivalent workers' groups published *Lutte Socialiste.*

While the student press was circulated within the ranks, hung on the walls of the Sorbonne, or sometimes disseminated as posters during May and June 1968, the wider French public was informed about the events through the mainstream media, mostly the transistor radio and the mainstream newspapers. Yet, French television and radio was under "firm governmental control," such that public broadcasting equated with state broadcasting, or as Daniel C. Hallin and Paolo Mancini in their comparative study of media systems argue, the French broadcasting under de Gaulle is a quintessential case of the "governmental model" of broadcast organization (Hallin and Mancini 2004: 30). In fact, the staff of the French Radio Television Française (RTF) was "appointed directly by the Minister of Information until 1964" and was "under tight political control even later" (Hallin and Mancini 2004: 106). Television programs such as *Panorama,* which used to give a weekly review of events, did not even mention the growing demonstrations and occupations in Paris and in the rest of the country on 10 May (Feenberg and Freedman 2001: 42). It was international radio, in particular Europe 1 and Radio Télé Luxembourg (RTL), available and willing to report from the heart of the barricades and demonstrations, that became the central means of information for French citizens (Scott 2008: 5). *Le Figaro,* France's oldest national daily, which enjoyed a comfortable existence as the voice of the conservative middle classes, *L'Humanité,* the official organ of the French Communist Party, and *Le Monde,* the left-of-center paper, were gradually losing the students' trust. This reinforced the growing confidence in the movement's own publications, not only within the movement but also in wider society, when journalists, producers, and technicians in the mainstream media joined the nationwide strike (Ross 2002: 15; Singer 2002: 19).

"Down with the Police State"

The students expressed their frustration with the learning process, their career and life prospects, the bureaucratic and hierarchical university structures, and the government's endeavors to limit access to higher education. Their demands were not restricted to the democratization and decentralization of the French educational system and the subsequent ending of class bias, the modernization of an outdated curriculum, and a decrease in unemployment. Their critique of the hierarchical university extended to a critique of societal hierarchies, as the slogan "De la Critique de l'Université à la Critique de la Société" ('From the Critique of the University to the Critique of the Society') reminds us. Their demands for radical reconstruction and democratization touched upon every sphere of life. The students critiqued capitalism, the culture of consumption, and the mass media, and questioned the oppression of women, discrimination against minorities, and the segregation of youth.

Although the students had a broad range of demands, they were all based on the principles of the "destructive critique."[5] "Destructive critique" is not meant to improve the existing societal conditions by the consolidation of political power, but is a critique that operates outside the rules, norms, and limitations of liberal parliamentary democracy and seeks to demolish the status quo and all its structures of inequality, subordination, and power. The student movement was ignited by the explosive power of "destructive critique" and its characteristics, namely, doubt, negation, irony, and destruction. The motto "De omnibus dubitandum" (Doubt everything) was omnipresent within the movement, which doubted the existing "system of order" and therefore demanded its destruction.

The target of the students was any form of power as exercised in factories, schools, universities, and the whole of society. Within this wide range of repressive forces, the police had a predominant position, personifying the oppressive and authoritarian nature of the existing government. As a response to their violent outbreaks on the streets of Paris and their instrumental role in securing the capitalist order, more and more people took to the streets. Activists, according to Ross, disrupted the natural "givenness" of places assigned by the police (Ross 2002: 24–25). This disruption consisted of physical dislocation of students, workers, and farmers, whose contact, although prevented by the police, became possible in meetings, which brought them together.

The way that the mainstream and activist media represented the protesters' efforts to disrupt the places assigned to them by the police suggest a substantial discrepancy, with photographs portraying the police in a disapproving light in the student publications unsurprisingly dominating. Numerous photographs show policemen in aggressive positions, being violent and using tear gas or confronting demonstrators with an aggressive attitude. Indicatively, *Action*'s front page in its first issue, published on 7 May, was covered by a photograph that depicted policemen blocking the entrance of the Faculté de Lettres. The headline "Repression: Faire Face!" (Repression: Stand Up!) equates police with repression. The following article entitled "Pourqoui nous nous battons" (This Is Why We Are Fighting) explains the reasons for the uprising, arguing against the television and radio misrepresentation of their mobilization. Photographs of policemen brutally beating protesters with truncheons appeared in almost all the issues of *Action,* rendering police the unmediated representative of an authoritarian and repressive state.

In many cases, photographs were seen together with cartoons, most of which were explicitly ironic toward the police. Indicative is the photograph published in *Barricades* (see figure 8.1) that shows a group of armed policemen beating a demonstrator. The headline "Les Voyous" (The Hooligans) creates an ironic inversion. Although the article that follows refers to the protesters, who performed acts of violence during the events, the immediate connection that can be made is to relate the headline to the policemen's thuggish behavior. This irony becomes even crueler if one takes into account the accusations of the mainstream press, both of the Right and the Left, accusing the students of insults, violence, and irresponsible acts (Singer 2002: 122–23). In contrast to these accusations, the article that accompanies the photograph gives reasons for the insulting behavior of a section of the students, presenting it as an unavoidable outcome of the social and economic inequalities of capitalist society. The cartoon underneath extends the sarcastic character of the page.

In fact, there were many examples of photographs of police being juxtaposed with cartoons that commented on their brutality. An interesting example is a photograph that was published in the first issue of *Action.* The photograph shows policemen lined up and is taken from the back, so that their faces are not visible. One cannot see any violence or conflict depicted, only some smoke on the right of the photograph. Nevertheless, the cartoon by Siné, just above the photograph, depicts the arrest of an injured student. The drawing of one policeman with a moustache like Hitler's and the ironic dialogue, "Il était armé? Oui, chef ... d'un diploma" (Was he armed? Yes, sir ... with a degree), are caustic comments on the police's extreme brutality against the students.

In contrast with the omnipresence of photographs of the police's brutal behavior in the student press, neither in *L'Humanité* nor in *Le Figaro* were these photographs customary. One of the few exceptions is the coverage on 7 May, when both newspapers published photographs of police on their front pages. In both cases, the photographs were positioned at the center of the pages and depicted a group of policemen attacking students, with the students hardly visible in the background. Despite these similarities, their headlines have an absolutely different tone indicating the political orienta-

Figure 8.1. Group of Armed Policemen Beating a Demonstrator. *Barricades,* no. 1, June 1968

tion of each newspaper. In fact, *L'Humanité* directly accused the government of being responsible for the escalation of the violence in the Latin Quarter, while *Le Figaro* presented the events in a rather neutral tone.[6] Nevertheless, photographs of the police never became the focus of the attention in the mainstream press, and gradually disappeared from their coverage at the end of May and during the month of June.

While negation and irony as characteristics of the students' destructive critique are depicted in many photographs, as shown in the examples from *Action* and *Barricades,* photographs depicting destruction are very rare. While there were many photographs taken by photojournalists that show students in violent and destructive gestures, similar images were absent from the students' publications.[7] An exception is a photograph published in the FAF's newspaper *Le Monde Libertaire,* where an open-air meeting of high school students is depicted (see figure 8.2). The meeting numbers only a few participants and looks like a spontaneous gathering of students rather than a well-organized meeting. Although the young people seem to look in different directions, there is a speaker among them. Nevertheless, neither the gazes of the students depicted nor the focus of the photograph directs our attention to him. Instead, the picture focuses on another student, who is lifting an object into the air. The student looks profoundly irritated and his gesture implies that he is under inordinate stress. There is no indication in the picture as to whether the student is pointing at something, nor does he seem to be confronting the police or any other material forces. Instead, he seems to be performing an act of violence without an immediate recipient. The focus is on the violent gesture, which, compulsive, dramatic, and aggressive as it is, functions as a signifier of destruction for its own sake. While this violent gesture may be the result of the repression of living with capitalist injustices and exploitation, destruction as such did not seem to be valued in the May movement.

"Ensemble: Etudiants, Travailleurs": Photography, Innovations, and Antinomies

The movement soon went far beyond its university origins to unite students, workers, and professionals in a common struggle against de Gaulle's regime. On 13 May, the students made a decision of decisive importance, to allow workers to enter the Sorbonne (Viénet 1992: 44). On the same day, the two main unions, the CGT and the CFDT, provoked by the students' mobilization, decided on a general workers' strike (Reader 1993: 117). Although the strike was initially small in scale, it provoked a chain reaction, and within a few days 7.5 to 9 million workers went on strike (Gilcher-Holtey 1998: 263). On 13 May, students and workers demonstrated together in Paris in a march led by both student leaders and trade unions. The next weeks saw extended occupations in schools and universities and strikes in factories, department stores, banks, public transportation, gas stations, and even newspapers and television all over the country.[8] The majority of the intellectual and literary world also expressed their support for and solidarity with the movement

Figure 8.2. Open-Air Meeting of High School Students. *Le Monde Libertaire* July–August 1968: 4

(Singer 2002: 159). By 24 May, France was paralyzed by the biggest strike that it and probably any other European country had ever known up to that time (Singer 2002: 156). This student-worker juncture was exceptional; in no other major Western country did the student and worker movements intersect as they did in France.

It seemed then that the slogan of the demonstration, "Students-Workers-Solidarity," was taken seriously for the first time. Soon student leaflets began to draw a parallel between student and labor demands. "Between your problems and ours there are certain similarities: jobs and opportunities, standards and work pace, union rights, self-management" read one of the students' leaflets (Feenberg and Freedman 2001: 124). As soon as the strike was announced, silkscreen posters by the Atelier Populaire promoted student-worker solidarity. On 14 May, the first posters that supported the student-worker alliance appeared with the slogans "Usines, Universités, Union" (Factories, universities, union), "Ensemble: Etudiants, Travailleurs" (All together: students, workers), and "Le Même Problème, La Même Lutte" (The same problem, the same struggle). The slogans became more concrete particularly at the Renault factory at Flins, including "Ouvriers, Etudiants, Population, Liaison Effective Flins" (Workers, students, the people in effective liaison at Flins) and "Solidarité Effective, Étudiants, Travailleurs" (Students, workers, effective solidarity) (Atelier Populaire 1969: 39).

Although the alliance between students and workers was verbally articulated in the students' posters and publications, there was no photographic equivalent of these statements. An indicative example is the photograph on the cover of *Action* on 21 May, which depicts a student demonstration (see figure 8.3). The caption underneath gives us the time and the place: "Friday, 17 May. For the first time in France, a student demonstration went to a factory occupied by the workers: Renault."[9] The students are presented in a frontal view, demonstrating outside Renault. What is worth noting, however, is that although the presence of workers is implied, there are no actual photographs of workers in the publication. The only reference to workers is the industrial background, to which the spontaneity and the impulsiveness of the students appear as a visual disruption. The background seems theatrical and overly contrived, and the sky and the banner are retouched heavily, so that the scene, although it may not be, seems constructed.

The majority of the photographs published in the student press depict young, passionate protesters full of revolutionary ardor. In many of them the students seem to be acting on a sudden irresistible impulse, which is related to their youthfulness. This omnipresence was at odds with the absence of photographs of older people and, specifically, of workers in these publications. A careful examination of the student press shows that photographs of workers occupying factories or marching along with the students did not appear in the student publications, even when the students had made an alliance with the workers. This is likely due to the physical dislocation of the protesters imposed by the police, which intended to isolate students in the Latin Quarter and workers in the factories (Ross 2002: 25). In many cases,

Figure 8.3. Students' Demonstration. *Action,* no. 3, 21 May 1968: 1

this physical isolation was not effective, when (mostly) young workers joined the students on the streets, but the photographic documents of the period did fail to portray this alliance.

One of the very few, if not the only, photographs of workers that appeared in *Action* on 11 June 1968 depicted workers standing on the balcony of their factory (see figure 8.4). The workers do not face the camera, and it is not known where they are looking. There is no action shown in the picture or any visual reference to their factory's occupation or their strike. Their static posture contradicts the students' militancy and suggests that this photograph could have been taken on a normal working day. Only the caption reminds us that the photograph was taken at Sud-Aviation in Nantes, the first factory that was occupied by workers on 14 May.

Photographs of revolutionaries posing in front of the camera first appeared as early as the Paris Commune in 1871, when the technology of photography was still primitive, making it impossible to take any action pictures: posed photographs of revolutionaries was a repeated theme in the French workers' movement. Similar poses can be seen in the images of the strikes of 1936 (Doy 1979: 16; Dell 2000: 599–621). This does not mean that there were not photographs of workers demonstrating; such photographs appeared to a great extent in *L'Humanité,* which is another indication of the different imagery that dominated the student and the mainstream press.

This difference was also evident in the photographs that depicted assemblies. In many photographs published in the student press, such as the photograph from *Le Monde Libertaire* discussed earlier, the students were depicted participating in nonhierarchically structured meetings. In a similar photograph published in *Action* depicting a meeting at the occupied Sorbonne, the student speaking is just one of the participants, and he does not seem to have a leading role within the movement. It is true that the movement was fiercely resistant to any kind of leadership and hierarchies within the university, the society, and in mainstream party politics. In the student meetings, anyone could have the floor and no order or opinion was imposed. This practice was also a negation of the traditional-conventional politics as understood within participatory organizational structures of the old labor and communist movement. The movement's originality was its break with the old world, and especially with the habits of the political establishment. The photographs reproduce exactly this refusal of any kind of leadership, hierarchy, or traditional political organization.

This lack of visually represented hierarchy is obvious when contrasted with photographs of workers' meetings, which were published in trade union publications such as *La Vie Ouvrière,* the weekly newspaper of the Confédération Générale du Travail (CGT), the largest French trade union, which took the largest part in controlling the workers' strikes during May 1968, and *L'Humanité.* One photograph reproduced in both papers is indicative. The photograph depicts a meeting of workers at Renault being addressed by the president of the CGT. The focus is on the speaker, while the workers on

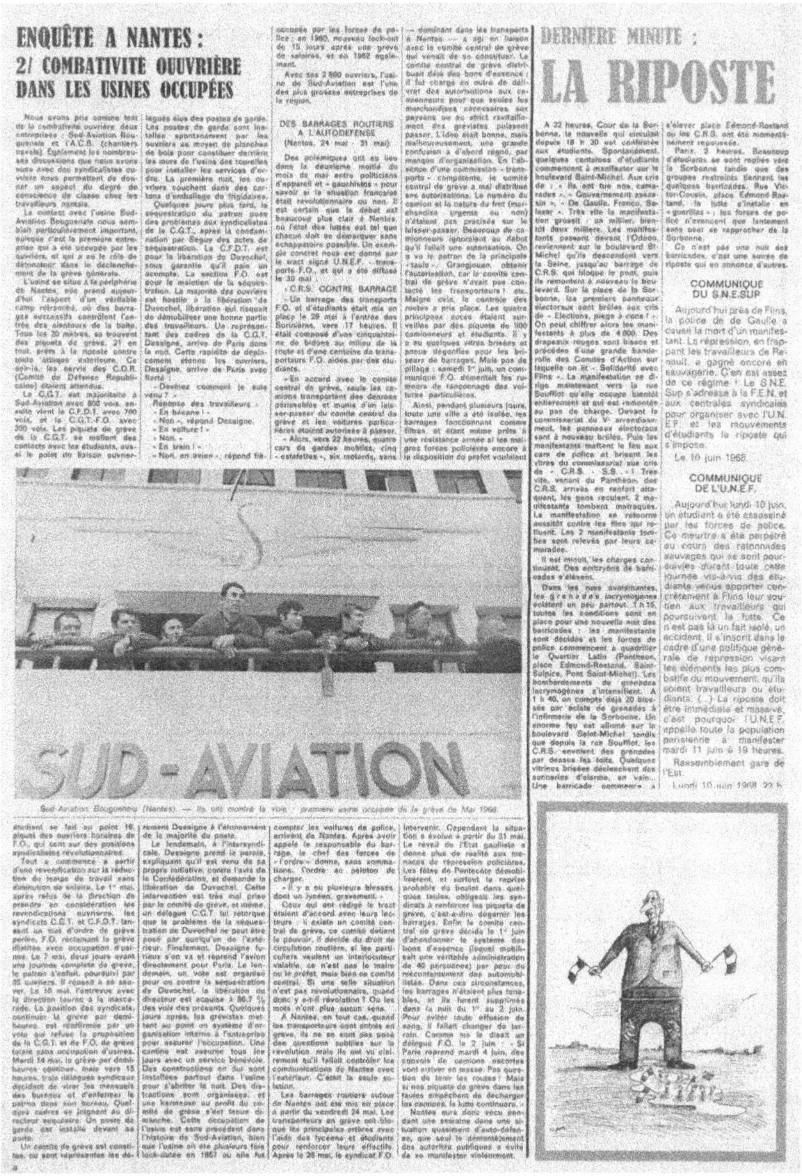

ENQUÊTE A NANTES :

2/ COMBATIVITÉ OUVRIÈRE DANS LES USINES OCCUPÉES

DERNIÈRE MINUTE :

LA RIPOSTE

Sud-Aviation Bouguenais (Nantes). — Ils ont montré la voie : première usine occupée de la grève de Mai 1968.

COMMUNIQUE DU S.N.E.SUP

Aujourd'hui près de Flins, la police de de Gaulle a causé la mort d'un manifestant. La répression, en frappant les travailleurs de Renault, a gagné encore en sauvagerie. C'en est assez de ce régime ! Le S.N.E. Sup s'adresse à la F.E.N. et aux centrales syndicales pour organiser avec l'U.N.E.F. et les mouvements d'étudiants la riposte qui s'impose.

Le 10 juin 1968.

COMMUNIQUE DE L'U.N.E.F.

Aujourd'hui lundi 10 juin, un étudiant a été assassiné par les forces de police. Ce meurtre a été perpétré au cours des ratonnades sauvages qui se sont poursuivies durant toute cette journée vis-à-vis des étudiants venus apporter concrètement à Flins leur soutien aux travailleurs qui poursuivent la lutte. Ce n'est pas là un fait isolé, un accident, il s'inscrit dans le cadre d'une politique générale de répression visant les éléments les plus combatifs du mouvement, qu'ils soient travailleurs ou étudiants. (...) La riposte doit être immédiate et massive, c'est pourquoi l'U.N.E.F. appelle toute la population parisienne à manifester mardi 11 juin à 19 heures.

Rassemblement gare de l'Est.

Lundi 10 juin 1968 22 h

Figure 8.4. Workers Standing on the Balcony of Their Factory. *Action,* no. 7, 11 June 1968: 4

strike are listening passively to their union delegate. The existing hierarchy and the separation between the party representatives and the public not only resemble older representations of the labor movement, but also remind us of the representation of mainstream politics. The photograph is divided into two levels: the upper stage, where the delegate addresses the crowd, and the lower level, where the mass of workers stand. As the photograph was taken from a high viewpoint, this division becomes even clearer, while the delegate occupies a significant proportion of the image, directing the viewer's attention toward the speaker and not the massed workers. In contrast to the delegate, who is clearly seen in the photograph, the crowd is represented as a mass, and it is difficult to distinguish the individuals' faces.

There seems to be a substantial difference in the way students and workers appeared in these photographic representations. The student press prioritized photographs of students, reproducing a specific idea about the movement being a spontaneous, impulsive youth movement. These photographs contradicted photographs published in the trade union publications and *L'Humanité*, which showed static workers posing in front of their occupied factories or participating in a hierarchically structured meeting that resembled mainstream politics.

In fact, photography visualized an existing dichotomy in the alliance between the student body and the workers and their trade unions. This contradictory character of the alliance has been nicely described by Feenberg and Freedman:

> A movement built on this alliance inevitably had two contrary faces. The one embodied the energy of student leaders, diffused and avowedly immoderate; this student energy had driven the police to commit brutalities that inspired a popular demonstration unequaled in the history of the Fifth Republic. The other aspect, that of the Communist Party and France's major union, the General Confederation of Workers (CGT), presented a reformist, almost moderate face. (2001: 28)

The students rejected the old ideas and organizational structures of the labor movement, and challenged the existing hierarchies in their political praxis, especially in student sit-ins and open meetings (Castoriadis 1997: 49). These antihierarchical and antiauthoritarian demands never gained the support of the communist-oriented CGT. The workers' initial demands, which prior to the May events were not fundamentally different from those of their unions, were soon rearticulated to include not only wage increases and a reduction of working hours, but also structural changes in industry, such as the reduction of hierarchies, workers' self-administration, and the reorganization of decision making.[10] But that applied only to a minority of workers. The major workers' organizations and, consequently, the majority of workers were not actually influenced by the goals of the student movement, continuing for the most part to restrict their demands to improvements in wages and working conditions and to the forging of electoral alliances.

The main trade union, CGT, not only attempted to prevent the alliance between students and workers, but also discouraged the students' demonstration at Renault, refused to support the students in public, and declined to meet with representatives of the UNEF (Feenberg and Freedman 2001: 49–50). In reality, the CGT struggled to keep students out of the factories on strike, calling them the "children of the big bourgeoisie" and trying to isolate the student movement (Katsiaficas 1987: 110). The CGT also aimed to direct "the protest into the orderly channel of a mediated settlement" (Katsiaficas 1987: 265). Therefore, in the middle of June, after a gradual decay of the movement, the workers' unions decided on a general return to work and agreed to resolve the conflict in reformist ways. The students were promised a democratization of the educational system and although occupations, demonstrations, and barricades continued for a while, the movement lost its strength and vitality, and thus was isolated and easily suppressed by force.

De Gaulle's electoral victory at the end of June was preceded by pro-Gaullist demonstrations. *Le Figaro,* in contrast with the student press and *L'Humanité,* covered the demonstrations in support of the general. In particular, the first demonstration in support of the government, which took place in Paris on 30 May 1968, made the front page of *Le Figaro.* On that day, General de Gaulle called for elections, announced the dissolution of the National Assembly, and asked French civilians to "undertake 'civil action' against subversion and the threat of 'totalitarian Communism'" (Caute 1988: 218). In response, thousands of his supporters marched up the Champs-Élysées holding national flags. The photograph published on the front page is of a massive demonstration, taken from a very high standpoint. The viewer is therefore confronted by a mass of people and a few banners, whose slogans are not distinguishable. The photograph resembled photographs of demonstrating students published earlier in the month in the mainstream press, except for the captions, which indicate the real purpose of the demonstration.

Conclusion

Photographs retrieved from the press that served the movement highlighted how the photographic medium represented the police, the student body, and the alliance between the students and the workers. It is true that when the students allied with the workers, they "had accomplished what the major unions had considered practically impossible, what the Communist Party had declared theoretically absurd, and what the government had never imagined" (Feenberg and Freedman 2001: 36). When the student mobilization was extended to the workers' body, the students' leaflets drew parallels between the students' and workers' demands, but the photographs failed to represent this alliance. Photographs focused on the youthful body of the uprising, participating in antihierarchical meetings and expressing their "destructive critique" against the state, while neglecting the middle-aged workers and professionals who vigorously participated in the events.

In comparison, photographs that portrayed workers striking and occupying factories were present in the mainstream press, and most particularly in *L'Humanité*. Photographs of posing workers in their occupied factories dominated the communist newspaper. Their resemblance to photographs of old labor movement meetings and mainstream politics was at odds with the students' rejection of conventional leftist perceptions of revolutionary practice and denunciation of the political status quo. The two different representations reveal the existing differences that the movement needed to overcome in order to find an effective way to transform society.

Notes

1. *Le Monde* did not publish photographs until February 1972, when it published a cartoon for the first time. A photograph on its first page appeared only in December 1983. See Kim Willsher (2005).
2. As Daniel Singer explains, the UNEF was in the hands of various radical leftist groups after the mid-1950s. Although in its heyday during the Algerian war, after the war the UNEF gradually lost its strength. The Gaullist government contributed to its decay, since it deprived it of its subsidy and sponsored a nonpolitical union, which definitely weakened the UNEF (Singer 2002: 55). For a similar discussion, see Seale and McConville (1968). Also, Robert V. Daniels (1989: 155) argues that the UNEF moved toward the radical Left under the militant president Jaques Sauvageot. In March 1968, UNEF joined the anti-Vietnam campaign, proving its radical orientation.
3. For more details on the 22 March movement, see Cohn-Bendit and Cohn-Bendit (2000: 46–53).
4. The Union des Jeunesses Communistes Marxistes-Leninistes (UJCML), along with the JCR, split from the orthodox Union des Étudiants Communistes (UEC, Union of Communist Students) (Singer 2002: 56–57).
5. For an interesting use of the terms "constructive critique" and "destructive critique," see Agnoli (2003: 25–38).

6. *L'Humanité*'s headline read "Escalade de la violence policière au Quartier latin: Le Responsible c'est le gouvernmement" (7 May 1968: 1). *Le Figaro*'s headline read "Violents Accrochages Hier jusqu'a 23 Heures" (7 May 1968: 1).
7. Photojournalists' coverage of the events appeared later in photobooks, such as: Claude Dityvon, *Mai 68* (Paris: Camera Obscura, 1988); Bruno Barbey, *Mai 68 ou l'Imagination au Pouvoir* (Paris: Galerie Beaubourg, Editions de la Difference, 1998); Hood Museum of Art, Darmouth College, *Protest in Paris 1968: Photographs by Serge Hambourg* (Hannover, NH: University Press of New England, 2006).
8. For a detailed overview of the various sectors' strikes, see Seidman (2004: 161–214).
9. The caption in French reads: "Le vendredi 17 mai, pour la première fois en France, une manifestation etudiante a pris le chemin d'une usine occupée par les travailleurs: Renault."
10. Ingrid Gilcher-Holtey (1998: 263) analyzes how the workers' demands evolved from requests for the increase of wages and the reduction of working hours to more complicated demands. The new term *autogestion,* coined mainly by the CFDT, embraced demands of an antihierarchical and antiauthoritarian nature.

Bibliography

Agnoli, J. 2003. "Destruction As the Determination of the Scholar in Miserable Times." In *Revolutionary Writing,* ed. W. Bonefeld. New York: Autonomedia.

Atelier Populaire. 1969. *Posters from the Revolution, Paris, May 1968.* London: Usine Université Union.

Castoriadis, C. 1997. *World in Fragments: Writings on Politics, Society, Psychoanalysis and the Imagination.* Palo Alto, CA: Stanford University Press.

Caute, D. 1988. *Sixty-Eight: The Year of the Barricades.* London: Hamish Hamilton.

Cohn Bendit, D. and G. 2000. *Obsolete Communism: The Left-Wing Alternative,* AK Press, Edinburgh, London & San Francisco.

Daniels, R. V. 1989. *1968: The Year of the Heroic Guerrilla.* London: Harvard University Press.

Dell, S. J. 2000. "Festival and Revolution: The Popular Front in France and the Press Coverage of the Strikes of 1936." *Art History* 23, no. 4 (November): 599–621.

Doy, G. 1979. "The Camera Against the Paris Commune." *Photography/Politics: I,* ed. T. Dennet and J. Spence. London: Photography Workshop.

Feenberg, A., and J. Freedman. 2001. *When Poetry Ruled the Streets: The French May Events of 1968.* Albany: State University of New York Press.

Fraser, R. 1988. *1968: A Student Generation in Revolt.* London: Chatto and Windus.

Gilcher-Holtey, I. 1998. "May 1968 in France." In *1968: The World Transformed,* ed. C. Fink, P. Gassert, and D. Junker. Cambridge: Cambridge University Press.

Hallin, D. C., and P. Mancini. 2004. *Comparing Media Systems: Three Models of Media and Politics.* Cambridge: Cambridge University Press.

Katsiaficas, G. 1987. *The Imagination of the New Left: A Global Analysis of 1968.* Boston: South End Press.

Reader, K. A. 1993. *The May 1968 Events in France: Reproductions and Interpretations.* New York: St. Martin's Press.

Ritchin, F. 2003. "1968: Unbearable Relevance of Photography." *Aperture* 171: 62–73

Ross, K. 2002. *May '68 and Its Afterlives.* Chicago: University of Chicago Press.

Scott, H. F. V. 2008. "May 1968 and the Question of Image." *Rutgers Art Review* 24; 1–18.

Seale, P., and M. McConville. 1968. *French Revolution 1968.* London: Penguin.

Seidman, M. 2004. *The Imaginary Revolution: Parisian Students and Workers in 1968.* New York: Berghahn Books.

Sekula, A. 1984. *Photography Against the Grain: Essays and Photoworks, 1973–1983.* Halifax: Press of the Nova Scotia College of Art and Design.

Singer, D. 2002. *Prelude to Revolution: France in May 1968.* Cambridge, MA: South End Press.

Touraine, A. 1971. *The May Movement: Revolt and Reform.* New York: Random House.

Viénet, R. 1992. *Enrages and Situationists in the Occupation Movement: France, May 1968.* New York: Autonomedia and London: Rebel Press.

Willsher, K. 2005. "Le Monde Lightens up." *Guardian,* 8 November. http://www.guardian .co.uk/media/2005/nov/08/pressandpublishing.france (accessed 7 May 2010).

Chapter 9

Guarding News for the Movement
The *Guardian* and the Vietnam War, 1954–70

Naoko Koda

Since the founding of the United States, dissident journalism has been integral to the political fabric of movements for social justice and political equality. The Boston-based abolitionist, William Lloyd Garrison, for example, published an antislavery weekly newspaper, the *Liberator,* between 1831 and 1865. A century later, the anti–Vietnam War movement produced a number of dissident newspapers that challenged the orthodoxy of the mainstream press. At the forefront of this movement was the *(National) Guardian*[1] newspaper, a radical leftist weekly based in New York City. During what the *Guardian* termed "America's imperial war against the Vietnamese," the weekly served both as a force against the war and an institutional fixture within the antiwar movement as a whole.

The *Guardian* was by no means the only major antiwar force that contributed to the antiwar movement. Without a central organization, anti–Vietnam War activities were ubiquitous and sustained by various, usually fragmented forces throughout the country. By 1969, the total number of antiwar organizations across the United States had mounted to seventeen thousand (Small 2002: 3). Groups such as Students for a Democratic Society (SDS), Women Strike for Peace (WSP), and Vietnam Veterans Against the War (VVAW), to name a few, made up the nucleus of the antiwar movement. The *Guardian,* hoping to play a centralizing role within the antiwar movement, called for the establishment of a massive antiwar movement consisting of a wide range of groups. The *Guardian* also played an important role as a critical space for debate and organization within the antiwar movement as a whole. Scholars have pointed out such places as GI coffee shops and university campuses as important sources of radicalism, where ideas and activities were developed and sustained. Yet, no one has approached the *Guardian* as a vital organ of the anti–Vietnam War movement. It is within this context that this article wishes to consider the monumental importance of the *Guardian* newspaper within the antiwar movement. It aims to fill this void of historical documentation of the anti–Vietnam War movement and argue that the *Guardian* played a crucial role as an alternative leftist newspaper.

My argument rests on the following claims. The *Guardian* was a mass medium, with a wide-scale national readership, that provided alternative information and analysis of the war with an unapologetic antiwar stance, challenging the mainstream media's viewpoint. It printed firsthand coverage of the war by its foreign correspondent in Vietnam, Wilfred Burchett, who reported from the areas controlled by North Vietnam. Rather than arguing whether the mass media or the *Guardian* was right or wrong, this chapter attempts to demonstrate how the *Guardian* provided alternative news reports that corresponded to leftist antiwar sentiments and reinforced doubts on the government and the US policy in Vietnam. It also aims to demonstrate that the Guardian was as a critical space for debate and an institutional fixture within the US anti–Vietnam War movement as a whole.

The *Guardian* before the Vietnam War

Professional journalists James Aronson and Cedric Belfrage started the *Guardian* to create a democratic newspaper in the United States. Aronson, who worked at the *Boston Evening Transcript* and the *New York Herald Tribune and Post,* and Belfrage, from the *London Express,* came to know each other while working on the denazification of the German press undertaken by the Psychological Warfare Division of the Supreme Headquarters Allied Expeditionary Force in 1945 (Aronson and Belfrage 1978: 5). While carrying out their mission to create a "democratic" press in West Germany, Aronson and Belfrage agreed that no such newspaper existed in the United States, and began creating their press shortly after their return to the United States (Aronson and Belfrage 1978: 5–6). Soon after they established their office on Murray Street in New York City, John T. McManus, a film critic of New York's moribund progressive daily *PM,* joined Aronson and Belfrage (Aronson and Belfrage 1978: 15–16). Believing there were some democratic principles to guard in America, the founders named their newspaper the *National Guardian* and issued its first publication on 18 October 1948 (Aronson and Belfrage 1978: 24).

After its debut, the *Guardian* played a crucial role in controversial issues, offering alternative views on events from a left-wing standpoint. In the Ethel and Julius Rosenberg case, the *Guardian* conducted its own investigation and uncovered the unjust legal procedures involved. The weekly launched a campaign called the National Committee to Secure Justice in the Rosenberg Case to fight against the "silence by death," which eventually sparked a global protest (Fineberg 1953: 33–35, 76). It also spoke out against racism in America. As early as 1948, the weekly covered notorious racist hate crimes and the unjust legal procedures of cases against African Americans (Aronson and Belfrage 1978: 130–31). W. E. B. DuBois wrote a total of 130 articles for the *Guardian* over 15 years, sharing his thoughts on racism and the lives of African Americans (Aronson and Belfrage 1978: 137–38).

The transparent leftist views of the *Guardian* attracted readers from a broad spectrum of the Left. Jack A. Smith, former chief editor of the *Guardian,* stated that "[the *Guardian*] viewed itself as a transmission belt from liberalism to a more enlightened progressive politics. The paper enjoyed the support of a broad spectrum of the Left from disenchanted liberals to communists" (Smith 1993: 100). By the end of its third year, the *Guardian* had become the largest leftist paper in the country, with a circulation exceeding seventy-five thousand readers (Aronson and Belfrage 1978: 157). In the mid-1950s, its circulation was reduced to roughly twenty-two thousand due to the political repression of McCarthyism, but the weekly survived and gained a new constituency in the 1960s.

New War, New Constituency

The *Guardian* attained a wide readership as a new generation of dissidents picked it up in the turmoil of the 1960s, when being status quo was frowned upon. It filled an informational vacuum for those who doubted the official reports on the war in Vietnam. Todd Gitlin, a former SDSer, said, "I already knew that the mainstream coverage of the [Vietnam] war was not reliable."[2] The *Guardian* reinforced the doubts about the official claims of the government. Gitlin recalled: "The liberal Governor G. Mennen Williams of Michigan … said John F. Kennedy was on the side of peace … and from reading the *Guardian,* I doubted" (Gitlin 1987: 87). For Gitlin, the *Guardian* was the major reinforcement that Kennedy was an "unnecessarily belligerent Cold Warrior," which he was against.[3] Many antiwar protesters charged that the mass media was publishing fabricated news against the leftist movements and giving blind support to the government. The mainstream media tended to be critical of the antiwar movement. In 1965, *Time* magazine called the antiwar activists the "Vietniks," encouraging communist hopes by giving them the expectation that "the U.S. does not have the stomach to fight it out in Vietnam" (quoted in Halstead 1978: 114).

The alternative leftist newspapers flourished as the 1960s began, calling themselves "underground press," copying the term from illegal publications that resisted governments in oppressive countries. In total, the Underground

Press Syndicate (UPS), a counterpart of the aboveground Associate Press, claimed approximately five million copies sold and thirty million readers, estimating that an average of six persons read each copy (Glessing 1970: 120). Smith recalled: "Likewise, great many of the new underground papers took their lead from the *Guardian* when it came to facts, figures, and analysis about the war" (1993: 100). Aronson and Belfrage wrote, "The young radicals seemed to trust us. They knew that the *Guardian* was the one constant to which they could turn for factual news of what was going on and as a bulletin board for what might be taking place" (1978: 320).

Challenging the Cold Warriors: 1954–63

The American mainstream media reported on the war in Vietnam based on its own selection of stories and sources with certain viewpoints. It largely depended on, first, the French army and then the US and Saigon governments as sources during the 1950s and well into the 1960s. Otto Friedrich, a senior writer for *Time* magazine, said:

> "[The wire service] had one basic source of news, the French Army communiqués … it was very economical for an American agency to depend on its Paris bureau, rather than Hanoi correspondents, to write the three or four daily war stories that were needed in New York or Chicago … Their chief function was to provide a certain legitimacy to our use of their byline and the magic dateline: Hanoi." (quoted in Wyatt 1993: 56–57)

When the French began retreating from Vietnam, the American and Saigon governments supplanted the French army as "[t]he largest and most influential purveyor of information" for the American mass media, which was trying to cover "all Asia with a mere handful of people" during this period (Wyatt 1933: 67). Clarence R. Wyatt critically called the press-government relationship at this time as "one of the blind leading the blind" (1993: 68).

The *Guardian,* on the other hand, relied on its nationally and internationally dispersed correspondents, and the most important source of wartime information was Wilfred Burchett, stationed in Vietnam. Burchett was an Australian journalist who had been following events in Vietnam since the early 1950s. He visited Vietnam for the first time in March 1954, which he later described as a fruitful journey that gave him a firsthand understanding of the Vietnamese struggle against foreign invaders (Burchett 2005: 425). In 1956, Burchett met Belfrage at the Journalist Congress in Helsinki (Burchett

2005: 467). Sharing the *Guardian*'s anti-imperialist stance, Burchett agreed to be the paper's foreign correspondent, and reported for the paper from the Soviet Union between 1956 and 1962, and then from Vietnam until the end of the war (Burchett 2005: 467, 510).

Throughout the war Burchett collected news stories in areas where other Western journalists could not access. The North Vietnamese Foreign Ministry granted Burchett a *laissez-passer* in 1955, a travel document that gave him the exclusive privilege to cover the parts of Vietnam they controlled for the next seventeen years (Burchett 2007: 89). Politically savvy North Vietnamese and National Liberation Front (NLF) fighters trusted Burchett, sharing not only their lodgings in jungle headquarters but also highly confidential information, including detailed hand-drawn military maps (Burchett 2005: 427–30). The Vietcong guerrillas even shared their secret tunnel systems with Burchett, even though these were their vital liaison and travel lines, connecting one shelter to another (Burchett 2005: 529–40). Burchett sent photographs from these areas in Vietnam that gave a certain legitimacy to his stories. In February 1965, the *Guardian* devoted a full page to print "Exclusive Pictures of a Revolution in Progress," sent from Vietnam, includeding Burchett interviewing NLF president Nguyen Huu Tho at his jungle headquarters and President Tho's son at the NLF's Liberation Radio station (*National Guardian* 1965a: 7). Burchett's firsthand coverage of the wartime situation in Vietnam was widely appreciated by the readers of the *Guardian*.

Against the Declaration of the "Undeclared" War: 1964

In 1964, President Lyndon Johnson faced growing conservative pressure that pushed the reluctant commander in chief to employ tougher action in response to NLF successes in South Vietnam, and the mass media followed suit. The mainstream newspapers' blind support for the government was apparent in their coverage of the Tonkin Gulf Resolution in August 1964. Congress gave near-unanimous approval (in the Senate the vote was 88–2, in the House it was 416–0) to a proposed resolution that gave Johnson authority to take "all means necessary" against communist aggression in Southeast Asia after the alleged North Vietnamese attacks on the USS *Maddox* and *C. Turner Joy*, which were conducting intelligence activities in the Gulf of Tonkin (Young 1991: 119). Despite the murky nature of the incident, the American mainstream newspapers reported the incident as proof of communist aggression in Vietnam. On 7 February, Johnson initiated an air strike, followed by a systematic bombing campaign, Operation Rolling

Thunder, starting on 2 March, making the fatal first step of the unstoppable escalation. On 17 February 1964, Joseph Alsop of the *Washington Post* wrote, "It is pleasant to report ... the deep trouble prevailing among our adversaries, rather than difficulties and dissensions on our side" (Alsop 1964: A15, 17). The rest of his article reflected the assumption that Kremlin and Beijing directed the Vietnamese communists; thus, the attack on North Vietnam meant an attack on world communist aggression. He wrote that allowing the North Vietnamese to attack South Vietnam and to enjoy peace at home had always been "illogical" (Alsop 1964: A15, 17). The mainstream presses' blind support for America's ideological war against alleged communist aggression and its traditional news gathering methods made the press an arm of US intervention in Vietnam. The *Guardian* criticized it as "voluntary collusion by the press with government" (*National Guardian* 1964b: 2).

In contrast, the *Guardian* framed the US intervention as America's "undeclared imperialist" aggression against the Vietnamese fighting to determine their own future. The weekly insisted on the idea that the Cold War "anticommunism" had become an ideological nucleus to rationalize undemocratic US activities against the Vietnamese, challenging Washington's Cold War justification for the war. The *Guardian* pointed out that the rise of political repression at home and the danger of nuclear destruction had been the consequences of the Cold War policy (*National Guardian* 1963: 1). In 1964, after Johnson initiated the bombing against the North Vietnamese, the *Guardian* warned:

> The struggle may be long drawn, but this is a war the U.S. cannot win. The Americans will spill more blood, their own and others, destroy more villages, wipe out more rice fields and buffalo, but that is about all ... This is the high road to oblivion. It starts from the blind remise that the people of South Vietnam ... prefer our invitation to death to the opportunity to build their own lives in their own land under governments of their own choosing ... The U.S. must get out and stay out of Vietnam. (*National Guardian* 1964a: 2)

The growing new generation of American leftists shared this pursuit of an alternative ground. In a letter to the *Guardian,* a reader insisted on the need of a new direction for the antiwar movement, led by the "post-McCarthy" generation (Schesch 1965: 2). Another reader expressed doubts about Washington's claim that the country was "defending freedom against Communism in Southeast Asia" (Bedacht 1964: 2). By 1965, the *Guardian* was printing strong antiwar voices, including its own, and outside the paper, such antiwar sentiments were coming together to organize a large-scale anti-war demonstration.

Celebrating "the Greatest Peace Demonstration in American History," 17 April 1965

The first major demonstration against the Vietnam War took place on 17 April 1965 in Washington DC, organized by the SDS. The SDS and one police officer estimated that twenty-five thousand people participated in the demonstration that day (Gitlin 2003: 56). The participants picketed at the White House and marched to the Washington Monument, where they listened to journalist I. F. Stone, radical history professor Staughton Lynd, civil rights activist Bob Moses, Senator Ernest Gruening, and SDS president Paul Potter giving inspiring speeches (Anderson 1996: 125). The crowd then walked peacefully to Capitol Hill and a small contingent presented Congress with a peace petition (Anderson 1996: 125). This marked the first major organized anti–Vietnam War demonstration in the United States.

The next morning, the mainstream press reported on the event, and there was a significant gap between what really happened and what was reported, as Gitlin (2003) has pointed out in his book. On the day after the demonstration, the *Washington Post* reported that sixteen thousand people were at the demonstration (1965: A1). The *New York Times* claimed the number to be fifteen thousand, and then reduced it to ten thousand the next day (1965a: 1, 3, 1965b: 6). By and large, these newspapers favored sensational and violent stories. The *New York Times* picked up a story of a man from the American Nazi Party arrested for "having stepped on a record player—apparently because he disliked the polka music it had been playing," and a Hungarian freedom fighter arrested for "shouting and making menacing advanced toward the students" (1965a: 3). The *New York Times* called the demonstration an unprofessional challenge by inexperienced noncommunist youth with "beard and blue jeans mixed with ivy tweeds and an occasional clerical collar" and "several girls" with "baby carriages" (1965b: 3).

On the other hand, the *Guardian* reporters, locating themselves within the antiwar movement, carefully observed the demonstration on that day. The *Guardian* celebrated the demonstration as "the greatest peace demonstration in American history," with twenty-five thousand people participating (Gitlin 2003: 56; Small 1994: 40). The *Guardian* printed antiwar messages from the main speakers and photographs of legible picket signs carried in the demonstrations (Gitlin 2003: 51, 53, 56) (see figures 9.1 and 9.2 for

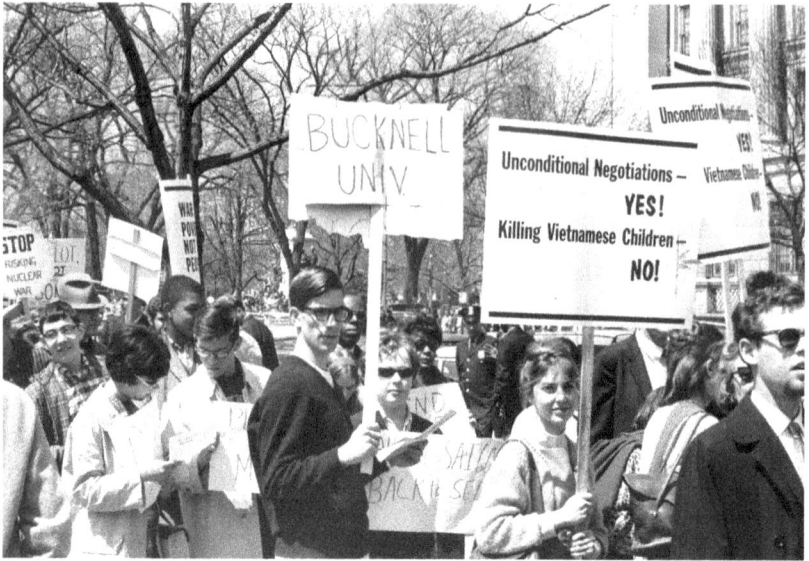

Figure 9.1. "Unconditional Negotiations – Yes! Killing Vietnamese Children – No!" Protestors Carrying Picket Signs during the Anti-Vietnam War Demonstration in Washington DC on 17 April 1965. National Guardian Photographs Collection, Tamiment Library, New York University. Photograph by Robert Joyce.

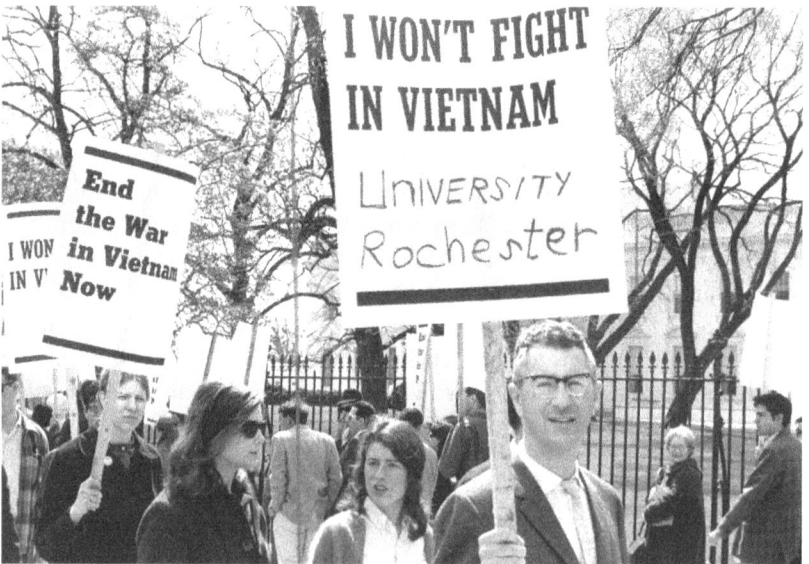

Figure 9.2. The Anti–Vietnam War Protestors Marching in the Front of the White House during the Demonstration in Washington DC on 17 April 1965 (*National Guardian* 24 April 1965: 3). National Guardian Photographs Collection, Tamiment Library, New York University. Photograph by Robert Joyce.

the *Guardian*'s photographs of demonstrators with legible picket signs). In the paper, it was reported that Iowa farmers, students, peace workers, pacifists, socialists, revolutionaries, freedom workers from the South, and the Old and New Left were there (Gitlin 2003: 56). Moreover, the writers of the *Guardian* emphasized that "[the demonstration] was a step toward integrating the movements for peace and civil rights" (*National Guardian* 1965b: 2). It celebrated such diversity, giving a completely different picture of the composition of the demonstration. Gitlin observes, "[T]he *Guardian* coverage is interesting here not as a model of the unexceptional or as a neglected story option at *the Times* ... but as a model of a rival cognitive possibility. It would be *de rigueur* to observe that the *Guardian* coverage was ideological. *The Times'* was no less so" (Gitlin 2003: 52–53). Small credits the *Guardian*'s coverage of the 17 April antiwar demonstration by saying, "[the] *Guardian* provided its limited readership with one of the most complete and professional accounts of the SDS demonstration on April 17, 1965, available in the American media" (Small 1994: 40).

Photographs Not Seen by the Mass Media

By mid-1965, Burchett's firsthand coverage of the war from "other side" of the seventeenth parallel had become one of the most important stories of the war found in the underground press. Readers named Bob and Sarah Cirese wrote to the *Guardian,* "[The articles by Wilfred Burchett] give one a real insight into the flesh-and-blood determination and cleverness of the National Liberation Front" (Cirese and Cirese 1967: 2). Smith recalls that Burchett's dispatches from Vietnam were "instrumental in developing what the Vietnamese termed their 'second front' in the war: the antiwar movement in the United States." He considered printing the Burchett reports the *Guardian*'s "political responsibilities to the antiwar movement" (1993: 103). Burchett's firsthand news stories undermined the legitimacy of the government, making it vulnerable to challenge by antiwar dissenters.

Arguably, Burchett's most significant leverage on like-minded people were his articles claiming that Vietnam would win the war against the United States. By January 1964, Burchett had concluded, "Win the war against the Communists. This is an absurdity ... And the end of the road for the policy for South Vietnam will be military defeat" (Burchett 1964: 3). Burchett emphasized the overwhelming popularity of the NLF and anti-American sentiments among the South Vietnamese, whom the United States was supposed to be fighting for. The *New York Times* also knew of the existence of such negative sentiments against the United States, but it reported that backwardness and xenophobia in Vietnamese society led to the conflict. On 24 April 1966, it stated that local anti-Americanism could be explained by Vietnamese men's feeling of shame at their wives and daughters working as bar waitresses for Americans and the "reluctance of the Vietnamese to abandon their easy-going daily routine" (Sheehan 1966: 3). In contrast, Burchett reported ruthless American "search and destroy" operations targeted at the Vietcong guerrillas in villages in South Vietnam as the source of the Vietnamese resentment of America (Burchett 1966b: 9). Using his knowledge of the Vietnamese language, Burchett interviewed a wide range of local Vietnamese, including former South Vietnamese officers who had shifted to the NLF side. In his report, Burchett quoted a Buddhist saying, "How can we remain indifferent when American troops and U.S. satellite armies have invaded South Vietnam, sowing death and suffering everywhere, destroying pagodas, massacring the people, including Buddhists" (Burchett 1966b: 9). Burchett emphasized that American brutality against the Vietnamese was turning the local population against the United States.

There were observers outside the American mainstream who trusted Burchett's accounts. David Dellinger, a leading figure of the antiwar movement, commented, "Burchett is committed not to the objective truth but to one side of a partisan conflict. Oddly enough, in view of all this, Burchett's reports and predictions turn out through the years to be remarkably accurate, whereas the American press never seems quite able to catch up with reality" (Burchett 1968: xi). Despite the American mass media's rejection of Burchett's reports, the Japanese major mainstream newspaper *Mainichi Shinbun*[4] ran a Burchett series. Minoru Omori, the foreign editor of the *Mainichi* who was in charge of publishing Burchett's reports, recalled, "The Burchett series, 'Inside the Liberated Zones' reassured things I had been reporting from Vietnam and never seemed propagandistic. I took the responsibility for printing the series, but there was no voice against my decision within the *Mainichi* office."[5] Impressed by Burchett's reports, the *Mainichi* even decided to broadcast video reports from Burchett on its own television station, TBS.[6]

Supposedly independent and free newspapers in the United States had ideological restraints and were pressured to confine themselves within the Cold War consensus, as the *New York Times* correspondent, Harrison E. Salisbury's case demonstrated. Foreign newspapers had been reporting the escalation of the US bombings and strikes on civilian areas, but the administration and the Pentagon denied this and blamed the North Vietnamese for inflicting damage in those areas, so the *New York Times* sent Salisbury to Hanoi to investigate and report on the case (Halstead 1978: 317). Helped by Burchett to gain access to the Communist side, Salisbury became the first journalist from the American mass media to report from North Vietnam (Aronson 1990: 253). Salisbury filed a total of fourteen articles during his two-week stay between 23 December 1966 and 7 January 1967, including reports about the damage American bombings had inflicted on the civilian population and facilities (Aronson 1990: 253; Wyatt 1993: 153; *New York Times* 1966: 3). When the *New York Times* printed Salisbury's stories revealing US bombings on civilian facilities, it infuriated the government, which saw a challenge to its denial in the nation's leading newspaper. The secretary of defense, Phil G. Goulding, condemned Salisbury's reports as a "national disaster" that contradicted the official statement that the American bombings were only attacking military structures and deployed a team of twenty to thirty people to examine Salisbury's reports, trying to find a way to discredit them (Small 1994: 65; Salisbury 1988: 146–47). Goulding condemned Salisbury's reports as mere copies of Hanoi's propaganda (Salisbury 1988: 147). Other major newspapers joined the battle, taking the side of the administration against Salisbury. Walter Lippmann of the *Washington Post* wrote that the government declared that Salisbury had made himself "a tool of enemy propaganda" and "we must remember that in time of war what is said on the enemy's side of the front is always propaganda" (Lippmann 1967: A15). To avoid being an enemy of the administration, the *New York Times*

Figure 9.3. Wilfred Burchett in Vietnam. Photograph Sent by Burchett from NLF Areas to the *National Guardian.* Burchett Is Standing on the Left with Two Vietnamese People in Front of Their Strategic Map. National Guardian Photographs Collection, Tamiment Library, New York University.

also ran stories to counter the report filed by its own correspondent. On 4 June 1967, the *New York Times* wrote that "Harrison Salisbury's report of his controversial trip to North Vietnam … has revealed so much new information on the situation in the North as to add a new debate. Salisbury showed a deplorable lack of professional journalistic skepticism in some of his dispatches to the *Times* from Hanoi" (Mecklin 1967: BR2). The American mass media's reaction to Salisbury's articles reflected the tenacious underlying assumption that "[n]othing written from a Communist country can be factual while anything written in the United States or any other part of the 'free world' is automatically true" (Aronson 1990: 258).

Salisbury's report came as no surprise to the readers of the *Guardian*. Burchett's reports had already described civilian causalities of "American aggression." In March 1966, Burchett dispatched reports that summarized "great victories of the U.S. air force," which included "destroying all 160 buildings, killing 139 and seriously wounding 80 lepers and medical personnel" in the Quang Binh province (Burchett 1966a: 1, 9). He also had revealed "a systematic and deliberate attack against schools, hospitals, sanatoriums, and most strictly defined civilian targets, protected by international law," which he witnessed in North Vietnam (Burchett 1966a: 1, 9). Small says, "The Salisbury story demonstrated that Burchett and *Guardian* had been correct all the time" (Small 1994: 66).

The Escalation of the War at Home: 1967

Another thing that worried Washington was the escalation of the antiwar movement at home. The number of US servicemen in Vietnam increased from approximately 385,200 at the end of 1966 to 485,000 by the end of 1967, and the number of antiwar warriors fighting on the second front at home increased as well. On 15 April 1967, the largest single antiwar demonstration to date took place, organized by a moderate umbrella organization, the Spring Mobilization Committee to End the War in Vietnam (Halstead 1978: 327). It was joined by an unprecedentedly broad coalition of antiwar forces. The Spring Mobilization coordinated a march, to be divided into contingents, that would leave Central Park at noon and move toward the United Nations building on First Avenue in lower Manhattan (Halstead 1978: 336). A radical segment of the rally, a group of few hundred people, gathered at Central Park's Sheep Meadow for a draft card burning (Halstead 1978: 333). The crowd size for the whole rally was so huge that one of the participants said that New York was "Antiwar City" that day (Halstead 1978: 335).

The demonstration dominated the front pages of newspapers the next morning. The *New York Times* and the *Washington Post* again downsized the number of antiwar protestors. The *New York Times* reported that police officers estimated the number of demonstrators outside the UN at between 100,000 and 125,000; however, it used the lowest possible number in its headline, "100,000 Rally at U.N. Against the War in Vietnam" (Robinson 1967: 1). To balance the two opposing views, the *Washington Post* cited a "salient majority" saying, "I will bet we could get 10 times this number out here to support the war if we made the same effort these people did" (Jeschke 1967: A6). These mainstream newspapers overemphasized minor sensational dimensions of the demonstration. Despite the fact that the draft burning at Sheep Meadow was not the chief aspect of the demonstration, the *New York Times* used it as a headline the next morning, which read, "Many Draft Cards Burned—Eggs Tossed at Parade." It also devoted considerable space to the NLF supporters, followed by the story of their confrontation with counterdemonstrators, who shouted at the antiwar protestors "Bomb the Hanoi" and "Dr. Spoke Smokes Bananas" (Robinson 1967: 1).

By contrast, the *Guardian* celebrated the "Biggest Anti-War Rally Ever" in every page of the first issue after the demonstration on 15 April. It reported on, "[a] massive Chunk of humanity—estimated at from 300,000 to 500,000 persons—[who] urged through midtown New York … The demonstration in New York alone was the largest peace mobilization in the U.S. history" (Price 1967: 1). The *Guardian* also mentioned the NLF flags and the draft card burning, but made it clear that they were "not interrupted by the march's sponsors, but neither were they part of the planned program" (Price 1967: 1). Michael Klare wrote for the *Guardian*, "Student participation in the New York peace march was tremendous … The Participants were not just isolated 'hippies' and radicals, but significant segments of student bodies" (Klare 1967: 8). In a "What they said at UN" piece, the *Guardian* devoted half a page to speeches given by Martin Luther King Jr., Stokely Carmichael, Professor Howard Zinn of Boston University, and Pedro Juan Rua of the Movement for Puerto Ricans, speeches that appeared sporadically in the *New York Times* and the *Washington Post* (*National Guardian* 1967: 2). The last major article on the demonstration to appear in the *Guardian* that week was Robert L. Allen's "Harlem Marchers Jolt Times Sq. in Detour," which gave a full-page account of the Harlem march organized by the Black United Action Front, which called for the "victory of liberation movements throughout the world" (Allen 1967: 4). The *Guardian* gave one of the most detailed accounts of the 15 April demonstration, as well as analyses by journalists involved with the movement.

Catching Up and Moving Away: 1968

The Tet Offensive of 1968 brought the realization that the escalation should be halted and eroded the confidence of the American mainstream press as well as the general public in the previously unquestioned American victory. In his speech on 29 September 1967, President Johnson claimed that Hanoi would "realize that it just can never win" (Johnson 1967). Within four months, the NLF and North Vietnamese proved their ability to launch a series of successful attacks, which became known as the Tet Offensive. It was the Americans who realized that they would not win the war. The series of successful strikes by the North Vietnamese made Johnson's "we're making progress" reiteration in November 1967 absurd. The *New York Times* wrote that the Tet Offensive "throw[s] doubt on recent official American claims of progress" and called it "a humiliating surprise" (quoted in Wyatt 1993: 187). *Newsweek* stated, "have not been given a realistic assessment of the situation in Vietnam." (quoted in Wyatt 1993: 187). And the press finally came to the conclusion that the cost of the war was too great to continue it with no clear victorious ending. The mainstream press's doubts and disagreements about the US policy in Vietnam became clear after the Tet Offensive.

By that time, the *Guardian* had the largest amount of subscriptions it had ever had and had expanded in size (Smith 1993: 103). It had twenty-eight thousand subscribers by 1968 and thirty-two thousand by 1969 (Raymont 1968: 34). Taking into account that it was common for the paper to be shared among groups of people, the *Guardian* was estimated to have approximately seventy-five thousand readers (Smith 1993: 99, 103). The paper established a dozen *Guardian* news/circulation bureaus to meet the wide national demand (Glessing 1970: 66). Even though the mass media became critical of the war and the government, the *Guardian* remained an important source of information for radical leftists.

By 1968, the *Guardian* became more focused on youth radicalism, dropping *National* from its name in May 1967 (Raymont 1968). After the transformation from an "Independent Progressive Weekly" to "Independent Radical Newsweekly," the paper increasingly identified itself with anti-imperialist struggles and the Third World revolutionaries. In May 1967, the departure of the last remaining original member of the *Guardian,* James Aronson, placed the paper completely under the operation of the New Left. It began providing more pages to present the diversity of perspectives that invigorated the antiwar discussion. In *Revolution in the Air,* Max Elbaum states that "[t]he paper [the *Guardian*] served as one of the main vehicle for left debate," and many prominent figures from the broad spectrum of the Left, including Julius Lester of the black liberation movement and Todd Gitlin and Carl Davidson of SDS, contributed their views (2002: 61).

In 1969–70, the *Guardian* was becoming one of the most prominent national advocates of revolutionary politics, with a special emphasis on class-based Marxism-Leninism (Elbaum 2002: 62). A small group within the paper disagreed with the *Guardian*'s criticism of ideas for armed struggles and physically seized the paper's office in April 1971. Failing to convince the rest of the staff, the group started their own independent revolutionary newspaper called the *Liberated Guardian* (Leamer 1972: 75). Elbaum credits the *Guardian* by saying, "Standing out as one of the few broad-based radical institutions of the 1960s to sustain itself into the 1970s, the paper's influence on activists just turning toward revolutionary ideas was immense" (Elbaum 2002: 62). The *Guardian* persisted for forty-four years after its establishment in 1948. The perseverance of the *Guardian* made it one of the most well-known and widely read newspapers of the American Left. Smith recollects that the *Guardian*'s coverage of the war and antiwar activities was "considered essential reading by leading activists and decision makers within the various antiwar, civil rights, student, feminist, and progressive movements throughout the country" (Smith 1993: 99).

Conclusion

The *Guardian* was a source of alternative information on the Vietnam War and antiwar activities, a dissenting voice, and a critical institutional fixture within the antiwar movement as a whole. Throughout the country, a significant number of American leftists of the Vietnam era picked up the *Guardian*, which shared their antiwar sentiments. It reinforced the antiwar dissenters' doubts about the US policy in Vietnam by providing news reports with an unapologetic antiwar stance. As a member of the antiwar movement, the paper participated in the movement's politics and played a crucial role by providing alternative news coverage of the war and the movement.

Notes

1. The name changed from *National Guardian* to *Guardian* in 1968. The newspaper is uniformly referred to as the *Guardian* in this chapter.
2. Author's interview with Todd Gitlin on 23 December 2008.
3. Author's interview with Todd Gitlin on 23 December 2008.

4. The *Mainichi* maintained a nationwide circulation between 3,474,826 and 4,409,757 during the 1960s, according to *Jiji Almanac 1962* (Jiji Tsuushinsha 1962: 129) and *Jiji Almanac 1969* (Jiji Tsuushinsha 1969: 129).
5. Author's interview with Minoru Omori on 9 May 2008.
6. Author's interview with Minoru Omori on 9 May 2008.

Bibliography

Allen, R. L. 1967. "Harlem Marchers Jolt Times Sq. in Detour." *National Guardian,* 22 April.

Alsop, J. 1964. "Matter of Fact: New Phrase in Viet-Nam." *Washington Post,* 17 February.

Anderson, T. H. 1996. *The Movement and the Sixties.* New York: Oxford University Press.

Aronson, J. 1990. *The Press and the Cold War.* New York: Monthly Review Press.

Aronson, J., and C. Belfrage. 1978. *Something to Guard: The Stormy Life of the National Guardian 1948–1967.* New York: Columbia University Press.

Bedacht, M. 1964. "The Mail Bag." *National Guardian,* 11 April.

Burchett, W. 1964. "Vietnam Rebel's Terms for a U.S. Settlement." *National Guardian,* 23 January.

———. 1966a. "'Great' Victories for U.S. Air Force." *National Guardian,* 26 March.

———. 1966b. "Vietnam's Buddhist Masses Turn Toward NLF." *National Guardian,* 12 November.

———. 1968. *Vietnam Will Win!* New York: The Guardian.

———. 2005. *Memoirs of a Rebel Journalist: The Autobiography of Wilfred Burchett,* ed. W. G. Burchett, G. Burchett, and N. L. Shimmin. Sydney: UNSW Press.

———. 2007. *Rebel Journalism: The Writings of Wilfred Burchett,* ed. G. Burchett and N. L. Shimmin. New York: Cambridge University Press.

Cirese, B., and S. Cirese. 1967. "The Mail Bag." *National Guardian,* 28 January.

Elbaum, M. 2002. *Revolution in the Air: Sixties Radicals Turn to Lenin, Mao and Che.* London: Verso.

Fineberg, S. A. 1953. *The Rosenberg Case: Fact and Fiction.* New York: Oceana Publications.

Gitlin, T. 1987. *The Sixties: Years of Hope, Days of Rage.* New York: Bantam Books.

———. 2003. *The Whole World Is Watching: Mass Media in the Making and Unmaking of the New Left.* Berkeley: University of California Press.

Glessing, R. J. 1970. *The Underground Press in America.* Bloomington: Indiana University Press.

Halstead, F. 1978. *Out Now! A Participant's Account of the Movement in the U.S. Against the Vietnam War.* New York: Pathfinder Press.

Jeschke, P. R. 1967. "Protestors on Coast Hold Biggest Rally." *Washington Post,* 16 April.

Jiji Almanac 1962. 1962. Tokyo: Jiji Tsuushinsha.

———. *1969.* 1969.Tokyo: Jiji Tsuushinsha.

Johnson, L. 1967. "Speech on Vietnam." Speech, National Legislative Conference, 29 September. http://millercenter.org/scripps/archive/speeches/detail/4041 (accessed 6 December 2008).

Klare, M. 1967. "The Students Turn Out in Full Force." *National Guardian,* 22 April.

Leamer, L. 1972. *The Paper Revolutionaries: The Rise of the Underground Press.* New York: Simon and Schuster.

Lippmann, W. 1967. "Today and Tomorrow: Harrison Salisbury in Hanoi." *Washington Post,* 10 January, A15.

Mecklin, J. 1967. "The Vietnam Story." *New York Times,* 4 June.

National Guardian. 1963. "Looking Forward—Our 16th Year." 10 October.

———. 1964a. "Get Out of Vietnam!" 13 February.

———. 1964b. "Vietnam Game." 27 February.

———. 1965a. "Exclusive Pictures of a Revolution in Progress." 6 February.

———. 1965b. "What the March Means." 24 April.

———. 1967. "What they said at UN," 22 April 22.

New York Times. 1965a. "15,000 White House Pickets Denounce Vietnam War." 18 April.

———. 1965b. "Picketing Kept Up at The While House." 19 April.

———. 1966. "No Military Targets, Namdinh Insists." 31 December.

Price, W. A. 1967. "Biggest Anti-War Rally Ever." *National Guardian,* 22 April.

Raymont, H. 1968. "Radical Editors Say Their Job is In 'Movement.'" *New York Times,* 12 February.

Robinson, D. 1967. "100, 000 Rally at U.N. Against Vietnam War: Many Draft Cards Burned—Eggs Tossed at Parade." *New York Times,* 16 April, 1.

Salisbury, H. E. 1988. *A Time of Change: A Reporter's Tale of Our Time.* New York: A Cornelia & Michael Bessie Book.

Schesch, A. 1965. "The Mail Bag." *National Guardian,* 15 May.

Sheehan, N. 1966. "Anti-Americanism Grows in Vietnam." *New York Times,* 24 April.

Small, M. 1994. *Covering Dissent: The Media and the Anti-Vietnam War Movement.* New Brunswick, NJ: Rutgers University Press.

———. 2002. *Antiwarriors: The Vietnam War and Battle for America's Hearts and Minds.* Wilmington, DE: Scholarly Resources Books.

Smith, J. A. 1993. "*The Guardian* Goes to War." *The Voices from the Underground,* vol. 1, Tempe, Ariz.: Mica Press, 1993, 99-106.

Washington Post. 1965. "Viet-Nam War Protest is Staged by 16,000." 18 April.

Wyatt, C. 1993. *Paper Soldiers: The American Press and the Vietnam War,* 1st ed. New York: W. W. Norton.

Young, M. B. 1991. *The Vietnam Wars, 1945–1990.* New York: Harper Perennial.

Chapter 10

From "We Shall Overcome" to "We Shall Overrun"

The Transformation of US Media Coverage
of the Black Freedom Struggle, 1964–68,
in Comparative Perspective

David Carter

Media coverage of civil rights demonstrations in the United States played a critical and well-documented role in arousing the national conscience and laying the groundwork for the landmark civil rights legislation of 1964 and 1965. Sit-ins, freedom rides, fire hoses, police dogs, and gas-masked figures on foot and on horseback swinging nightsticks amid roiling clouds of tear gas against a silhouetted steel structure: together these and other images form the iconography of the civil rights era. Civil rights veteran John Lewis, whose own activist trajectory intersected so many of these visual tableaux, argues that "if it hadn't been for the media—the print media and television—the civil rights movement would have been like a bird without wings, a choir without a song" (quoted in Roberts and Klibanoff 2007: 407).

Lewis's colorful language describing the power of media to shape public understandings of the civil rights movement helps to explain the extraordinary success of the African American freedom struggle from World War II to the passage of the Voting Rights Act in 1965. The media helped to indelibly fix in the public's imagination—and America's historical memory—critical events like the Supreme Court's *Brown v. Board* decisions in 1954 and 1955, the Emmett Till lynching in 1955, the Montgomery bus boycott from 1955 to 1956, the Little Rock school desegregation crisis in 1957, the sit-in movement in and after 1960, the freedom rides in 1961, the Birmingham campaign in the spring of 1963, the March on Washington later that summer, and voting rights struggles in the Mississippi Delta and in Selma, Alabama, in 1964 and 1965, to name but a few of the particularly deeply etched protest events from that period. Typically, the common denominator that helped to convey the moral urgency of the movement was the riveting drama of white violence directed against nonviolent African American protesters (and occasionally their white allies).

From emancipation onward, African American activists crafted media strategies designed to maximize favorable press coverage of their causes, from abolition to antilynching to concerted efforts to win civil rights and a greater measure of economic justice. They pointed to the glaring hypocrisy of an American political system that trumpeted egalitarian ideals while tolerating the festering social and economic ills of segregation and other forms of racial proscription. Their ability to call members of America's white majority to conscience was central to the success of black media strategies over the course of decades. Martin Luther King Jr. spoke of "redeeming the soul of America," and when white activists and observers sympathetic to the black freedom struggle asserted that their *own* freedom and citizenship were diminished by America's own version of racial apartheid, the civil rights movement enjoyed its greatest successes.

Popular treatments of the movement remain hostage to an ahistorical periodization that suggests that social protest emerged out of nowhere in 1954 with the Supreme Court's *Brown* decision and faded to black in 1965 with the passage of the Voting Rights Act. (The assassination of King in 1968 is treated as a tragic coda, but the intervening years are typically glossed over.) As part of this metanarrative historians typically devote obligatory attention to a handful of dramatic events, mass protests, and acts of violence, treading on what one scholar has called "sacred ground" (Hogan 2007: 10).

Moreover, much of the history of the American civil rights movement as it is currently taught in schools and portrayed in the media ignores the organizing efforts of African Americans in the cities of the urban North and West. Few historians make the necessary geographic detours above the Mason-Dixon line, and if historical accounts do visit the riot-torn geography of northern urban neighborhoods, it is no longer in the narrative and analytical context of civil rights, and seldom with a focus on the structural underpinnings of economic racism and the sociological roots of disorder.

Instead, historians resemble too closely those uneasy reporters who in the second half of the 1960s arrived to cover the "race riots" of the "long, hot summers," with the armored personnel carriers of the National Guard as their insulating escort. Like most journalists, scholars depart from this unfamiliar non-southern urban geography with the last firefighting crews—and television cameras—the ashes still smoldering in their wake with the task of analysis incomplete or ignored.

Scholars still need to explore more fully the impact of media depictions of ongoing efforts at civil rights reform and urban unrest in the United States in this later time period, as well as the ways in which movement activists sought to influence that coverage through evolving and competing media strategies. Such historical inquiry, moreover, would benefit from comparative research and transnational approaches. Jeremi Suri perceptively notes that although "the observation that the events of 1968 were global in scope is quite common (almost cliché) … the dominant analytical frame for understanding social and political change remains national in scope" (2007: xi). Even if individuals challenging the status quo in different national contexts were not always aware of participating in global patterns of protest, studying activism across national borders can yield important insights. Governmental attempts to suppress protest and the often violent dynamic between social insurgency and state response merit similar comparative scrutiny (Suri 2007: intro.). Until scholars break out of the pattern of studying the civil rights struggle within a restrictive periodization and a rigidly national framework, historical interpretations of the linked struggles for civil rights and economic justice in the United States will remain dangerously myopic.

Despite the preoccupation with the "glory days" and "greatest hits" of the civil rights era, the years 1965 to 1968 can stake their own claim as the era of the media-defined watershed. Events playing out in the news appeared all the more stark and all-determining because of heightened expectations. Had African Americans "overcome" by 1965, in the words of the freedom song and civil rights anthem? Was the "dream" articulated by King in his famous 1963 address in Washington DC a dream fulfilled or a dream deferred? Fashioning coherent media strategies remained one of the central challenges of activists and protesters. For as events were recast in print, and especially as they were refracted through the camera lens and manipulated at editing consoles in television network newsrooms, the fundamental and seemingly ever-growing power of reportage to shape public perception, even public discourse, was more and more evident. And television was the main battleground.

"Like nothing else before it," one historian has suggested, TV "exposed the contradiction between liberty and white supremacy" (Norrell 1991: 72–73). It could circumscribe, and—less often—open up avenues of initiative within the US federal government and the broadening spectrum of the civil rights movement. Arguably more than at any time in the past, the media in and after 1965 played a critical role in fashioning national political culture and delimiting the perceived boundaries of political possibilities and agendas for reform. Television had furthered the goals of the southern-based civil rights movement up through the Selma campaign in 1965; in the three years that followed, its flickering images would increasingly fuel white backlash with incendiary coverage of urban rioting, Black Power, and other perceived manifestations of African American "militancy."

One can fairly easily summarize the prevailing historiographical trends in examining the relationship between US-based print and visual media and the African American civil rights movement. In their recent Pulitzer Prize–winning account *The Race Beat: The Press, the Civil Rights Struggle, and the Awakening of a Nation* (2007), veteran journalists Gene Roberts and Hank Klibanoff devote twenty-two chapters and nearly four hundred pages to the relationship between the mass media and the struggle for black equality from World War II to the passage of the Voting Rights Act in 1965. They then allocate just over twelve pages to the period from 1965 to 1968 in a single chapter entitled simply, "Beyond" (Roberts and Klibanoff 2007: 395–407). Julian Bond and Jenny Walker are more proportional in their treatment of the evolution of media coverage of the movement during the post-1964/65 period, but their thoughtful essays in Brian Ward's edited collection *Media, Culture, and the Modern African American Freedom Struggle* are in many respects exceptions that prove a larger rule (Bond 2001: 16–40; Walker 2001: 41–66).

Historian Hugh Davis Graham offers a promising point of departure for understanding a critical shift in media coverage, suggesting that civil rights and antipoverty reform after 1965 "harbored a vulnerability in the mercurial image of [their] chief clientele" (1990: 234). "During 1965–1966," Graham notes, "the Negro image in America was sharply transformed … In the spring of 1965 the dominant symbol was a petitioning black voter being brutalized by Sheriff Jim Clark in Selma [Alabama]. By 1966 this had been countered, if not displaced in the volatile world of *Time* and *Newsweek,* by the rampaging ghetto rioter in Watts, or the black racist harangues of an H. Rap Brown [a militant black activist from the period]" (Graham 1990: 234). Veteran civil rights activist and Pulitzer Prize–winning journalist Roger Wilkins echoed this analysis in 2008 when he noted in the days leading up to the fortieth anniversary of the assassination of Martin Luther King Jr.: "By 1968, a lot of white people had gotten tired of civil rights and thinking of race … The picture of docile black people holding hands and singing freedom songs had been replaced by images of poor blacks rampaging through cities, looting and burning" (quoted in Blake 2008: website).

Scholars and other commentators on the 1960s have long pointed to the role of the Watts riot in south central Los Angeles in August 1965 as a turning point in public perceptions of race relations. According to this viewpoint, Watts served as a wake-up call to the national dimensions of a problem that sociologist Gunnar Myrdal had perceptively labeled "an American Dilemma" in 1944 when he sought to redefine the "Negro problem" in the United States in fundamentally national rather than strictly regional terms. Watts was certainly not the first modern "race riot" in US history, but for a number of reasons it overshadowed earlier instances of urban disorder in the 1960s, including several outbreaks of unrest in black neighborhoods in Harlem and Rochester in New York and elsewhere in the summer of 1964 and earlier urban flare-ups in 1963.

Less than two weeks after the 1965 violence and property destruction in Los Angeles had finally subsided, President Lyndon Johnson's press secretary George Reedy struggled to understand the riot and its consequences for the Johnson administration's antipoverty and civil rights programs. "One need only drive through the impoverished and desperate slums," Reedy reflected, "to understand that the mere existence of a segregated community in modern society creates a 'we and they'—a 'friend and enemy'—psychology … People are not going to live peacefully under such circumstances unless they are cowed and this country has passed the point where Negroes can be cowed even if the majority of whites desire to do so" (quoted in Carter 2009: 60).

Reedy was also aware of the way in which the new media shaped public responses to the issue of civil rights. It was not simply that the camera had begun to shift its gaze from long-suffering black victims to angry rioters; it was the way in which the powerful images of urban disorder threatened even the most respectable middle-class black activists. "Unless they are extraordinarily careful, the Civil Rights leaders run the risk of identifying their movements with ordinary hooliganism and savagery," warned Reedy (quoted in Carter 2009: 60). His musings were prophetic, for many white Americans would increasingly see black America through the prism of civil disorder and violent cities. The vision that many idealistic Americans had not wished to acknowledge as an accurate reflection of national ideals of liberty and equality in the pre-1965 period was now inverted, oversimplified, and transformed into a grotesque distortion of reality by the "Coney Island mirrors of the media" (Lawson 1984: Reel 11, 0499-0502; Hodgson 1998: 170).

Increased attention within the Johnson White House to media coverage (and a growing attention to public opinion polling) could and did generate both action and self-conscious inactivity. It would not be too farfetched to argue that the administration took its cue from the early successes of the civil rights movement in seeking to anticipate how a wide range of issues would play on television. If television could be seen to be "turning against the movement," with skewed coverage of urban disorder and the most incendiary language of self-proclaimed African American militants, it became very difficult for civil rights advocates within the Johnson administration to press their case for ongoing racial and economic reform.

Another turning point in the transformation of media coverage of the movement came in the summer of 1966 during the "Meredith March Against Fear," when black militancy gained a new face and voice. James Meredith, who had earlier desegregated the University of Mississippi, had sought to march across the Magnolia State, only to be ambushed and wounded by a shotgun-wielding white Tennessean. Civil rights leaders, including Martin Luther King Jr. of the Southern Christian Leadership Conference (SCLC), Floyd McKissick of the Congress of Racial Equality (CORE), and Stokely Carmichael of the Student Nonviolent Coordinating Committee (SNCC), visited a recovering Meredith in the hospital on 7 June and promised to complete the fallen activist's march. They resumed his interrupted route that very afternoon, and were promptly assaulted by Mississippi state troopers, who shoved them to the shoulder of the road, knocking SNCC's Cleveland Sellers to the ground and almost provoking Carmichael to violence.

King later recalled hearing "words [that] fell on my ears like strange music from a foreign land." Angry foot soldiers urged their leaders to make the affair an "all-black march" and declared, "We don't need any more white phonies and liberals invading our movement." "If one of these damn white Mississippi crackers touches me," threatened one demonstrator, "I'm gonna kick the hell out of him." King hoped the singing of the benedictory anthem "We Shall Overcome" would restore a degree of harmony to the tense marchers, but the volume of singing fell appreciably during the stanza "Black and White Together." "This is a new day," a marcher told him, and the lyrics should be rewritten as "We Shall Overrun" (King 1967: 25–26).

Unnerved by the growing radicalism of SNCC and CORE, Roy Wilkins and other representatives of the National Association for the Advancement of Colored People (NAACP) elected not to participate in the march. As an example of the sophistication of SNCC's media strategy, Carmichael explicitly sought to alienate Wilkins and the more moderate NAACP. But the young SNCC chairman recognized the imperative of keeping King as a part of the march; his presence alone guaranteed major media coverage.

White violence continued to plague the march in subsequent days, and after Stokely Carmichael was arrested by local white Mississippi authorities and then released, he used the opportunity to test-drive a new slogan. When he yelled the question "What do you want?!" to a carefully primed audience of Mississippi blacks at an evening rally, the crowd exploded in unison: "Black Power!!!" Most observers were unaware that this appearance of spontaneity had been carefully crafted by SNCC activist Willie Ricks's advance work. Camera flashes lit the gathering and national reporters hurried to file stories on a slogan many whites would soon deem to be incendiary and menacing.

Journalist Paul Good, covering the 1966 march as a freelance writer, was disgusted by what he saw as shallow and superficial media coverage. At the first sign of conflict between marchers, wire service reporters and television cameramen "shoot from the[ir] truck like flushed quail," wrote Good. Mile after mile of open-bed trucks filled with black field hands passed by, "heading for their $3 a day in the sun, serfs in a cotton industry receiving a billion [dollars] a year in federal subsidies." But the newsmen showed little interest in this or the hundreds of dilapidated shacks "where the essence of the march was made flesh in the lives of Negroes … whose atrophied political instincts were still held in check despite the Voting Rights Act, by threats of dispossession from the land, firing from job, or other retaliation." Too often, reporters could only see how chronicling dissension within the ranks of civil rights leadership made for good copy as they stared "straight through the realities of a Deep South that was changing grudgingly and only when pressure grew too great to bear" (Good 2003: 500).

Black Power—with its overtones of black militancy—became the focus of news coverage of the march, diverting attention from its concrete program, the attempt to register new black voters, and its earlier symbolic focus on blacks' refusal to be cowed by a state legendary for its climate of institutionalized intimidation and racism. Even though King, McKissick, and Carmichael struck a bargain agreeing to forswear the use of the slogans "Freedom Now" and "Black Power" during the remaining stages of the march, the genie was out of the bottle, and both SNCC and the headline-hungry white media would find the new story line irresistible (Lawson 1985: 57; Fairclough 1987: 316–19; Roberts and Klibanoff 2007: 398–400).

When marchers tried to pitch their overnight tents on the grounds of a black elementary school in Canton, Mississippi, state troopers and local police fired off dozens of canisters of tear gas and waded into the protesters swinging their billy clubs. As one journalist said, police, state troopers, and sheriff's deputies "came stomping in behind the gas, gun-butting and kicking the men, women and children. They were not arresting, they were punishing" (*New York Times* 24 June 1966). Dr. Alvin Poussaint, a representative of the Medical Committee for Human Rights, had accompanied the march, and he and another doctor were up all night treating the victims. It was, he said, like a war zone in the aftermath of a battle (Dittmer 1994: 485–86).

A year earlier, the "Bloody Sunday" Selma, Alabama, bridge beatings had ignited national outrage. But in the summer of 1966, the violence in Canton barely registered among most whites. Far more interesting were the fault lines in the movement that grew sharper as marchers ignored their leaders' unity agreement and chanted "Freedom Now" and "Black Power" in a competitive black antiphony; what conceivably could have been alternating theme and descant now sounded like jarring and deliberate dissonance. The reality of white-on-black violence now seemed less newsworthy than evidence of ideological discord within the movement and the specter of black-on-white mayhem.

Martin Luther King Jr. feared the Black Power slogan would "confuse our allies, isolate the Negro community, and give many prejudiced whites, who might otherwise be ashamed of their anti-Negro feeling, a ready excuse for self-justification" (quoted in Carson 1981: 210). But Carmichael and other SNCC and CORE leaders represented an increasingly vocal constituency, one committed to a movement where blacks would call the shots and unite under a powerful—and to most audiences a novel—rallying cry.

When Mississippi governor Paul Johnson called Black Power "the greatest threat to law and order and domestic tranquility ever heard in this country," his response was shared by most whites across the nation, who reacted as though struck by a thunderbolt (Johnson 1966). These unfamiliar new militants and their sloganeering drew white media like moths to a flame. A Herblock cartoon in the *Washington Post* depicted Black Power as a "Dangerous Genie" (7 July 1966); for its part, *Time* magazine wasted little time in labeling the Black Power slogan the clarion call of "the new racism" (8 July 1966). Two perceptive writers spoke to the heart of the matter when they described Black Power as a "fright concept" that deeply divided civil rights activists and alarmed white moderates, who saw it as a form of reverse racism (*Nation* 24 October 1966).

Few whites were willing to be similarly analytical in reflecting on the new rallying cry. While warning that in its clumsiest iteration Black Power "gives too many Negroes a chance to escape responsibility," National Urban League head Whitney Young pointed out that "Stokely didn't really make the backlash they're all talking about. He just gave [white critics] an excuse to come out publicly where they had been hesitant otherwise" (quoted in Parks 2003: 559). Roy Wilkins of the NAACP, widely viewed as the standard-bearer for civil rights "moderates" and without doubt the African American leader closest to Lyndon Johnson's White House, saw no need for nuance, however. Equating Black Power with "black death," he insisted that "no matter how endlessly [its proponents] try to explain Black Power, the term means anti-white ... It has to mean going it alone. It has to mean separatism ... This offers a disadvantaged minority little except the chance to shrivel and die" (quoted in Parks 2003: 559).

For other African Americans, national leaders, grassroots activists, and everyday citizens seeking to make sense of the din of the hyperbolic national media conversation, the new slogan Black Power summoned emotions rooted in their long search for self-determination and self-identity. It also represented *new* dimensions of anger and bitterness at the failure of the United States to respond to their entreaties for civil rights. The potency of the phrase overshadowed King's usual monopoly of the limelight, and thrust a young Stokely Carmichael into the glare of national media attention. One SCLC staffer captured Carmichael's predicament: "Stokely didn't get a chance to give any meaning to black power. He threw the words out, and before he could explain it the press had taken it and used it as a bludgeon" (quoted in Fairclough 1987: 319).

In its conceptual elasticity, Black Power was bigger than Stokely Carmichael, bigger even than the memory of Malcolm X, who along with novelist Richard Wright had used the phrase before white media and white viewers and readers suddenly seized on it in 1966 against the backdrop of the Meredith March Against Fear (Carson 1981: 207–11). And that slogan, propagated extensively by the mass media, soon drove a wedge into the coalition of African Americans and white liberal allies, a fissure compounded by the escalating Vietnam War and the fault lines it revealed in President Johnson's "liberal consensus." When many of the same northern white churches that had offered critical moral support to the Civil Rights Act in 1964 and the Voting Rights Act in 1965 failed to close ranks behind the 1966 civil rights package Johnson had sought to move through Congress, media commentator Mary McGrory observed, "The music has gone out of the movement" (*Evening Star* [Washington] 5 August 1966).

Even more than weekly news magazines and daily newspapers, during the period from 1965–68 television played a critical role in the displacement of favorable media coverage by often sensational negative coverage. Increasingly, images swamped ideas, and a carefully calibrated media strategy could come unraveled depending on the way media framed protest events and rhetoric. This was both the promise and the trap of African American militancy as its proponents interacted with a media accustomed to depicting black protest through attention to interracial violence, both actual and rhetorical (Joseph 2009).

From 1966 forward, many whites in America came to view Black Power along with urban unrest as part of a radioactive, if hypnotic, pairing. Media coverage of the urban riots also exhibited a voyeuristic quality, lending an immediacy to the images that emerged in direct counterpoint to earlier coverage of white repression of nonviolent African American protesters in the US South. For juxtaposed against the American public's abhorrence of the violence represented by the riots that flared between 1964 and 1968 was a fascination on the part of many whites with the condition of African Americans in the nation's inner cities, a desire to peer behind the tenement curtain to see how "reality" comported with their stereotyped visions of blighted urban lives and landscapes. The relatively recent advent of live television feeds and the saturation coverage of urban unrest went a long way toward satisfying this voyeurism, even as it helped to fuel a backlash against the civil rights reform agenda the Johnson administration professed to be dedicated to fulfilling.

Portraying the civil rights struggle in terms of white violence directed against nonviolent African American demonstrators had been the dominant interpretive frame in terms of how television had related the civil rights struggle to national audiences in the first decade of the black freedom struggle. Now *black* violence—or the implicit threat of such violence—took center stage once again as the media sought to frame the perceived growing militancy of black activists and the seasonal flare-ups in the nation's cities. African Americans complained that this coverage of urban unrest and ideological militancy came at the expense of other civil rights narratives and was alienating erstwhile white supporters.

Some thoughtful white journalists willingly conceded the point. "Had it not been for television showing us Bull Connor and his dogs in Birmingham and the march on Selma, there would not have been the momentum to push the civil rights acts through the Congress," *Atlanta Constitution* editor Ralph McGill perceptively noted. Television "performed a magnificent service by showing violence, but now it finds itself trapped in carrying on in the same manner and seems to be incapable of providing anything except violence." McGill was explicit in calling for the written word to lend the nuance that television coverage could seemingly not convey, perhaps not surprising given his position as a newspaperman representing an industry that would increasingly be besieged by the growing influence of television news (McGill, quoted in Roberts and Klibanoff 2007: 400–401). But there is little evidence to suggest that mainstream print media was any more capable of redefining this frame in the tumultuous years following passage of the Voting Rights Act than their colleagues at the editing consoles in the television newsrooms—or the protesters themselves, for that matter, whose media strategies failed to yield the sympathetic coverage they sought.

As scholars continue to explore the roles of print and television media in "translating" protest and social activism for domestic audiences in the United States, it is equally important to consider that challenge of translation in a transatlantic context. Tom Hayden (2008) writes eloquently of his impressions of "restless youth" acting across borders in a globally based "generation of '68" in his afterword to the anthology *1968 in Europe.* That volume itself, published in 2008, heralded an important new trend, for with each passing year both emerging and established historians and social scientists are publishing new research examining both the American civil rights movement and other nationally based (and transnationally connected) protest movements. These scholars recognize the merits of examining protest and media coverage of dissent across international borders and within the context of the Cold War, antiwar movements, cultural and "countercultural" trends, and other variables (Hayden 2008: 325–31).

In this vein, Martin Klimke's recent work examining student movements in the United States and West Germany from a transatlantic comparative perspective offers a promising example of the possibilities for such historical approaches. His scrutiny of some of the shared wellsprings of ideological inspiration between student movements on both sides of the Atlantic and his discussion of how German students could be at once anti-American and identify with members of the US student-based Left—"with America against America"—sets a standard worthy of emulation (Klimke 2004: 35–54).

Some US activists in and beyond the diverse civil rights movements and New Left/antiwar/counterculture movements saw themselves as part of a larger international struggle, a tendency that became especially pronounced as student opposition to the Vietnam War escalated in the second half of the 1960s. Malcolm X and John Lewis were influenced by a decolonizing Africa (Malcolm X and Haley 1965; Lewis and D'Orso 1998). Tom Hayden met both Vietnamese and Czech antiwar activists in Czechoslovakia in 1967, just months before the Prague Spring (Hayden 2008: 327). Two years later, Margot Adler traveled to an embargoed Cuba with a contingent of Americans, joining the international Venceremos Brigade to participate in the sugarcane harvest (Adler 1997: 262-72). But the international identification of American protest activists has been poorly integrated into the historical narrative of American civil rights history.

One detects a noticeable trend to remedy this deficit, however, in recent publications from both American and international scholars engaged in an interdisciplinary conversation. A complementary literature is emerging that discusses protest in and beyond Europe as part of a global network of protest activism whose members were participating in vibrant exchanges over both ideology and concrete tactical approaches to challenging state authority.

Scrutiny of protesters' media strategies is at the heart of these inquiries. As one example of the insights afforded by a comparative approach, historian Mike Sewell, in his analysis of how British media and the broader public responded to the American civil rights movement, notes that many voices in Great Britain in the 1960s were eager to "pounce" upon evidence suggesting racism was less a regional phenomenon in the United States than a truly national characteristic. Those in the United Kingdom who monitored US news most carefully found confirmation of their suspicions in the electoral success of Alabama governor George Wallace outside the South in and after 1964 and in conflicts over de facto school desegregation and other examples of racial discrimination in the Midwest and the urban Northeast. Sewell also notes how British media coverage often made comparisons between racial unrest in the United States and England's own racial strife. British media producers, and their consumers, seem to have mirrored the mainstream American unease about Black Power, alarmed by the race riots that rocked the United States and the ideological tenor of those African American leaders labeled "extremist" on both sides of the Atlantic (Sewell 1996: 194–212).

Extensive coverage of the 1967 Newark and Detroit riots in British newspapers suggests the ways in which the lines blurred between editorial critiques of American domestic political turmoil and its controversial foreign policy. A 25 July 1967 cartoon in the (London) *Times* during the peak period of violence in Detroit depicted two African American infantrymen deploying from a helicopter and dodging bullets in Vietnam against the backdrop of a burning thatched hut while one remarks, "This is proving to be excellent training for civilian life."

The same day the *Times* asserted in an editorial entitled "The Pattern of Violence" that American race riots were no longer "sporadic," but had reached the point of being an "epidemic"; the rioters were "affected by a new and dangerous philosophy. It is that any rioting, any destruction, any killing of white-skinned people is a battle won in the cause of Negro emancipation." Mirroring the penchant for sweeping overgeneralization so much in evidence in the editorial slant of US media, the London editors spoke condescendingly of the naïveté of both the rioters themselves—members of the "mob in being"—and the voices of African American militancy egging the deluded rioters on: "Moderate civil rights movements had been superseded by racial militancy—indeed race war. It becomes meritorious to hit out, and hit back, defy the law, and shake society for society is to be forcibly changed." As with the cartoon featured in that same day's edition, the *Times*' editors placed US foreign and domestic policy decisively in the same frame when they tabulated the global significance of urban racial strife in Newark, Detroit, and elsewhere: "America's world standing, which derives so much from social coherence and political morality, will suffer" (Modood 1996: 181–93).

On 27 July 1967, just as the violence of the Detroit riots was finally subsiding, the *Times* posed the question, "Could it possibly happen here?" Identifying "smoke signals" in the ways in which British West Indian immigrants had faced barriers in assimilating into the neighborhoods of "English people," the *Times*' editors ultimately concluded that while America's urban discord should serve as a wake-up call, the circumstances faced by marginalized African Americans in the United States and West Indian immigrants in the UK were more different than they were similar. In an interesting flattening out of American urban geography that downplayed regional differences between the US South and North for stylistic reasons, the editorial concluded:

> Birmingham, Alabama, and Birmingham, England, are, in the end, quite different. We have a social problem, not a war. We have worry, ignorance, superstition, fear and dislike: we do not have much hatred based on colour, and nobody carries a gun. In the matter of riots we shall get no more of them than we deserve.
>
> (*The Times*: 27 July 1968)

Still, complacency was conditional: it paid to quarantine England from the virus of American racial militancy where practicable, and the following day, on 28 July 1967, the *Times* paired its story of Lyndon Johnson's establishment of the National Advisory Commission on Civil Disorders, headlined "President Opens Riot Inquiry," with a headline reading "British Ban on Stokely Carmichael." The accompanying story related that SNCC's Carmichael, who had visited England just days earlier, would not be permitted to return to British soil, his ban justified by the Home Secretary in classic bureaucratic understatement: "Having considered a report on this man's recent activities I have decided that his presence here is not conducive to the public good." The *Times* listed complaints characterizing Carmichael's transatlantic rhetoric in the United Kingdom as "virulently anti-white and call[ing] for racial violence."

Such comparative analysis can be tied to the ways in which images of the US civil rights movement played a role in shaping both European and world views of American race relations during this period, particularly given the heightened international stakes of the Cold War, decolonization movements, and other transnational phenomena. Although American historians have on balance been slower to embrace transnational approaches, there is now a vibrant transatlantic dialogue emerging, and a growing number of scholars are charting how global currents directly affected protest and reactions to dissent in the United States and how American events in turn shaped events abroad. This trend in comparative and transnational histories of protest and media coverage of protest can be seen as important steps in the ongoing effort to break out of that "dominant analytical frame" based on national history critiqued by Jeremi Suri (2007: xi).

These new studies illuminate the need for even more systematic analysis of both domestic and international media coverage of American urban unrest and ideological developments in the civil rights era. Comparative examination of trends in media coverage will enrich understandings of how the struggle for black equality in the United States informed the freedom struggles and protest cultures of students, political dissidents, and other dispossessed and marginalized historical actors around the world in the "global 1960s," and how those actors in turn influenced American activists. A more expansive and inclusive historical canvas will surely be the result.

Bibliography

Adler, M. 1997. *Heretic's Heart: A Journey Through Spirit and Revolution.* Boston: Beacon Press.

Blake, J. 2008. "King's Final Crusade: The Radical Push for a New America." http://www.cnn.com/2008/US/04/01/mlk.final.crusade/index.html (accessed 7 May 2008).

Bond, J. 2001. "The Media and the Movement: Looking Back from the Southern Front." In *Media, Culture, and the Modern African American Freedom Struggle,* ed. B. Ward. Gainesville: University Press of Florida.

Carson, C. 1981. *In Struggle: SNCC and the Black Awakening of the 1960s.* Cambridge, MA: Harvard University Press.

Carter, D. 2009. *The Music Has Gone Out of the Movement.* Chapel Hill: University of North Carolina Press.

Dittmer, J. 1994. *Local People: The Struggle for Civil Rights in Mississippi.* Urbana: University of Illinois Press.

Fairclough, A. 1987. *To Redeem the Soul of America: The Southern Christian Leadership Conference and Martin Luther King, Jr.* Athens: University of Georgia Press.

Good, P. 2003. "The Meredith March." In *Reporting Civil Rights, Part Two: American Journalism, 1963–1973,* ed. C. Carson, D. Garrow, B. Kovach, and C. Polsgrove, comp. New York: Library of America.

Graham, H. D. 1990. *The Civil Rights: Origins and Development of National Policy.* Oxford: Oxford University Press.

Hayden, T. 2008. "Afterword." In *1968 in Europe: A History of Protest and Activism, 1965–1977,* ed. M. Klimke and J. Scharloth. New York: Palgrave Macmillan.

Hodgson, G. 1998. "Heresies of Liberalism." *Media Studies Journal* 12, no. 3 (Fall): 164-71.

Hogan, W. 2007. *Many Minds, One Heart: SNCC'S Dream for a New America.* Chapel Hill: University of North Carolina Press.

King, Jr., M. L. 1967. *Where Do We Go from Here: Chaos or Community?* New York: Harper and Row.

Johnson, P. B. 1966. Statement submitted to Senate Judiciary Committee, Subcommittee on Constitutional Rights, in opposition to Senate 3296, 89th Congress (undated, fall). Paul Johnson Papers, Folder 10, Civil Rights Bill [1966], Box 110, McCain Library and Archives, University of Southern Mississippi, Hattiesburg, Mississippi.

Joseph, P. E. 2009. "The Black Power Movement: A State of the Field." *Journal of American History* 96, no. 3 (December): 751–76.

Klimke, M. 2004. "Between Berlin and Berkeley, Frankfurt and San Francisco: The Student Movements of the 1960s in Transatlantic Perspective." In *Taking Back the Academy! History of Activism, History as Activism,* ed. J. Downs and J. Manion. New York: Routledge.

Lawson, S. F. 1985. *In Pursuit of Power: Southern Blacks and Electoral Politics, 1965–1982.* New York: Columbia University Press.

———, ed. 1984. *Civil Rights During the Johnson Administration, 1963–1969,* Part I, "The White House Central Files." Lyndon Baines Johnson Library, Austin, TX; Frederick, MD: University Publications of America, Inc., microfilm, Reel 11, 0499-0502.

Lewis, J., and M. D'Orso. 1998. *Walking With the Wind: A Memoir of the Movement.* New York: Simon and Schuster.

Malcolm X and A. Haley. 1965. *The Autobiography of Malcolm X.* New York: One World.

Modood, T. 1996. "The Limits of America: Rethinking Equality in the Changing Context of British Race Relations." In *The Making of Martin Luther King and the Civil Rights Movement,* ed. B. Ward, and T. Badger. New York: New York University Press.

Myrdal, G. 1944. *An American Dilemma: The Negro Problem and Modern Democracy.* New York: Harper and Row.

Norrell, Robert J. 1991. "One Thing We Did Right: Reflections on the Movement." In *New Directions in Civil Rights Studies,* ed. A. L. Robinson and P. Sullivan. Charlottesville: University Press of Virginia.

Parks, G. 2003. "Whip of Black Power." In *Reporting Civil Rights, Part Two: American Journalism, 1963–1973,* ed. C. Carson, D. Garrow, B. Kovach, and C. Polsgrove, comp. New York: Library of America.

Roberts, G., and H. Klibanoff. 2007. *The Race Beat: The Press, the Civil Rights Struggle, and the Awakening of a Nation.* New York: Vintage.

Sewell, M. 1996. "British Responses to the Civil Rights Movement." In *The Making of Martin Luther King and the Civil Rights Movement,* ed. B. Ward and T. Badger. New York: New York University Press.

Suri, J. 2007. "Introduction: 1968 as History." In *The Global Revolutions of 1968,* ed. J. Suri. New York: Norton.

Walker, J. 2001. "A Media-Made Movement? Black Violence and Nonviolence in the Historiography of the Civil Rights Movement." In *Media, Culture, and the Modern African American Freedom Struggle,* ed. B. Ward. Gainesville: University Press of Florida.

Chapter 11

Taking the Revolution to the Big Screen

A Taxonomy of Social Movements' Uses of Cinema in the 1960s and 1970s

Stefan Eichinger

The 1960s and 1970s witnessed social movements around the world engender a flurry of episodes of political contention. Among these movements featured student and labor movements in North America and Western Europe; antidictatorial movements in Eastern and Southern Europe as well as Latin America; and national independence movements in Africa and colonialist vestiges elsewhere.[1] Social movements in the 1960s and 1970s drew on a wide media repertoire for propagating their political claims. One element of that repertoire that has thus far been largely understudied, however, is their varied uses of cinema. This chapter, then, intends to remedy that omission by proposing a taxonomy of the manifold ways in which cinema was harnessed by social movements in the 1960s and 1970s for political claim making.

To be sure, the 1960s and 1970s were not the first time that cinema was put to use by social movements in advancing political claims. On the contrary, traces of such political filmmaking reach back to cinema's origins as a mass medium at the turn of the twentieth century.[2] Filmmaking by social movements in the 1960s and 1970s nonetheless exhibits two traits that invest it with a larger significance for studying political uses of cinema by social movements. The first trait is a heightened geographical dispersion: instances of political filmmaking by social movements did not remain confined to a few highly industrialized countries, but occurred on every continent. The second trait involves the appropriation of cinema also by smaller and less cohesive actors inside social movements than political parties, trade unions, or similarly structurally evolved organizations. This tendency is, for example, illustrated by the Groupes Medvedkine, two spontaneously emerging factory workers' collectives that, between 1967 and 1974, produced about a dozen films as part of the French labor movement (see Iskra 2006).

The taxonomy proposed here is three-tiered and builds on ideas encapsulated in the public forum model of public discourse in Gamson (2004) and Ferree, Gamson, Gerhards, and Rucht (2002b), and the media taxonomy sketched in Jacobs (2005). In the next section, I will elucidate a taxonomic framework for analyzing possible uses of cinema by social movements for political claim making. I will consider the choice of tiers and the respective parameters associated with each tier in the framework. In subsequent sections, I will develop, on the basis of this framework, a taxonomy of social movements' uses of cinema for political claim making in the 1960s and 1970s. For each tier, I will derive a set of categories from the corresponding parameters in the framework, and show how various examples of films can be analyzed through these categories.

Taxonomic Framework

To begin with, let us clarify what we mean by political claim making. Social movements aim to promote attitudes and opinions with respect to certain political issues that challenge those espoused by elites and authorities. Such promotional activity is called claim making.

Now, the public forum model of public discourse presented in Gamson (2004) and Ferree, Gamson, Gerhards, and Rucht (2002b) offers a convenient conceptual tool for analyzing how public discourse (notably, media discourse) is shaped by political actors, including social movements.[3] The model starts from the observation that public discourse occurs in a variety of public forums. A *public forum* is, at a bare minimum, an instance where someone (the *speaker*) contributes to public discourse through some discursive intervention (the *speech*) in some location (the *arena*). Traditional examples of public forums are parliamentary sessions, party conventions, town hall meetings, etc. These public forums are marked by the fact that the speaker, in delivering his speech, must be physically present in the arena. An important class of public forums is that of mass media, such as newspapers, radio, television, or cinema. (In contrast to more traditional public forums, these do not require the speaker's physical presence in the arena.) Applying the tripartite scheme of speaker-speech-arena to cinema gives us a public forum where someone (the *filmmaker*) makes a discursive intervention by particular audiovisual means (the *film*) in some location where the intervention is screened (the *projection venue*). Thus, social movements—or more precisely, political actors partaking in them—can make use of cinema for political claim making by capturing their claims on film and showing the latter to audiences in a projection venue.[4]

Drawing on the model's three-component structure of public forums, we can analyze possible uses of cinema for claim making in public discourse through the components of filmmaker, film, and projection venue, respectively. This yields three tiers on which to base the framework. Next, we need to address the question of how to classify, with respect to each tier, the range of possible uses of cinema by social movements for political claim making. My proposal is to identify for each tier a pair of parameters from which determinate sets of categories can be derived; every possible use will then be assignable to some category.

First Tier

The *first tier* requires classifying possible filmmakers contributing to public discourse (regardless of the particular political issues on which a discourse may bear). My approach is to categorize filmmakers based on the discursive stance they assume, that is, the way in which they choose to intervene in some discourse. To this effect, I propose two parameters for the filmmaker component:

1. *Filmmaker intentionality:* How does the filmmaker intend to relate to the discourse?
2. *Filmmaker positionality:* How does the filmmaker position his discursive contribution in relation to those of other discourse participants?

The *first parameter* concerns the ways in which a filmmaker may intend to relate to public discourse. Frequently, in making a film, a filmmaker may intend to actively contribute to the evolution of public discourse on some topic. Yet there are other intentions a filmmaker may conceivably have. For instance, a filmmaker may not have intended a certain film as a contribution to some particular discourse, even though it is construed in this light by other participants in that discourse. In that case, the filmmaker intervenes in the discourse unintentionally. The parameter of filmmaker intentionality thus aims to capture the full range of relations a filmmaker may intend to entertain with respect to public discourse.

The *second parameter* allows us to further differentiate the set of discursive interventions intended as actively contributing to discourse, which presumably constitutes the most prominent way of relating to discourse. Given that social movements intervene in discourse in order to challenge political elites and authorities, such discourse will involve different parties advocating opposing discursive stances. Now, the second parameter aims to account for the ways in which a filmmaker positions himself, by virtue of his discursive intervention, with regard to other discourse participants. For instance, does he remain nonaligned, considering issues impartially on their own merits? Or does he align himself with other participants by toeing the line of some party or movement?

Second Tier

The *second tier* aims to classify the types of films a filmmaker may use for his discursive interventions. To capture the many different types of films potentially available, we must select sufficiently general parameters:

1. *Filmic reference mode:* What reference mode does the content of the filmmaker's film have?
2. *Filmic content structure:* How is the content of the filmmaker's film structured?

The *first parameter* accounts for the ways in which the content of a filmmaker's discursive intervention may refer. Broadly speaking, the content of a film either refers to factual or fictional persons, events, and circumstances. In principle, there is a broad spectrum of conceivable reference modes, ranging from highly fictional to purely factual content, with many modes mixing factual and fictional elements.

The *second parameter* regards possible ways of arranging filmic content into a coherent structure. One prominent way of structuring filmic content is offered by narratives. A narrative, roughly speaking, gives structure to content by embedding characters in relatively well-defined spatial settings and arranging events involving the characters into relatively well-defined temporal sequences. Other ways of structuring filmic content may rely on more abstract organizing principles, such as argument and counterargument.

Third Tier

The *third tier* aims to classify the types of projection venues in which a filmmaker makes his discursive contribution. Given that a projection venue is a location where filmmakers connect with potential audiences through their films, my choice of parameters is meant to distinguish between different venues based on their audience accessibility across time:

1. *Projection venue accessibility:* How accessible is the projection venue?
2. *Projection venue regularity:* How regularly is the projection venue available?

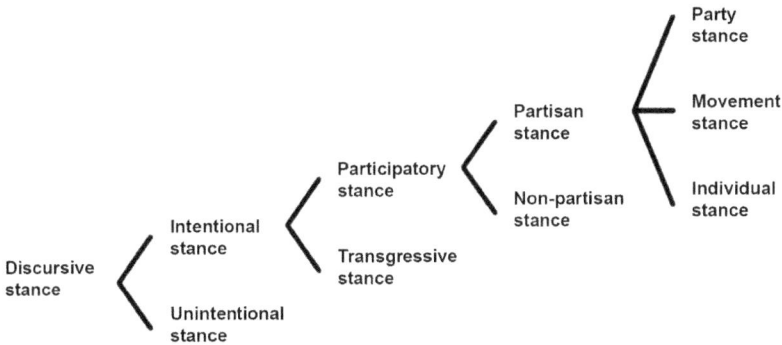

Figure 11.1. Tree Diagram of Categories of Discursive Stance

The *first parameter* concerns the accessibility of projection venues to potential audiences: some venues may be easily accessible to large and demographically diverse audiences, whereas others may only be open to audiences composed from more specific groups. The *second parameter* considers how regularly a projection venue is potentially available for screening films. Here the spectrum ranges from venues that are persistently available to one-time venues that are specifically made available for a particular occasion. Jointly, the two parameters determine a projection venue's overall audience accessibility. It should be emphasized that the notion of projection venue covers more than what in common parlance are called movie theaters. Indeed, any public or private location used for screening a film thus becomes a projection venue.

First Taxonomic Tier: The Filmmaker

Based on this framework, we can now develop a taxonomy of social movements' uses of cinema in the 1960s and 1970s. This section analyzes the set of categories related to the first tier (see figure 11.1), which corresponds to the filmmaker component in the framework. The categories are derived from the parameters of filmmaker intentionality and positionality and thus represent specific discursive stances available to a filmmaker.[5]

Intentional vs. Unintentional Stance

The most general distinction of discursive stances opposes the categories of *intentional* and *unintentional stance*. In making a film, a filmmaker submits to the possibility that he will be construed by participants to some public discourse as intervening in the discourse—regardless of his actual intentions.

In particular, social movements that are locked in a discursive struggle with elites and authorities over some political issue may construe a filmmaker as intervening on their behalf in the struggle. The distinction between intentional and unintentional stances captures two fundamental options concerning filmmaker intentionality: the former category covers the case where the filmmaker intends to intervene; the latter accounts for the case where he is unintentionally drawn into the discourse by (some members of) a social movement.

The locus classicus of social movements enlisting filmmakers against their intentions is the attitude adopted by the film critics of *Cahiers du cinéma* in the early 1970s toward their own former aesthetic predilections. Following the upheavals of May 1968 in France, the *Cahiers* writers sought to align themselves with the French left-wing movement by justifying their film criticism as supporting the Left's struggle against the establishment. To this end, they argued that films like John Ford's *Young Mr. Lincoln* (1939), a traditional Hollywood biopic that they had previously championed on purely aesthetic grounds, could be interpreted as exposing—contrary to initial appearances—the internal contradictions of "the dominant ideology" espoused by the establishment (Bickerton 2006). Thus, in the very catholic view of the *Cahiers* writers, even some seemingly entirely apolitical films were construed as intervening discursively on behalf of the French left-wing movement.

Participatory vs. Transgressive Stance

The category of intentional stance can be subdivided into the categories of *participatory stance* and *transgressive stance*. The distinction, again, bears on the parameter of filmmaker intentionality: participatory stances are stances where the filmmaker intends to actively participate in some discourse; transgressive stances, on the other hand, are stances where the filmmaker intends to expose and transgress prevailing discursive norms and boundaries, rather than submit to them by participating in the discourse. The rationale for assuming a transgressive stance lies in the view that prevailing discursive norms and boundaries are inherently unsuitable to producing good discourse on a given issue. In particular, social movements seeking to challenge elites and authorities may come to the view that current discursive arrangements form a severe obstacle to the success of their efforts. In that case, they may consider it advantageous first to demand a redressing of existing discursive norms and boundaries, rather than engage their opponents in adverse discursive arrangements.[6]

Given this rationale, it is not surprising that the proliferation of movements calling for radical social or political change in the 1960s and 1970s was accompanied by various filmmakers opting for a transgressive stance. For in order to be able to properly discuss such radical change, it was argued, existing discursive practices would have to be changed first. A classic reference point in this regard is an interview of Marcelin Pleynet and Jean Thibaudeau, both members of a French literary avant-garde movement, in *Cinéthique* in 1969 (see Pleynet and Thibaudeau 1969). In this interview, Pleynet and Thibaudeau claimed that the films genuinely advancing the cause of the contemporary French left-wing movement were those that deconstructed the ideological presuppositions concealed in standard modes of filmic representation. Hence, a film's political utility did not depend on what content it conveyed, but whether it questioned conventional modes of conveying content. As an example of a film in which the filmmaker assumes a transgressive stance, Pleynet and Thibaudeau mention *La Méditerranée* (The Mediterranean Sea, 1963) by Jean-Daniel Pollet and Philippe Sollers. The film eschews reference to any overt political content in favor of an emphasis on a highly experimental form, which consists largely of sequences of landscape images.

Yet taking a transgressive stance is not incongruent with reference to political content per se, as evidenced in the films of the Groupe Dziga Vertov such as *Tout va bien* (Everything Is Fine, 1972) and *Letter to Jane* (1972). While the former examines the representation of labor struggles (ranging from traditional union activities to more spontaneous and aggressive forms such as factory occupations) in post–May 1968 France, the latter deconstructs the use of visual imagery in Vietnam War discourse. What qualifies both as examples of a transgressive stance is their investigation, and transgression, of existing discursive norms on disputed political issues.

Partisan vs. Nonpartisan Stance

In the category of participatory stance there is a further distinction between *partisan* and *nonpartisan stance,* which bears on the parameter of filmmaker positionality. Whereas a filmmaker taking a nonpartisan stance purports to approach a given discourse from a neutral point of view, a filmmaker taking a partisan stance does so under a perspective that is biased toward specific sets of political beliefs. We should note that neutrality is not to be read here as implying that a filmmaker who, in making a film, assumes a nonpartisan stance is ever fully impartial. Rather, it should be understood as implying that he holds himself publicly to the standard of impartiality. (Consequently, a filmmaker assuming a nonpartisan stance can sensibly be rebuked for failing to meet that standard. No such reproach can be leveled against a filmmaker with a partisan stance, however, as he acknowledges his partiality.)

A good illustration of why this distinction is relevant is supplied by the evolution of Argentine political cinema in the 1960s and 1970s. A fair amount of early political filmmaking in Argentina was dedicated to documenting, in a more or less ethnographic vein, the social misery in remote provinces of the country. In doing so, the filmmakers can be seen as participating in the discourse on national and economic development that pitted the military establishment and economic liberals against the Peronist movement and a more fragmentary left-wing movement. Typical instances of this cinematic strand are *Ocurrido en Hualfín* (It Happened in Hualfín, 1966) by Raymundo Gleyzer and Jorge Prelorán or *Muerte y pueblo* (Death and Village, 1969), made by Nemesio Juárez with assistance from Gerardo Vallejo. Although these films are plausibly construed as exposing the abject living conditions of the people they portray, their tone remains largely descriptive. *Muerte y pueblo,* for instance, depicts in dispassionate images and commentary the death rites and daily lives of villagers. Thus, these films do not yet offer any indication of the unmistakable political partisanship characteristic of later works by Gleyzer and Vallejo, in which they aligned themselves closely with radical left-wing parties and trade unions.

Party, Movement and Individual Stance

Within the category of partisan stance we can further distinguish between the categories of *party, movement,* and *individual stance.* The distinction, which accounts for the source of partisanship, is based on the parameter of filmmaker positionality. The category of party stance involves a filmmaker assuming a stance that represents the collective political beliefs of some political party (or similarly structurally evolved organization) without any discernible modification. Thus, films in which the filmmaker takes a party stance allow him to contribute to some discourse precisely by giving voice to the discursive position of the institutional actor with which he has aligned himself.

A notable example of party stance is the *Noticiero ICAIC Latinoamericano* newsreels that began to be regularly exhibited in Cuban cinemas in the 1960s. Initiated little more than a year after the Cuban Revolution by ICAIC, the recently established national Cuban film institute, the newsreels were intended as an audiovisual mouthpiece for the Castro-led group Movimiento 26 de julio, which was trying to consolidate its grip on power in the aftermath of the revolution. Another example are the *cinegiornali* newsreels of Terzo Canale, produced between 1968 and 1974 by the Italian Communist Party to diffuse its views on momentous contemporary political events, both domestic and foreign, at a time when political conflict between Italy's Left and Right was rapidly intensifying.

Films in which the filmmaker adopts a movement stance are films whose partisanship is grounded in the collective political beliefs of a social movement. Thus, in a sense, this category serves as an intermediary between the categories of party and individual stance. On the one hand, a filmmaker can only contribute to the goals of a social movement if his partisanship remains in accordance with the collective beliefs espoused by the movement. In this respect, movement stance is similar to party stance. On the other hand, social movements tend to be less cohesive political actors than parties, trade unions, etc. As such, their collective beliefs tend to be more vaguely defined, allowing more leeway for voicing individual opinions.

A typical example of movement stance is Fernando Solanas and Octavio Getino's *La hora de los hornos* (The Hour of the Furnaces, 1968), which analyzes the events in recent Argentine history that led to the ousting of Perón from his presidency by a military coup and weighs various strategies for the Peronist movement to reclaim power. Solanas and Getino provide their analysis while identifying themselves as part of the movement. Moreover, as noted above, through the late 1960s to the early 1970s, several other influential figures in Argentine political cinema underwent a shift in participatory stance, as filmmakers like Gerardo Vallejo and Raymundo Gleyzer turned from films displaying a nonpartisan stance to films displaying a movement stance. For instance, in 1971 Vallejo made *El camino hacia la muerte del Viejo Reales* (Viejo Reales's Long Way Journey to Death), which threw its weight behind the reinvigorated Peronist movement, and especially currents around FOTIA, a powerful sugarcane workers' union in the country's northwest. In a similar vein, Raymundo Gleyzer's Cine de la base films reveal close ties to the FAS movement, a short-lived socialist conglomerate of parties, trade unions, and guerrilla groups.

Finally, films in which the filmmaker adopts an individual stance are those in which a filmmaker's individual political beliefs serve as the source of partisanship, in contrast to the collective beliefs of a party or movement. A case in point would be some of Joris Ivens and Marceline Loridan's Asian films from 1965 to 1976, such as *Le dix-septième parallèle: La guerre du peuple* (The Seventeenth Parallel: The People's War, 1967), in which the filmmakers depict the daily hardships of North Vietnamese villagers at the border of the demarcation line between North and South Vietnam, or *Le peuple et ses fusils* (The People and Their Guns, 1970), which shows the life of Pathet Lao guerrillas in underground caves during the Laotian civil war. What makes such films plausible specimens for films with individual stance is that the partisanship evident in the films reflects Ivens and Loridan's own political beliefs, rather than merely reiterating those of the North Vietnamese government, Pathet Lao, or the French antiwar movement.[7]

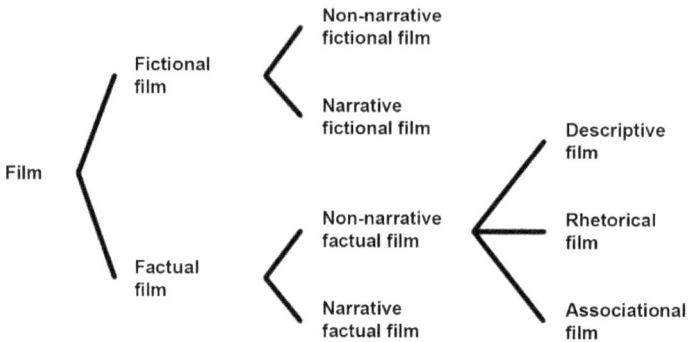

Figure 11.2. Tree Diagram of Categories of Film

Second Taxonomic Tier: The Film

In this section I turn to the set of categories associated with the second tier (see figure 11.2), which corresponds to the film component in the framework. The categories are derived from the parameters of filmic reference mode and content structure and thus represent specific types of films that the filmmaker can use to contribute to discourse.

Factual vs. Fictional Film

The most general distinction among types of film, which involves the parameter of filmic reference mode, is that between *factual* and *fictional film*. The difference between these two categories is that factual films refer to actual persons, events, and circumstances in an unmediated way, whereas fictional films do not. As a result, a film that presents itself as factual (e.g., by displaying the conventional hallmarks of a documentary) incurs a commitment to depicting only factual content. What implications such a commitment entails exactly is in practice often a source of considerable dispute. While there is broad agreement over requirements such as that persons be represented as possessing precisely those elementary personal characteristics that they actually possess (e.g., someone represented as a factory worker on strike should actually be a factory worker on strike, and not someone impersonating a factory worker on strike or an actual factory worker playing to be on strike), other aspects seem more controversial. (For instance, to what extent is it acceptable to stage particular scenes for greater rhetorical concision, or to reenact scenes that were not filmed when they originally occurred?)[8]

Although fictional films do not refer to actual persons, events, and circumstances as directly as factual films, it does not follow that fictional films cannot relate to actual events and persons in ways that would be relevant to social movements for political claim making. Besides very general allusions to contentious political events or discourse, which often require substantial interpretive work on the part of audiences to perceive the intended connection, there are myriad strategies for filmmakers to link fictional content to actual events more conspicuously. I shall illustrate this point with two examples.

The first example is *Theptida rongraem* (Hotel Angel, 1974), a Thai film made by Chatrichalerm Yukol one year after student protesters had successfully put an end to nearly two decades of military dictatorship and ushered in a period of democratic reform in Thailand. Though seemingly a story about a provincial girl's trials and tribulations in Bangkok, a skillful montage sequence toward the end interlaces the girl's struggle with documentary footage of the student protests, thereby implying an alignment between her path toward individual emancipation with Thai society's path toward political emancipation. In *Theptida rongraem,* therefore, the connection between fictional filmic content and political reality rests on the audience's ability to appreciate the analogy offered in a single key sequence in the film. The second example consists of another Thai fictional film, *Tongpan* (1977), which exhibits many stylistic features characteristic of factual films despite the explicit staging of scenes. Even though our suspicions about the exact status of the scenes, many of which are in fact reenactments of actual events, are never fully resolved, this state of limbo reinforces the impression that the depicted events have a close bearing on political reality.

Narrative vs. Nonnarrative Factual Film

Within factual film we can further distinguish between the categories of *narrative* and *nonnarrative factual film.* This distinction bears on the parameter of filmic content structure: narrative factual films are factual films whose content structure is predominantly in a narrative mode, while nonnarrative factual films are factual films whose content is structured according to nonnarrative principles. More precisely, we can characterize narrative factual films as factual films that embed characters in well-defined spatial settings and arrange events involving these characters into well-defined temporal sequences. Thus, the stories of this type of film involve the development of characters and events along fairly conspicuous spatial and temporal dimensions.[9]

As typical examples of narrative factual film about specific protest events we can mention films by Guillermo Cahn, Carlos Flores, and Samuel Carvajal, such as *Casa o mierda* (Home or Shit, 1970) or *Nutuayin Mapu, recuperemos nuestra tierra* (We Reclaim our Land, 1971). Produced shortly after the Unidad Popular coalition of left-wing parties came into government for the first time in Chile, these films depict land occupation operations instigated by radical left-wing opposition movements like MIR, which tried to force the newly elected government's hand on the long-disputed issue of land reform. In *Casa o mierda,* for example, we first see images of daily life in one of the shantytowns (poblaciones) on the outskirts of Santiago. The next scenes show how some of the residents start organizing, with the help of MIR cadres, a nightly land seizure operation. The film ends with large numbers of people thronging the freshly occupied land, thus establishing a perspicuous story arc.

Rhetorical, Associational, and Descriptive Film

The category of nonnarrative factual film can be divided into the following subcategories: *descriptive, rhetorical,* and *associational film.* Descriptive films are films that depict events and characters' actions in well-defined spatial settings, but do not arrange them into well-defined temporal sequences. Frequent examples are found among (quasi-)ethnographic films such as *Muerte y pueblo* (see description above), which shows scenes of the villagers' life and rituals without relating the scenes to each other by means of an overarching temporal structure. The film remains, for instance, ambiguous as to the time frame in which the depicted events take place.

The category of rhetorical film comprises films that, unlike narrative films, are structured in accordance with rhetorical principles such as argument and counterargument. Given the generality of these principles, rhetorical films often marshal a wide range of events and characters, situated at divergent locations and times, in support of its central argument. The unifying thread connecting events and characters is typically provided through voice-over commentary or intertitles. A classic example in this respect is Solanas and Getino's *La hora de los hornos,* which provides a vast panorama of Argentine politics in the thirteen years following Perón's removal from the presidency through a coup in 1955, followed by tentative arguments about how Peronism might successfully reclaim power. The arrangement of its content based on rhetorical principles is particularly apparent in the first part, which is segmented into several chapters aiming to explore the symptoms of neocolonialism in Argentine society.

Associational films differ from the previous two categories in that they are neither descriptional nor are they structured on the basis of rhetorical principles. Instead, associational films try to establish a single argumentative point or theme—frequently through juxtaposing images and sound/music while relying little via spoken or written commentary. Prime examples of associational films are some of the short films Santiago Álvarez made for the Cuban film institute, such as *Now* (1965) or *L.B.J.* (1968). *Now,* for instance, constitutes a propagandistic attack on racial discrimination in the United States, showing through a montage of images the abuse suffered by blacks at the hands of white police. The juxtaposition of these images with the unequivocal lyrics of an Afro-American protest song serves as a call to decisive action against racial injustice.[10]

Narrative vs. Nonnarrative Fictional Film

As for fictional films, it is evident that the overwhelming majority of them are narrative. Indeed, narrative fictional films are so ubiquitous that one might wonder whether there exist instances of nonnarrative fictional films at all. One example may be Jacques Doillon's *L'an 01* (The Year 01, 1973), a fictitious account of the entire world abandoning any form of organized society. The film provides a panorama of life in this utopian state in the style of a traditional report on factual events. Considering that the film moves from one character to the next, without establishing the type of temporal sequences among depicted events that are characteristic of narrative films, we seem justified in classifying *L'an 01* as both fictional and nonnarrative. Another example is Rodolfo Kuhn's *Prologue* to the collective work *Argentina, mayo 1969: Los caminos de la liberación* (Argentina, May 1969: The Paths of Liberation, 1969). Kuhn's film offers a fictitious (and highly satirical) account of the authoritarian nature of contemporary Argentina under the military's rule from the perspective of a pigeon. Central to the film is the idea to offer a panoramic view of Argentine society from an unusual perspective. As such, its content is arranged more in accordance with descriptive or rhetorical film, rather than narrative film. Thus, we can view Kuhn's *Prologue* as another example of nonnarrative fictional film.

Third Taxonomic Tier: The Projection Venue

Finally, we turn to the set of categories tied to the third tier (see figure 11.3), which corresponds to the projection venue component in the framework. The categories are derived from the parameters of projection venue accessibility and regularity, and thus represent specific types of projection venue in which the filmmaker may choose to screen his film.

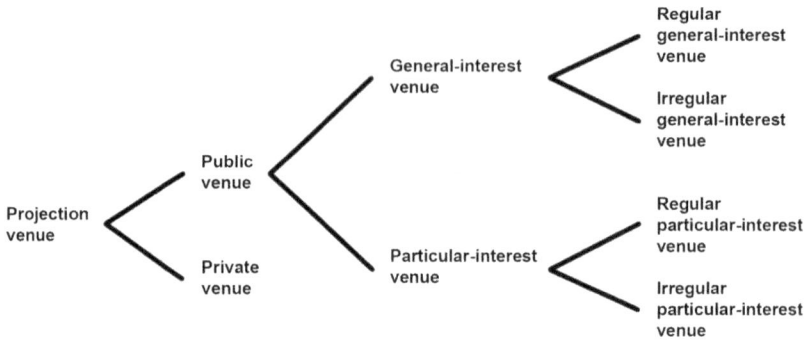

Figure 11.3. Tree Diagram of Categories of Projection Venue

Public vs. Private Venue

The first distinction, which is based on the parameter of projection venue accessibility, opposes the categories of *public* and *private venues.* By private venues we mean projection venues with a highly restrictive accessibility, where access tends to be denied to all but those audience members that are actively admitted by gatekeepers. Public venues, on the other hand, comprise all those projection venues with no such restrictions.

Given that private venues are marked by highly selective accessibility, private venues are important for two reasons. First, restrictions on what films may be shown are generally much weaker for them than in the case of public venues. Consequently, films that have been banned from public venues may still be shown in private venues. This was the case, for example, with *Pueblo armado* (A People in Arms, 1961), a film made by Joris Ivens shortly after the Cuban Revolution during his visit to the island. Amid heightening tensions in the confrontation between Cuba and the United States, the French authorities decided to bar *Pueblo armado* from being shown in easily accessible public venues, on account of its unmitigated pro-Cuban partisanship. Instead, it had to be screened behind closed doors at a French-Cuban association in Paris (cf. Schoots 1995). Second, the restrictive accessibility of private venues can be turned into an advantage by specifically targeting select groups of decision makers that wield substantial influence on policy issues addressed by a film. An example of a film that was used in this way is *Tongpan* (see description above). Initially, *Tongpan,* which takes aim at the exclusive nature of the deliberative process on the utility of a large-scale dam-building project for national economic development, was intended as a critical contribution to development debates that took place in Thailand in the brief democratic reform period between 1973 and 1976. The film, however, was also given a screening at the World Bank headquarters in Washington DC (see Peagam 1979).

General Interest vs. Particular Interest Venue

Public venues can be subdivided into the categories of *general interest* and *particular interest venues*. This distinction, borrowed from Jacobs (2005), bears on the parameter of projection venue accessibility and is analogous to the more familiar opposition between broadcasting and narrowcasting media. Roughly, general interest venues provide access to heterogeneous and potentially unrestricted audiences, while particular interest venues give access to socially, occupationally, or otherwise circumscribed segments of society. Among both types of projection venue we can further distinguish between regular and irregular venues—a distinction bearing on the parameter of projection venue regularity.

Regular vs. Irregular General Interest Venue

The category of *regular general interest venue* comprises general interest venues that exhibit films on a regular basis. This usually also implies a fixed location for screening. Prototypical examples of such venues are ordinary movie theaters, art house cinemas, etc. Venues of this category offer the advantage that films are more frequently accessible and thus offer the possibility of relatively large audiences, which however makes them also more vulnerable to censorship from authorities and negative intervention from opposed pressure groups. Consequently, filmmakers may have to moderate their discursive stance in order to gain access to such venues. In addition, there are further, perhaps less obvious constraints. For instance, since regular general interest venues are primarily used for entertainment, it is not surprising, given the close connection between narrativity, fictionality, and entertainment, that the majority of films showing at these venues are narrative fictional films. Thus, aiming for access to regular general interest venues may impose considerable constraints on the types of film from which a filmmaker can choose for his discursive intervention.

In contrast, the category of *irregular general interest venue* comprises general interest venues that function as projection venues on an irregular basis. The range of irregularity may vary from occasional to one-time venues. Besides circumstances where they are the only means to guarantee film supply to certain areas, mobile cinemas have also been used in industrialized countries to show films that were barred from more regular venues. An example in this respect is *Sekigun—PFLP: Sekai senso sengen* (Red Army—PFLP:

Declaration of World War, 1971) by Wakamatsu Koji and Adachi Masao. Seeing no chance of screening their film at regular general interest venues, the authors set up a mobile projection unit touring Japan to show the film at universities and other public institutions (see Hirasawa 2003). Thus, irregular general interest venues frequently become attractive when regular ones are not accessible, because interference from authorities and pressure groups tends to be much weaker.

Regular vs. Irregular Particular Interest Venue

The category of *regular particular interest venue* consists of venues that cater on a regular basis to particular social groups. Typical examples of such venues are universities, schools, or union halls. To be sure, the degree of regularity attained by all but few such venues is substantially lower than that of most regular general interest venues. Furthermore, some venues such as universities or schools may be used to cater either to a wider public (general interest) or exclusively to students (particular interest). As examples we can name *Assatsu no mori* (Forest of Oppression, 1967) and *Gennin Hokokusho* (Report from Haneda, 1967), which were made by Ogawa Shinsuke together with core members of the student collective Jieiso. Jieiso employed its extensive network among university students to distribute the films from its Tokyo headquarters to universities throughout the country (see Nornes 2007). According to an internal year-end report by the collective, in one month alone *Assatsu no mori* had "around sixty screenings in every part of Japan" (Nornes 2007: 48). What is remarkable is not only the expanse of Jieiso's network but also the regularity with which it was tapped for various films in support of the Japanese student movement throughout the years, as it evolved into Ogawa Productions.

Finally, the category of *irregular particular interest venue* consists of venues that cater to particular groups on an irregular basis. Such venues tend to impose the least constraints on films compared to other types of projection venues, since their irregular nature and circumscribed audiences lower possibilities as well as incentives for authorities or pressure groups to intervene in their projection. For that reason, this category is a favored type of venue with political actors seeking to address large audiences without the knowledge of authorities. On the one hand, particular interest venues are still directed toward sizeable audiences in comparison with private venues. On the other hand, they are less exposed to outside intervention than either general interest or regular particular interest venues. An example for this category is supplied by the projection practices of Grupo Pueblo de Rosario, the mobile projection group that assumed the task of secretly showing *La hora de los hornos* in the Argentine city of Rosario between 1968 and 1972. In an internal memorandum, the group describes its efforts to separately target three distinct social strata in different types of locations: artists, intellectuals, and professionals in middle-class family homes; high school and university students at universities, schools, and in the homes of militant students; and workers and other youth in union halls and in working class neighborhoods (see Mestman 2001). While the first type of location can be analyzed as private venues, the other two types of locations provide examples of irregular particular interest venues.[11]

Conclusion

The taxonomy presented in this chapter furnishes three tiers of categories for analyzing how social movements used cinema in the 1960s and 1970s for political claim making. Every possible such use can therefore be viewed as instantiating a triad of categories, one in each tier. Take, for instance, *La hora de los hornos* by Solanas and Getino, which, as discussed above, arguably falls into the categories of movement stance and rhetorical film with respect to the first and second tiers. In addition, the film was screened by a mobile projection group in irregular particular interest venues. Hence, one use that Solanas and Getino made with *La hora de los hornos* for political claim making can be described as instantiating a categorial triad of *movement stance/rhetorical film/irregular particular interest venue.* But we also noted that the mobile projection group showed the film to diverse audiences in different locations. Some locations constituted irregular particular interest venues; other locations (such as the middle-class family homes used for showing it to artists, intellectuals, and professionals) count rather as private venues. Hence, another use made *of La hora de los hornos* for political claim making can be analyzed as instantiating a categorial triad of *movement stance/rhetorical film/private venue.*

In discussing various examples of films above, I attempted to illustrate how, for each tier, the selection of categories enables one to make sense of films as discursive interventions in the political struggles of social movements. The empirical salience of individual categories will of course have to be evaluated on the basis of additional filmic examples. There is also scope for further conceptual refinement as regards individual categories. I noted, for instance, that the parameter of filmic reference mode, with its basic distinction between factual and fictional films, remains still relatively underdeveloped. Finally, I was able to forge some conceptual connections between cinema and other mass media. There are two ways in which this taxonomy achieves that. First, the taxonomy is based on a framework derived from a general model of public discourse. In this model cinema is but one specific public forum; the parameters of the taxonomic framework are thus also generalizable to other public forums. Second, the selection of categories was such that many categories should be pertinent for application to other types of mass media.

Acknowledgments

A preliminary draft of this chapter was presented at a conference at Volda University College, Norway (26–28 November 2008). I would like to thank the organizers for their invitation and the participants in the panel discussion for helpful suggestions. I would also like to express my gratitude to Mariano Mestman, who generously provided me with difficult-to-locate material on Argentine political cinema, and Paijong Laisakul, for discussing with me the finer points of Thai political cinema in the 1970s. Finally, I would like to thank Kathrin Fahlenbrach for her editorial guidance and commentaries on several different drafts.

Notes

1. This threefold scheme ought to be regarded only as a rough indication of the variety of social movements relevant here, as it would otherwise obscure consideration of many other movements. In the United States, for instance, one may think of the civil rights movement, the peace movement, or the women's movement. The closest umbrella term for the entire class of relevant social movements is, to my knowledge, Immanuel Wallerstein's notion of antisystemic movement (see Wallerstein 2002).

2. For a detailed account of political uses of cinema by, for example, the US labor movement in the first two decades of the twentieth century, see Ross (1991).

3. The name for the model is mine; the authors do not seem to reserve for the model any specific term. Furthermore, it should be observed that this presentation of the model deviates in some respects from the original model. For comparison with the original, see Gamson (2004: 242–43) and Ferree, Gamson, Gerhards, and Rucht (2002b: 9–13).

4. Note that my talk of speaker and filmmaker is rather generic here. There is no need for a speaker or filmmaker to be an individual. They could just as well be some collective actor such as a political party, trade union, or a writers/filmmakers collective.

5. I shall discuss examples of films predominantly for categories at terminal nodes in the tree diagrams in figures 11.1, 11.2, and 11.3, as they can also serve as examples for higher categories.

6. There is a connection between transgressive stance and so-called constructionist discourse theories. Constructionist theories—whose pivotal figure is Michel Foucault and whose proponents include Nancy Fraser, Seyla Benhabib, or Iris Marion

Young—emphasize how discursive structures are shaped by mechanisms of power. Consequently, discourses are not simply unencumbered exchanges of opinion, but may reflect through their structure prevailing power relations among discourse participants. For constructionists, good discourse is therefore not merely a matter of discussing political issues within a given discursive setting; it also involves exposing hidden inequalities in discursive structures (see Ferree et al. 2002a).

7. Much of what generally counts as propaganda film probably falls into the category of partisan stance. Yet, these two concepts are not identical. Propaganda normally refers to a specific way of arguing for an opinion (i.e., by appealing to emotions rather than rational argument and by providing distorted or one-sided information). Partisan stance, on the other hand, refers to a filmmaker siding with a particular discourse participant on some contested issue—regardless of rhetorical style.

8. The term "factual film" is preferred over the term "documentary" because it is the proper complement of fictional film (i.e., factual films are distinct from fictional films only in terms of their reference mode.) The term "documentary," on the other hand, gained currency in the 1920s and 1930s to denote nonfictional films with certain stylistic ambitions as opposed to more prosaic types of nonfictional films called actualities—a meaning which it has largely retained (see Wolfe 1993).

9. For further elaboration of the concept of narration, see Bordwell and Thompson (2001: chap. 3).

10. The categories of associational and rhetorical films are inspired by similar categories found in Bordwell and Thompson (2001: chap. 5). While the notion of rhetorical film here is more or less synonymous with the corresponding notion in Bordwell and Thompson, the notion of associational film here incorporates what Bordwell and Thompson call abstract, categorical, and associational films.

11. Jacobs (2005) suggests three pairs of categories (nonpartisan vs. advocacy media, news vs. fictional media, and general interest vs. particular interest media) for differentiating between types of mass media. Jacobs's taxonomy formed an important source of inspiration, which can be seen from the fact that his pairs of categories correspond to the tiers/components of public forums here.

Bibliography

Bickerton, E. 2006. "Adieu to *Cahiers.*" *New Left Review* 42 (November–December): 69–97.

Bordwell, D., and K. Thompson. 2001. *Film Art: An Introduction.* 6th ed. New York: McGraw-Hill.

Ferree, M. M., W. A. Gamson, J. Gerhards, and D. Rucht. 2002a. "Four Models of the Public Sphere." *Theory & Society* 31, no. 3 (June): 289–324.

Ferree, M. M., W. A. Gamson, J. Gerhards, and D. Rucht. 2002b. *Shaping Abortion Discourse: Democracy and the Public Sphere in Germany and the United States.* Cambridge: Cambridge University Press.

Gamson, W. A. 2004. "Bystanders, Public Opinion and the Media." In *The Blackwell Companion to Social Movements,* ed. Snow, D. A., S. A. Soule and H. Kriesi. Oxford: Blackwell Publishing.

Hirasawa, G. 2003. "Ecstasy of the Angels." In *Art Theatre Guild: Unabhängiges japanisches Kino 1962–1984,* ed. R. Domenig. Vienna: Vienna International Film Festival.

Iskra. 2006. *Les Groupes Medvedkine.* Booklet in DVD collection. Paris: Éditions Montparnasse.

Jacobs, R. N. 2005. "Media Culture(s) and Public Life." In *The Blackwell Companion to the Sociology of Culture,* ed. M. Jacobs and N. W. Hanrahan. Oxford: Blackwell Publishing.

Mestman, M. 2001. "La exhibición del cine militante." In *La herida de las sombras,* ed. Colorado, L. F. and P.C. Cantero. Madrid: Academia de las Artes y las Ciencias Cinematográficas de España. Actas del VIII Congreso de la Asociación Española de Historiadores de Cine (AEHC).

Nornes, A. M. 2007. *Forest of Pressure: Ogawa Shinsuke and Postwar Japanese Documentary.* Minneapolis: University of Minnesota Press.

Peagam, N. 1979. "'Tongpan': A Cinema Review." *Bulletin of Concerned Asian Scholars* 11, no. 1 (January–March): 32–51.

Pleynet, M., and J. Thibaudeau. 1969. "Économique, idéologique, formel … entretien realisé par Gérard Le Blanc." *Cinéthique* 3: 7–14.

Ross, S. J. 1991. "Struggles for the Screen: Workers, Radicals, and the Political Uses of Silent Film." *American Historical Review* 96, no. 2 (April): 333–67.

Schoots, H. 1995. *Gevaarlijk leven: Een biografie van Joris Ivens.* Amsterdam: Uitgeverij Jan Mets.

Wallerstein, I. 2002. "New Revolts Against the System." *New Left Review* 18 (November–December): 29–39.

Wolfe, C. 1993. "The Poetics and Politics of Nonfiction: Documentary Film." In *Grand Design: Hollywood as Modern Business Enterprise, 1930–1939,* ed. T. Balio. American Cinema History Series 5. New York: Charles Scribner's Sons.

Chapter 12

Challenging Television's Revolution
Media Representations of 1968 Protests in Television and Tabloids

Todd Michael Goehle

This chapter surveys the media politics surrounding West German public television and its representation of social and student protest movements around 1968. The meanings attached to public television and its representation of social and student protest did not develop in isolation but rather inside a dynamic media system, one in which numerous interests, including television personalities, print elites, social and student activists, and audiences, looked to satisfy political agendas and entertainment desires from varying sites of power. Diverse personal factors, for example, an individual's political ideology, status in media conflicts, and media preferences, also shaped representations of social and student protest. Additionally, television aesthetics and journalistic standards blurred the lines between information and sensation. As this chapter details, the emotions associated with television representations of 1968 resulted from not only the viewer's opinion of student and social protest but also the individual's relationship with the television medium.

Popular histories of the period surrounding 1968 depict television as a revolutionary medium that altered West German politics with its ability to cross time and space and to deliver visual news coverage in the home. Offering greater nuance, the media historian Meike Vogel distinguishes between the television medium, which could serve a democratizing function by allowing a plurality of responses about student and social protest, and the televisual message. Among other insights, Vogel argues that television executives, in response to the violence that followed the shooting of West German Sozialistische Deutsche Studentenbund (The German Socialist Student League, SDS) leader Rudi Dutschke in April 1968, normalized the view that the Außerparlamentarische Opposition (Extra Parliamentary Opposition, APO) was a left-wing student movement opposed to parliamentary rule and in the process overlooked the APO's heterogeneous identities (Vogel 2005, 2006).

On this latter point, Vogel is similar to, albeit less deterministic than, Todd Gitlin, the student activist turned sociologist who assessed the ways in which television networks framed representations of the American Students for a Democractic Society (SDS) (1980). Social movement scholars have revisited and revised Gitlin's approach, tacitly confirming that television placed limits on the representation of activism and yet remained malleable to subversive politics (Gitlin 1980). Kathrin Fahlenbrach, for example, explores how West German student and social activists defined and influenced their targeted television public, youth audiences, through their clothing, language, and use of gesture (Fahlenbrach 2001). West Germany's 1968 became "a revolt against the media and a revolt by means of media," (Fahlenbrach 2001: 179) an idea echoed by the "chronicler of 1968," Wolfgang Kraushaar (Kraushaar 2001: 317–47).

Increasingly, German historians have also situated television representations of 1968 in a broader frame of media transformation, generational change, and post–Third Reich democratization. Christina von Hodenberg credits the progressivism exhibited by many of the era's media personalities and products not to the activism of 1968 but rather to a larger process of media democratization beginning in the late 1950s, when *zeitkritisch* journalism (critical-contemporary journalism) challenged the antitotalitarian[1] and consensus-forming rhetoric of Cold War conservatives and media elites (von Hodenberg 2006). Von Hodenberg also convincingly reveals how *zeitkritisch* journalism made positive contributions to the development of West Germany's democratic political culture through its willingness to discuss taboo topics such as everyday life in East Germany, the preparedness of the West German military, and, eventually, the student movement. Still, questions remain about the audiences responsible for the genre's popularity. Acknowledging von Hodenberg's impressive examination of numerous mediums, Corey Ross nonetheless believes she deploys a too narrow focus on "serious journalism and critique" and downplays the influence of important "market segments such as the tabloid sector" (Ross 2008: 306–9). Inspired by both Ross's criticisms and von Hodenberg's multiple media approach, this chapter reveals the extent to which traditional sources of news and information, including television news programs and documentaries but also print tabloids and programming guides, shaped public opinion in and around 1968.[2]

There are a number of reasons that justify my inclusion of these latter sources in general and the publications of Springer Verlag, including the tabloid *Bild-Zeitung* and the broadcast guide *Hörzu*, in particular. First, Springer Verlag and *zeitkritisch* television programs frequently engaged in bitter debates about the politics of post-WWII reform. Unsurprisingly, such battles also occurred over each medium's coverage of 1960s activism. Thus, representations of student and social protest not only offer commentaries about contemporary activism but also insights into cross-media rivalries. Second, Springer's tabloids and television guides dominated their respective markets and were influential conservative voices in West German media. Despite the publications' sensationalism, many readers consumed Springer Verlag's negative coverage about radical activism and public television, making the tabloids important sources for television criticism. Lastly, unlike traditional forms of print media, which emphasized text over image, Springer's broadcast guides and tabloids created layouts with effects closely comparable to the visual aesthetics of television. In ways similar to television, tabloids were believed to trigger sudden emotions and create an "intense" media experience for the user (Goehle 2009: 125–27).

Ultimately, however, the comparative, multimedia approach used in this chapter allows for a more nuanced view of the motives and responses that shaped West German television's representations of social and student protest. Certainly, television executives, officials, and reporters believed the medium to be a vehicle that could champion democratic impulses, educate audiences about important political issues, and assist West Germany in overcoming its authoritarian past. Still, broadcast policies that promoted politically diverse programming and forums, when combined with television's willingness to broadcast social and student activists, left the medium vulnerable to the subversive acts of protestors, accusations of political bias, and claims that its news coverage threatened the stability of West German democracy. Here especially, the legacies of the Third Reich, the Nazi Party's use of media and mass spectacle, and the effects of these devices on German citizens, loomed large. Despite the public officials' best intentions, television representations of student and social protest, with few exceptions, appear to have seldom altered the opinions of viewers outside of a program's intended audience. Rather, in many instances, television representations about student and social protest seemingly reinforced the audience's preexisting political biases. While this chapter's investigation into television representations of student and social protest reveals the primary intentions of television reporters and executives, it also exposes the hardening opinions of media competitors, diverse media publics, and consumers.

Television and Springer Verlag before the Student Movement

Beginning in the late 1950s, institutional, technological, and professional developments helped make public television a preferred medium for news and entertainment. The introduction of Magnetic Recording Technology (MAZ) in 1959 allowed the regional branches of the ARD (The Working group of public-law broadcasting institutions of the Federal Republic of Germany) to record, reproduce, and store live film footage with greater ease and a higher degree of quality (Hickethier 1998: 123). The initial broadcasts of the second public television network, ZDF (Second German Television), in April 1963 as well as a third channel of programming first offered in 1964 encouraged greater competition and improvement in the television product. Introduced in August 1967, color television also raised viewer expectations and intensified production demands. Specifically, the growth of the medium increased costs and demanded greater specialization among members of the production staff, developments that placed additional pressures upon writers, directors, and editors (Zielinski 1993: 153).

These improvements secured viewership and affected how audiences thought about other forms of media. Assessing television's meteoric rise, media scholar Siegfried Drescher believed the mix of the verbal and the visual would reduce the viability of competing media forms over time and make television an overwhelmingly more believable source of information than newspapers or radio broadcasts (Drescher 1968: 3). For Drescher, television's ability to trigger a viewer's emotions was key. While admittedly lacking empirical evidence to support these claims, researchers such as Drescher found television, unlike other media, "struck the human ability to experience" and sought ways to measure this effect (Drescher 1968: 3).

The popularity of television, combined with an economic recession that caused a spike in already mounting production costs, concerned many in the print industry, including the owner of Springer Verlag, Axel Springer. Accused by many *zeitkritisch* journalists and student activists of owning a media monopoly and in turn manipulating public opinion, Springer possessed mixed motives. On the one hand, Springer was fearful of lost revenues. On the other hand, Springer wished to expand his influence across media and into television. Subsequently, Springer championed reforms that would lead to the privatization of public television. *Bild-Zeitung*'s editors published stories questioning public television policies and channeling the financial concerns of the tabloid's lower-middle-class audiences.[3] References to "customers," "competition," and "rights" portrayed television's executives as despotic.[4] Allusions to rights also raised questions of fairness and objectivity, claims that stemmed from the growing influence of the Social Democrats (SPD) and progressively minded officials in public television administrations. Grievances were expressed privately as well. In June 1967, Springer complained bitterly to Christian Democratic (CDU/CSU) party officials about a political bias existent among broadcast officials, who accepted the programming petitions of liberal and left-of-center printers but ignored similar proposals by Springer (Springer 1967). Likewise, conservative television officials exaggerated their alarm about the "ultra-left Mafia" that "had cunningly isolated the influence of CDU broadcast directors and advisor boards" and pursued a "neo-Marxist reeducation of the German people" (*Exclusiv-Dienst* 1967: 12). Even before 1968, then, right-of-center fears about the left-leaning politics of public television were well-established. Such fears only intensified when television officials proved willing to broadcast a wide range of news and opinions about student and social protests.

Television Representations of 1968

As stated in the introduction, *zeitkritisch* television programming aired controversial political topics that were intended to engage and provide audiences with the information needed to make educated political decisions. Perhaps the best-known of these programs was *Panorama*. Under moderator Peter Merseburger, *Panorama* willingly discussed SDS- and APO-related issues, provided critical remarks following the death of student protestor Benno Ohnesorg on 2 June 1967, and presented reports on anti–Vietnam War and anti–Emergency Laws protests (Lampe and Schumacher 1991: 171, 177). *Panorama* also offered extensive commentary about the Easter protests of 1968, when students and social activists engaged in massive street demonstrations after the attempted assassination of SDS leader Rudi Dutschke. Rumors that the shooter drew inspiration from Springer publications inflamed passions and inspired some protestors to attack Springer property. In subsequent weeks, *Panorama* blamed *Bild-Zeitung* for the violence, an argument that drew upon the tabloid and the program's contentious past.[5]

In their quest to provide controversial yet critically informative programming, *zeitkritisch* journalists pursued interviews with charismatic protest leaders such as Dutschke. Fearing such dialogues falsely promoted the individual over the group and thus contradicted the antiauthoritarian principles of the APO, Dutschke nonetheless understood television's ability to reach large audiences and subsequently agreed to appear on the 3 December 1967 edition of *Zu Protokoll* with host Günter Gaus. As argued by Fahlenbrach, Dutschke, like other activists, developed a series of dissent strategies that were attuned to the standards and aesthetics of the television medium (2001: 179). Using emotionally charged rhetoric and demonstrative body language, Dutschke contrasted the somber and relatively passionless tone exhibited by Gaus, who championed the progressive ideals of *zeitkritisch* journalism by expressing his hope that the interview would provide information for his viewing audience (von Hodenberg 2006: 407). Contrasts in lighting and long-standing camera shots also contributed a sense of intimacy that activated viewers' emotions and evoked sympathy for the student leader (Fahlenbrach 2001: 205–11). In their attempts to provide provocative programming, *zeitkritisch* journalists directly as well as inadvertently provided mediated sites of dissent in which students and social activists could challenge West German politics and media structures.

Domestic politics was not the only topic broached by television. For example, the *zeitkritisch* program *Report* detailed a variety of emerging international countercultures, including "San Francisco Hippies, LSD trips, Rockers, and the Amsterdam based Provos movement" (von Hodenberg 2006: 407). Similar to Merseburger, the journalists of *Report* presented stories that seemingly blurred information and personal opinion. In a story on San Francisco's hippies, *Report*'s Dagobert Lindlau presented himself as both an expert and a sympathizer of the counterculture by enjoying a drive over the Golden Gate Bridge in a Ford Mustang convertible and listening to Jimi Hendrix's "Purple Haze," among other activities (Lampe 2000: 156–60). Mixing personal experience, critical engagement, and an interest in taboo political topics, *zeitkritisch* programs retained progressively minded audiences and yet provided critics with "evidence" of collusion between television and student activists.

Presenting student-based dissent was not the same as supporting it, however. Although the situationist-inspired provocations of *Kommune I* attracted a great deal of attention, many television commentators dismissed the antiauthoritarian commune's provocations and contended, "the love of crude humor covered up their real goals and made good-intentions unbelievable" (quoted in Vogel 2005: 161). Opportunities also existed for opponents of student activism. Axel Springer willingly participated in a planned 28 August 1968 television special, "A Few Days in the Life of Axel Springer."[6] The program sought to communicate Springer's core beliefs on "the problem of Israel, co-determination, Berlin, social politics, and finally the press" and also to reinforce comments he made in an interview on 8 February 1968 with ZDF reporter Klaus Harpprecht (Böddeker 1968). For Springer, such opportunities provided the chance to generate public support and to present himself as a "symbolic figure of the Bundesrepublik" (Böddeker 1968).

Television administrators also allowed for critiques of their own medium. As both a reporter for Springer Verlag's respectable daily *Die Welt* and a contributor to the ARD, Matthias Walden declared in a 29 May 1968 televised report "Appraisal: Youth Rebellion,"

> the radical rebellion, ladies and gentlemen, rehearses the overthrow of a society, in which the Revolutionaries do not sit in prison, but in

front of the television camera, benevolently publicized, presented, applauded, so that they continue to be experienced over the course of this program as wholly typical. (NDR 1974)

For Walden, television normalized student violence, an argument juxtaposed by images of open fires and burning newspapers, symbols that visually awakened memories of the book-burning ceremonies of National Socialism (Vogel 2005: 161). This mixture of language and image criminalized, if not fully demonized, student protestors as "left fascists" (NDR 1974), a familiar antitotalitarian trope that complemented the consensus-seeking denouncements of conservative politicians and publications, including *Bild-Zeitung*. Walden's denouncements of both student and social movements and public television revealed the era's diverse programming and also complemented the negative representations of the television medium and student protest previously presented in Springer-owned publications.

Tabloid Representations of Television and 1968

Long before Walden's comments, *Bild-Zeitung* and *Hörzu* engaged in wider debates about student protest and the television medium. Specifically, these publications commonly quoted conservative commentators who criticized television's relationship with student and social activism and represented the medium as one capable of reawakening the "irrational emotions" associated with the Third Reich. The commentary of Helmut Thielicke, an outspoken television critic, student movement opponent, and theologian, typified this latter memory constellation. Released just prior to Dutschke's interview with Gaus in 1967, Thielicke's article "Rap the Fingers of Television" attacked television's presentation of radical activism and especially its quest for scandal and sensation. According to Thielicke, television enabled student violence and in the process threatened West German democracy. Similar to Walden, Thielicke believed camera shots and editing techniques allowed "the exception to appear as the rule" and provided the "exception an inflated publicity" (Thielicke 1969: 96). Amounting to a reactionary rendition of McLuhan's "the medium is the message," Thielicke feared that

an optically generated, visual neurosis threatens to fall forever upon us. For Germans this is particularly dangerous, because one deteriorates with greater ease into uncontrollable emotion in this country than elsewhere. With it, the television appears not only to *report* the story—distortedly!—but also to *make* the story. Television not only visually depicts the confusion, but it creates and intensifies it. The Radikalinski rehearses the emergency and the television provokes the rehearsal. (1969: 96–97)

Evoking memories of the mass political spectacles of the Nazis, Thielicke and his controversial comments were frequently cited in Springer publications and varied according to each publication's intended audience.[7] In *Bild-Zeitung*'s front-page editorial "And the Television Is There," Thielicke's critique of television as a visual form of communication was deemphasized. Rather than explore the poisonous effects of the televisual medium, the editorial warned of television's collusion with student activism and demanded officials vigilantly defend public order and state authority, since "freedom was paramount" (*Bild-Zeitung* 1967: 1). Consistent with its previous criticisms, *Bild-Zeitung* emphasized the failures of broadcast executives to serve the best interests of the West German people.

In contrast, *Hörzu* frequently referenced to Thielicke's arguments about the visual medium, especially in its coverage of Dutschke's interview with Gaus. For example, in its final editorial of 1967, *Hörzu* mentioned the theologian's ideas of optical neurosis and reestablished the connectedness of the students' gestures, television's coverage of student protest, and the spectacle politics of the Nazi past (*Hörzu* 1967: 6). In the next week's editorial, cooler heads prevailed. Television was depicted as both a useful tool to educate the public and a possible threat to social order. Here again, however, the editorial emphasized the spectacle of student unrest and declared democratic journalism "must stand the test" against such tactics. For *Hörzu,* television news programs failed in this task, since they would "rather produce emotion and even neuroses than the pursuit of truth" (Vagts 1967–68: 6). Television's mission was to present the news objectively and "to place the facts on the table." Only through the impartial presentation of "the facts" could audiences determine "where the protest is reasonably justified and where the distorted agitation begins" (Vagts 1967–68: 6).

These arguments resurfaced after Easter 1968, when *Hörzu* once again attacked television for its inability to offer balanced journalism. *Hörzu* also championed its consistent positions against student activism and quoted judiciously from its previous editions' warnings about the student threat (Vagts 1968: 6). Once more, it was argued that, unlike *Hörzu,* television stirred sensation and left citizens uninformed about student demands. For columnist Hermann Vagts, "the fact is, in the leading evening programs, something constantly was seen about Hippies and LSD, but we heard almost nothing before Easter about the SDS, *Hochschule* reform, the agenda of the APO or the views of Professor Habermas" (1968: 6). With West Germany facing "open revolt," television's mission was to overcome human emotions and to serve the interests of "this—relatively—viable state" (Vagts 1968: 6).

Statist discourses informed *Bild-Zeitung*'s coverage as well. Citing the *Münchner Merkur*, a regional newspaper known for its television critique, *Bild-Zeitung* outlined how public broadcasting, "because of anticipatory news reporting, became the ideal information mediums for the demonstrators." Viewers, listeners, and, more troubling, protestors were said to "know already in the morning, what would occur in the evening." Television coverage also evoked sympathy for the students, since viewers "saw clubbing police officers, water cannons in action, horses and barb-wire, but no malicious students ... Coverage is more strongly distorted through images than through words" (*Bild-Zeitung* 1968: back page). Whereas the editorials of *Hörzu* presented television's misguided coverage of the student movement as easily correctable, *Bild-Zeitung* embraced a far more ominous tone and continued to mix antitotalitarian discourses with the claim that students and television executives worked in tandem to undermine a democratic West German state.

Television, Tabloids, and Audiences in 1968

Across mediums then, contributors and critics associated with television's representation of 1968 expressed their concerns about the visual medium's effects on West German audiences. With memories of the Nazi past still looming large, television audiences themselves became both real and rhetorical objects of debate. Yet what were the roles and responses of West German media users in relation to television's representations of student protests in and around 1968?

A critical analysis of market and opinion research can provide some speculative answers. In one notable study, the Institute for Applied Social Sciences (INFAS) analyzed West Germany's "oldest and best known television magazine *Panorama*" to determine "how *zeitkritisch* programs were regarded, who watched them, and what value they can have on shaping of public opinion" (Institut für Angewandte Sozialwissenschaft 1968). Released in May 1968, the survey found *Panorama* offered viewers information and critical perspectives, a conclusion declared to be evidence of the program's important public function by anchor Gerhard Bott (Bott et al. 1970: 7–9).

Ignored by Bott was the issue of media effects and, specifically, *Panorama*'s influence on the politics of the viewer. To answer this latter question, researchers devised a comparative, multimedia approach and searched for print publications that, in their opinion, exhibited the authoritative qualities that

Panorama looked to "neutralize." Despite disclaiming that "reading a boulevard newspaper alone certainly does not produce an authoritarian mindset," INFAS selected *Bild-Zeitung* and asked survey respondents a series of questions about media usage and authoritarian tendencies (see table 12.1).

From the data, INFAS argued that *Bild-Zeitung* readers were "consistently more irrational, emotional, and authoritative than the rest of the population," a condition only intensified following regular viewings of *Panorama* (Institut für Angewandte Sozialwissenschaft 1968: 36). Ironically, *Panorama* actually reinforced the reactionary mind-sets of many of its viewers, which included *Bild-Zeitung* readers, and had little impact on anyone aside from those who already possessed similar political viewpoints (Institut für Angewandte Sozialwissenschaft 1968: 36). INFAS's findings were not universally accepted, however. Elisabeth Noelle-Neumann of the Allensbach Institute dismissed the study, since it mistakenly operated from Paul Lazarsfeld's theory that only a few media-savvy individuals, and not mass audiences, were

Table 12.1. Media and Characteristics Representative of Authoritarian Tendencies

Selected Opinions		Frequently watches *Panorama* Reads *Bild*	Frequently watches *Panorama* Does not read *Bild*	Infrequently watches *Panorama* Reads *Bild*	Infrequently watches *Panorama* Does not read *Bild*
Germany needs an energetic leader who thinks of his own people first.	Yes	70%	60%	60%	62%
	No	30%	40%	40%	38%
It is a fact that there are people of different races and colors in the world. They will always struggle against one other. This is natural law.	Yes	39%	29%	30%	36%
	No	61%	71%	70%	74%
National Socialism also had its good sides. At least order and discipline prevailed.	Yes	67%	55%	56%	56%
	No	33%	45%	44%	44%
The Jews have no claims to reparations. It would have been better if Germany had not given even a penny to the Jews.	Yes	24%	12%	22%	17%
	No	76%	88%	78%	83%

Source: Institut für Angewandte Sozialwissenschaft (1968)

able to make sense of the news (Noelle-Neumann 1977: 115–26). Irrespective of Noelle-Neumann's criticisms, the survey confirmed the fears of television executives who conceptualized television as a democratizing medium, especially since the INFAS survey seemingly exposed a media environment in which television programs activated the audience's emotions but that personal characteristics, in tandem with the use of multiple media, ultimately influenced the reception of television representations on 1968.

Television, Critics, and Audiences after Easter 1968:
Obscenity as Social Criticism

After 1968, public officials continued to see television as a democratizing medium that could encourage open-minded viewers to develop their own political positions (Vogel 2005: 163). Third-channel networks proved especially important in this regard. Regional in scope, third-channel networks aired cultural and educational broadcasting that could provide both artistic and political opportunities for activists.[8] One such example was *Obscenity as Social Criticism,* an NDR (North German Broadcasting)-produced documentary shown on 20 October 1970. Written and directed by progressive filmmaker Thomas Ayck, the film discussed the rise of explicit sexual content in the public sphere—termed the "porn" or "sex wave"—and asked if the sexual revolution of the 1960s precipitated the commoditization and not the liberation of sex. The film also explored the ways in which activists used politicized tactics of a sexual nature—deemed obscenities by bourgeois standards—to overcome normative standards of sex and pornography and to awaken citizens from their sexually repressive states. Ayck inventively blended quotations from Marcuse and film footage from Andy Warhol with interviews of American playwright Arthur Miller, Spanish surrealist Fernando Arrabal, and Vienna *Aktionismus* cofounder Otto Mühl, among others. Acts of sexual provocation were also incorporated, including footage of the touring sex troop "The American Living Theater," and an interview with a Flensburg activist who placed garden gnomes simulating acts of masturbation in front of the city's administration building (NDR 1970a).

Through sight and sound, the documentary itself functioned as a thought-inducing obscenity. For example, the music of child singing sensation Heintje accompanied photographs of the garden gnome, a sequence linking the child's pop music with masturbation. Catholic officials quickly voiced confusion over "what tendencies the author proposed" with this segment, one of twenty points raised in a memorandum submitted to NDR by the local bishop's office (Brünning 1970). Echoing the previously noted sentiments of Thielicke, church and conservative commentators continued to express concern about how left-wing activism, in tandem with television's visual images, inspired irrational drives among West German audiences. In response, NDR programming director Dietrich Schwarzkopf acknowledged the documentary's "optical problem" and that the topic might have been more appropriate for a nonvisual medium such as radio. Still, Schwarzkopf defended the film and argued, "an abstract handling of the theme without sources, for example in a discussion, appears to us as a flight from reality, especially when the viewer is confronted at different occasions in their daily routine with the question of obscenity's borders" (1970). For Schwarzkopf, "abstraction" and "flight from reality" were not the effects of the program or the medium, but rather dangerous sentiments that could deprive audiences of the information needed to develop reasoned positions.

Schwarzkopf's logic assumed television was a progressive medium that developed progressive attitudes in the public. Yet similar to the findings of the aforementioned INFAS study, many viewers rejected this logic. Two weeks after *Obscenity as Social Criticism* first aired, NDR officials received 633 viewer letters about the program, 490 of which offered negative assessments (NDR 1970b: 1). An unofficial report resulting from the backlash soon emerged, and included press clippings, excerpts from viewers' letters, and a table that noted the frequency and appearance of certain words or ideas (see table 12.2).

Viewer letters provide additional context. Unsurprisingly, letters signed "anonymous" exhibited the most aggressive language. One letter threatened, "what fortune for your coworkers that the brown flag in Germany has vanished, or else you could have all had a good romp in a concentration camp" (NDR 1970b: 13). Although signed letters critical of the program were sometimes linked to these anonymous respondents through their referencing of the Nazi past, they were typically more restrained and embraced religious, anticommunist, and cultural decline arguments. Combining all three sentiments, one man argued:

> This scandal … stinks to high heaven. Programs of this type serve the degradation of national morals and national character and with it the expansion of communist Moscow's imprint, just like the laws for the exemption of punishment of Homosexuality and Pornography. You awaken in many viewers emotional opposition and the call for the strong man, who can then deliver these pigs where they belong, in the work camp. You have not served the goal of democracy with your program. Was that perhaps your underhanded intention? (NDR 1970b: 15)

Table 12.2. Negative and Positive Criticisms of *Obscenity as Social Criticism*

Negative Criticisms

- Scolding the contributors as "filthy pigs, wild pigs"; of the event as "swinishness, mess, filth": 30%
- Additional vocabularies of protest: "foul, bullshit, trash, crap, rubbish, shit, smutty, unacceptable, obscene, rude, outrageous, nauseating, decadent, sordid, revolting, tasteless, depraved, disgusting, perverse, vulgar, shocking, brutal, scandalous, primitive, banal, fallacious": 22%
- Moral-religious objections: "unmoral, immorality, irresponsibility, shamelessness, damnability, lack of reverence, nihilism, violation of human dignity, demoralization, sin, destruction of moral worth, Barbary": 17%
- The criticism of society served as an excuse; it treated itself much more like a porn program, a sex film: 12%
- Punishment for coworkers and responsible individuals: "dismissal, workhouse, jungle, concentration camp": 11%
- Concern for youth, the "dignity of woman," the preservation of the family: 10%
- Concern for the nation: "Poor Germany! Control of the healthy national sentiment": 8%
- Formal protest without an argument, without revilement: 8%
- Participants were politically identified as "SPD-People, Leftists, Red, Communist": 6%
- Confessed response of shock: 5%
- Elaborated—altogether negative—dispute of the theme, obscenity and social criticism: 4%
- Sexuality does not belong in public: 4%
- Revilement of the contributors: "Communist pigs, psychopaths, shits, abnormal, pervert, homosexual, psychopath, bugger, abnormal, impotent, uninhibited creatures, parasites, sadists, perverse anarchists, *Phallusoph* (Marcuse), hermaphrodites (Giese), senile lechers": 3%
- Anti-Semitic arguments, yearning for Hitler: 3%
- Purely aesthetic/formulistic critiques: 5%

Positive Criticisms

- The appropriate viewing circles gave their thanks for the "bravery, the civil courage," for a "worthwhile, many-sided illustration," for "the best program of the year."
- Elaborate, in total positive, the examination of the theme, obscenity and social criticism: 25%
- Wrote a comment because of the widely open public denouncement: 25%
- Requests for manuscripts on the further treatment of this theme: 22%
- Wish it would be repeated: 15%

Source: NDR (1970b: 2–3)

In his dismissal of the film, the letter writer displayed an antitotalitarian ideology and denounced public television as a despotic institution, discourses previously expressed in the publications of Springer Verlag. Still, anticipating conservative criticisms, many viewers wrote NDR to defend the program. One respondent described the critics' "vocabulary as obscene" (NDR 1970b: 20). A woman who identified herself as "no hippie, but a 43-year-old housewife and mother" could "only agree with Marcuse's words. The critics of your program have almost completely overlooked the meaning of your program … It simply should illustrate a documentation of the present societal order. I hope that you would also include in the future a critical analysis of the present [debate] in your program" (NDR 1970b: 23). Viewers who supported *Obscenity as Social Criticism* seemingly embraced television's mission of providing information and analysis on controversial public debates. At least speculatively, viewer responses to the film confirm that *zeitkritisch* programs influenced like-minded audiences and triggered negative sentiments among viewers who possessed opposing political perspectives. On topics concerning social and student protest, divisions remained among the intended or expected reception of programs produced by *zeitkritisch* television personalities and the actual responses of diverse viewing audiences.

Conclusion

Throughout 1968 and its immediate aftermath, public television's representations of West German social and student protests were heterogeneous. Especially on the level of production, officials pursued a democratizing mission and sought to satisfy viewer demands by offering programs that varied in purpose, content, and ideology. The diverse perspectives of filmmakers, screenwriters, news moderators, and program participants also ensured conflicting opinions about social and student protests. For every Peter Merseburger there was a Matthias Walden, whose employment with Springer Verlag ensured not only a dismissal of social and student activism but also a discussion about media competition and television objectivity. Still, television representations of social and student protest reflected a commitment to create and ultimately educate the public, a platform that left the medium vulnerable to subversive tactics as well as accusations of conspiracy and lacking objectivity.

Democratization through production did not necessarily lead to the democratization of the viewer. In constructing a historically based, social geography[9] of television in the late 1960s, this chapter has sketched two layers of reception that complimented and contributed to representational production. The first layer was composed of those actors, ranging from commentators with cultural capital to newsmakers of the moment, who engaged directly with the television medium. The second layer consisted of those individuals who responded indirectly to television's representations through surveys and the writing of letters. In this latter layer, composed of ordinary viewers and audiences, representations of social and student activism were filtered through an individual's politics, cultural values, or even media preferences. If television representations of social and student protest affected audiences, they did so by triggering and subsequently reinforcing preexisting biases and prejudices. Identifying the varied levels of production and reception reveals a much more complex view of how representational meaning was produced and obtained. In the initial and immediate moments of 1968, television representations of student and social protest, which were intended to democratize through variety, seemingly only further atomized a fragmented viewing public.

Notes

1. Antitotalitarianism was an at times militant ideology based upon the thoughts of Hannah Arendt and her "totalitarianism" thesis. Antitotalitarianism was used to maintain Cold War consensus and ostracize "extreme" right- and left-wing interests deemed possible threats against the West German state. For antitotalitarianism and German memory, see Kansteiner (2006). For antitotalitarianism and its influence on news coverage during 1968, see Goehle (2009).

2. Space limits my discussion to these "news-oriented" sources. Other forms of television programming, such as fictional television films, also informed and entertained viewers. For example, in 1969, the NDR production *Alma Mater* addressed the question of student activism. For Dieter Meichsner, the noted screenwriter who was responsible for *Alma Mater,* successful television films needed "to engage in reality" (Hickethier 1998: 249), a perspective that informed the film's controversial depiction of student activism as violent and irrational.

3. For a discussion of the tactics used prior to 1967, see Kain (2003).

4. See, for example, Müller-Ebert (1967a: 6, 1967b: 6, 1967c: 1).

5. For a brief overview of this contentious past, see Hickethier (1998: 173–75).

6. The program did not officially air until 1970.

7. Throughout the 1960s, Thielicke occasionally wrote editorials for a number of Springer Verlag publications. Topics ranged from sex and morality in society to blessings at Easter and Christmas.

8. Limits nonetheless existed, as television executives proved willing to cancel activist-produced programming without notice, especially if administrators believed the program posed a threat to the general welfare of the nation. Perhaps the most famous example of such censorship was the cancelation of Ulrike Meinhof's television film *Bambule*. Scheduled to air on 24 May 1970, NDR executives feared *Bambule* would encourage audiences to emulate the acts of Meinhof, who ten days earlier famously

freed Andreas Baader from incarceration, a first step toward the formation of the Red Army Faction (see Kersting 2006).

9. Wulf Kansteiner has used the term "social geography" to describe the conflicting memory interests existent in postwar German society. The term is useful for categorizing the different media players and their positions of power within the West German media sphere of the late 1960s. For more on this concept, see Kansteiner (2006: 316–33).

Bibliography

Bild-Zeitung. 1967. "Und das Fernsehn ist schon da!" Hamburg Ausgabe, 2 December, 1.
———. 1968. "Fernsehen half dem SDS." 18 April, back page.
Böddeker, G. 1968. "Betr: Fernsehndung 'Einige Tage aus dem Leben des Axel Springer.'" 7 March. Unternehmensarchiv des Axel Springer Verlags (ASV-UA), Nachlaß Horst Mahnke, Band 2, Title 1.0/1967-1968.
Bott, G., U. Happel, B. Hesslein, E. Hollweg, L. Lehmann, P. Merseburger, and P. Schier-Gribowsky, eds. 1970. *Panorama: Berichte, Analysen, Meinungen.* Hamburg: Rowohlt.
Brünning, W. 1970. "Report in response to *Obszönität als Gesellschaftskritik?*" 20 November. Staatsarchiv Hamburg (StAH), 621-1/144, Nachlaß Norddeutscher Rundfunk, file 2849.
Drescher, S. 1968. "Zur Wirkung des Fernsehens als Informationsquelle über das Welt- und Tagesgeschehen." Speech for the 115th Sitzung des Programmbeirats für das Deutsche Fernsehen (ARD). StAH, 135-1 VI Staatliche Pressestelle VI, 1454, NDR 1955–1968.
Exclusiv-Dienst. 1967. "Störungen im Fernsehen." Vol. 48 (30 November): 12.
Fahlenbrach, K. 2001. *Protestinszenierungen: Visuelle Kommunikation und kollektive Identitäten in Protestbewegungen.* Wiesbaden, Germany: Westdeutscher Verlag.
Gitlin, T. 1980. *The Whole World Is Watching: Mass Media in the Making and Unmaking of the New Left.* Berkeley: University of California Press.
Goehle, T. 2009. "Embracing International Revolution, Upholding Domestic Consensus: Tabloid News and the Uses of the Prague Spring in West Germany's 1968." In *1968: Des sociétés en crise: Une perspective globale,* ed. P. Dramé and J. Lamarre. Montreal: Presses de l'Université Laval.
Hickethier, K. 1998. *Geschichte des Deutschen Fernsehens.* Stuttgart, Germany: Metzler.
Hörzu. 1967. "Brauchen Sie den Krawall." Vol. 52 (22–29 December): 6.
Institut für Angewandte Sozialwissenschaft. 1968. "Zeitkritik im Fernsehen: Zuschauer, Einstellungen, und Wirkungen." May. ASV-UA, Nachlaß Horst Mahnke, Band 12, 4.04.
Kain, F. 2003. *Das Privatfernsehen, Der Axel Springer Verlag und die deutsche Presse: Die Medienpolitische Debatte in den sechziger Jahren.* Münster, Germany: LIT Verlag.
Kansteiner, Wulf. 2006. *In Pursuit of German Memory: History, Television, and Politics after Auschwitz.* Athens, OH: Ohio University Press.
Kersting, F.-W. 2006. "Juvenile Left-wing Radicalism, Fringe Groups, and Anti-psychiatry in West Germany." In *Between Marx and Coca-Cola: Youth Cultures in Changing*

European Societies, 1960–1980, ed. A. Schildt and D. Siegfried. New York: Berghahn Books.

Kraushaar, W. 2001. "1968 und Massenmedien." *Archiv für Sozialgeschichte* 41: 317–47.

Lampe, G., and H. Schumacher. 1991. *Das Panorama der 60er: Zur Geschichte des ersten politischen Fernsehmagazins der BRD.* Berlin: Volker Spiess.

Lampe, G. 2000. *Panorama, Report, und Monitor: Geschichte der politischen Fernsehmagazine, 1957–1990.* Konstanz: UVK/Haus des Dokumentarfilms.

Müller-Ebert, G. 1967a. "Wir wollen mehr Fernsehen! Alle sind dafür -nur das Fernsehen sagt 'nein'!" *Bild-Zeitung* Hamburg, 30 September 1967: 6.

———. 1967b. "Wer zahlt, darf meckern!" *Bild-Zeitung* Hamburg, 30 September 1967: 6.

———. 1967c. "Fernseher, bitte anschnallen!" *Bild-Zeitung* Hamburg, 6 October 1967: 1.

NDR. 1970a. *Obszönität als Gesellschaftskritik.* Manuscript, 20 October. StAH, 621-1/144, Nachlaß Norddeutscher Rundfunk, file 2849, Beschwerden zur Fernseh-Sendung "Obszönität als Gesellschaftskritik?" von Thomas Ayck.

———. 1970b. "Pressekritik und Zuschauerpost zu 'Obszönität als Gesellschaftskritik'?" StAH, 621-1/144, Nachlaß Norddeutscher Rundfunk, file 2849.

———. 1974. *Zeitgeschehen im Fernsehen: Studentenunruhen.* Manuscript, 14 November. Archiv des Hamburger Instituts für Sozialforschung (HIS), RUD 460,01.

Noelle-Neumann, E. 1977. "Der getarnte Elefant." In *Öffentlichkeit als Bedrohung: Beiträge zur empirischen Kommunikationsforschung,* ed. J. Wilke. Munich: Alber.

Ross, C. 2008. "Writing the Media into History: Recent Works on the History of Mass Communications in Germany." *German History* 26, no. 2 (April): 299–313.

Schwarzkopf, D. 1970. "Stellungnahme: Zu der Fernsehsendung 'für die Wochenzeitung *Publik.*'" 3. StAH, 621-1/144, Nachlaß Norddeutscher Rundfunk, file 2849.

Springer, A. 1967. "Vortrag von Axel Springer vor dem rundfunkpolitischen Arbeitskreis der CDU/CSU, 9 June 1967 in Eichholz." ASV_UA, Reden Axel Springers von 1946–1985.

Thielicke, H. 1969. *Kulturkritik der studentischen Rebellen.* Tübingen, Germany: Mohr.

Vagts, H. 1967–68. "Armes Deutschland" *Hörzu* 53 (30 December 1967–5 January 1968): 6.

———. 1968. "Ist einer ohne Schuld? *Hörzu* 18 (4–10 May 1968): 6.

Vogel, M. 2005. "Außerparlamentarisch oder antiparlamentarisch? Mediale Deutungen und Benennungskämpfe um die APO." In *Neue Politikgeschichte,* ed. U. Frevert and H.-G. Haupt. Frankfurt: Campus.

———. 2006. "Der 2. Juni 1967 als Kommunikationsereignis: Fernsehen zwischen Medienritualen und Zeitkritik." In *Medialisierung und Demokratie im 20. Jahrhundert,* ed. F. Bösch and N. Frei. Göttingen, Germany: Wallstein.

von Hodenberg, C. 2006. *Konsens und Krise: Eine Geschichte der westdeutschen Medienöffentlichkeit, 1945 bis 1973.* Göttingen, Germany: Wallstein.

Zielinski, S. 1993. "Zur Technikgeschichte des BRD-Fernsehens." In *Geschichte des Fernsehens in der BRD: Band 1: Institution, Technik, und Programm,* ed. K. Hickethier. Munich: Fink.

Chapter 13

Protest in Television
Visual Protest on Screen

Kathrin Fahlenbrach

The rise of television as a leading mass medium in the 1960s marks a turning point in the history of protest movements in Western democracies. Public attention via television became a relevant currency of political power, and political actors have since had to adapt to its criteria of news coverage.[1] This implied a change of political discourses in public: since then, according to the criteria of media selection, they have to concur today not only in terms of political programs and goals, but also in terms of media adequacy.[2]

The first part of this chapter will elaborate on the 1960s as a historical turning point in regard to media coverage on protest. The second part will discuss general tendencies in the interrelation between television and protest actors after 1968 up to today, especially in regard to the visual staging of protest. The chapter will scrutinize different interests, motives, and strategies, both of protest actors and television networks, for visually "performing" protest on the screen.

Protest and Television in the 1960s: A New Symbiosis

As mentioned above, the rise of television as a leading mass medium during the 1960s in Western societies fundamentally changed the rules of political discourses in public and opened new possibilities for protest actors to become "visible" in the public spheres of mass media.

A relevant background for this development is the professionalization and diversification of television at this time. While television channels were established in most Western countries after 1945 for mass media use, a considerable consolidation of the medium can be observed during the 1960s.[3] In the UK and in Germany, for example, TV networks such as BBC or ARD increased the number of channels so that they could address more specifically different publics. In order to address diverging interests, producers had to expand their programs and develop new formats. Especially the young generation was discovered as a new target group, both in the consumer industry and in television. Pop formats and TV shows addressed young people directly and presented themselves as a forum of global youth cultures (cf. Bodroghkozy 2001).[4]

At the same time, in Germany and other Western countries, a new, critical journalism evolved, influenced by the investigative standards of British and US journalism.[5] In the 1960s, the public TV stations in Germany generally had to consolidate democratic infrastructures, which were inaugurated after 1945 under the influence of the Allies. Although governmental influence on the medium, with its totalitarian tradition in Germany, could not be fully banned from institutional and journalistic decisions, officially, the public stations had to contribute to the democratization of West Germany. During the 1960s a new generation of journalists personally and ideologically subscribed to that duty and developed new political TV formats, such as *Panorama*.[6]

Besides the institutional and thematic proliferation of television during this period in different Western countries, the technological standards of production and distribution became highly evolved. Around 1967, color TV was installed in most European countries; new forms of live broadcasting were developed, and electronic video recording was standardized; US networks installed the first TV satellite, enabling global live broadcasting; and new journalistic formats on foreign affairs were established, eminently enlarging the public's horizon of domestic perceptions. The cross-national distribution of television broadcasting was pushed forward in this period, especially by the European Broadcasting Union (EBU). This network of European broadcasters was a relevant institution for the international flow of news on protest events.[7] Furthermore, the expansion of news agencies contributed to the cross-national distribution of media coverage of protest issues around 1968. As Werenskjold (2011) argues, international news agencies such as VISNEWS (Visual News) and UPITN (United Press International Television News) were important for networks in smaller countries.

All these developments, to mention only the most prominent ones, established new forms of media participation at social events—both on the side of media producers and recipients. According to a slogan globally used by TV producers, the medium was held as a "window to the world," and its images were experienced mostly as authentic documents, giving people the impression of participating closely at distant events all over the world. Thus, another relevant field of innovation and consolidation, which also had significant consequences on political discourses, was visual representation on the TV screen.

Characteristically enough, until the end of the 1960, TV shows and news had presented a rather fixed aesthetic, more focused on language and on "talking heads" than on pictures. The visual standards of TV broadcasting were, until the end of the 1950s, influenced by print media, radio broadcasting, and theater, because most journalists and actors had their professional origins in these older media. But in the context of a growing professionalization of technological and production standards, visual designs and broadcasts were also modernized. This was reinforced by the increasing concurrence with print magazines, which developed ambitious visual aesthetics in order to confront the new dominance of television (cf. the new style of photo journalism in *Life* magazine).

Hence, we may observe a shift from linguistic to visual strategies in public discourses during this period, meaning that visual representations in the mass media adopted a dominant role in the attraction of public attention by both different social actors and the mass media. As I will show below, this "visual turn" appears paradigmatically in television coverage of the student movement during the 1960s in Germany. Still, there were further interrelations between protesters and television that have to be considered beforehand, and that illuminate the deeper interest of the networks in the movement, as I will demonstrate by largely focusing on the case of West Germany.

Student Movements and Television: The West German Case

In West German television, single journalists took a sympathetic interest in the democratizing effects of the student revolt. As mentioned earlier, there existed a young generation of journalists in public TV stations that subscribed to a new code of ethics in German journalism: to be neutral, objective, and critical toward the political establishment (cf. von Hodenberg 2006a, 2006b). Even if they distanced themselves from the radical ideas of the Marxist-Leninist groups around the SDS (Sozialistischer Deutscher Studentenbund), these journalists generally welcomed the students' fight for liberalization and democratization of German society, as well as for an open and critical public sphere. Between 1967 and 1968, German television reported on student issues like: "The Political Engagement of the Students" (Bayerischer Rundfunk 4 August 1967), "Revolt against Authorities" (Westdeutscher Rundfunk 11 November 1968), and "The Outer-Parliamentary Opposition" (Sender Freies Berlin 20 February 1968). Such broadcasts offered their public a deeper insight into the political but also the social and expressive motivations of the contesting students.[8]

As Vogel (2005, 2006, 2010) demonstrates in her empirical studies on television coverage of the student movement in West Germany, public networks had been concerned with the movement since its very beginnings around 1966. Even before it received broad attention in the course of escalating social and political conflicts between 1967 and 1968, single TV stations reported about the emergence of an "outer-parliamentary opposition" at German universities (cf. Vogel 2005). One of the reasons for this was that several journalists were themselves discontented with the missing opposition in German parliament at this time. Even if they did not subscribe to most of the students' political visions (e.g., the idea of a socialist "Räte-Republik"), they welcomed their goal of building an opposition to the reigning "Grand Coalition" of the two biggest parties (The Christ Democrat Party: CDU and the Social Democrat Party: SPD).

Yet, not all public stations and their journalists sympathized with the protesters. Especially in Berlin, mass media, including television, added fuel to anticommunist fears and resentments of the citizens, who were surrounded by the socialist German Democratic Republic (GDR). Vogel (2006) analyzes the case of television coverage on the protests against the shah of Persia in Germany in June 1967, which escalated violently with the death of the student Benno Ohnesorg. She shows that TV stations differed eminently in their evaluation of the protests and the student's death, caused by a policeman. Although all networks celebrated affirmatively the visit of the shah as a spectacular media event, leading networks like WDR (Westdeutscher Rundfunk) or NDR (Norddeutscher Rundfunk) also gave attention to critical perspectives toward the shah, thereby legitimating the motives of the protesters. This was especially the case in political journalistic formats such as *Panorama,* which were relevant outlets for the new critical journalism mentioned above. Vogel's insightful analysis demonstrates that political reports in these broadcastings even opposed positive attitudes towards the shah, which were aired in the coverage of his visit on the same networks.

In contrast, the Berlin channel SFB (Sender Freies Berlin) had a widely negative attitude toward the student demonstrations against the shah. In its news, they were presented as troublemakers, bothering a dignified and relevant state visit. Thus, television coverage on students' demonstrations and their confrontations with the police were not always positive. As Gitlin (2003) describes regarding the American situation, German news also often focused on aggressive struggles between activists and police, especially in their images and films. Nevertheless, the discursive climate in a lot of German public networks was rather positive toward the students, and the activists quickly recognized the chances that this sympathy offered them.

One strategy for the students to be "visible" in TV (and other mass media) was to provide the journalists with charismatic representatives for the movement. Although many activists were critical toward this kind of personalization, contrasting with their antihierarchical and antiauthoritarian postulates, it was obviously one of the most effective ways of achieving media access. Around 1968, interviews with prominent activists such as Rudi Dutschke or members of the *Kommune I* were so popular in the media that they could even demand growing fees for their meetings with journalists.[9]

Yet, the SDS organizers could hardly control the media's choice concerning the movement's representatives. While there were several possible spokesmen for the political part of the student movement, such as Bernd Rabehl or K. D. Wolff, the media very quickly focused on Rudi Dutschke—even though his position within the movement was internally criticized. It was his visual and televisual attractiveness that made him the perfect "leader of the revolution" for the mass media. He was interviewed by several leading print journals,[10] and invited to a prestigious talk show.[11] In this show, the journalist Günter Gaus gave Rudi Dutschke the opportunity to explain the aims and motives of the German student movement to a large public (cf. a close analysis in Fahlenbrach 2002: 206ff.). In another portrait of Dutschke, broadcast by the network WDR in 1968 (WDR III 19 April 1968), the journalist Wolfgang Vernohr interviewed him in the backseat of a car on his way to a protest event. Dutschke announced here that he wanted to retire from the media spotlight, shortly before he was shot down in the street (in April 1968). Although he clearly recognized the mechanisms of media selection as concentrating on himself, and even though he objected to it ideologically, he conformed perfectly to this very mechanism in his public appearances in order to make the movement "visible."

Thus, as mentioned earlier, the interrelation between rebellious students and mass media, especially television, was highly complex and ambiguous during the 1960s. While the students in Germany, but also in other Western democracies, complained about conservative commonsense policies and commercial interests in television, they also profited from the medium in various ways. But in many countries, such as the United States, television was rather dismissive or even hostile toward the activists and treated them as marginal, radical groups (cf. Gitlin 2003). At the same time, its journalists and photographers were fascinated by the revolting youth, who offered them spectacular pictures of confrontations with the establishment and of provocative actions that excited the collective emotions of their public.

In West Germany around 1968, television quickly discovered the visual attractiveness of the students' protest actions. The activists, for their part, recognized that they could enter the mass media public sphere rather easily by staging their protests unconventionally and spectacularly. The French activist Daniel Cohn-Bendit reported later that the students at that time explicitly addressed the selective criteria of news coverage when planning their protest actions:

> We used the media, which—against all dissociations in their commentaries—acted as a huge diffusion machine, disseminating our leaflets, our ideas, and our action forms to all corners of the country. We simply offered the best action and we knew this. It seemed as if we were not focusing on arguments, but on actions and on images. During demonstrations—our most powerful weapon due to their media effectiveness—we positioned ourselves; we presented ourselves as one social body, and performed for the cameras. (Cohn-Bendit 1988: 111, my translation)

The students developed different forms of protest techniques that were attractive for the media. Based on situationist and antiauthoritarian attitudes, they used protest techniques such as sit-ins, go-ins, teach-ins, and other peaceful events in order to symbolically occupy relevant public spaces (cf. Fahlenbrach 2002). Besides this, traditional forms of manifestation were arranged for the cameras, which attracted media attention not only in order to present a mass of contesting people in confrontation with the police, but also because they were equipped with provocative placards, images, and slogans.

Apart from such symbolic techniques, the students used pictures from the press and television as material for their placards and leaflets. This was especially important for anti-Vietnam demonstrations. The war in Vietnam, considered today as the first "television war," demonstrated the new symbolic, emotional, and political power of images in the early era of television.[12] While television and students used these pictures with widely different motives, their public image use coincided and produced—even against the intention of single TV producers—strong political pressure on the US administration.

Thus, in the 1960s, the interrelation between television and rebellious students was highly controversial and symbiotic at the same time. In Germany, TV journalists partly sympathized with their fight for more democracy and liberalization in political and social institutions. As in other Western countries, television discovered protest actions as image or media events, which ensured them broad attention. Being part of political, social, and generational conflicts during the 1960s, these protests were loaded with intensive collective emotions.

As a result, around 1968, activists received new access to mass media and developed new strategies for using this resource. Following Dieter Rucht's

(2004, and in this volume) distinctions of media strategies in social movements, I would argue that the rebellious students developed four prominent media attitudes and strategies that were established and professionalized later on by further movements: absence, attack, alternatives, and adaption. After having experienced phases of *absence* from the mass media, they developed an array of internal *alternative* media (journals, magazines, leaflets, etc.). Some of these were not only directed at the internal public sphere of the movement, but also a broad public.[13] Furthermore, they harshly *attacked* the mass media, analyzing the economic and political interests guiding their public world constructions and their effects. Finally, they generated several strategies for media *adaption,* organizing protest actions as spectacular events, with visual and symbolic material that addressed the visual focus of television and print media. They arranged press conferences and offered the media prominent and charismatic spokesmen to make the movement visible. Finally, they performed spectacular pseudoevents, calculating subversively the reactions of the media and exposing their discursive rules, stereotypes, and frames.

Hence, for the first time in the history of protest movements, the activists around 1968 were broadly visible in the mass media—a fact that was essentially promoted by the structural change of the public sphere, initiated by the new dominance of television. In this historic situation, most of the characteristics of and problems in the interrelation between protest movements and mass media evolved into the way in which they exist today.

Protest on Television after 1968: An Outlook

Getting Protest on the "Tube": Media Strategies after 1968

Although the mass media public sphere has become more accessible for protest actors since the 1960s, when television discovered the news values of protest phenomena, they have since had to deal with the growing concurrence for public attention. Protest movements not only have to share it with established political actors, but also with an increasing number of other contentious actors. Apart from political or social movements, staging public protest has been discovered by many social groups as an effective way of achieving collective interests. Farmers, company workers, soldiers' mothers, or doctors take to the streets to claim specific interests and rights. The more their protest touches the interests and collective emotions of a broader public, the higher their chances are to receive the attention of television and other mass media.

Hence, protest movements have to make their claims relevant to the needs and concerns of a wider public. In this regard, many of them have developed pragmatic attitudes of media *adaption* since the 1960s (cf. Rucht 2004). While the student movement relied on idealistic and romantic ideas of society, current movements often use "marketing" strategies to convince the media and their public of the necessity of specific political, social, or economic changes. Therefore, movements often organize institutional forms like nongovernmental organizations (NGOs), parties, or research institutes that act professionally in public and in political spheres, thereby professionalizing media strategies discovered in the 1960s (cf. Delli Carpini and Williams 2001). Probably the most relevant lesson that these movements learned from this period is that protest issues have to be performed in a visually and symbolically evident and attractive manner for television and other visually focused mass media.[14] This is all the more important today, as many protest issues refer to complex and often widely invisible processes and risks such as climate change or economic globalization.

With the help of professional agencies, movement organizations like Greenpeace or Attac arrange visual "performances" that concretize the processes mentioned above in single images or films. For such NGOs, traditional protest marches and demonstrations lose their dominant role. At the same time, they enlarge the public space for protest actions, using not only the street as a place of contestation but also places where they can make their claims specifically visual. The ecological movement, for example, performs protest and media events at places of acute environmental damage. In this regard, Greenpeace set new benchmarks. In one of their most successful protest actions, they occupied the oil platform Brent Spar that Shell intended to plunge into the sea in 1995. Live television reporting from the platform showed the aggressive efforts of Shell to banish the activists. These images showed a strong company violently attacking a small group of vulnerable activists. The fact that the protesters risked physical harm and even death to protest the company's destructive plan gave them high moral credibility. The "David vs. Goliath" framing of this performance (cf. Juliane Riese, this volume) in news coverage provided the Greenpeace activists with broad solidarity and sympathy in the mass public. In contrast to this, the images caused massive damage to Shell's reputation, and the company finally decided to stop the immersion of the platform. Since then, Greenpeace regularly invites television journalists and cameramen to accompany them on their confrontational trips against militaries, companies, or whale hunters at sea in order to provide them with privileged and spectacular pictures that might then help them to apply public pressure on their adversaries.

Thus, protest actions in public space are today often elaborated media campaigns that not only address the local attendees, but also, first and foremost, television and its global public sphere. It is in this way that their organizers finally address the political and economic elites as parties responsible for a certain problematic situation.

Nevertheless, collective protest action in public space is still a relevant form for many protest groups and movements in order to become visible in mass media, especially in television, which is still the leading mass medium in Western countries. This implies marginalized movements, which have only low public resources, and grassroots movements, which refuse professional and centralized organization of media campaigning. The same is the case for transnational movements, which mostly communicate in online virtual spaces and thus need collective protest actions in order to become physically visible as a collective actor. They all address the mass media public sphere when positioned as a collective body of contesters, providing the cameras with significant symbols, pictures, and banners that should transport at least their most relevant claims onto the screen.

Every movement that seeks to apply public pressure on their addressees[15] therefore has to adapt more or less to the most relevant news values, which are:

- *Visualization:* Presenting attractive image material.
- *Personalization:* Providing media with eloquent spokespersons who might act as representatives of the movement and as experts in news, talk shows, and magazines.
- *Relevance:* Relating protest issues to collective interests and the needs of a broader media public (or specific interests and needs of a specific media public[16]).
- *Dramatization:* Claiming acute urgency of a problem, adapting to television's focus on dramatic crisis and alarmist rhetoric.

Finally, activists use potential alliance partners in television and other mass media as possible gatekeepers for their topics and issues. As I showed in the first part of this chapter, the political and discursive climate in German television around 1968 provided the student movement with several potential alliance partners. Since then, the interrelation has become much more economic: activists have to "sell" protest issues to journalists as hot news, offering them material to keep the viewer's attention on their channel.

Still, the political and ideological attitudes of journalists and networks are relevant aspects that influence if and how protest actors are represented on TV. As Gitlin (2003) and Gamson (2006) convincingly show, protest actors may find considerable sympathies in TV if their aims and values widely conform to those of the network journalists. This is especially the case for moderate movements, which do not seek to change society as a whole but concentrate on specific issues that contribute to social, political, or ecological modernization and progress. Thus, the ecological movement or the consumer critical movement refer to values that are generally shared by Western TV journalists, concerning, for example, human health and the safety of our environment. Since these values touch on the existential needs and interests of their public, they are also relevant in terms of news values.

At the same time, the discourse on such issues might become dominated by television, giving other, established actors space for public statements and pushing activists into the background. As Gitlin (2003) argues, such movements thus often have to pay a high price for getting their issues onto the agenda of television. Besides the risk of being marginalized in the public debates they initiated, mass media, and especially television, tend to simplify and soften their claims.

Thus, some protest groups have developed subversive strategies in order to confront television and its public with more radical perspectives on a given problem. After subversive concepts of guerrilla communication was discovered by the student movement, such groups adapted their messages in an overaffirmative way to the criteria of news coverage, thereby first hiding their proper intentions.

One of the most prominent groups successfully performing guerrilla tactics in order to implement radical claims on prime-time television are the Yes Men. In 2003, one of their activists succeeded in being invited to an interview on BBC World as a representative of Dow Chemical. In this role he announced full compensation for the victims of the chemical catastrophe in Bhopal in 1984, which caused thousands of deaths. Since the company until then had renounced such a broad compensation and had never officially apologized for the accident, this statement was top news, with the BBC even broadcasting the interview twice. In the two hours until Dow realized the hoax, CNN reported a Dow stock loss of two billion dollars. Dow ultimately distanced itself from its false spokesman and stated that it would not pay any compensation, thereby making their ignorance more obvious than ever to a global television public and causing massive image damage for the company. With this subversive media event, the Yes Men succeeded in making a global public aware of the Bhopal catastrophe and the failure of the people behind it to take responsibility.

This example demonstrates how an overaffirmative adaption to news criteria might be used to subversively implement a contentious message within a media reality. As such, it might have powerful consequences on its addressees outside the media.

Protest As a Standardized Topic in Television News

After the student movements in the 1960s, protest has been established in television news as a recurrent topic. Collective protest actions on screen have some general news values; since protest action is always the result of social conflicts, these images make problems and crises in a society visible, which are otherwise difficult to represent on screen. Moreover, protest actions help to reduce complex conflicts to single actors and fronts. While protesters themselves confront specific addressees, television mostly performs such confrontations by additionally polarizing the fronts. As diverse studies demonstrate, television tends to select moments of violent confrontations, introducing the frame of "protesters vs. police." Although the behavior of these two sides is generally evaluated antithetically, clearly confronting "good" and "bad" behavior, the attribution of such evaluation might change between these two sides. Depending on the values and aims of the protesters and those of the police, both sides might be described as "legal" or "illegal." McLeod (1995) analyzed a street protest by an autonomous group that was covered by one US TV channel as radical and seeking violence. The pictures focused on aggressive activities of the protestors on the one hand and on injured policemen on the other. This is a prototypical schema in the news coverage of activists that do not conform to key values of a network and its public, and that tend to be marginalized and radicalized in comments and pictures. Gitlin (2003) and McLeod (1995) observed recurring strategies for delegitimizing protest actors in their studies. Apart from visual polarizations between "violent" actors and "protective" policemen, this is often carried out in commentaries by *delegitimizing strategies* such as:

- The radicalization of protest actors.
- The marginalization of protest actors, emphasizing their social deviance.
- The implicit or explicit quest of protests aims and issues.
- The trivialization of protest aims and issues.
- The reduction and simplification of protest aims and issues (e.g., by reductive citation of their slogans and claims).
- The decontextualization of protest actions (e.g., by focusing on non-representative violent moments during a manifestation or by presenting policemen as victims of the activists' violence).

In contrast to this, protesters might also represent the main values and worldviews of a network and its public and thus delegitimize aggressive behavior by the police (cf. Rucht 2004). This is especially the case in the coverage of protests in nondemocratic countries like Iran, where protesters are regarded as the victims of a totalitarian government. However, news coverage on such protests might even become part of political propaganda. After the US military invasion of Iraq in 2002, US soldiers assisted some Iraqis in toppling a statue of Saddam Hussein in the center of Baghdad. American networks, who were part of the "public diplomacy" of the US administration,[17] presented this event as a large collective protest action. Some unofficial photos revealed later that there were only a few people around the statue and no crowd at all. Thus, television only presented a very selective perspective, creating the impression that Iraqis were enthusiastic about the fall of Saddam and grateful to the US military for bringing his government down.

Nonetheless, protest actions are a recurrent topic in television news. Since the 1960s, protest has obviously been considered a relevant characteristic of democratic and pluralistic societies. A screening of CNN and BBC News on two days (11–12 March 2010) supported this observation: four top news stories that were repeated several times referred to protest events in Thailand, Greece, Nigeria, and South Africa.[18] All these reports presented social and political protest as a significant expression of democratic needs. Hence, and apart from the reasons mentioned above, I follow Gitlin's thesis that television in Western countries favors protest topics in order to perform the idea of a vital political public sphere, allowing very different actors to express their interests and ideologies. The networks thus present themselves as "social centers" of democratic societies (cf. Couldry 2003: 3). Therefore, reporting about protest in nondemocratic countries legitimizes a television network's self-understanding of being a democratic institution. This role is also performed visually: often, reporters are shown in the midst of the protesters, part of a collective upheaval against an authoritarian government. In the CNN feature about peoples' protests in Nigeria, for example, a shaking camera shows the excited reporter in the crowd, his shirt wet with sweat. Such images act as authentic documents, evidencing not only the close participation of television in social events around the world but also suggesting that it is part of democratic processes at their roots. In these reports legitimizing protest actions, television uses, again, recurring *legitimizing strategies,* such as:

- Selection of favorable pictures, focusing on peaceful demonstrators or presenting them as "victims" of violent policemen.
- Contrasting visually "peaceful" protesters with "aggressive" policemen (mostly of a nondemocratic country).

- Portrayal of closeness: the close participation of reporters at a protest event invites the public to anticipate the collective emotions of the protest actors.
- Presentation of interviews with activists, giving them the possibility to explain their motives.
- Portraits of representative participants concerned with a given (social, political, etc.) problem at the center of protesters' claims.
- Background reports about a given (social, political, etc.) problem at the center of protesters' claims.

Finally, television profits in a rather pragmatic way from protest activities. They provide television with new topics and issues for news, journalistic broadcasts, and reports in diverse formats.

Furthermore, television might adapt perspectives and attitudes that were once proclaimed by specific protest movements and assimilate them into their own worldview. This is, for example, the case with environmental issues. As news coverage on the climate summit in Copenhagen in 2009 demonstrated, the claim for a worldwide change in environmental politics is nowadays part of a broad consensus in Western postindustrial countries. Thus, television presented itself in many countries as being itself a critical observer of the global political establishment. In German television, for example, protesters in Copenhagen were portrayed extensively. In one feature by the news magazine *Tagesthemen* (ARD, 12 December 2009, 10:45), a single young activist was accompanied over several days in Copenhagen while she met with other activists, talked about her wishes and claims concerning the results of the summit, and protested in the streets. Single sequences on violent confrontations with the police showed her as being part of the "peaceful" protesters. Furthermore, background features on climate change were recurrently broadcast on German television, always emphasizing the necessity for a global agreement on climate politics.[19]

Apart from being representative of a general discursive change, another reason for the high value of environmental issues in television news is its dramatic characteristics. As mentioned before, television generally favors topics that allow dramatic scenarios to be presented, appealing to collective fears and giving the chance to formulate alarmist prophecies. Again, this stabilizes its role as a "social center," also offering people possible solutions to a crisis and providing them with background information and interpretative frames. Since protest movements often act as early-warning systems in a society, one might consider a structural bind between movements and television: although they often follow quite different aims and motives, they both focus on latent and overt crises and conflicts in a society, they both struggle for public attention, and they both use dramatic visual policies to get it.

Conclusion

From the 1960s to today we may observe a growing professionalization and reutilization in the interaction between television and protest movements. While social or political protest is a recurrent and even popular topic in television news, journalists and photographers use highly stereotyped discursive and visual frames of reference that reduce their observation and interpretation of protest phenomena to established commonsense perspectives. What protest movements have to deal with today, however, is not the missing interest in protest per se, but stereotyped media framings that turn contentious semantics into already established patterns of explanation—especially on the level of visual representations.

Concerning visual policies, we may observe today two general tendencies of protest actors seeking to appear on TV. First, a *pragmatic adaption* to the established patterns of news coverage: simply offering television the polarizing pictures they are used to and thereby communicating rather simple messages (as in the case of traditional pictures of street protests and struggles). Second, a *subversive adaption,* based on the elaborate planning of media events, which communicate more complex messages to the television public by overaffirmatively assimilating news values and image frames (as in the case of the guerrilla communication of the Yes Men).

Generally, and looking beyond visual policies, we may conclude that since 1968, Western television has also adapted to protest discourses and strategies in many ways and helped at least moderate movements to change the established consensus—even if this is partly the result of unintended effects.

Notes

1. Consequently, politics became a "largely mediated experience," as Delli Carpini and Williams state: "political attitudes and actions result from the interpretation of new information through the lenses of previously held assumptions and beliefs" (2001: 161).
2. The interrelation between media and protest movements are closely analyzed in, for example, Gitlin (2003), Fahlenbrach (2002), Koopmans (2004), Gamson (2006), and Werenskjold (2008).
3. For the consolidation of television as a leading mass medium in the US, see Spigel and Curtin (1997).

4. In the UK, for example, the music shows "Top of the Pops" (BBC) and "Ready Steady Go" (Rediffusion TV), or the German "Beat Club" (ARD/Radio Bremen).

5. See von Hodenberg's (2006a, 2006b) studies on new journalistic criteria in West Germany after 1945.

6. *Panorama* is still today a political format that presents critical and often provocative background reports (see a close analysis in Lampe [2000]).

7. I owe this information to Rolf Werenskjold, who analyzed the cross-national diffusion of news on protest issues around 1968 (Werenskjold 2011).

8. In research at the German Archive for Broadcasting (Deutsches Rundfunkarchiv) in 1998, I found thirty-four German television broadcasts between 1967 and 1968 that were solely or partly concerned with the student movement. For a more encompassing empirical analysis of television coverage of the student movement, see Meike Vogel (2005, 2006, 2010).

9. Cf. an interview with Rudi Dutschke in the economic magazine *Capital* (Dutschke 1968).

10. Cf. Dutschke (1967a, b).

11. The show of Günter Gaus was called "Zu Protokoll" and it was aired by the *SWF (Südwestfunk)* on December, 3th, 1967.

12. In the United States, news from the Vietnam front had been broadcast on television since the beginning of the war. There is much research on the Vietnam War and television (e.g., Anderegg 1991).

13. Such as the German print magazine *Agit 888*.

14. Delicath and DeLuca (2003) analyze "image events" as forms of effective public form of visual argumentation.

15. There are other nonpublic ways to pursue protest issues, such as lobbying, building of research networks, or providing activists with independent information about a certain problem, such as in the consumer industry or in ecology.

16. Some media campaigns are directed at specific media and their target groups; consequently, specific interests and needs are addressed.

17. Only selected journalists from US networks and journals were allowed to report from Iraq. The US administration treated them as "embedded journalists": they would take part in the front line of the war, providing the global public with authentic pictures from the front. As this example demonstrates, the media often fell prey to this strategy and became part of military propaganda.

18. Protest news on CNN and BBC News included: "Strikes and Protests in Greece" (CNN 11 March 2010); "Greek Strike Protest" (BBC News 11 March 2010); "Nigeria's Myriad of Problems" (CNN 11 March 2010); "Protesting Broken Promises" (BBC); "Thailand Braces for Massive Political Protests" (BBC News 12 March 2010); and "Thailand Readies for Protests" (CNN 12 March 2010).

19. E.g., ZDF, *Auslandsjournal XXL,* 9 December 2009, 10:45 p.m.

Bibliography

Anderegg, M. A. 1991. *Inventing Vietnam: The War in Film and Television.* Philadelphia, PA: Temple University Press.

ARD. *Tagesthemen.* 12 December 2009, 10:45 p.m. [Television News Magazine]

Bodroghkozy, A. 2001. *Groove Tube: Sixties Television and the Youth Rebellion.* Durham, NC: Duke University Press.

Cohn-Bendit, D. 1988. "Tyrannei der Mehrheit: Tyrannei der Betroffenheit." In *Medien ohne Moral: Variationen über Journalismus und Ethik,* ed. L. Erbring. Berlin: Argon.

Couldry, N. 2003. *Media Rituals: A Critical Approach.* London: Routledge.

Delicath, J. W., and K. M. DeLuca. 2003. "Image Events, the Public Sphere, and Argumentative Practice: The Case of Radical Environmental Groups." *Argumentation* 17, no. 3 (September): 315–33.

Delli Carpini, M. X., and B. Williams. 2001. "Let Us Infotain You: Politics in the New Media Environment." In *Mediated Politics: Communication in the Future of Democracy,* ed. W. L. Bennett and R. M. Entmann. Cambridge: Cambridge University Press.

Dutschke, Rudi. 1967a. Interview. *Spiegel* 29, no. 10: 29–33.

———. 1967b. Interview. *Stern* 48, no. 11: 72.

———. 1968. Interview. *Capital* 4: 42-50.

Fahlenbrach, K. 2002. *Protestinszenierungen: Visuelle Kommunikation und kollektive Identitäten in Protestbewegungen.* Wiesbaden, Germany: Westdeutscher Verlag.

Gamson, W. 2006. "Bystanders, Public Opinion, and the Media." In *The Blackwell Companion to Social Movements,* ed. D. Snow, S. A. Soule, and H. Kriesi. Malden, MA: Blackwell.

Gaus, G. 1967. "Zu Protokoll". *SWF,* 3 December 1967. [Television Talk Show]

Gitlin, T. 2003. *The Whole World Is Watching: Mass Media and the Making and Unmaking of the New Left.* Berkeley: University of California Press.

Koopmans, R. 2004. "Movements and Media: Selection Processes and Evolutionary Dynamics in the Public Sphere." *Theory and Society* 33, nos. 3–4 (June): 367–91.

Lampe, G. 2000. *Panorama, Report und Monitor: Geschichte der politischen Fernsehmagazine 1957–1990.* Konstanz, Germany: UVK.

McLeod, D. M. 1995. "Communicating Deviance: The Effects of Television News Coverage of Social Protest." *Journal of Broadcasting and Electronic Media* 39, no. 4: 4–19.

Rucht, D. 2004. "The Quadruple 'A': Media Strategies of Protest Movements since the 1960s." In *Cyber Protest: New Media, Citizens and Social Movements,* ed. W. van den Donk, B. D. Loader, P. G. Nixon, and D. Rucht. London: Routledge.

Spigel, L., and M. Curtin, eds. 1997. *The Revolution Wasn't Televised: Sixties Television and Social Conflict.* New York: Routledge.

Vogel, M. 2005. "Außerparlamentarisch oder antiparlamentarisch? Mediale Deutungen und Benennungskämpfe um die APO." In *Neue Politikgeschichte: Perspektiven einer historischen Politikforschung,* ed. U. Frevert and H.-G. Haupt. Frankfurt: Campus.

———. "Der 2. Juni als Kommunikationsereignis: Fernsehen zwischen Medienritualen und Zeitkritik." In *Medialisierung und Demokratie im 20. Jahrhundert,* ed. F. Bösch and N. Frei. Göttingen, Germany: Wallstein.

———. 2010. *Unruhe im Fernsehen: Protestbewegung und öffentlich-rechtliche Berichterstattung in den 1960er Jahren.* Göttingen, Germany: Wallstein.

von Hodenberg, C. 2006a. *Konsens und Krise: Eine Geschichte der westdeutschen Medienöffentlichkeit 1945–1973.* Göttingen, Germany: Wallstein.

———. 2006b. "Der Kampf um die Redaktionen: 1968 und der Wandel der westdeutschen Massenmedien." In *Wo "1968" liegt: Reform und Revolte in der Geschichte der Bundesrepublik,* ed. C. von Hodenber, and D. Siegfried. Göttingen, Germany: Vandenhoek & Ruprecht.

Werenskjold, R. 2008. "The Dailies in Revolt: The Global 1968 Revolts in Major Norwegian Newspapers." *Scandinavian Journal of History* 33, no. 4. (December): 417–40.

———. 2011. "The Revolution Will Be Televised: The Global 1968 Protests in Norwegian Television News." In *Between Prague Spring and French May: Opposition and Revolt in Europe 1960–1980,* ed. M. Klimke and J. Scharloth. New York: Berghahn Books.

ZDF. *Auslandsjournal XXL.* 9 December 2009, 10:45 p.m. [Television Show]

Part III

Professional Strategies of Protest across the Media after 1968

Chapter 14

Representing Black Power

Handling a "Revolution" in the Age of Mass Media

Craig J. Peariso

After attending a Black Panther Party press conference in 1967, a reporter for the San Francisco *Chronicle* wrote, "If a Hollywood director were to choose them as stars of a movie melodrama of revolution, he would be accused of typecasting" (quoted in Moore 1971: 257). While this reporter quickly backed away from suggesting that there was anything suspicious about the Panthers' media-friendly tactics—saying that party founders Bobby Seale and Huey Newton "are not actors and this is not Hollywood"—others were not so politic. Drama critic Robert Brustein, for example, wrote that the party's press conferences and photo-ops suggest that their "actions and rhetoric are an extension of theatricality, and proceed through the impulse to impersonation" (Brustein 1970: 14). Even the party's alleged murder of a police informant, he continued, "bore sufficient similarities to the plot of a recent movie ... to make one suspect that life was imitating art." By the early 1970s, even those affiliated with the Black Power and antiwar movements had begun to wonder if the Panthers might have mistaken pictures of sensationalized confrontations for "revolution."

In a discussion of activism, one might ask if it would necessarily be a bad thing for life to imitate art. After all, one of the hallmarks of modern art is its purported opposition to the status quo. From Courbet to the surrealists, any number of nineteenth- and early twentieth-century artists understood their work in terms of an uncompromisingly radical, utopian political agenda. However, the mixture of art and activism Brustein worried about was not a marriage of radical politics and utopian aesthetics, but a reconciliation of grassroots action and mass culture. In this chapter, therefore, I would like to focus on the "impulse to impersonation" that he and others recognized in the Panthers' various attempts to reach out to the media, and to look, in particular, at the ways in which the party's early efforts to gain national publicity seemed almost to invite cinematic comparisons. What interests me is not the obvious way that social movements of the late 1960s began to see the media as a potential means of broadcasting their messages to large numbers of supporters and fellow travelers. Rather, I would like to focus on the way "revolutionary" organizations like the Panthers reached out to journalists and cameramen, how they made themselves available and appealing to the mass media. Several historians and critics have described the Panthers' public image as theatrical, but few have attempted to address the importance of the media in the formulation of this political theater (see, e.g., Heath 1976; Pearson 1994; Rhodes 1999). Attending to this aspect of the Panthers' performance of Black Power politics will suggest that the party's work of self-formulation presents a challenge not only to the way we think about calls for "revolution," but also to our understanding of late twentieth-century culture.

Even before Newton and Seale founded the Black Panther Party in October 1966, the pair had looked to devise ways of communicating the potential power of black liberation politics. They needed to make grassroots action appeal, as Newton later wrote, to the "street brothers," those more likely to be found in pool halls than at political rallies. So they spent the summer of 1966 in the ghettos of the San Francisco Bay Area, speaking to groups of disaffected youths about their constitutional right to bear arms, and the collective force African Americans might assert if they were to take up weapons in self-defense. Those who listened, according to Newton, "were interested but skeptical about the weapons idea. They could not see anyone walking around with a gun in full view" (Newton 1995d: 115). Though Newton and Seale repeatedly emphasized the legality of their plans, those who had grown up in the slums of Oakland, San Francisco, Berkeley, and Richmond, who had witnessed and felt the violent rage of certain police officers, recognized, rightly, an incredible risk. To convince these "street brothers," Newton and Seale would have to stage a demonstration. They would have to show that it was indeed possible to stand up to the police, to let the police know that violence and aggression against black victims would no longer be tolerated.

What they devised was the "Panther Patrol." Shortly after the Party's official founding, Newton, Seale, and a couple of friends began to follow and "observe" the actions of officers from the Oakland Police Department. When the officers made traffic stops or questioned someone on foot who looked "suspicious," the Panthers, each carrying either a pistol or a shotgun, climbed out of their own car to observe the interaction from a "safe" distance. The patrols were entirely legal—laws concerning the possession of firearms and interference with police procedures were studied scrupulously in their planning—but for the officers they were unnerving. In Oakland, a city in which accusations of police brutality were common, a group of armed black men (and eventually women) roaming the streets citing laws and legal codes regarding arrest procedures and encouraging members of the community to join them constituted a profound reversal of long-standing power relations. And although these patrols gave rise, in turn, to a focused campaign of harassment by the Oakland Police Department, they nonetheless earned the Panthers a local reputation as something like the vanguard in the struggle for black liberation.

Their growing reputation prompted an invitation from a separate group calling itself the Black Panther Party of San Francisco to provide armed security for Malcolm X's widow, Betty Shabazz, at an upcoming rally. As the San Francisco Panthers were concerned primarily with issues of cultural nationalism rather than armed revolution, members were reticent to carry loaded weapons for fear of running afoul of the law. Newton and Seale, who saw themselves and their own Black Panther Party for Self-Defense as Malcolm X's true legatees, leapt at the opportunity. To them, it seemed the perfect way to generate greater publicity, and to show the people of the Bay Area which Panthers were truly serious in their revolutionary aspirations. On the day of the rally, a cadre of Oakland Panthers arrived, fully armed, to meet Shabazz at the airport. The police, watching anxiously, were effectively helpless to stop them, for, as always, their carrying of firearms conformed precisely to the letter of the law. The Panthers thus made their way through the airport fully armed, and escorted Shabazz to the San Francisco offices of *Ramparts* magazine, where she sat for an interview with Eldridge Cleaver. When Shabazz emerged from the building surrounded by Newton and the Panthers, a local television cameraman stepped in for a clearer view. As Shabazz had asked that no photographs be taken that day, Newton placed a magazine in front of the camera's lens. When the cameraman grabbed the magazine and tried to push Newton out of the way, Newton sensed a golden opportunity. He dropped the magazine, punched the cameraman, and demanded that his adversary be arrested for assault. The police, of course, refused, telling Newton that if anyone were to be arrested it would be he. In response, the Panthers spread out and surrounded the police with their shotguns and rifles drawn. The few officers that were there, each carrying only a revolver, were outnumbered and overpowered. In front of cameras and reporters, the Black Panther Party for Self-Defense had once again rendered the police impotent.

One of the most interesting things about this standoff, at least for my own purposes, is Cleaver's reaction. Recounting the incident, Cleaver said that when *Ramparts* staff members asked him who that was challenging an officer to draw his gun, he told them only that it was "the baddest motherfucker I've ever seen":

I was thinking, staring at Huey surrounded by all those cops and daring one of them to draw, "Goddamn that nigger is c-r-a-z-y!"

Then the cop facing Huey gave it up. He heaved a heavy sigh and lowered his head. Huey literally laughed in his face and then went off up the street at a jaunty pace, disappearing in a blaze of dazzling sunlight. (Cleaver 1969: 35–36)

Cleaver's description was undoubtedly embellished, but it nevertheless points to something quite important. Though surprising to the officers, the particular way in which Newton chose to give form to this act of defiance was all too conventional. More than just stereotypical, Newton's "revolutionary" tactics were, arguably, mass cultural. The "vanguard" of the struggle for black liberation looked as if it had been pulled straight from a Saturday matinee. Armed outlaws fighting for "the people," standing up to police acting on behalf of a cruel, oppressive system, were all too common in film and television. As the San Francisco *Chronicle* reporter quoted earlier put it, to cast Newton and the Panthers as revolutionaries in a Hollywood film would have seemed cliché. The party seemed almost *too* perfect for the role of American guerrilla warriors. Their actions rendered the formal similarities between the modern revolutionary and too many underdog heroes of Hollywood film almost undeniable. The Panthers' popularity with local media, therefore, seemed both shocking and, at the same time, entirely predictable.

Not surprisingly, supporters of Black Power politics soon began to ask if the Panthers' actions might be little more than publicity stunts. In the summer of 1967, Newton responded to the party's critics, writing that it would be a mistake for revolutionaries to shy away from publicity, as the "sleeping masses must be bombarded with the correct approach to struggle and the party must use all means available to get this information across to the masses" (Newton 1995a: 17). For Newton, to be a "real" revolutionary one had to be willing to risk one's own extinction, to stand in the face of the "dog power structure" not to ask for equal rights, but to show that one would take them by any means necessary. To move the masses to make a revolution themselves, the vanguard party would have to inspire them. True revolutionaries would make themselves visible.

Thus, he continued, the Watts riots, much as the violence may have caused many young blacks to fear the repercussions of openly defying authority, were nevertheless a powerful revolutionary catalyst. They did not bring about substantive change—their immediate effect, after all, was the death of large numbers of young blacks—but for Newton that was not the point. On one hand, the riots provided an expression of the intense frustration of the inner-city poor. They were, as Frantz Fanon called the anticolonial uprisings in 1950s Africa, "the sign of the irrevocable decay, the gangrene ever present at the heart of colonial domination" (Fanon 1968:

130). On the other hand, Newton was equally interested in the way these actions seemed to appeal to the media. While any riot was destined to end disastrously for its participants, the riots in Watts had been "transmitted across the country to all the ghettoes of the Black nation. The identity of the first man who threw a Molotov cocktail is not known by the masses, yet they respect and imitate his action" (Newton 1995a: 14). Whatever damage the riots had caused, they provided a truly stunning image, one as inspiring for many young blacks as it was dreadful for whites. As T. V. Reed recently put it, these images appeared to have "awakened countless numbers of Negroes into African Americanness" (Reed 2005: 51). For this reason, Newton argued, as important as it might be to organize in individual neighborhoods, if the vanguard party hoped to foment real revolution, local interventions would never be sufficient. They would need to distribute images of their activities to a mass audience. "Millions and millions of oppressed people may not know members of the vanguard party personally," Newton wrote, "but they will learn of its activities and its proper strategy for liberation through … the mass media" (Newton 1995a: 17). To "capture the imagination" of the people, the vanguard party would have to engage the press.

Of course, disagreements over whether, or how, civil rights or Black Power advocates should employ the media as a tool were nothing new. From the March on Washington to the Selma-to-Montgomery voting marches of 1965, questions about the media's role in depicting and defining the civil rights movement were quite familiar by the time the Panthers arrived on the scene. Speaking of the 1963 March on Washington, for example, Malcolm X, who had appeared on television numerous times in the late 1950s and early 1960s, denounced organizers for having played so obviously to the cameras. The problem was not that the media distorted the demonstrators' message; reporters had no need to misrepresent what had happened, for the entire event had been created just for them: "The marchers had been … told *how* to arrive, *when, where* to arrive, *where* to assemble, when to *start* marching, the *route* to march … even where to *faint* … Hollywood couldn't have topped it" (Malcolm X and Haley 1966: 280–81). What struck people as new in the Panthers' actions, therefore, was not so much their opportunistic staging, but the forms they chose to appropriate.

Both Martin Luther King Jr. and Malcolm X had formulated their media personae in opposition to stereotypes of black masculinity. Newton and the Panthers, on the other hand, seemed to revel in them. In their various confrontations with the police, the Panthers virtually embodied what psychologists William Grier and Price Cobbs described in 1968 as the "bad nigger," one who "no doubt accounts for more worry in both races than any other single factor" (Grier and Cobbs 1992: 66). The "bad nigger" was, in

Grier and Cobbs's terms, the "defiant nigger," the "savage rapist-Negro" who might, at any moment, "turn on his tormentors" (Grier and Cobbs 1992: 66). Designing and courting armed standoffs with the police, Newton forced to the surface one of the most pervasive and persistent stereotypes of black masculinity, thereby making many Americans, both black and white, incredibly anxious. Where the earlier generation of civil rights leaders looked to bury these stereotypes, Newton, like many black males of his generation, seemed to feel that these ostensibly regressive myths could be transformed into a viable political tactic. As Robyn Wiegman (1995) has argued, by inverting the power relations of white and black men that had been in place since the era of Reconstruction, they attempted to turn the mythical potency of the black male into one of the animating concepts of the Black Power movement. By the late 1960s, regardless of its liabilities, the myth of the hypermasculine black male seems to have provided young men like Newton with a ready-made form for the performance of social antagonism.

And in what one might call a televisual counterpoint to the 1963 March on Washington, Newton, Seale, and Cleaver, who, after the standoff in front of the *Ramparts* offices, quickly signed on as the party's new minister of information, orchestrated what would become the party's most famous action: the invasion of the California State Capitol building in Sacramento on 2 May 1967. Responding to a proposed bill that would outlaw the carrying of firearms by private citizens, thirty party members, twenty of whom were visibly armed, traveled to Sacramento seeking to make a public statement during a meeting of the legislature. The group made its way to the floor, but was quickly ushered into a separate conference room, where, in front of a gathering of photographers and journalists, Seale read a prepared statement entitled "Executive Mandate Number One" denouncing the proposed legislation for attempting to remove guns from the hands of the lower classes. Where, in Washington, any suggestion of anger or violence was virtually forbidden, lest Congress and television viewers get the impression demonstrators were attempting to force the passage of civil rights legislation, the Panthers deliberately courted that perception. "That we would not change any laws was irrelevant, and all of us … realized that from the start … Since we were resigned to a runaround in Sacramento, we decided to raise the encounter to a higher level in the hope of warning people about the dangers in the Mulford bill and the ideas behind it" (Newton 1995d: 147). In 1967, marches and sit-ins were no longer newsworthy. The Panthers needed to offer reporters something more dramatic.

Later, Newton lamented this sensationalism. Though he admitted that the party had carried guns into the Capitol to capture the attention of reporters, he insisted that the degree to which the press was fascinated by the weapons had come as a shock. Seeing the news on television that afternoon, he wrote, he was astounded. By carrying guns into a meeting of the legislature, the Panthers had ensured themselves a spot on the evening news. But the assembled journalists, and much of the viewing public, had failed to recognize the Panthers' "revolutionary" message: "Executive Mandate Number One" was "definitely going out ... Bobby read it twice, but the press and the people ... were so amazed at the ... Panthers' presence, and particularly the weapons, that few appeared to hear the important thing" (Newton 1995d: 149). Wanting to correct any potential misunderstanding, Newton and Seale planned a special edition of the party's newspaper, *The Black Panther,* to tell "The Truth About Sacramento." As Seale later explained, it was important for the Panthers to provide their side of the story, as "there were so many lies about the Black Panther Party ... Lies by the regular mass media—television and radio and the newspapers—those who thought the Panthers were just a bunch of jive, just a bunch of crazy people with guns" (Seale 1991: 182). *The Black Panther* would thus offer an account of the events that took place in Sacramento in the words of those who were there. It would counteract the media's sensationalism, Seale and Newton believed, with the truth.

Upon Cleaver's urging, however, the "truth" about Sacramento ran alongside what would become the most reproduced of all Panther images: a photograph of Newton seated in a wicker throne, holding a spear in one hand and a rifle in the other. Far from telling the "truth" about party activities and ideologies, the photograph embellished the mythology of Newton and the Panthers. Presenting him in full party uniform—white shirt, black pants, black shoes, black leather jacket, and a black beret—and surrounding him with a collection of objects connoting what one might call, following Roland Barthes, a stereotypical "Africanicity," the photograph drew a hackneyed parallel between the struggles for black liberation being waged on the two continents (1978). Though the African liberation struggles were certainly fought with guns, this juxtaposition of rifle and spear, Black Panther wardrobe and tribal shields, Huey Newton and what looked to be props from *Sanders of the River,* served to encode the Panthers' project not only in racial but also in mass cultural terms. Ironically, Newton claimed to dislike the image for this very reason. On one hand, from the time of the party's founding, he and Seale had taken great care to emphasize the Panthers' opposition to cultural nationalism and racial separatism. On the other hand, the photograph appeared to place undue emphasis on Newton, thereby betraying the party's efforts to forge a collective, community-based movement. Presenting himself as a celebrity, the new messiah of black liberation, risked sending conflicting messages to *The Black Panther*'s readers. Not unlike Brustein, it seems, Newton felt that the image suggested something like a rapprochement of the vanguard and kitsch.

To Newton's dismay, this seemed to be precisely what Cleaver wanted from the photo. Cleaver, along with Beverly Axelrod, the attorney who had helped negotiate Cleaver's release from prison in 1966 and at whose house the Panthers had worked on the newspaper, assembled these props and arranged for a "white Mother Country radical" to take the photograph. Upon seeing the final prints, Cleaver demanded that the image be featured in each subsequent issue of *The Black Panther,* that local party offices display it prominently, and that copies be made available for sale in the form of a sixteen-by-twenty poster. As Cleaver's longtime friend Stew Albert recalls, Newton was not alone in his skepticism:

> Cleaver showed up at my pad and wanted to put up a large personality poster of Huey … Because Eldridge was so happy with his new friends, I agreed. But when he gave me a bunch of posters for my "associates," I felt unspoken reservations about their corniness … [P]ersonality posters were relatively new. Even our … rock stars hadn't as yet made use of them. They seemed narcissistic and quasi-cultic, not really ideal food for egalitarian revolutionaries. (Albert 2002: 189)

Like Newton, Albert was uncomfortable because the image presented the Panthers less as the leaders of a "people's revolution" than as unwitting mirrors of the society they claimed to despise. Rather than using images to describe a potential future liberation, or to expose the wrongdoings of those in power, Cleaver seemed to be reveling in the most regressive forms of popular culture.

These concerns regarding Cleaver's "revolutionary" images and tactics only intensified in the months that followed. In October 1967, Newton was imprisoned and charged with the murder of Oakland police officer John Frey, and Seale was involved in the conspiracy and murder trials of the Chicago 8 and the Panther 21. In their absence, Cleaver assumed the role of leader and spokesman, inaugurating what David Hilliard called the "second life of the Party" (Hilliard and Cole 1993: 3). Cleaver spent the next year building on the media coverage of actions like Sacramento, playing upon mass media imagery of the party and the struggle for black liberation. He traveled the country, appearing on television talk shows, giving speeches to large audiences on college campuses, gaining celebrity endorsements from stars like Marlon Brando, and running for president on the Peace and Freedom Party ticket.

For Newton, in jail, regardless of the support Cleaver had secured for the Panthers, these tactics were a concern. Like many, he became increasingly worried that Cleaver's rhetoric would both provoke official retaliation and alienate the community. Following his acquittal and release in 1970, therefore, Newton began to distance the party from Cleaver's increasingly outrageous pronouncements. References to guerrilla warfare were eschewed, members who endorsed violent struggle were excommunicated, and social initiatives like the Breakfast for Children program, in which the Panthers provided poor, inner-city children with free breakfast each day before school, became official talking points. Seale campaigned for local office in Oakland; the Black Panther Party for Self-Defense became, simply, the Black Panther Party; and Newton renamed his position. No longer the minister of defense, he asked first to be known as the party's supreme commander, and later, finding that title too self-important, settled on supreme servant.

Finally, in February 1971, after an ugly disagreement on a local television talk show, Newton officially expelled Cleaver from the party. Shortly thereafter he published an essay in *The Black Panther* explaining that this step had been inevitable. The party's leadership had learned from past mistakes. They now discouraged "actions like Sacramento ... because we recognized that these were not the things to do in every situation" (Newton 1995c: 48). They had come to see these acts as failures, for "the only time an action is revolutionary is when the people relate to it in a revolutionary way." Though these performances had once provided a model for the party, they had proven more costly than anyone had imagined. The community, Newton suggested, had simply been unprepared to interpret the Panthers' imagery correctly. As a result, the party had never connected with the people in the way that he and Seale had hoped. His initial willingness to present the Panthers as an organization of "negroes with guns" had backfired, and Cleaver had merely perpetuated a damaging myth. "Under the influence of Eldridge Cleaver," Newton wrote, "the Party gave the community no alternative for dealing with us except by picking up the gun" (Newton 1995c: 51). In spite of the party's apparent growth, Cleaver's continued emphasis on stereotypical imagery in Panther publicity had left the organization hamstrung.

Surprisingly, just four months later, Newton penned a "revolutionary analysis" of *Sweet Sweetback's Baadasssss Song*, by Melvin Van Peebles, praising the film for its clever deployment of stereotypes. The film, which details the flight from the law of a young black fugitive named Sweetback, was, in Newton's estimation, no less than a revolutionary call to arms, which "the corporate capitalist[s]" had made available to the public only because they had "fail[ed] to recognize the many ideas in the film" (Newton 1995b: 113). When distributors watched *Sweetback,* they saw not a parable of radicalization, but a tale of picaresque heroism revolving around a character that embodied the stereotype of the hypersexual black buck. By playing this role, appropriating and resignifying images that had been used to oppress black men for more than a century, Van Peebles secured national distribution for his film (though not without some effort), allowing his encoded "revolutionary" messages to reach millions. What made *Sweetback* radical, in other words, was not, as David Joselit has argued, Van Peebles's insistence on operating outside the studio system (Joselit 2007: 126–31). Rather, it was his ability to make radical politics appear utterly conventional: "Van Peebles is showing one thing on the screen but saying something more to the audience" (Newton 1995b: 114). Sweetback's sexual escapades are "always an act of survival and a step toward his liberation … The real meaning is … so deep that you have to call it religious" (Newton 1995b: 118). For Newton, when Van Peebles depicted sexual intercourse in the film, he did so not to titillate, but to re-present the stereotypes of black masculinity, to manipulate them as symbols, to "signify." Apparently, where Cleaver used stereotypical images only to propagate misunderstandings, Van Peebles had devoted his work to correcting them. By providing young black men and women with this "revolutionary analysis" and urging them to see the film again, Newton hoped to awaken them to the deeper, "religious" truths of its imagery.

As Henry Louis Gates Jr. (1988) explains, however, the political potential of the practice known as signifying—or "Signifyin(g)," as Gates writes it—is not so simple. Signifying is not one operation per se, but an umbrella term encapsulating the various modes of figurative language used in African American writing and speech. It is tempting to think of these practices—as Newton apparently did—as a type of direction through indirection, a way of drawing on a preexisting language while inserting critical connotative differences. But as Gates makes clear, while signifying may imply the speaker's disdain for those with whom that preexisting language is associated, the practice nevertheless underscores the hegemonic power of that language. It suggests a "protracted argument over the nature of the sign" by emphasizing "the chaos of ambiguity that repetition and difference … yield in either an aural or a visual pun" (Gates 1988: 45). One must therefore think of signifying not as a traditionally oppositional or revolutionary tactic, but as a process akin to the Freudian dreamwork. That is to say, the real importance of the signifying gesture lies neither in the signifier nor in the signified (the manifest or the latent content), but in the ways in which the utterance somehow exceeds the limitations of the sign itself, exerting pressure on the signifier's form to indicate a desire that is constitutively repressed because its articulation in existing language is impossible. What is at stake in the practice of signifying is not revolution, but the ability to read something like an African American subjectivity out of its stereotypical formulations.

To those versed in the literature of contemporary art criticism, this talk of stereotypes, images, and minority identities should sound familiar. In the 1980s, after all, when appropriation became the dominant mode of artistic production, any number of critics attempted to explain the way that preexisting signs could be, or had been, used to indicate a subversive or oppositional identity. In two of the most famous essays on this topic, Craig Owens (1992) came to a series of conclusions regarding the work of photographer Barbara Kruger that are, in the end, quite similar to the points made by Gates. While a number of artists took on the problem of stereotypy in the 1980s, Kruger's work was unique insofar as she was the only artist to acknowledge that the stereotype was not simply imposed upon the individual, and thus easily shaken. Instead, Kruger's work treated the stereotype as integral to the formation of individual subjectivity. By combining appropriated photographs with text that "oscillates perpetually between the personal and the impersonal," her works ask the viewer to confront the impossibility of separating subjectivity from subjection (Owens 1992: 192). However, for Owens, Kruger's emphasis on the canned, the preformulated, the impersonal language that purportedly signifies our individuality may have held a strategic value. Whereas Michel Foucault suggested that the panoptic model of discipline functioned to neutralize desire, for Owens, the question of desire is central when attempting to understand the enactment of an imaginary control over women through visual technologies (1992). It is thus important, Owens argues, to tell the other "half of the story," to supplement Foucault's disciplinary model of subject formation with the insights of Lacanian psychoanalysis.

In Lacan's conception of the gaze, the visual exercise of power is inseparable from the desire to achieve a complete mastery over the other (1998). While much feminist film criticism of the 1970s worried over the "male gaze," the look of the implicitly heterosexual, masculine viewer intent on denying female agency through the visual objectification of women, Owens notes that, for Lacan, any attempt at visual mastery will necessarily fall short. Unlike the Sartrean concept of the gaze (1993), which was linked to the act of looking, the gaze as conceived by Lacan emphasizes the other as the site of the object-cause of desire. As such, it is the opposite of the look. It is the point from which the object sees me, a point I can never successfully locate. The gaze thus resides not in the spectator, but in the object, the other. I can never master it, as it always already looks back at me. The gaze, that is, marks a split in the object, a split that renders it a subject. According to Owens, Kruger's artistic practice emblematizes this model of the gaze. "Kruger reflects the stereotype back on itself," seizing upon the necessary failure of its will to power to enact what is perhaps the only mode of agency available to those subjected to contemporary apparatuses of visual discipline (Owens 1992: 198).

Though Owens stresses the singularity of Kruger's work, it is important to recognize that more than a decade before these essays appeared in print—and two years before Kruger held her first one-person show in New York—Betye Saar, an African American artist from Watts, began exhibiting a series of mixed-media assemblages featuring stereotypical images of black women. The series, entitled *The Liberation of Aunt Jemima*, recycled found images of the "mammy" character—the obese female servant with dark skin and exaggerated features—turning a "derogatory image" into a commentary on empowerment. In the first of these works, from 1972, the viewer finds a wooden box lined with Aunt Jemima baking mix labels. In the middle of that box, standing amid tufts of cotton, is a notepad holder in the shape of a different Aunt Jemima, that of the nineteenth-century minstrel show, in which the character would have been played by a white man in blackface and drag. In place of the sheets of paper this figure would have held, Saar inserted an image of a third "mammy," the house slave charged with taking care of the master's children. Upon closer inspection, one finds critical differences inserted with each of the image's repetitions. In the central figure of the house slave, from the waist down her dress has been covered over by a clenched fist cut from the pages of a Black Power newspaper; in the second mammy, we find that Aunt Jemima's left hand, originally designed to hold a pen or pencil, now clutches a rifle, while her right holds a broom. These allusions to the contemporary struggle for Black Power lead one to ask why, if the piece was about black liberation politics, Saar did not begin with images of Kathleen Cleaver, Elaine Brown, Betty Shabazz, or even Coretta Scott King. The answer to this question, according to Saar, is that she wanted to "take the figure that classifies all black women and make her into one of the leaders of the revolution."

Saar's phrasing reveals that her juxtapositions of Black Power and servitude, of liberation and exploitation, were not just a call to radicalize the unenlightened, nor were they simply an effort to denounce the ways in which whites, and men in particular, imagine black women. By redeploying the popular iconography of racism and sexism, Saar pointed to the role this iconography played in determining, as she put it, "how we saw ourselves." Her works thus stage a paradox similar to the one found in Kruger's images: that of the individual struggling to achieve subjectivity, only to discover that that subjectivity is unthinkable apart from the subjection s/he seeks to transcend. Not unlike Gates's "Signifying Monkey," Saar's Aunt Jemima, even in the process of her liberation, is inseparable from the character of the mammy. Like Kruger's photographs, Saar's assemblages confront the viewer with "the techniques whereby the stereotype produces subjection, interpellates him/her as subject." But in contrast to "the immobility of the pose," one might say that these works "propose the *mobilization* of the spectator" (Owens 1992: 199).

Philosopher Brady Heiner suggests that Foucault's work of the 1970s— not just his theory of discipline but his genealogical method more generally—may have been rooted in and inspired by the philosopher's exposure to the writings of the Black Panther Party. Working alongside Jean Genet in the Groupe d'Information sur les Prisones in 1971, Foucault knew and admired the work of the Panthers. Their desire to unearth displaced historical knowledges, along with their "analyses of the prison system as a strategic mechanism in the consolidation of American governmental authority," Heiner argues, exerted a profound influence on Foucault's theorization of power (Heiner 2007: 321). And although there was no direct connection between Saar and the Panthers, given the obvious similarities between her Aunt Jemima and the photograph of Huey Newton discussed earlier, one cannot help but ask if the "other half of the story," the critical potential of the pose as described by Owens, might also find its antecedent in a similar place. Though Saar's assemblage has been read as a rejoinder to the Panther's photograph and the sexism so widespread among Black Power leadership, Newton's insistent criticism of Cleaver, his repeated attempts to distance the party from Cleaver's stereotypical images, actions, and performances, and his regret that these media tactics seemed to invite a variety of misinterpretations prompt one to ask if it may have been Cleaver himself who was signifying. Certainly, some advocates of Black Power called in earnest upon an authentic blackness as the key to maintaining one's critical distance from the workings of American culture and society. Might Cleaver's posing have been an attempt to indicate that that distance was itself nothing more than an illusion, that any "authentic" blackness was circumscribed by the very culture it opposed? Could this be the potential power of the "impulse to impersonation" condemned by Brustein? Were Cleaver's recitations of a stereotypical black masculinity, like Van Peebles's, not a failure of identity politics, but a politics of failed identity?

Bibliography

Albert, S. 2002. "White Radicals, Black Panthers, and a Sense of Fulfillment." In *Liberation, Imagination, and the Black Panther Party,* ed. G. Katsiaficas and K. Cleaver. London: Routledge Press.

Barthes, R. 1978. *Image-Music-Text.* New York: Hill & Wang.

Brustein, R. 1970. "Revolution As Theater." *New Republic,* 14 March.

Cleaver, E. 1969. "The Courage to Kill: Meeting the Panthers." In *Eldridge Cleaver: Post-Prison Writings and Speeches,* ed. R. Scheer. New York: Random House.

Fanon, F. 1968. *The Wretched of the Earth.* Trans. C. Farrington. New York: Grove Press.

Gates Jr., H. L. 1988. *The Signifying Monkey: A Theory of African American Literary Criticism.* Oxford: Oxford University Press.

Grier, W. H., and P. M. Cobbs. 1992. *Black Rage.* New York: Basic Books.

Heath, G. L. 1976. *Off the Pigs! The History and Literature of the Black Panther Party.* Metuchen, NJ: Scarecrow Press.

Heiner, B. T. 2007. "Foucault and the Black Panthers." *City* 11, no. 3 (December): 313–56.

Hilliard, D., and L. Cole. 1993. *This Side of Glory: The Autobiography of David Hilliard and the Story of the Black Panther Party.* Boston: Little, Brown, and Co.

Joselit, D. 2007. *Feedback: Television Against Democracy.* Cambridge, MA: MIT Press.

Lacan, J. *The Four Fundamental Concepts of Psychoanalysis.* New York: W.W. Norton & Co., 1998.

Malcolm X and A. Haley. 1966. *The Autobiography of Malcolm X.* New York: Grove Press.

Moore, G. 1971. *A Special Rage.* New York: Harper & Row Publishers.

Newton, H. P. 1995a. "The Correct Handling of a Revolution: July 20, 1967." In *To Die for the People,* ed. T. Morrison. New York: Writers and Readers Publishing.

———. 1995b. "He Won't Bleed Me: A Revolutionary Analysis of *Sweet Sweetback's Baadasssss Song.*" In *To Die for the People,* ed. T. Morrison. New York: Writers and Readers Publishing.

———. 1995c. "On the Defection of Eldridge Cleaver from the Black Panther Party and the Defection of the Black Panther Party from the Community." In *To Die for the People,* ed. T. Morrison. New York: Writers and Readers Publishing.

Newton, H. P. 1995d. *Revolutionary Suicide.* New York: Writers and Readers Publishing.

Owens, C. 1992. "The Medusa Effect, or, The Specular Ruse." In *Beyond Recognition: Representation, Power, and Culture.* Berkeley, CA: University of California Press.

Pearson, H. 1994. *The Shadow of the Panther: Huey Newton and the Price of Black Power in America.* Reading, MA: Addison Wesley Publishing Co.

Reed, T. V. 2005. *The Art of Protest: Culture and Activism from the Civil Rights Movement to the Streets of Seattle,* Minneapolis: University of Minnesota Press.

Rhodes, J. 1999. "Fanning the Flames of Racial Discord: The National Press and the Black Panther Party." *The International Journal of Press Politics* 4, no. 4 (September): 95–118.

Sartre, J. P. 1993. *Being and Nothingness.* New York: Washington Square Press.

Seale, B. 1991. *Seize the Time: The Story of The Black Panther Party and Huey P. Newton.* Baltimore, MD: Black Classic Press.

Wiegman, R. 1995. "The Anatomy of Lynching." In *American Anatomies: Theorizing Race and Gender,* ed. R. Wiegman. Durham, NC: Duke University Press.

Chapter 15

Throwing Bombs in the Consciousness of the Masses

The Red Army Faction and Its Mediality

Hanno Balz

When we look at the research on "terrorism,"[1] urban guerrillas, and militant struggles in contemporary history, the role of the media has been strongly emphasized in publications during the last two decades.[2]

One historic example of great prominence is the Red Army Faction (RAF), whose urban guerrilla struggle had an enduring effect on West German society, especially during the 1970s. Recently, the role of the media in the conflict between the RAF and the West German state has been examined more thoroughly (see Balz 2008; Elter 2008). In this chapter, I will discuss the chosen media strategy adopted by the RAF and how it triggered mass media responses either by means of coercion or persuasion. In this regard, describing a mere "depiction" of the RAF in the media would be too limited; instead, the RAF will be regarded as an actor in the struggle for public hegemony. The questions I raise here will deal with the nature of the interconnectedness between the mass media and the policy of the West German RAF. Furthermore, the chapter explores in which ways the RAF saw the media as a primary target for their actions, both ideologically and physically.

First, I will present a brief overview of the RAF's armed struggle in the 1970s and how it affected state and society in West Germany. Following this, theories that interpret "terrorism" as a form of communication will be referred to, and I will then present the public relations (PR) strategy of the RAF between 1970 and 1977. This implies an analysis of the group's communiqué and its overall strategic agenda in provoking the established power. Beyond the discursive level of declarations, the performative aspects of the "propaganda of the deed" the RAF called upon along with older concepts of anarchism will then be examined. The aim of the RAF's media policy was to demonstrate the mere possibility of militant attacks on the state, as well as violently forcing the mass media to report on political issues that had been neglected previously. Also, the RAF's "propaganda of the deed" served as a call to arms for the radical Left after the revolt of '68 had diversified and radicalized it. In conclusion, I will evaluate to what extent the RAF was able to get its message across and whether we can speak of a successful PR policy of the urban guerrilla. My approach, which features an analysis of the RAF's discursive as well as performative practices, will therefore broaden the current academic debate on the relationship between the RAF and the media, as it is able to show the antagonisms of the RAF's PR strategies more than other research on the topic, however fruitful the works of Andreas Elter, for example, still are.

As was mentioned above, the relationship between "terrorism" and the media has been considered in great depth during the last years, in particular after 9/11. However, the phenomenon is not a new one, and by studying the developments of the 1970s, and particularly the West German example, in greater detail, we can learn about the difficult relationship existing between the mass media and "terrorism." They are codependent, since the phenomenon of "terrorism" is partly constructed within media discourses.

An analysis of the relationship between "terrorists" and the media is complicated by the fact that labels such as "terrorist" are not neutral signifiers but are themselves part of a wider dynamic of delegitimization. The careful examination of language is therefore vital to understanding the real dynamic that unfolds in the public domain when so-called terrorists strike. Such an analysis is particularly important when we look at perceived moments of national crisis, such as in West Germany during the autumn of 1977 or after 9/11, when stereotypes are activated more easily.

Stereotypes, such as of intellectuals "supporting terrorism" and of an urban guerrilla that consists of "manic criminals," seem to have survived for longer periods than would have been assumed. Thus, we find strategies of ideological naturalization at work: in ideological clashes over the signifiers and the signified, hegemony has its expression in words and meanings.

The struggle over words used for the terror phenomenon seen as the biggest threat to society in postwar German history was at least as constitutive for state and society as the militarization of the police and the massive tightening of the law. It can be argued that the "terrorism" discourse manufactured consent on a wide scale; never again was the divide between society and state as small as during the escalation of the "German autumn" in 1977.

During 1977, the Red Army Faction's first-generation cadres, Andreas Baader, Gudrun Ensslin and Jan-Carl Raspe, were imprisoned at the Stammheim high security prison. Police had arrested them in June 1972 after a series of bomb attacks on US Army facilities in Frankfurt and Heidelberg, as well as on Augsburg police headquarters and the Hamburg branch of the Springer Publishing Company. In April 1977, the remaining three accused—Ulrike Meinhof had committed suicide in 1976—were sentenced to life imprisonment after a two-year long, highly controversial trial that was held in a newly erected "bunker" courtroom on the grounds of the Stammheim prison. Shortly before the end of the "trial of the century," as it was known in the press, a new RAF commando killed the federal attorney general Siegfried Buback and his escort on an open street. This was the first assassination of a leading "representative of the system" in West Germany. During the following "77 offensive," as the commando called it, the federal government was pressured to release the RAF prisoners. The first attempt to kidnap an important representative of the German economic elite failed: in July 1977, the chairman of the Dresdner Bank's management, Jürgen Ponto, was shot when he resisted kidnappers.

Still, just a few weeks later on 4 September, the RAF succeeded with their plans when they kidnapped Hanns-Martin Schleyer and killed his escort of three bodyguards and a driver. Schleyer was at that time the most influential, but also most controversial, economic leader in West Germany. In 1977 he was head of the Confederation of German Employers' Associations, which made him the "boss of the bosses." For the Left he was a prominent enemy, personifying the continuity from National Socialism to late capitalism: Schleyer had previously been a middle-ranking SS officer and became known for his tough stance on striking workers (Hachmeister 2004: 14).

The six weeks that followed are still considered to be the worst existential crisis of the Federal Republic of Germany (FRG). The federal government, and especially Chancellor Helmut Schmidt, was adamant in not giving in to the kidnapper's demands to release the Stammheim prisoners. During these weeks, an extralegislative administration was established, beyond any parliamentary control, where all affairs were handled by a special crisis squad led by former Wehrmacht officer Helmut Schmidt. A news ban was called into immediate effect and even the reintroduction of the death penalty was discussed (Balz 2008: 278ff.). To take the escalation even further, a Palestinian commando hijacked a Lufthansa airplane with German tourists on 13 October to support the RAF's demands. When, four days later, all hostages were freed by the new paramilitary German GSG 9 squad, it became clear that the RAF's "77 offensive" was in tatters. The next morning, on 17 October, Andreas Baader, Gudrun Ensslin and Jan-Carl Raspe were found dead in their high-security cells.[3] Schleyer was found dead in the trunk of a car a day later.

While the so-called German autumn was the most referred-to phase of the RAF's attack on the state, it must be seen as a culmination of what had happened in the years before. In the 1970s, the conflict between the RAF and the West German state proved to be a paradigm for the growing political polarization of communication in German society. It can be said that the "terrorism" debate was the struggle over the state of the nation, and so the discursive, political and moral boundaries were heavily disputed, as the renowned political scientist Kurt Sontheimer observed in the late 1970s (1979: 112). In this regard, the mass media must be considered the decisive structure of political communication: "Regarding societal conflicts, mass media, taking its enormous contribution into account, perform a strategic function: To develop as a social conflict, a problem must be published in any case" (Franz 2000: 58).

The main assumption in this chapter is that especially in long-term political conflicts, "semantic struggles" take a leading role, being fought in the mass media as well as in government. It took some time until the term "terrorist" was naturalized in German discourse, when no one could question that those in the RAF were mere "terrorists," unless the individual was willing to risk exclusion from societal consensus. In the early years of the urban guerrilla, or roughly between 1970 and 1975, the group was mainly called either the "Baader-Meinhof group" or the "Baader-Meinhof gang." Each label was determined by the political position of the speaker and proved to be highly controversial during these years: speaking of a "Baader-Meinhof group" eventually led to accusing one of being sympathetic with the RAF. Following the official ideological assumption that the RAF had to be defined as a mere criminal phenomenon, the usage of the label "gang" was seen as an expression of loyalty to the West German state. On the other hand, the "proper" name "Red Army Faction" was meant to conjure up emotional images of the World War II archenemy. Through its label, the RAF promoted its fundamental opposition to the West German state and its legacy.

In my recent research, I examined the media discourse on the RAF. Here it can be stated that the dominant discourse aimed at implementing some hegemonic explanation and therefore condemnation of the urban guerrilla and, furthermore, of the whole generation of revolt in the early 1970s (Balz 2008). Following this, the "terrorism" discourse does not necessarily describe those actors it names. Therefore, it focused less on the RAF members in prison or underground, but rather on the impact that this challenge to the power monopoly would have on society. The media strategies ranged from creating instances of moral panic to the denunciation of those actors who refused to denounce the armed struggle.

According to the slogan of the urban guerrilla, to throw bombs into the consciousness of the masses, the hegemonic discourse was also aimed at the consciousness of the masses. Both sides were not only fighting each other by means of physical force, but also by means of propaganda.

In times of moral and political crisis, discourses revolve around fundamental questions regarding the juridical system, the generation gap and consent in society in general. In the end, I argue that the "terrorism" discourse in West Germany constructed a formation of society by means of delimitation.

"Terrorism" As Communication?

"Terrorism" became a metaphenomenon that affected the responses of actors as well as recipients on all sides. It has been argued that the discursive and medial struggle regarding meaning can be regarded as some form of a "theater of terror." As Weimann and Winn have pointed out: "Modern terrorism can be understood in terms of the production requirements of theatrical engagements. Terrorists pay attention to script preparation, cast selection, sets, props, role playing, and minute-by-minute stage management" (1994: 52).

Scholars from the United States have tried to explain the communicative aspects of "terrorism" with the "theater of terror" model. However, this model appears to be too superficial, as it implies an "open stage" model, where anyone could enter the stage, to participate both on the side of the urban guerrilla and of the state. Still, with its attacks against representatives of the state, the military and the economy, the RAF was dependent on the media's attention. Yet the representatives of the political institutions also acted on the media stage. Thus, the media texts regarding "terrorism" incorporate a performative practice that, by its ritual discourses, produces the effects that it names.

In the example of the Red Army Faction and its "media campaign" that I will now address, we can find a significant metamorphosis in the 1970s, when the group shifted its focus from public sympathy to public attention.

(Public Relations) Strategies of the Red Army Faction

I would now like to focus on the role the Red Army Faction itself played in the media discourse of the 1970s. How can the RAF be seen as both a subject of discourse as well as beyond discourse? Regarding its militant practice, has the RAF been an autonomous actor in the conflict? Furthermore, how did the RAF refer to the media discourse and thus follow a corresponding publicity strategy?

A distinguishing characteristic of the first RAF generation was the fact that those individuals who went underground in 1970 and declared the construction of a "Red Army" were already prominent figures. For example, Ulrike Meinhof was editor of the left-wing *konkret* magazine and a radio personality; her political radio features were quite popular and well-known by both the radical Left and more politically moderate audiences. Similarly famous was Horst Mahler, who as a solicitor defended Rudi Dutschke, the leader of the Extraparliamentary Opposition (APO), in court. Finally, Andreas Baader and Gudrun Ensslin gained substantial media attendance in 1968 when they were sentenced for an arson attack in a Frankfurt shopping center. Taking the publicity of the RAF founders into account, a paradoxical situation emerged in which the players in the early urban guerrilla were prominent personalities, yet the political program was hardly known at all. Being a VIP "terrorist" influenced to some extent public perception, as well as modes of personalization of the RAF in the media.

After visiting a Palestinian guerrilla training camp in Jordan, the first RAF members left the organization and gave their accounts to the press. Shortly after he returned from the camp in November 1971, Peter Homann, for example, told the news magazine *Der Spiegel* about the military education he received in Jordan (22 November 1971: 47–62). The media quickly became interested in the Baader-Meinhof story. However, since their "informants" were most often former members who had left due to personal conflicts within the group, the discourse quickly shifted from the story of the glamorous and famous gone underground to assumptions about the internal structure of the group. One particular target of interest was the provocative figure Andreas Baader, so attention as to who was the new "leader of the gang" grew stronger in the media.

With increased media interest, the RAF not only communicated with a radical scene they thought would support them, but also with the West German mass media. After fleeing underground in 1970, Ulrike Meinhof sent *Der Spiegel* magazine an audiotape in which she explained the idea behind the RAF. This statement from life underground bore a certain strategy of authenticity: Meinhof did not send a written statement to the editors, but rather delivered her statement in the true form of the radio journalist she used to be.

Contacting the press directly was not an uncommon public relations policy for the RAF: in early 1972, the leading German tabloid *BILD* spread a rumor that Baader was about to quit the armed struggle and would hand himself over to the authorities. Shortly after that, Baader sent a RAF statement to all news agencies denying any plans to surrender and instead referred to Meinhof's previously penned "Concept of the Urban Guerrilla" paper. Baader "stamped" the letter with a fingerprint to prove its authenticity. At this point, the story interest of *BILD* and other newspapers was cunningly played with and undermined; a fugitive criminal identified himself publicly by sending a forensic mark of himself and then declared, as *BILD* dramatized, "that he wants to destroy our state with his gang" (25 January 1972: 1).

The publishing of communiqués, mainly through the mass media but sometimes via counterpublic channels, as, for example, in radical and clandestine magazines or leaflets, has played an important role for (urban) guerrillas and militant organizations of the twentieth century. This is even more true if contemporary "terrorist" strategies are taken into account. While the Irish Republican Army (IRA) in the 1970s and 1980s had the military weight to publicly let a spokesman declare its attacks on the British Army, the RAF and other urban guerrilla groups had to declare themselves clandestinely. However, the RAF could not rely on broader sympathies from the public or journalists, who would not print their political statements. In the end, the bombings, assassinations, and kidnappings were a means of coercion to propagate the RAF's message in the media.

In its programmatic writings, the RAF continuously claimed the ideology of the "primacy of practice." In declaring this priority over other means of political activism, it reduced the heterogeneity of societal contradictions to simple answers. Emphasizing the simple, existential phrase "Just do it!" as an apparent answer to Lenin's historic question "What is to be done?" was meant to focus on an appeal. Moreover, the reduction of the simple has some cathartic value for a revolutionary, who left behind a life of legality and then wanted to have a clear revolutionary front line before him. As Jochen Reiche summarized: "Things are simple, not complex. They are clear and visible. There are not any problems of analysis, of constructing theory and awareness. The only problem there is, that of practical experience, that is the decision for armed struggle" (1978: 18).

The policy of the early RAF was one of escalation or, as Peter Waldmann has put it, a "provocation of power" (1998: 32ff.). It is the offensive breaking of norms on a symbolic level, amplified by public discourse and charged with emotionality. In particular, the guerrilla theory of French revolutionary Régis Debray inspired this strategy. Debray placed strong emphasis on the exemplariness and therefore emblematic nature of revolutionary violence, so that it would be "armed propaganda" that would be responsible for the movement's success. In the United States, the ex-Students for a Democratic Society (SDS) faction and later urban guerrilla group Weathermen/Weather Underground referred to Debray in a similar way as the RAF: "In Debrayism, Weathermen found an alternative to the 'basebuilding' approach of much of the American left, as well as a rationale for engaging immediately in violence" (Varon 2004: 57).

Apart from Debray, it was the guerrilla strategy of Mao Zedong that was relevant for the RAF as well as for other (urban) guerrillas, insofar as Mao made clear that it was not about defeating the enemy in the first place, but about winning over the public. In the case of classic guerrilla warfare, it can be said that "the effect of a violent act, rather than the violent act itself, mattered" (Schmid and de Graaf 1982: 20). Having said this, the analytical dichotomy between "terrorism" and guerrilla warfare, as it is represented by the majority of "terrorism" researchers, should be brought into question (see, e.g., Laqueur 1982: 10ff.; Münkler 1980: 299–326; Kraushaar 2006: 31–32; Waldmann 1998: 14ff.; Tuman 2003: 5ff.). A common definition sees "terrorism" as a strategy of communication, whereas the guerrilla actually strives to overthrow the government. Schmid and de Graaf therefore suggest "to interpret terrorism as communication, activated and amplified by violence" (1988: 54). This definition is problematic insofar as the actions of guerrilla fighters as well as of international conflicts are to be understood as a communicative strategy. If one looks at the massive US bombing of Baghdad in 2003, which was officially named "Shock and Awe," then this strategy of overwhelming the enemy implies the dissemination of *terreur* in a classical sense.

The question remains as to what extent a state (especially in a democratic media society) that fights a "terrorist" threat can act on such symbolic levels as well. Ultimately, it can be stated here that the discourses on "terrorism" are always about staging politics to a certain extent.

A Provocation of Power

In the beginning, between 1970 and 1972, the RAF seemed less politically isolated than in later years. Their first generation hoped to gain support from the post-APO activists and from social fringe groups, such as institutionalized teenagers, single mothers, the unemployed or migrants—groups regarded as the new revolutionary subject, not only by the RAF. Between 10 and 20 percent of West Germans were seen by the RAF as potential supporters for an urban guerrilla movement that was believed would be the instigator of mass revolt (Fetscher et al. 1981: 63). Even after realizing that cooperation with the legal Left proved impossible under the pressure of state persecution, the RAF claimed to be part of the radical Left.

To a certain extent, the RAF knew the role it played and its limits. At least in the beginning of their armed struggle, the urban guerrillas seemed to be aware of the symbolic dimension of their actions. As Meinhof articulated in the "concept of the urban guerrilla" in 1971:

> The concept of the urban guerrilla originated in Latin America. Here, the urban guerrilla can only be what it is there: the only revolutionary method of intervention available to what are on the whole weak revolutionary forces. … The student movement, for one, realized something of what the urban guerrilla can do. It can make concrete the agitation and propaganda which remains the sum total of left-wing activity. … The urban guerrilla's aim is to attack the state's apparatus of control at certain points and put them out of action, to destroy the myth of the system's omnipresence and invulnerability. (Rote Armee Fraktion 1997: 41–42)

As expressed by Meinhof, the provocation of power aims at staging a reversal of roles: the attackers should be regarded as the attacked and vice versa (Waldmann 1998: 34). In this context, a precondition was the experience of powerlessness during the protests of the Extra Parliamentary Opposition (APO) of the 1960s. During the student revolt, the "revolutionary" activists saw themselves being exposed to the powers of the police and the courts. A feeling of powerlessness resulted from a lack of political patience, as activists sought to bring down the state as soon as possible and to motivate the revolutionary subjects, as the theory actually promised. Therefore, the RAF that saw itself as an expression and agent of a global revolutionary struggle, much as the armed avant-garde of the German ex-APO did when they challenged state power.

Provoking the national power monopoly through specific guerrilla attacks, the strategy of the RAF was to eventually unveil the "open fascism" of West German politics. Thus, the only answer to the provocation would be massive repression by the state. It was believed that, in the face of this escalation, the state would drop its "democratic mask" and a revolutionary situation would follow. By conjuring up the repression, which the Left would have to and actually did endure in the first place, this strategy embodied a cynical "ends justify the means" rationality that was common to the whole RAF ideology. Assuming the revolutionary process was not emancipation from present living conditions, but passage through a "new fascism," the RAF detached itself from the foundation of the New Left (Gilcher-Holtey 2003: 122–23). With its strategy of provocation, the urban guerrilla did put pressure on the political elite, forcing Hans Dietrich Genscher, federal minister of the interior, to reply: "We won't do the gang the favor of reacting in an authoritarian and fascist way. That is merely what they want" (*Der Spiegel* 5 June 1972: 19–32).

Propaganda of the Deed

The RAF's symbolism always embodied the order to decipher their actions beyond any criminal classification as being political in its nature. But it is with this claim that the failure of the RAF becomes clear. In fact, the common interpretations, most of them medial, were generally moralistic. Additionally, the few political evaluations concerning the RAF ranged from "counter-revolutionary" to "putschist" and even "left-wing fascist." Could the "concept of the urban guerrilla" in its propagandistic approach be seen as a didactic play, like Brecht's *The Measures Taken*?

After all, the RAF, in reference to the ideological theory of "false consciousness," propagated the symbolic effect of its actions: "We throw the bombs against the repressive apparatus also into the consciousness of the masses" (Rote Armee Fraktion 1997: 100). Thus, the militant act itself constitutes a public statement, which, in the historic tradition of nineteenth-century anarchism, the RAF called "propaganda of the deed." Accordingly, the performative dimension of a revolutionary practice becomes evident. The deed, argued the RAF, explains itself and therefore must be understood as a discursive intervention.

From this rationalization, a major contradiction of the urban guerrilla can be observed: if it was the practice that is determining in the final instance, it wouldn't have been necessary to explain oneself in such an elaborate way as the RAF did in their papers between 1970 and 1972. Rather, the impression remains that a theory was made fit for a militant practice.

Accordingly, it has been argued that modern "terrorism" should be classified with regard to a general theory of communication. According to this line of reasoning, it is predominantly the use of violence that constitutes the communicative act; therefore, the violent "propaganda of the deed" would make "terrorism" a media phenomenon (see Tuman 2003; Alexander and Latter 1990; Paletz and Schmid 1992; Weimann and Winn 1994; Livingston 1994).

Regarding the RAF, its "propaganda of the deed" expressed some kind of distorted communication, because its aim was not to evoke an open public debate (Musolff 1996: 10). Moreover, the claims of the urban guerrilla to submit to its urban guerrilla strategy are essentially authoritative. In addition to its authoritative nature, the communicated message of the RAF contained a mode of persuasion. With regard to the respective receiver of the message, this can be categorized according to four grounds:

1. The Left should be persuaded that the qualitative step from opposition to urban guerrilla is necessary and "objectively right." At the

least, a solidly united Left should accept the legitimacy of trying to start an armed struggle and, if possible, support it.

2. A greater, politically neutral public should be convinced that the varnish of the democratic order of the FRG barely covers the traditional "fascist" character of this state.

3. The decision makers in the political apparatus should be persuaded to take the RAF seriously as a fundamental enemy. The urban guerrilla wanted to demonstrate its ability to challenge the state as a warring party.

4. The mass media should be persuaded that the voice of the RAF in public discourse, manifested by its "propaganda of the deed," is of such importance that it cannot be excluded. More than this, it is essential for the RAF to demonstrate that they are not a small and isolated group of "Desperados," and instead that they are a legitimate opponent with widespread support. At first, this consists of the supposed naturally revolutionary social fringe groups, and later of the people of the "Third World" who fight for liberation.

The practice of the RAF in its coaction of *performativity* (the speech acts of the RAF's communiqués) and *performance* (the violent acts of its staging) represented the basic pattern of a communicative effect, with the RAF declaring the "truth" in a ritualized act. Proclaiming the start of an armed struggle establishes social facts. The fundamental texts of the RAF, as well as their later statements, themselves resembled something ceremonial.

The RAF was aware of the effect of its publicity and hence acted as if all attention was placed on it. Still, RAF representatives emphasized the defensive role they "had" to play, because initially it would have been the governmental persecution that made the urban guerrillas publicly known: "We have been active now for less than 12 months, much too short a time to start speaking of 'results.' However the great attention being lavished on us by Messrs. Genscher, Zimmermann & Co. has given us the opportunity to mull a few things over, even at such an early stage" (Rote Armee Fraktion 1997: 31).[4]

The RAF saw itself as representing the excluded and the oppressed—shifting between social fringe groups in the FRG and an ideologically extraterritorialized global proletariat. In the end this implies that the political subject constitution of the RAF via an armed struggle does not express a substitutional leading role toward the revolutionary *subjects,* but rather a mandate over the revolutionary *objects,* from whom mere reactions are to be retrieved in the first place. When the RAF later considered itself to be at eye level with its enemy, it attacked the "representatives of the system." Did then, following this self-concept, an *avant-garde* compete against an *elite*?

In rejecting the analogy of "terrorism" and "theater" that was referenced earlier, it should be asked if the symbolic dimension of "terrorism" has more in common with performance art and its framework of real time and an open ending (Sabatini 1986). Using methods of performance analysis, we should rather speak of a structure of "social drama," which is organized in and around rituals (Turner 2002: 196–97).

The performativity and mediality of the RAF goes hand in hand. Even though the RAF wanted to take over parts of the state power via guerrilla strategies, the "question of power" (*Machtfrage*) could be asked primarily on a symbolic level, which actually is easier than generating a people's uprising (Varon 2004: 206). With the obvious absence of such an uprising, the symbolic dimension became solely dependent on its own dynamic. However, it would be shortsighted to speak of the RAF as only a media revolt. The strategic use of media, on the one hand, was part of its symbolic policy, but on the other hand, it was part of its declaration of war against the state. Furthermore, the practice of the urban guerrilla can hardly be reduced to its symbolic dimension even if this is inherent within the performative act. For example, the bombing of the Springer newspaper building in Hamburg was beyond the demonstration of protest; it was first and foremost a direct violent act. This bombing was not a symbolic revolt against the media, but an attempt at direct intervention against the "representatives" of the publishing company.

A Revolt by Means of and against the Media

From the beginning, the RAF knew about its medial significance, or its role as "super-entertainers," to borrow Walter Laqueur's (1982) term. Part of the concept of the urban guerrilla was a symbolic policy, as well as some kind of public relations, like sending statements to international press agencies. Within this strategy, the tradition of the revolt of 1968 is evidenced, as it was the first protest movement "that orientates its forms of public protest with the requirements of the mass media theoretically and practically" (Fahlenbrach 2002: 176).

It may seem paradoxical that the 1968 movement was a media revolt in two senses; it was both "a revolt against the media and a revolt by means of the media" (Fahlenbrach 2002: 179). On the one hand, the revolt was aimed at the media as an instrument of representing and constructing a hegemonic public. On the other hand, it designed its symbolic and expressive actions according to the media's requirements for aestheticized events.

Bommi Baumann, who was active in the militant Movement 2 June, criticized the media policy of the RAF as early as 1975 when he stated that the

> RAF said the revolution wouldn't be built through political work, but through headlines, through appearances in the press, over and over again, reporting: "Here are guerrillas fighting in Germany." This over-estimation of the press, that's where it completely falls apart. Not only do they have to imitate the machine completely, and fall into the trap of only getting into it politically with the police, but their only justification for their actions comes through the media. (Baumann 1977: 129)

By examining the texts of the RAF, its status with the media, and in particular the ambivalence of revolting against and by means of the media, becomes clearer. On the one hand, the RAF's critique focused repeatedly on the reporting of the press and television. It even tried to intervene in this press discourse by publishing rectifications:

> Virtually all the stuff written about us in the newspapers are [*sic*] lies—that's clear. Apparent plans to kidnap Willy Brandt make us look like political buffoons, underhanded methods are used to try and connect us with planning a child-kidnapping.... Whoever imagines that the organization of an illegal armed resistance can be based on medieval forms of justice like the Volunteer Corps or right-wing militias, is intent on initiating their own pogrom. (Rote Armee Fraktion 1997: 28)

The RAF repeatedly addressed the public and the media, not only with their programmatic texts but also by releasing "official" press statements. After the assault on the Springer building in 1972, the RAF demanded in a communiqué that Springer stop its agitation against the Left and that "the Springer press prints this declaration" (Rote Armee Fraktion 1997: 146).

The short communiqués of RAF commandos after 1975, which merely aimed at freeing the Stammheim prisoners, were no more than expressions of the group's ideology, serving as ex post facto justifications for actions that lacked a clear political agenda (Varon 2004: 65). Nevertheless, the second RAF generation was able to professionalize their communicative technique, as evidenced by the well-known video images of the hostage Schleyer in September 1977. During the Schleyer kidnapping, it was of prime importance for the commandos to introduce anti-images of the economy leader into the public. The images of a worn and suffering Schleyer would have increased pressure on the German government enormously. So the state apparatuses, with the implemented "news blockade" in the autumn of 1977, withheld any RAF-produced video and photographic images. The RAF was eventually successful in launching an image of the captive Schleyer by circumventing the state news blockade and sending photographs to foreign news agencies. French newspapers printed the photo of the kidnapped Schleyer on 8 September; German newspapers reluctantly followed two days later (Balz 2008: 271). In the end, this PR coup proved unsuccessful, as the adamant determination of the federal government not to submit to the kidnapper's demands remained in place. Analyzing the RAF's strategy, the actions pursued could no longer be thought of as a "media revolt," but rather as the tactical usage of media to free the Stammheim prisoners. In contrast, the RAF left deep traces in the collective memory via the symbolic dimension of its policy: "In essence, the RAF redefined its 'place' in German politics by asserting that despite its apparent marginalization, it was at the nerve center of state-power" (Varon 2004: 228).

The role the mass media played in the RAF turned out to be manifold: it traditionally served as a publication channel for the RAF's communiqués and as an amplifier for the "propaganda of the deed," which manifested itself in different attacks. In its aim to pose the "question of power" (*Machtfrage*), the RAF challenged not only the state's monopoly of power but also the discursive power of the hegemonic media system.

In summary, the RAF, employing its performative and discursive strategy, was definitely an actor in "terrorism" discourse. It temporarily achieved an initial goal: to set a partial medial agenda. This was especially the case when it was possible for its members to stylize themselves as victims, which became clear in the broad discussion over prison conditions. In this case, the mass media exposed the state of the German prison system as never before. The most distinct proof that the RAF was able to prevail as an actor in discourse was its essential demonstration of the possibility of an armed counterforce.

Finally, I would like to ask, in the spirit of Judith Butler, whether the "terrorism" discourse might be "itself a restaging of the performance" of the RAF (Butler 1997: 14). After all, the hegemonic discourse, despite its massive efforts to delegitimize the actions and arguments of the RAF, served as an amplifier for the urban guerrilla's modes of communication.

Notes

1. The term "terrorism" will be used in quotation marks, to avoid any normative, and therefore problematic, predefinition.
2. For the last ten years, research has mainly focused on "new terrorism," such as al-Qaeda. For "older" forms of social revolutionary violence and the media, see, for example, Weimann and Winn (1994), Tuman (2003), Paletz and Schmid (1992), Nacos (2002), Musolff (1996), and Waldmann (1998).

3. It remains a controversial issue up to the present day—laden with conspiracy theories—as to whether this was suicide or state-founded murder. There is no room here to go into detail.
4. Hans-Dietrich Genscher was the federal minister of the interior during this time; Eduard Zimmermann used to be the anchorman on a well-known crime investigation show on German TV.

Bibliography

Alexander, Y., and R. Latter. 1990. *Terrorism and the Media: Dilemmas for Government, Journalists and the Public.* MacLean, VA: Brassey's.

Balz, H. 2008. *Von Terroristen, Sympathisanten und dem starken Staat: Die öffentliche Debatte über die RAF in den 70er Jahren.* Frankfurt: Campus.

Baumann, B. 1977. *Wie alles anfing.* Frankfurt: Karl Marx Buchhandlung.

Butler, J. 1997. *Excitable Speech: A Politics of the Performative.* London: Routledge.

Elter, A. 2008. *Propaganda der Tat: Die RAF und die Medien.* Frankfurt: Suhrkamp.

Fahlenbrach, K. 2002. *Protestinszenierungen: Visuelle Kommunikation und kollektive Identitäten in Protestbewegungen.* Wiesbaden, Germany: Westdeutscher Verlag.

Fetscher, I., H. Münkler, and H. Ludwig. 1981. "Ideologien der Terroristen in der Bundesrepublik Deutschland." In *Ideologien und Strategien,* ed. I. Fetscher and G. Rohrmoser. Opladen, Germany: Westdeutscher Verlag.

Franz, B. 2000. *Öffentlichkeitsrhetorik: Massenmedialer Diskurs und Bedeutungswandel.* Wiesbaden, Germany: DUV.

Gilcher-Holtey, I. 2003. *Die 68er Bewegung.* Munich: Beck.

Hachmeister, L. 2004. *Schleyer: Eine deutsche Geschichte.* Munich: Beck.

Kraushaar, W. 2006. "Zur Topologie des RAF-Terrorismus." In *Die RAF und der linke Terrorismus,* ed. W. Kraushaar. Hamburg: Hamburger Edition.

Laqueur, W. 1982. *Terrorismus.* Frankfurt: Suhrkamp.

Livingston, S. 1994. *The Terrorism Spectacle.* Boulder, CO: Westview Press.

Münkler, H. 1980. "Guerillakrieg und Terrorismus." *Neue Politische Literatur* 25, no. 3: 299–326.

Musolff, A. 1996. *Krieg gegen die Öffentlichkeit: Terrorismus und politischer Sprachgebrauch.* Opladen, Germany: VS Verlag.

Nacos, B. 2002. *Mass-Mediated Terrorism: The Central Role of the Media in Terrorism and Counterterrorism.* Lanham, MD: Rowman & Littlefield.

Paletz, D. L., and A. P. Schmid. 1992. *Terrorism and the Media.* Newbury Park, CA: Sage.

Reiche, J. 1978. "Zur Kritik der RAF." In *Jahrbuch Politik,* vol. 8, ed. B. Herzbruch and K. Wagner. Berlin: Wagenbach.

Rote Armee Fraktion. 1997. *Texte und Materialien zur Geschichte der RAF.* Berlin: ID-Verlag.

Sabatini, A. J. 1986. "Terrorism and Performance." *High Performance* 9, no. 2: 29–33.

Schmid, A. P., and J. de Graaf. 1982. *Violence as Communication: Insurgent Terrorism and the Western News Media.* London: Sage.

Sontheimer, K. 1979. *Die verunsicherte Republik.* Munich: Piper.

Tuman, J. S. 2003. *Communicating Terror.* Thousand Oaks, CA: Sage.

Turner, V. 2002. "Dramatisches Ritual—Rituelles Drama: Performative und reflexive Ethnologie." In *Performanz: Zwischen Sprachphilosophie und Kulturwissenschaften,* ed. U. Wirth. Frankfurt: Suhrkamp.

Varon, J. 2004. *Bringing the War Home.* Berkeley: University of California Press.

Waldmann, P. 1998. *Terrorismus: Provokation der Macht.* Munich: Gerling Akademie Verlag.

Weimann, G., and C. Winn. 1994. *The Theater of Terror: Mass Media and International Terrorism.* New York: Longman.

Chapter 16

On Dynamic Processes of Framing, Counterframing, and Reframing

The Case of the Greenpeace Whale Campaign in Norway

Juliane Riese

Greenpeace is famous for the media successes it achieves through flamboyant and often confrontational as well as emotional communication; simple and powerful framings of issues; the use of strong visual imagery and symbolism; and snappy, often vernacular rhetoric (Livesey 2001; Tsoukas 1999; Murphy and Dee 1992). This chapter discusses a case in which this media-savvy organization was unsuccessful: the campaign against whaling in Norway. This campaign not only failed to put a stop to Norwegian whaling, but was actually counterproductive with regard to the public impression it helped form in Norway.

Benford (1997: 412) argues that studies of "negative cases" like the present one, in which framings by social movement organizations fail to stimulate (the desired) collective action and, ultimately, social change, are lacking. He further argues that there is a tendency in movement framing literature to focus on frames as static "things" rather than on the "dynamic processes associated with their social construction, negotiation, contestation, and transformation" (Benford 1997: 415; see also Goodwin and Jasper 1999; Broad et al. 2004).

In this chapter, I describe Greenpeace's actions and reactions to other groups' actions, as well as to negative media coverage, in the Norwegian whale campaign over a twenty-year period. I analyze the dynamic *processes* of framing, counterframing (by Greenpeace's adversaries), and reframing in the campaign, in the Norwegian cultural and political context. Based on this analysis, I suggest some hypotheses on the outcomes of framing/counterframing "contests" (Ryan 1991) more generally. By thus focusing on framings as context-dependent, contested processes, the study of this particular campaign contributes to research on the conditions in which protest communication via the media produces, or fails to produce, certain effects (cf. Giugni 1998; Heitlinger 1996).

The next section summarizes the most relevant theoretical points from the literature on frames and framing. I then discuss the framing activities concerning the whaling issue in Norway in historical order.

Frames and Framing: Characteristics and Functions

The term "frame" goes back to Goffman (1974: 21) and denotes a schema of interpretation that enables individuals "to locate, perceive, identify, and label" occurrences.[1] Frames allow people to make sense of events, organize experience, and guide action, whether individual or collective (Snow et al. 1986: 464). "Frame" as a metaphor has two related but different meanings: on the one hand, a frame is a grammar, "a structure in which meaning is contained in and conveyed by the relationships among the elements" (Williams and Benford 2000: 129). On the other hand, a frame, as in a window- or picture-frame, "acts as a boundary that keeps some elements in view and others out of view" (Williams and Benford 2000: 129–31). It is useful to think of the latter function dialectically. As Gamson (1988: 221) points out, one cannot keep a theme in view without also making its countertheme relevant.[2] Therein lie opportunities for social movement organizations (SMOs) such as Greenpeace, who often challenge existing frames.

Indeed, frames should not be thought of as static "things" (Benford 1997; see also Goodwin and Jasper 1999). They are constructed, contested, and reconstructed in everyday life. SMOs, together with other organizations or groups, representatives of local governments and the state, and the media, are "actively engaged" in processes of "production of meaning" (Snow and Benford 1988: 198) in an ever-changing "discursive opportunity structure" (Benford and Snow 2000; Gamson 2004). The media, to a great extent, provide the arena in which SMOs engage in framing activities.

SMOs need to "frame … relevant events and conditions in ways that are intended to mobilize potential adherents and constituents, to garner bystander support, and to demobilize antagonists" (Snow and Benford 1988: 198). Fulfilling all three tasks with one framing is a formidable challenge for SMOs (Gamson 2004: 250).

According to Snow et al. (1986: 464), movement participation depends on the degree to which SMOs achieve frame alignment, that is, manage to link their own and potential participants' interpretive orientations "such that some set of individual interests, values and beliefs and SMO activities, goals and ideology are congruent and complementary." A number of factors that affect the mobilizing potency of SMOs' framing activities have been identified in the literature.

First of all, SMO framing will be more successful the better it attends to the core framing tasks of diagnostic, prognostic, and motivational framing (Snow and Benford 1988, 1992). Diagnostic framing identifies a problem and attributes blame or causality for it. Prognostic framing suggests solutions to the problem and identifies strategies, tactics, and targets. Motivational framing provides a call to arms, or a rationale for action.

Furthermore, SMO framing activities will mobilize more support the more central, or salient, the values or beliefs these organizations seek to promote are to the larger belief system of their audience. The success of framing activities also depends on the degree of empirical credibility, experiential commensurability, and narrative fidelity the framings have for the audience (Snow and Benford 1988). Empirical credibility refers to the fit between the framing and the events. If there is evidence for the framing, it will be more credible to the audience. Experiential commensurability concerns whether the framing harmonizes with the personal experiences of the audience. Even if evidence for some framing can be provided, it might be very far from people's everyday lives. Narrative fidelity describes "the degree to which proffered framings resonate with cultural narrations, that is, with the stories, myths, and folk tales that are part and parcel of one's cultural heritage" (Snow and Benford 1988: 210).

We can subsume centrality, empirical credibility, experiential commensurability, and narrative fidelity as all contributing to, or constituting a part of, the degree of resonance a framing has for or with its audience (Benford and Snow 2000: 619–22). Clearly, affects have considerable influence on resonance. According to Berbrier (1998), culture and values are internalized into individuals' affective systems. Persuasion can therefore be explained in terms of "appeal to people's fundamental sentiments about things in society" (Berbrier 1998: 440). SMOs can achieve frame alignment if they employ frames that correspond with these fundamental sentiments.

For the case discussed here, the concept of counterframing—attempts to "rebut, undermine, or neutralize a person's or group's myths, versions of reality, or interpretive framework" (Benford 1987: 75, quoted in Benford and Snow 2000: 626)—is particularly relevant. Such counterframing often spawns reframing activity on the part of those who are being counterframed, with the goal of, in turn, countering the damage done by the counterframing (Benford and Snow 2000: 626). I interpret the case of the Greenpeace whale campaign in Norway as a sequence of framing, counterframing, and reframing activities by Greenpeace and its opponents.

For the case study this chapter is based on, twenty-five semistructured in-depth interviews with twenty-two current and former Greenpeace employees, from activists to executive directors, were carried out in 2005 and 2006. All interviewees had worked for Greenpeace in Scandinavia, but not all were from Scandinavia originally. Furthermore, internal and public Greenpeace materials and articles from newspapers in Norway and other countries were analyzed. The next section describes the original Greenpeace framing of the whaling issue.

The Original Greenpeace Framing: "Whales As Symbols, Greenpeace As David, Whalers As Goliath"

The first Greenpeace actions against whaling in Norway took place in the 1980s. From my interviews with Greenpeacers, the following interpretation appears to have been dominant within the Greenpeace organization for a long time. The whale, because of its perceived special qualities, such as intelligence and peacefulness, is a symbol of the precious but vulnerable environment. The environmental destruction in the case of whaling is particularly tangible and visible—wonderful animals being hit by harpoons and bleeding—as well as particularly unnecessary, because there are substitutes for all whale products. Whalers are "bloody butchers" (original Greenpeace terms) who commit an unnecessary crime against defenseless Mother Nature to make a profit. The protection of whales, then, is a symbol of environmental protection generally. The theme here is, "If we can't save the whales, then what can we save?" Greenpeacers who ride small rubber dinghies between big harpoon boats and fleeing whales are environmental "Davids" confronting the butchering "Goliaths."

The solution to the problem identified in this framing was simple: whaling must be stopped with legislation making it illegal. This could be achieved by a great number of people (including nonwhaling nations' governments) exerting pressure on whaling nations and their governments to pass such legislation. This framing, particularly for its motivational part, depended a lot on the "fundamental sentiments," which, according to Berbrier (1998), are the result of internalization of values or culture. If people were appalled at the pictures of peaceful whales bleeding to death, that is, if these pictures managed to evoke an *emotional* response, people would take action.

It was always clear to Greenpeacers that the only way they could stop whaling was by mobilizing public attention and outrage. This is the idea of "bearing witness" (Carmin and Balser 2002: 378): if you cannot stop it yourself, expose it to the world. Without (mass) media presence, Greenpeace's actions won't work.

The Greenpeace campaign against whaling did indeed attract a lot of media attention worldwide, and the extensive media coverage did mobilize international opposition to whaling. In many countries, the original framing of the whale campaign was thus successful.

Limited Success of the "Whales as Symbols" Framing in Norway

In Norway too, the Greenpeace campaign against whaling attracted a lot of media and public attention. But it did not achieve frame alignment with the Norwegian audience. To understand why this was so, we need to understand a number of things about Norway.

On the one hand, Norway, with its population of 4.5 million, is a socially and culturally homogenous society with a strong orientation toward egalitarianism, solidarity, and social cohesion (Hveem et al. 1984; Strømsnes et al. 2009: 399; see also Hansen and Holt-Jensen 1982; Barnes 1954). Norway was what Kramer (1984: 92) calls an "underdeveloped colony" (my translation), first of Denmark and then of Sweden, for more than five hundred years, until 1905 (see also Barnes 1954), when Norwegians rejoiced in finally gaining national independence. The proud young nation was traumatized by the Nazi occupation of Norway during World War II. My Norwegian interview partners emphasize that Norwegians have a strong dislike of foreigners "coming up here and telling them what to do." To this day, Norwegians continue to be friendly toward their nation-state and its institutions: Grendstad et al. (2006: 133–34) report trust rates of between 50 and 80 percent in most Norwegian institutions, with a trust rate of 77 percent for both the legal and the national political system (cf. Sørhaug 1984).

On the other hand, Norway is a *diverse* society in the sense that it has what Strømsnes et al. (2009) and Grendstad et al. (2006) call the "local community perspective." For centuries, there were practically as many local cultures in Norway as there were local settlements, given the geographical isolation of most of them because of mountains and fjords, and the relative freedom, self-confidence, and economic independence of Norwegian farmers vis-à-vis any kind of ruling class (Hansen and Holt-Jensen 1982; cf. Sørhaug 1984). Of course, when speaking of such freedom and independence, it must immediately be added that until after World War II, Norway was rather poor. Only a small part of Norwegian territory is arable land; thus, many farmers were also fishermen, hunters, whalers, and sealers, and had to be to survive. This meant that the local cultures were directly tied to the local resources for sustenance (Hansen and Holt-Jensen 1982). Nature was and is seen as a taskscape, an environment where people make a living

(Strømsnes et al. 2009; Grendstad et al. 2006). To the average Norwegian, using the environment, killing animals, and so forth is in no way a violation of nature (Strømsnes et al. 2009; Grendstad et al. 2006).

Norwegian society can seem somewhat surprising to non-Norwegians in that, while national feelings in the sense explained above are strong, the small local community has traditionally been seen as the heart of Norwegian identity and culture (Grendstad et al. 2006). Even today, it is important to most Norwegians to emphasize their bond to the local community they come from. It is often seen as a problem that the population in the more remote parts of the country has been diminishing for decades. Since the 1960s, official government policies have been in place to maintain a decentralized settlement structure (Hansen and Holt-Jensen 1982; see also Norwegian Ministry of Foreign Affairs 2003). Support for whaling is a (small) part of these policies.

As for contemporary Norwegian whaling, it must be noted that it is carried out by fairly small fishing boats with crews of a few men, which go out for whales for a few weeks per year and for fish for the best part of the year (cf. Whale and Dolphin Conservation Society n.d.). Norwegian whalers have only hunted small or minke whales since the 1970s (Statistics Norway 2006). Yearly catches were below one thousand from 1984 (Statistics Norway 2010), and although catch quotas have recently been raised to above one thousand, whalers find it difficult to exhaust them (Doyle 2009; Fouché 2008). It is unlikely that this hunt threatens the existence of the minke whale population in question. The common minke whale is not viewed as threatened, according to the International Union for Conservation of Nature (IUCN) Red List of Threatened Species (www.iucnredlist.org). However, it can be argued (as many Greenpeacers indeed do) that any legal whaling also encourages illegal whaling, as well as lobbying for greater catch quotas and for encroachment on other whale species (see, e.g., High North Alliance 2002; Sollied 1994).

Norwegians today are "politically involved, ... well educated, and tied with Japan for the highest level of newspaper readership in the world" (Norgaard 2006: 353–54). Thus, with a resonant framing, an organization like Greenpeace would have a good chance of mobilizing people via the media. Taking into account what has been said about Norwegian history and culture, however, it is easy to see the shortcomings, in the Norwegian context, of the "whales as symbols, Greenpeace as David, whalers as Goliath" framing.

First of all, while the "protection of nature" would certainly be a value that is central to the belief system of most Norwegians, the "protection of an animal" is not seen as equivalent or symbolic of that and is not a central value at all. For most Norwegians, the fact that an animal is beautiful, intelligent, or peaceful is just not an argument for why you should not kill and eat it, as long as the population of animals is not threatened.

Second, the contention that the minke whale population was threatened had little empirical credibility for Norwegians. The Norwegian government was controlling whaling and setting catch quotas, and Norwegian scientists were quoted in newspapers saying that the Norwegian minke whale hunt was sustainable. Why should Norwegians not trust them?

Third, the original Greenpeace framing was not commensurable with Norwegians' own experiences. A picture showing a whale being killed would have looked normal and familiar, rather than outrageous, to most Norwegians. Many Norwegians went hunting and fishing themselves (and still do), and many of them had met whalers in the local communities where they had their roots. They knew that whalers are fishermen, normal people, fathers and grandfathers, so to frame them as "bloody butchers" or "criminal greedy Goliaths" was very far from an average Norwegian's perspective (cf. Strømsnes et al. 2009).

Finally, the Greenpeace framing, for Norwegians, possessed little narrative fidelity. Apart from the fact that Norwegian whalers caught a limited number of whales from small vessels, rather than great numbers of whales from factory ships, which did not really fit a framing of "Norwegian whalers as greedy Goliaths" anyway, Norwegians saw *themselves* as a tiny nation that had been oppressed for a long time by bigger nations. *They* were David. Opposition against whaling could be interpreted as an attack on small local communities that had to make a living, and most Norwegians had a sense of solidarity with these communities, and felt that they were what Norway was really about.

For these reasons, the original Greenpeace framing, while successful in mobilizing supporters in other countries, was unsuitable to achieve frame alignment with the Norwegian audience. Norwegians' "fundamental sentiments," the result of their socialization into the Norwegian cultural system, were different from those of Greenpeacers. Worse still, the original Greenpeace framing made it easy for Greenpeace's antagonists in Norway to frame the whaling issue according to *their* interests.

The Norwegian Counterframing: "Greenpeace as Goliath, Norway as David"

There are several prowhaling lobby organizations in Norway, the foremost of which is the High North Alliance (HNA). Norwegian whalers and their allies successfully counterframed the whaling issue. The diagnostic part of the counterframing by the prowhaling lobbyists can be summarized as follows. Tiny whaling communities, who had lived in a "merciless" (a whaler quoted in Jonassen 1993: 12, my translation) natural environment for centuries and really understood this environment, were dependent on whaling for their survival (Wallace 1992; Lloyd-Roberts 1991). They were being threatened by a "protest industry" (a whaler quoted in Helle and Stenerud 2003: 10, my translation) staffed by "urban environmentalists" (a whaler quoted in Lloyd-Roberts 1991: 15) who knew "fish and meat only from the supermarket freezer" (a whaler quoted in Jonassen 1993: 12, my translation) and wanted to stop whaling. These people based their arguments on emotions rather than facts, turning the whale into an "urban totem" (a whaler quoted in Maddox 1992: 46) instead of acknowledging that there are many different whale species and that minke whales are not all that special (Barrett 1993). They were trying to destroy traditional ways of life in Norway, telling Norwegians how to run their lives (a whaler quoted in Lloyd-Roberts 1991: 15), and practicing "cultural imperialism" by imposing their foreign values on Norwegians (a whaler quoted in Maddox 1992: 46).

The outside world had mixed up David and Goliath:

> "People in the U.S. are totally misinformed," said Georg Blichfeldt, secretary of the High North Alliance … "They think there's a big whaling industry, factory ships … We're just a bunch of stupid little boats owned by families fighting for our rights. The only big organizations living off the whales today are Greenpeace and the Whale and Dolphin Society that use them as symbols for money raising." (Darnton 1993: 1; see also the quotes in Helle and Stenerud 2003).

The prognostic part of the prowhaling lobbyists' framing followed logically from the diagnostic part: Norwegian David must resist these Goliaths and their "environmental protection hysteria" (a whaler quoted in *Associated Press* 1986). Norwegian politicians should defend traditional Norwegian rights.

The counterframing "answered" the Greenpeace framing by taking up its themes and promoting corresponding counterthemes (cf. Gamson 1988). The theme "Whales are wonderful and symbolic" was countered by "You are misinformed sentimental city-dwellers who don't understand that minke whales are not special," while the theme "Greenpeace are environmental Davids and Norwegians are butchering Goliaths" was countered by "You are mixing up David and Goliath—in fact, *we* are David." The counterframing also promoted a value that was higher to Norwegians than the value promoted by the Greenpeace framing, namely, preservation of a particular practice as an expression of national sovereignty, heritage, culture, and identity (cf. Kramer 1984). The counterframing can thus be said to have not only acknowledged the Greenpeace framing, but also transcended it.

The prowhaling lobbyists' counterframing of the whaling issue was more resonant with the Norwegian audience than the Greenpeace framing. Not only was the value it promoted central in the belief system of this comparatively young nation, but also, prowhaling lobbyists' assurances that they understood nature and knew what they were doing were credible to Norwegians. Furthermore, the idea that Norwegian whaling communities simply kept up certain traditions and at the same time were very close to nature had a high degree of experiential commensurability for many people. Finally, the prowhalers' framing had a much greater degree of narrative fidelity than the Greenpeace framing. It made more sense to Norwegians to see themselves as pressured by powerful greedy foreigners who knew nothing about their way of life than to see other people as Davids and Norwegians as greedy Goliaths. If Greenpeace's actions mobilized public support in countries like Germany—which they did—then this would only strengthen the impression that the antiwhaling protest community was a foreign power wanting to take away Norwegians' rights, putting pressure on them to stop something they had done for centuries. The prowhalers' framing successfully evoked affective responses from Norwegians that supported it.

Outcome of the Framing Contest

It should be noted that some Greenpeacers, particularly Norwegian Greenpeacers, were quite aware that the Greenpeace communication in the whale campaign was problematic in Norway, and understood the reasons for this. They therefore tried to use arguments, in the Norwegian context, that they deemed to be more convincing to the Norwegian audience than those along the lines of whales being special animals. The problem with these attempts was that, in the end, Greenpeace as an organization was sending out so many different messages to the media and the public that the impression it gave was rather inconsistent and chaotic (see Bragli Alstadheim 1992; Schmidt 1992; Straume 1992; Waagbø 1992). Thus, the awareness of some Greenpeacers that the Greenpeace framing described above was problematic in Norway did not lead to Greenpeace communicating in ways that were anywhere near as resonant with the Norwegian audience as the prowhaling lobby's counterframing.

As it was, a major discursive conflict developed around the whaling issue in Norway. Indeed, Norwegian media called it the "whale war" (Furuly 1993; Johannessen and Bertinussen 1995; Jonassen 1993; Mathismoen 1992). The outcome of this "war" was that most people in Norway were bystanders on the whaling issue with a leaning toward the prowhaling cause, with Greenpeace virtually unable to mobilize any support at all for the anti-whaling cause. Grendstad et al. (2006: 109) report survey results according to which "about 80 percent of the general Norwegian population said that to prohibit Norwegian … whale hunting was either 'not very important' or 'not important at all.'" My Norwegian interviewees stated that people in the streets of Oslo would wear T-shirts saying "And I eat dolphins, too" or "Intelligent food for intelligent people."

Norwegian politicians sided with the prowhaling lobby. They argued that this was about the right to preserve a cultural heritage, while freely admitting that whaling was not actually economically important to Norway (Maddox 1992). Foreign minister Johan Joergen Holst is quoted in Brown (1993: 8) as saying, "It's important that small states … are able to resist pressure from major powers which … disregard agreements and regulations for the management of natural resources." Greenpeace was discounted as being in it for fundraising purposes (Barrett 1993). "Prime Minister Brundtland said Norway had a long tradition of … using resources without depleting them. … 'Of course we feel dictated to,' she said. 'It's a completely illogical, irrational, wrongly based campaign'" (Darnton 1993: 1).

Norway defied the International Whaling Commission (IWC)'s moratorium on commercial whaling from 1986 to 1987, and again from 1993 to the time of writing, while in the period from 1988 to 1992 small numbers of whales were caught for the "purposes of scientific research" (Statistics Norway 2010).

The Greenpeace Reframing: "Norway Should Respect International Agreements"

In 1999, Greenpeace designed a new strategy for the campaign against Norwegian whaling. This strategy can be interpreted as an attempt to reframe the whaling issue in Norway in order to counteract the prowhalers' counterframing of Greenpeace's original framing and to counteract the confusion in Greenpeace's own communications. It was based on the results of a focus group study on "average" Norwegian attitudes to whale hunting, receptivity to arguments against whaling, attitudes to Greenpeace campaigning against whaling, and general knowledge of whales, which Greenpeace had commissioned in 1998 from a professional researcher in Oslo. As part of the study, the researcher had presented a number of arguments against whaling (provided by Greenpeace) to the participants and documented their reactions and the ensuing discussions.

The participants judged all of the arguments against whaling presented to them to be unconvincing—except one: that Norway was defying an international agreement by continuing whaling. The participants opined that obedience to international law was more important than personal or national convictions; if Norway disrespected international law, then other countries might disrespect international law as well. Therefore, Norway should end whaling, even though they personally did not have any objections to it. (That Norway had technically "exempted" itself from the IWC moratorium by lodging a reservation does not really alter this argument, as international agreements will only be effective if those who are put at a disadvantage by them also respect them.) This argumentation is consistent with the Norwegian "David against Goliath" attitude. Norway is a tiny country with little military or other power and has suffered in the past because bigger countries did not follow the rules. Therefore, it makes sense that Norwegians are anxious to ensure that everybody respects the rules.

The diagnostic part of Greenpeace's reframing, based on the results of the focus group study, was that Norway was defying international agreements. The prognostic part was that this should be stopped through legislation by the Norwegian government in accordance with international agreements. The motivational part relied on the simple argument that it must be in the interest of all Norwegians to respect international rules.

In the same way that the prowhalers' counterframing can be said to have "responded to" Greenpeace's original framing, Greenpeace's reframing can be said to have "responded to" the prowhalers' counterframing. It promoted counterthemes to the prowhalers' themes. While the prowhaling lobby's counterframing implied that "a foreign Goliath is trying to destroy traditional Norwegian ways of life," the Greenpeace reframing suggested that "Norwegian David has to respect international agreements if he wants foreign Goliaths to respect them as well." This made it harder for prowhalers to suggest that little Norwegian David was being pressed down by a protest industry that only played on emotions. Greenpeace also took up the "Greenpeace are sentimental idiots" theme by using the slogan "Drit i Greenpeace, men redd hvalene" in 1999, which can be translated as "Fuck Greenpeace, but save the whales." Greenpeace consciously communicated to Norwegians that they were free to think Greenpeace a bunch of sentimental idiots, but that the issue in question was really international cooperation rather than anything to do with Greenpeace.

The reframing also promoted a value, namely, international cooperation, which can be seen to rank higher than the value promoted by the prowhalers' counterframing, namely, preservation of a particular practice as an expression of national sovereignty, culture and identity. National sovereignty can only be preserved in a well-functioning system of international cooperation (as Norwegians, historically, have learned the hard way). Such reasoning would be convincing to many Norwegians. Thus, the reframing can be interpreted as acknowledging as well as transcending the themes and the value of the counterframing.

Not only did the Greenpeace reframing promote a value that was central in the Norwegian belief system,[3] it also possessed empirical credibility, as it was possible to provide evidence that the international agreements in question existed. The framing may possibly not have had a great degree of experiential commensurability, because international agreements do not usually figure prominently in average people's lives. But it did possess narrative fidelity, because it was consistent with Norwegians' identity to insist on compliance with international rules. The new framing could thus be expected to be more resonant than the original Greenpeace framing.

Success of the Reframing Strategy

There are some signals that Greenpeace's reframing strategy had the desired effect. There were media reports that must have been quite satisfactory for Greenpeace (Mikalsen 1999; *NTBtekst* 1999; *Dagbladet* 1999; *Dagens Næringsliv Morgen* 1999; Olaussen 1999; Tonstad 1999). A leader from *Dagens Næringsliv Morgen* (a national Norwegian newspaper comparable to the *Financial Times*) of 15 July 1999 compared the profit from whaling to the expenditures on research, as well as the expenditures on diplomatic activity, "as a consequence of the many protest actions since the catch started again in 1993." It came to a conclusion of the "Fuck Greenpeace, but note the rational argument against whaling" type. "Should the hunt continue? We don't believe so. The only argument is, as far as we can see, that it's not fun to give in because of Greenpeace actions" (*Dagens Næringsliv Morgen* 1999: 2, my translation).

Ultimately, it is difficult to judge whether the reframing strategy achieved a good degree of frame alignment between Greenpeace and Norwegians. One reason for this is that, for organization-internal reasons, it was replaced by a different strategy in 2000. This strategy put the whaling issue into the broader context of the Greenpeace oceans campaign, and avoided confrontational measures against Norwegian whaling such as direct actions, thereby toning down emphasis on the whaling issue as a single issue. The 1999 strategy's chances for success must have been limited because of its short life span alone. However, Greenpeace does still use the "international agreements" argument in Norway (see Helle and Stenerud 2003).

Discussion and Conclusion

The specific effect of counterframing is that it constrains an SMO's choices and keeps it in a rather more narrow, or predetermined, "discursive opportunity structure" than it would prefer to be in (cf. Fetner 2008). Opponents may not be able to entirely undo the effects of an SMO's framing. (Despite the fact that the Norwegian prowhaling lobby successfully counterframed the whaling issue in Norway, Norway was still under pressure from other countries to stop whaling.) But if counterframing is successful, the counterframed SMO has to implicitly or explicitly refer to it, and take it into account in its reframing. The opponents thus force the SMO to move away from its original framing(s), and to relate to its opponents (Broad et al. 2004; Evans 1997; Esacove 2004; McCaffrey and Keys 2000; cf. Fetner 2008).

I have argued that both Greenpeace and its opponents in Norway used strategies of acknowledging and transcending their respective opponents' framing. These strategies promoted counterthemes to their opponents' themes, and values that were perceived to be of a higher order than those promoted in their opponents' framing. I suggest that the success of an SMO's reframing will depend on the degree to which it is able to find a resonant framing that does just that. The reframing needs to promote a higher value than the counterframing, or represent a mind-set in which the counterframing can be included and acknowledged, in order to rebut the counterframing. (The same applies to counterframings in relation to original framings.)

However, in order to promote a higher-order value or to be able to incorporate the counterframing, the reframing will probably have to be less issue-specific and more abstract than the original framing and the counterframing. This probably comes at a cost to resonance among the original audiences or adherents (cf. Evans 1997). Indeed, Greenpeace in Norway traded in an issue-specific framing ("whales are wonderful and symbolic") with strong resonance among its non-Norwegian audiences for one that was less issue-specific ("Norway should respect international agreements") and probably less resonant among non-Norwegian audiences to counter the counterframing that had successfully been used against Greenpeace in Norway. Thus, successful counterframing is likely to put an SMO in a situation where it faces tradeoffs regarding resonance among different audiences. How SMOs handle such tradeoffs in order to ultimately achieve their goals is an interesting question that warrants further investigation.

Acknowledgments

I am indebted to my interviewees for making this research possible. I am grateful to Frank den Hond, Deborah Rice, Bert Klandermans, Jacquelien van Stekelenburg, Dunya van Troost, Jacomijne Prins, Saskia Welschen, Marjoka van Doorn, Marije Boekkooi, Anouk van Leeuwen, Frank de Bakker, Maaike Matelski, and the reviewers and editors for valuable feedback on earlier versions of this chapter.

Notes

1. Goffman (1974: 7) explains that the term "frame" was proposed by Bateson (1983, first published 1955) in roughly the sense in which he employs it.
2. Gamson (1988: 220) uses the term "cultural themes" to indicate "frames and related symbols that transcend specific issues and suggest larger world views."
3. Norway is a founding member of NATO, the UN, and the European Free Trade Association, and contributes with forces in different international missions, works as third-party mediator in international conflicts, and so on (Gross and Rothholz 1997).

Bibliography

Associated Press. 1986. "Carrier Nimitz Met By Protesting Norwegian Whalers." 29 August.

Barnes, J. A. 1954. "Class and Committees in a Norwegian Island Parish." *Human Relations* 7, no. 1 (February): 39–58.

Barrett, G. 1993. "Whalers Fight to Preserve a Way of Life." *Age,* 25 May.

Bateson, G. 1983. "Eine Theorie des Spiels und der Phantasie." In *Ökologie des Geistes: Anthropologische, psychologische, biologische und epistemologische Perspektiven,* 2nd edition, ed. G. Bateson. Frankfurt: Suhrkamp.

Benford, R. D. 1997. "An Insider's Critique of the Social Movement Framing Perspective." *Sociological Inquiry* 67, no. 4: 409–30.

Benford, R. D., and D. A. Snow. 2000. "Framing Processes and Social Movements: An Overview and Assessment." *Annual Review of Sociology* 26, no. 1: 611–39.

Berbrier, M. 1998. "'Half the Battle': Cultural Resonance, Framing Processes, and Ethnic Affectations in Contemporary White Separatist Rhetoric." *Social Problems* 45, no. 4 (November): 431–50.

Bragli Alstadheim, K. 1992. "Berthiniussen tar ikke avstand fra Sea Shepherd." *Klassekampen,* 25 July.

Broad, K. L., S. L. Crawley, and L. Foley. 2004. "Doing 'Real Family Values': The Interpretive Practice of Families in the GLBT Movement." *The Sociological Quarterly* 45, no. 3 (July): 509–27.

Brown, P. 1993. "Norway Set to Defy World Whaling Ban." *Guardian,* 19 May.

Carmin, J., and D. B. Balser. 2002. "Selecting Repertoires of Action in Environmental Movement Organizations: An Interpretive Approach." *Organization & Environment* 15, no. 4 (December): 365–88.

Dagbladet. 1999. "Slakter Norge." 8 July.

Dagens Næringsliv Morgen. 1999. "Hvalskuddene." 15 July.

Darnton, J. 1993. "Norwegians Claim Their Whaling Rights." *New York Times,* 7 August.

Doyle, A. 2009. "Norway Whale Catches Fall To Lowest In A Decade." *Thomson Reuters,* 28 August.

Esacove, A. W. 2004. "Dialogic Framing: The Framing/Counterframing of 'Partial-Birth' Abortion." *Sociological Inquiry* 74, no. 1 (February): 70–101.

Evans, J. H. 1997. "Multi-Organizational Fields and Social Movement Organization Frame Content: The Religious Pro-Choice Movement." *Sociological Inquiry* 67, no. 4: 451–69.

Fetner, T. 2008. *How the Religious Right Shaped Lesbian and Gay Activism.* Minneapolis: University of Minnesota Press.

Fouché, G. 2008. "Whaling Under Fire As Norway Catches Only 50 Percent of Its Quota." *Guardian,* 22 August, http://www.theguardian.com/environment/2008/aug/22/whaling.endangeredspecies, accessed 2 August 2013.

Furuly, J. G. 1993. "'Hvalkrigen' starter i april." *Aftenposten,* 4 March.

Gamson, W. A. 1988. "Political Discourse and Collective Action." In *From Structure to Action: Comparing Social Movement Research Across Cultures,* ed. B. Klandermans, H. Kriesi, and S. Tarrow. Greenwich, CT: JAI Press.

———. 2004. "Bystanders, Public Opinion, and the Media." In *The Blackwell Companion to Social Movements,* ed. D. A. Snow, S. A. Soule, and H. Kriesi. Malden, MA: Blackwell Publishing.

Giugni, M. G. 1998. "Was It Worth the Effort? The Outcomes and Consequences of Social Movements." *Annual Review of Sociology* 24, no. 1: 371–93.

Goffman, E. 1974. *Frame Analysis: An Essay on the Organization of Experience.* New York: Harper & Row.

Goodwin, J., and J. M. Jasper. 1999. "Caught in a Winding, Snarling Vine: The Structural Bias of Political Process Theory." *Sociological Forum* 14, no. 1 (March): 27–54.

Grendstad, G., P. Selle, K. Strømsnes, and Ø. Bortne. 2006. *Unique Environmentalism: A Comparative Perspective.* New York: Springer.

Gross, H., and W. Rothholz. 1997. "Das politische System Norwegens." In *Die politischen Systeme Westeuropas,* ed. W. Ismayr. Opladen, Germany: Leske & Budrich.

Hansen, J. C., and A. Holt-Jensen. 1982. *Det moderne Norge: Ressursene våre.* Oslo: Gyldendal Norsk Forlag.

Heitlinger, A. 1996. "Framing Feminism in Post-Communist Czech Republic." *Communist and Post-Communist Studies* 29, no. 1 (March): 77–93.

Helle, K.-E., and D. Stenerud. 2003. "Spekk, Løgn & Hvalfangst." *Folkevett* 6: 8–16.

High North Alliance. 2002. "Whale Export Resumed." 15 July. http://www.highnorth .no/news/nedit.asp?which=294, accessed 31 May 2006.

Hveem, H., S. Lodgaard, and K. Skjelsbæk. 1984. *Det moderne Norge: Vår plass i verden.* Oslo: Gyldendal Norsk Forlag.

Johannessen, B. A., and R. S. Bertinussen. 1995. "Det store Baste-taket." *VG,* 4 June.

Jonassen, A. M. 1993. "Den store HVALKRIGEN." *Aftenposten Morgen,* 7 April.

Kramer, J. 1984. "Norsk identitet—et produkt av underutvikling og stammetilhørighet."
In *Den norske væremåten: Antropologisk søkelys på norsk kultur,* ed. A. M. Klausen.
Oslo: J. W. Cappelens Forlag.

Livesey, S. M. 2001. "Eco-Identity As Discursive Struggle: Royal Dutch/Shell, Brent
Spar, and Nigeria." *Journal of Business Communication* 38, no. 1 (January): 58–91.

Lloyd-Roberts, S. 1991. "Endangered Species Nobody Wants to Save; Whalers Are Demanding the Right to Work." *Independent,* 27 May.

Maddox, B. 1992. "Return of the Whale Killers: Norway Defends the Hunt as 'Cultural
Preservation.'" *Financial Post,* 3 August.

Mathismoen, O. 1992. "Krigen Norge vil tape." *Aftenposten Morgen,* 8 August.

McCaffrey, D., and J. Keys. 2000. "Competitive Framing Processes in the Abortion Debate: Polarization-vilification, Frame Saving, and Frame Debunking." *The Sociological Quarterly* 41, no. 1 (January): 41–61.

Mikalsen, Ø. 1999. "Skjøt ikke for å treffe: Bastesen forsvarer skudd mot hvalfangstde-
monstranter." *Dagbladet,* 13 July.

Murphy, P., and J. Dee. 1992. "Du Pont and Greenpeace: The Dynamics of Conflict
Between Corporations and Activist Groups." *Journal of Public Relations Research* 4,
no. 1: 3–20.

Norgaard, K. M. 2006. "'We Don't Really Want to Know': Environmental Justice and
Socially Organized Denial of Global Warming in Norway." *Organization & Environment* 19, no. 3 (September): 347–70.

Norwegian Ministry of Foreign Affairs. 2003. "Der Fang von Zwergwalen in Norwegen."
http://www.norwegen.no/misc/print.aspx?article={4ac13188-5cac-44c9-99bd-
0a1576ee0f48} (accessed 12 July 2006).

NTBtekst. 1999. "Greenpeace skriver til tusener av nordmenn." 31 May.

Olaussen, L. M. 1999. "Bastesen angrer ikke skytingen." *Aftenposten Morgen,* 14 July.

Ryan, C. 1991. *Prime Time Activism: Media Strategies for Grassroots Organizing.* Boston,
MA: South End Press.

Schmidt, N. 1992. "Nordmenn er spyttslikkere." *VG,* 24 July.

Snow, D. A., and R. D. Benford. 1988. "Ideology, Frame Resonance, and Participant
Mobilization." In *From Structure to Action: Comparing Social Movement Research
Across Cultures,* ed. B. Klandermans, H. Kriesi, and S. Tarrow. Greenwich, CT: JAI
Press.

———. 1992. "Master Frames and Cycles of Protest." In *Frontiers in Social Movement
Theory,* ed. A. D. Morris and C. McClurg Mueller. New Haven, CT: Yale University
Press.

Snow, D. A., E. B. Rochford, S. K. Worden, and R. D. Benford. 1986. "Frame Alignment
Processes, Micromobilization, and Movement Participation." *American Sociological
Review* 51, no. 4 (August): 464–81.

Sollied, K.-A. 1994. "Hval: Grave en grav." *Nordlys Morgen,* 15 December.

Sørhaug, H. C. 1984. "Totemisme på norsk: Betraktninger om den norske sosialdemo-
kratismes vesen." In *Den norske væremåten: Antropologisk søkelys på norsk kultur,* ed.
A. M. Klausen. Oslo: J. W. Cappelens Forlag.

Statistics Norway. 2006. "Kvalfangst." http://www.ssb.no/aarbok/2006/fig/fig-375.html
(accessed 21 April 2011).

————. 2010. "Småhvalfangsten." http://www.ssb.no/histstat/tabeller/15-7.html (accessed 15 April 2011).

Straume, K. E. 1992. "Hvalfangernes skrek." *Nordlys Morgen,* 21 July.

Strømsnes, K., P. Selle, and G. Grendstad. 2009. "Environmentalism between State and Local Community: Why Greenpeace Has Failed in Norway." *Environmental Politics* 18, no. 3: 391–407.

Tonstad, P. L. 1999. "Skyter hval ulovlig Norsk gavepakke til Greenpeace." *Dagbladet,* 11 July.

Tsoukas, H. 1999. "David and Goliath in the Risk Society: Making Sense of the Conflict between Shell and Greenpeace in the North Sea." *Organization* 6, no. 3 (August): 499–528.

Waagbø, A. J. 1992. "Greenpeace-sjef går av i protest." *Dagbladet,* 2 August.

Wallace, A. 1992. "Norway Plans to Resume Whale Hunting in 1993." *United Press International,* 29 June.

Whale and Dolphin Conservation Society. n.d. *Subsidies in the Norwegian Whaling Industry.* http://www.wdcs.org/dan/publishing.nsf/c525f7df6cbf01ef802569d600573108/4bfbf08e3461f1d2802568f10038ab85/$FILE/subs.pdf.

Williams, R. H., and R. D. Benford. 2000. "Two Faces of Collective Action Frames: A Theoretical Consideration." *Current Perspectives in Social Theory* 20: 127–51.

Websites

High North Alliance: www.highnorth.no
International Union for Conservation of Nature: www.iucnredlist.org
Norwegian government: www.regjeringen.no
Statistics Norway: www.ssb.no

Chapter 17

The Limits to Transnational Attention

Rise and Fall in the European
Social Forums' Media Resonance

Simon Teune

In the wake of the World Social Forum (WSF), the idea of an open space for critics of neoliberal globalization to convene spread throughout the world (Smith et al. 2011). Becoming a public stage and part of the infrastructure of global justice movements (GJMs), local, regional, and national social forums were organized based on the WSF charter of principles. The charter envisions a global process that opens up alternatives to neoliberal globalization.[1] As part of this process, social forum events are organized to facilitate debates among diverse political actors without aiming at joint action.

Global justice activists in Europe decided to organize the first European Social Forum (ESF) in Florence in November 2002. Within the framework of a highly integrated polity, the meeting of European activists has been understood as being more than an exchange between people from neighboring countries. It is a gathering of Europeans who in their vast majority support the continental integration, while being critical of neoliberal policies implemented by European institutions (della Porta 2010). ESF meetings are spaces that allow such criticism to be expressed and light to be shed on those aspects of Europe that are blocked out in governmental public relations. War, environmental hazards, illegalization of migrants, and social and gender inequalities are some of the issues discussed at the European iterations of the WSF. However, in order to gain momentum, the "other Europe" that ESF participants strive for has to be visible outside the venue.

To reach this goal, ESF organizers make use of several channels to make the forum public (Mosca et al. 2009). Among other actions, they create a website, organize demonstrations, facilitate meetings of participants and local citizens, and print banners and leaflets. To convey their message to a large number of citizens, social forum activists also have to address commercial and public mass media: TV and radio stations, as well as newspapers and magazines.

This chapter aims to reconstruct to what extent the first four ESFs were successful in attracting media attention. For this purpose, the coverage of twelve European newspapers is analyzed. The chapter addresses three questions: How does the context of an ESF influence the media coverage of it? Does the public relations (PR) concept of the organizers play a role? And do journalists embrace the European character of the gathering, or do national interests prevail?

This introduction is followed by a theoretical section sketching the relationship of social movement events and mass media. The subsequent section reconstructs the respective contexts that shaped the public perception of the individual ESF events. This information is then referred to in the following section in order to understand the differences in media coverage and the importance journalists attached to the ESF.

Mass Media and the Making of Social Movement Events

Notwithstanding cyclical ups and downs, social movements are active on a continuous basis. The political groups and organizations that constitute these movements meet regularly to discuss strategies and form opinions. They communicate via the internet, telephone, and in face-to-face meetings. While these persistent activities are mostly limited to activist circles, social movements also generate public events such as demonstrations, direct actions, and conferences to gain visibility. By definition, protest is a public endeavor. It aims at a public display of dissent, at a visualization of problems that are otherwise concealed or unnoticed. In this context, social movement events seek to reach "reference publics" (Lipsky 1968) that are needed as part of a transformative process.

In order to address an external audience, social forum activists may distribute leaflets to bystanders at a demonstration; they might start a door-to-door campaign, as happened in preparation for the ESF in Florence, to inform citizens about upcoming events. Usually, these direct forms of communication require considerable resources and are necessarily limited in scope. For this reason, protest communication is largely dependent on mass media (Gamson and Wolfsfeld 1993; Koopmans 2004). They are an important channel to reach a mass audience, transporting messages and images sent out during social movement events. However, rather than being an amplifier for movement messages, mass media follow their own logics and work with different criteria than that of the protesters. Journalists turn toward protest events only if they consider them to be newsworthy. Confronted with a daily flood of news, journalists act as gatekeepers who decide what is published and what is hidden. This selection is far from accidental. Criteria underlying such decisions in the editorial office have been labeled news values (Staab 1990). Characteristics of a protest event that come into play as news values include its size and location and the level of conflict (McCarthy et al. 1996; Oliver and Meyer 1999), as well as the presence of celebrities.

Connected to the problem of selection for coverage is a dilemma: on the one hand, the message that social movement activists want to send out is usually a complex critique that calls into question hegemonic beliefs. On the other hand, journalists are attentive to social movements only in extraordinary moments, when the chances to convey a message are limited. Aspects of social movements that attract media interest, such as mass demonstrations and images of conflict, are more or less incompatible with the activists' wish to see their story told. While street protests may under certain circumstances be attractive to journalists, activist messages have to be condensed into slogans or images. However, the chances that journalists take these up and interpret them in the intended way are rather slim. Events that allow a detailed understanding of the challengers' discourses and motives, such as congresses, hearings, or social forums, are less likely to enchant journalists.

There are a number of aspects beyond the reach of event organizers that influence the public perception of protest events. A social movement event is confronted with specific discursive opportunities, those "aspects of the public discourse that determine a message's chance of diffusion in the public sphere" (Koopmans and Olzak 2004: 202). Koopmans and Olzak (2004) mainly explore three facets of discursive opportunity. The first, *visibility*, is connected to what was stated previously: an event must pass the editorial desk. The placement of messages in media outlets is likely to be more prominent if the second aspect comes into play. Other public speakers who react to an event provide *resonance*, either consonant or dissonant, which deepens the impact of an event. Finally, the *legitimacy* attributed to social movement activities has an influence on the public perception of them.

The reactions of journalists and third parties who are integrated into the concept of discursive opportunity can be explained with reference to a more general issue-related constellation. Discursive opportunities are more likely to be beneficial if the setting allows links to be established with the social movement event. Does the event add to the understanding of important developments? Can it be connected to relevant issue attention cycles (McCarthy et al. 1996)? Does the event resonate with cultural knowledge?[2] If these contextual aspects are beneficial, we can speak of a *kairós*, an opportune moment for a social movement event to be received in public discourse.

Identifying this moment and framing the event accordingly is a matter of hard work, experience, and imagination.

Lefébure and Langneau's (2001) analysis of the coverage of labor-related protests in Europe shows that a central question of this chapter—are European social movement events perceived as continental phenomena—can only be answered with reference to such contextual factors. Two European marches against unemployment, insecurity, and exclusion resulted in different news frames. In light of previous events and an initiative of the socialist French government to tackle unemployment Europe-wide, the first Euromarch on Amsterdam in 1997 was perceived as a genuine European event. The second march to the European summit in Cologne in 1999, set in a less dynamic environment, was hardly mentioned and was not framed as a European protest (Lefébure and Langneau 2001).

Finally, the media resonance of social movement events does not only impinge on the public perception of social movements, but also has an effect on the dynamics of the movements themselves. First, reflection in the media influences the configuration of a movement. The image of social movement events conveyed in commercial and public mass media fluctuates between appeal and threat (Lipsky 1968). Thus, it can either spur or inhibit participation (Gitlin 1980). It may also promote certain strands or organizations of a movement (Kolb 2005) that are portrayed as positive, while others are ignored or disapproved of. Second, activists usually observe media coverage closely and act with the awareness that they are being observed by the commercial and public mass media (Fahlenbrach 2002). Being recognized by mass media and confronted with external perspectives are important aspects in the self-perception of challenging groups that contribute to the building of a collective identity. As a consequence, internal discussions are shaped significantly by the public image of a movement.

The ESFs in Context

As seen in the previous section, the press resonance to the ESFs cannot be understood without putting the events into context. How receptive were journalists vis-à-vis the respective ESFs? How did other actors in the public sphere comment on the ESFs? And what was the political constellation in which the ESFs took place? These questions will be addressed for each ESF event individually. They are not, however, independent from the media coverage that is analyzed in the following section of this chapter. Media receptiveness, third-party activities, and other contextual factors are shaped by a public image of an event that is constructed in advance. For instance, political decision makers will only comment on the forum if they are under the impression that it is a significant event—something that is very unlikely to happen if the media do not cover the forum. Moreover, intermedia agenda setting plays an important role for editorial staff deciding on the extent of their coverage. If the major news media report on the ESF, this is an incentive for other journalists to take up the issue. To control the effect of ESF organizers' media relations on the press resonance, this aspect is also sketched briefly.[3]

The first ESF that took place on 6–10 November 2002 was perceived against the backdrop of two earlier events, which had partly diametric effects. In January 2002, the WSF took place for the second time. It inspired enthusiastic participants from Europe to transfer the process to their own continent. However, the WSF was more than an activist playground. After the colorful but somehow ephemeral protests in Seattle (1999, on occasion of a WTO meeting) and Prague (2000, targeting a joint meeting of World Bank and International Monetary Fund), the WSF was also recognized by a wider public as an event that offered serious alternatives to the policies promoted in the Swiss resort of Davos, where the World Economic Forum meets annually. The second event, which played an even more decisive role for the setting of the first ESF, was the G8 summit in Genoa in 2001. What was remembered about the large demonstrations against the summit was mainly the violence that peaked in the death of the protester Carlo Giuliani. Denying the extreme extent of violence on behalf of the police, the Italian government portrayed global justice activists as prone to violence and a threat to the cultural heritage in the ESF host city, Florence. Prime minister Silvio Berlusconi envisioned protesters that would "break the arm of Donatello's David" and called the ESF "lunacy" (*Corriere della Sera* 31 October 2002). Although the left-leaning regional government was supportive of the ESF, the atmosphere was tense both in the city and in the rest of Europe. Nevertheless, approximately sixty thousand participants[4] attended to discuss strategies "against war, racism and neoliberalism" (the ESF motto).

The organizers of the first ESF offered journalists daily press conferences and a selected program for journalists, typically including well-known organizations or celebrities. Several activists were identified as available for media contacts, and press releases were produced in a collective procedure. After the media resonance to the Genoa protests was dominated by one spokesperson of the local social forum, the ESF organizers intended to disperse media attention to a wider range of activists.

The atmosphere surrounding the second ESF, which took place in Paris on 12–16 November 2003, was certainly more beneficial. The first ESF and a large demonstration in that context had taken place without a critical incident—a sharp contrast with the previous hysteria about projected violence. It was only too obvious that Paris would not have to fear violent incidents. On the contrary, the mobilization that provided the context for the second ESF was the unprecedented transnational protests against the US-led war on Iraq, which had been interpreted as the advent of a European public sphere.[5] As the governments of France and Germany rejected the war, there seemed to be consonance with the protesters. This constellation facilitated the response to an event such as the ESF (although it was not widely known that the peace protests were initiated at the first ESF). Both the national and local governments in Paris were supportive of the event, providing considerable resources. Moreover, the ESF in Paris met with a decisively positive media environment. *Le Monde Diplomatique,* a monthly left-wing journal that played an important role in the foundation of the alterglobalist organization Attac and as a site for a critical debate of globalization, was a natural ally of the ESF organizers. Other left-wing media welcomed the forum as a chance to reaffirm their identity and put pressure on the conservative government. The number of participants in Paris was fifty thousand.

The organizers of the second ESF considered interaction with mass media to be a key problem. Their solution was a professionalization of the PR network. A press center at the venue was accessible for accredited journalists only, and two spokespersons were hired on a part-time basis. They distributed press releases in French, English, Spanish, and Italian to two thousand journalists.

In London, where the third ESF was held on 15–17 November 2004, the support of local authorities went even further, to an extent that proved to be problematic for the social forum process. The left-leaning mayor, Ken Livingstone, embraced the idea of an ESF in the British capital very early on. His administration provided considerable resources (such as free transportation for the participants at a cost of four hundred thousand pounds) and even became part of the organizing process, for instance, by administering the official ESF website. This appropriation of the ESF by a party politician was criticized by many grassroots activists. The role of Livingstone and the dominance of his Greater London Authority, as well as that of trade unions, NGOs, and the Socialist Workers Party, triggered a confrontation of "verticals" versus "horizontals," peaking in the disruption of a plenary session and a demonstration against the official ESF (Papadimitriou et al. 2007). Because of these conflicts in the preparatory process as well as disenchantment after two rather enthusiastic events, the London event attracted only approximately twenty-five thousand participants. The GJMs that were observed with interest when they entered the European stage in the early 2000s had lost appeal some years later.

The ESF in the British capital had a similar PR layout to its forerunner in Paris. However, the adaptation to the needs of commercial journalism was even more visible in London. A press officer was hired, and, as a service for journalists, the London website was the first ESF site to include a section to access press releases and information about accreditation. According to the website, six hundred journalists registered to report on the ESF.

Like the event in London, the Athens ESF, scheduled on 4–7 May 2006, did not trigger much excitement on the side of the national government, let alone abroad. The government concentrated a massive police presence in the capital to control what was expected to be one of the largest demonstrations of the radical Left beyond the Communist Party. However, this provision was made without exaggerated public statements, as in Italy in 2001. The ESF as such seemed to be accepted as routine. While there was also something of a routine among long-standing participants, the Athens ESF succeeded in integrating many activists from Central and Eastern Europe. According to the organizers, thirty-five thousand participants registered for the event.

As a reaction to the criticism of the London ESF, the media work in Athens was performed collectively by a group of five activists, one of them identifiable as an ESF press officer. The concept of the press team was akin to that developed by the organizers of the Florence ESF. They aimed at facilitating contacts between journalists and activists rather than providing a professional service to the mass media. The team also issued press releases that were available in Greek and English.

Journalistic Frames: Press Resonance to the ESFs

This section will explore the press coverage of the ESFs in the four host countries and in two further countries—Spain and Germany—where no ESF had taken place. For each country, the analyzed newspapers comprise a conservative and a liberal outlet. The labels "liberal" and "conservative" refer to the assumption that an editorial slant affects the selection of news and the opinion published in a paper.[6] The selected national newspapers tend to either the conservative (first media outlet mentioned in the following list) or the liberal pole in the political spectrum (second outlet). These are, for Italy: *Corriere della Sera* and *La Repubblica;* for France: *Le Figaro* and *Le Monde;* for the UK: the *Telegraph* and the *Guardian;* for Greece: *Kathimerini* and *Eleytherotypia;* for Spain: *El Mundo* and *El País;* and for Germany: *Frankfurter Allgemeine Zeitung* and *Süddeutsche Zeitung.*

The analysis is straightforward. Relevant articles were identified using the search phrase "European Social Forum" in the respective language on the newspapers' websites. For a period of one month before the event, during the event, and one month after, this search yielded a total of 531 articles. Formats included reports, news, reportages, interviews, op-eds, and letters to the editor. While saving time and money, this method is problematic inasmuch as the content available on the website differs from one newspaper to the other. In some cases, it was not possible to tell in which section of the newspaper the article was published or if it was part of the printed issue at all. Due to such problems, an elaborated quantitative analysis was not possible without investing considerably more resources. As a consequence, the following results are based on a simple count of articles and a content analysis that identifies central issues in the coverage and the general attitude vis-à-vis the ESF.

Florence, 2002: Novel Event in the Wake of Violence

Extensive media coverage of the anti-WTO protests in Seattle 1999 and the annual WSF paved the way for broad attention to a European iteration of the social forum. Riots and police brutality in the context of protests against the G8 summit in Genoa in July 2001 added to the attentive attitude of the media toward the Florence ESF. As a novel event for the European context, the first ESF in Florence triggered broad media coverage (see figure 17.1). None of the newspapers analyzed ignored the event. However, the conservative outlets emitted an explicitly hostile tone. Many of them echoed the excitement of the national government, which expected the worst. Accord-

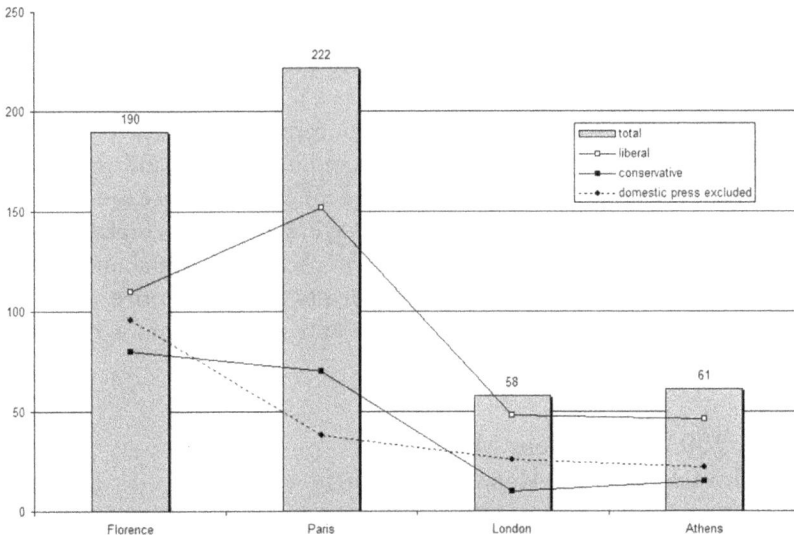

Figure 17.1. Coverage of the ESFs in Twelve European Newspapers

ing to the *Corriere della Sera,* Florence prepared for the "no global [label used in Italian for global justice activists] risk" (6 October 2002). The day after the official start of the forum, the newspaper published an open letter to the citizens of Florence written by resident journalist Oriana Fallaci:

> Close everything, pull down portcullises, put up the sign like the braves in 1922 when Mussolini's fascists made the march on Rome. "Closed for mourning" ... Impose yourself a sort of curfew, feel as you felt in 1944 when the Germans had blown up our bridges. (*Corriere della Sera* 7 November 2002)

While conservative papers seemed to agree with Fallaci—the *Telegraph,* for instance, quoted "the prominent Florentine author and journalist" and her portrait of global justice activists as "people who respect Saddam Hussein, love Osama bin Laden, and bow before the military and theocratic regimes of Islam" (9 November 2002)—liberal newspapers took a different stance. For example, the German *Süddeutsche Zeitung* qualified Fallaci's statements as "insults that are typical for her" (8 November 2002).

A member of the ESF press team remembers that:

> During the days of the forum, several correspondents mentioned the pressure exerted by their directors and editorial staff to report negatively on the event. The correspondent of the most important Italian newspaper, *Corriere della Sera,* decided to quit his job after some of his articles reporting positively about the forum were censored by his director. (interview, Lorenzo Mosca)

Rather than addressing the content of the forum, the Florence ESF was presented as the sequel of the anti-G8 summit of Genoa and the forum participants as people who would vandalize the city. Reference to the European dimension of the forum was only made in some articles explaining the meeting as an iteration of the global forums. Articles in liberal outlets that emphasized the novelty of the format tended to be more positive about the event. Some were even euphoric about the advent of a forum for European civil society.

Paris, 2003: Benevolent Media in the Homeland of *Le Monde Diplomatique*

In Paris, the interest of the media proved to be impressive even before the start of the event. Three to four hundred journalists attended a press conference prior to the ESF. Thanks to the strong interests of some left-leaning[7] newspapers in the forum, media coverage was not only extensive, but also positive. *L'Humanité, Libération,* and *Le Monde* all outbid each other in publishing special issues, columns, and announcements that encouraged the French to participate in the forum (Lévêque 2005: 92). Some papers even published the daily program. Photographs showed likeable young people, evoking a positive image of the event. The hype in the newspapers of the Left had a pull effect on media at the other end of the political spectrum. According to Sandine Lévêque, many local newspapers also featured the forum on their front pages thanks to Agence France Press, which distributed comprehensive material on the ESF. It is only the extensive domestic coverage that explains why the Paris ESF received the highest number of articles in the twelve European newspapers analyzed compared to the three other ESFs (see figure 17.1). In contrast to the coverage of the Florence ESF, there are two obvious tendencies. First, the gap between Right and Left newspapers covering the Paris ESF shows the enormous interest of the latter in taking up the event. Second, the interest of foreign media fell significantly after the first ESF. Obviously, the ESF was not considered important on the whole continent. However, among the most important issues mentioned by the French mass media were the expected effects of the forum on French and European politics. The presence of established political players such as the Socialist Party was of particular interest to the media. Another issue was the integration of Muslims in Europe, triggered by the appearance of the Swiss orientalist Tariq Ramadan. Right-leaning papers tended to invoke the impression that an anti-Semitic paper written by Ramadan was not rejected by the GJMs and Attac France in particular. With this in mind, it is no wonder that half of the fifty-four articles published in *Le Figaro* refer to the contested Muslim participant. The importance of the ESF as an arena of exchange for critical Europeans goes unnoticed in the conservative press.

London, 2004: A Low Point in Media Attention

With the exception of the ESF media partner the *Guardian,* who announced the event as "the most important political gathering in Britain" (17 December 2003), the ESF in London attracted the least attention among the newspapers analyzed. All articles on this event add up to a total of fifty-eight, which is a quarter of the articles published on the ESF in Paris. The scarce resonance was also lamented by activists. Susan George wrote in the *Guardian* that "not many Britons are aware that tens of thousands of thinkers and activists from across Europe and beyond gather this week in London for the third European Social Forum" (15 October 2004). Among the conservative papers in ESF host countries, the *Telegraph* shows the least interest in the forum, publishing only three articles containing the name of the event. The *Telegraph* denounces the ESF as a "world full of alarming contradictions" (17 October 2004) where capitalism is rejected and at the same time Che Guevara sweatbands are sold for ten pounds. The *Economist*—a magazine not represented in the quantitative analysis—demeans the forum as "fringe politics" (28 October 2004). More generally, conservative newspapers all over Europe lost interest in the forum and stated an "*altermondialiste* fatigue" (*Le Figaro* 22 October 2004). The main issues in the London coverage were the war in Iraq, the ambivalence of Labour's mayor of London, Ken Livingstone, as a supporter and usurper of the event, and the participation of Che Guevara's daughter Aleida in a panel discussion. Although there was one article in the *Guardian* about the contested domination of the forum by the GLA and national trade unions, this topic tended to be belittled in other articles within this newspaper.[8] Again, Europe was not the frame in which journalists presented the ESF.

Athens, 2006: Surefire News Value

The subsequent forum in Athens attracted just as little attention as the meeting in London. This applies even to newspapers that were open-minded about the social forum idea. For example, the *Guardian,* which had observed the forum in London with sympathy, now referred to the "cuddly anarchists" (23 April 2006), who were seen as a minor threat by the authorities after 11 September 2001. In Greece, the host country of the ESF, national attention was directed to the forum by a mere coincidence. A major football match was postponed because the necessary police force was in Athens during the mass demonstration. Even though one might presume that the threat to a national sport might raise hot tempers, the ESF coverage was not affected in a negative way. The example of Athens shows that hopes of drawing media attention to the forum by organizing a large final demonstration is highly ambiguous. The most positively perceived event in this respect was probably the peaceful demonstration in Florence, which contrasted sharply with the fear mongering of the Italian government and the conservative media. The demonstration four years later in Athens was, in contrast, accompanied by clashes between anarchists and the police. As surefire news value, the violence attracted the most space in the media coverage for the entire ESF. In Germany, the majority of the newspapers reduced their coverage to this particular incident, and the forum as such was of secondary importance only. Protests involving or even marginally associated with violence can hardly expect media coverage that includes the basic facts, such as the most important claim or the group organizing the event. As a colorful and spectacular event, particularly if associated with violence, a demonstration tends to trigger episodic forms of press coverage, focusing on the specific features of that one single event. The forum event is admittedly less attractive to journalists, but as a rather discursive happening it favors thematic coverage reflecting processes and contexts. It is not hard to imagine that without the clashes that accompanied the demonstration, the ESF in Athens would have undercut the media resonance of the previous forum in London.

Media Attention and Judgment: A Bad Success Story

Looking at the media coverage of the ESFs over time and comparing the newspaper reports from six countries, three trends are obvious: (1) conflict and proximity were the key explanatory factors for the amount of press coverage; (2) the media interest in the event decreased over time; and (3) liberal and conservative media differed widely in their coverage during the first two forums, while their coverage of the last ESFs tended to converge.

The analysis has shown that the coverage in the respective ESF host country is more extensive than in other countries (particularly in France, where the number of articles in the domestic press skyrocketed). The centrality of the issue panders to reports in domestic media that include more than just the basic facts (which is usual when the forum takes place in other countries). However, proximity to the ESF is not only a matter of geography. It is also related to the question of how the event can be connected to ongoing domestic debates that are perceived as important. Particularly in the first three forums, the attitude of the national and local government toward the event was a major issue for the press. Whereas the first forum was condemned by the national government in Italy but supported by the local authorities of Florence and Tuscany, the discussion around the Paris and London ESFs focused on the financial and logistical support by officials. In terms of the discursive opportunity structure model, the reaction of officials is a form of resonance that increases media attention for the forum.

The ESF was also taken as an opportunity to discuss domestic issues such as security (Italy), Muslim integration (Paris), the Iraq War (London), or the ban on police presence on campuses (Athens). In the same vein, an ESF held in a foreign country becomes an issue as soon as domestic politics are affected. In France, for instance, the coverage of the ESF started even before the first meeting in Florence because there had been prior discussion on whether the first ESF would be held in Paris or Florence. In Spain, the ESF in Athens attracted media attention as soon as Rafael Díez Usabiaga, a Basque trade unionist charged with supporting the illegal Batasuna party, was allowed to exit the country to attend it. This issue is mentioned in four of the five articles in both *El Mundo* and *El País* that mention the ESF (albeit in the domestic section of the newspaper). In sum, most newspapers do not follow global justice activists in their scale shift to the European level. Rather, they utilize a domestication frame that points out those aspects of the forum that are considered important for a national discourse.

The prevalence of the national context does not foreclose reference to Europe. *El País* and the *Guardian* label ESF participants as "Europeans." While articles written by journalists who attach hopes to the ESF (e.g., "Rattling the Bars," *Guardian* 18 November 2003) are almost exclusively published in liberal papers,[9] conservative papers do also occasionally transport the message of constructing "a more democratic Europe" (*El Mundo* 11 November 2003). However, the European frame connected to a thematic coverage vanishes as soon as the number of articles decreases. These observations converge with the finding of scholars on the European public sphere: a Europeanization of the public sphere has taken place on the level of monitoring the European Union (EU) government, while discursive exchange and mutual observation are rare (Brüggemann et al. 2006).

A great deal of the articles connected to the ESF focus on conflict, especially in Florence and Athens. While in Florence the shadow of Genoa and the hysteria of conservatives contributed to the making of the ESF event, the demonstration in Athens provoked well-known images that could not be linked to substantial claims. Also, the controversy related to Tariq Ramadan in Paris became a focus at least for conservative media outlets.

Beyond the national characteristics in the aspects being reported, the extent of press coverage continuously decreased. In the evaluation of the London forum, a fleeting "newness" was identified as a reason for the sparse press resonance (Lee 2004: 12). This was probably true not only for the specific ESF event, but also for GJMs in general. Figure 17.1 shows that this trend is particularly significant if newspapers from the host country are excluded.

Another lesson from the coverage of ESF events is the high degree of independence of media dynamics from the offers made by social movement activists. The professionalization of media relations seems to have had no impact on the coverage of the ESF whatsoever. While organizers in Florence and Athens followed a bottom-up approach that contradicted the habits and expectations of journalists, media relations in Paris and London were adjusted to the needs of journalists. Despite this variation in PR efforts, the resonance in newspaper coverage decreased over time. In London, where the ESF came closest to the PR approaches of organizations, companies, or governments, the event had the lowest press resonance. A professional press officer, an exclusive media center, and a website that fulfilled journalists' needs could not raise attention to the levels received during the preceding forums due to contextual factors. This is not to say, however, that media strategies of social movement activists are irrelevant. On the contrary, in a facilitating context professional PR can multiply the impact of an event or participating organizations (Kolb 2005). The example of the ESF shows, however, that social movements cannot generate interest by providing convenient working conditions for journalists alone.

When liberal and conservative newspapers are compared over time, their view of the ESF is not diametrically opposed. However, liberal newspapers tend to devote more space to the forums. They also emphasize different aspects and, initially, they grant more legitimacy to the forums. Regarding the first ESF in particular, liberal media applauded the congregation of critical activists. The sporadic euphoria in view of an "alternative citizenship" (*El País* 15 November 2002), partly written in the style of pamphlets, however, fades away during the London forum at the latest. At that point, the forum became just a "receptacle for do-gooders" (*Süddeutsche Zeitung* 18 October 2004), even for liberal newspapers. Yet the interest in the forum among conservative newspapers fades away faster than in their liberal counterparts. The percentage of conservative articles sinks from 42.1 percent in Florence to 17.2 in London. In Athens, the interest of conservative papers rises slightly (to a quarter) because of the violence at the demonstration. This does not foreclose positive articles in conservative newspapers. An article about the London ESF in *El Mundo* (18 October 2004), for instance, is written in a supportive style and provides a quote from the declaration of the assembly of social movements in which ESF participants sum up their criticism and list upcoming mobilizations.

Conclusion

Social forum activists are in a delicate position when they want to deliver their message to a larger public. Commercial and public mass media, one of the most important channels in which to raise public attention, are not very likely to be interested in the ESF as such. The attraction rises, however, if the event involves conflict, or if it can be related to debates relevant to the editorial staff. The analysis of twelve Western European newspapers showed that the initial interest on behalf of journalists, sometimes even accompanied by sympathy, dwindled very early.

It is obvious that many journalists do not conceive the later ESFs as important events of pan-European interest. This supports Pierre Lefébure and Eric Langneau's analysis of labor-related protests in Europe. They hold that "it is not enough for social actors to identify themselves as 'European' ... for the media to define their actions as such" (2001: 203). The fatigue on behalf of the mass media is met with a loss of enthusiasm among the ESF constituency, and it is hard to define the interplay between both findings. Is the decline in mass participation and hope attached to the ESF a result of or an influencing factor for a dwindling and often spiteful coverage?

The analysis of the press coverage of the ESFs does provide evidence for the impact of external factors on the extent of media resonance and the image of an event that emerges in the mass media. While issue attention cycles, domestic agendas, and the behavior of third parties shape the coverage to a great extent, the media relations efforts of activists organizing such an event prove to play a minor role. It is their task to be sensitive to the right moment and possible cross-references that might increase the pressure for journalists to cover their story.

Acknowledgments

This chapter draws from collaborative research with Lorenzo Mosca, Dieter Rucht, and Sara Lopez Martin within the EU-funded research project "Democracy in Europe and the Mobilization of Society" (http://demos.iue.it). I owe Antigoni Memou and Nikos Papadogiannis a debt of gratitude for identifying and translating the articles in Greek. I also thank Ariane Jossin and Christoph Haug for sharing their knowledge of the ESF with me.

Notes

1. The charter can be found at http://www.choike.org/documentos/wsf_s111_wsfcharter.pdf.
2. Especially in transnational social movement events, the conversion of different cultures of protest will be interpreted against the backdrop of national tradition in the host country.
3. A comprehensive comparison of PR efforts can be found in Mosca et al. (2009).
4. All numbers of participants are those declared by ESF organizers. They may be based on different methods of estimation.
5. Jürgen Habermas and Jacques Derrida took this stance in an essay that was part of a series of contributions by European intellectuals published in major European newspapers (*Frankfurter Allgemeine Zeitung* 31 May 2003; *Libération* 31 May 2003).
6. An editorial slant in German newspapers was first verified by Schönbach (1977) and confirmed in subsequent research.
7. Since the labels "liberal" and "conservative" are not appropriate for the French context, where liberal is associated with economic liberalism, the respective newspapers are idiomatically labeled "Left" and "Right."

8. Critics of the unions' and authorities' dominance were compared to Margaret Thatcher, who understood the trade unions as the "enemy within" the country (*Guardian* 16 October 2004).

9. Among the negligible articles portraying ESF participants as representatives of another Europe are op-eds authored by externals (e.g., "Construir Europa, hoy" by green activist and MEP Raül Romeva i Rueda in *El País* [28 October 2004]).

Bibliography

Brüggemann, M., S. Sifft, K. Kleinen-von Königslöw, B. Peters, and A. Wimmel. 2006. *Segmented Europeanization: The Transnationalization of Public Spheres in Europe: Trends and Patterns.* TranState Working Papers 37. Collaborative Research Center 597 Transformation of the State.

della Porta, D. 2010. "Reinventing Europe: Social Movement Activists as Critical Europeanists." In *The Transnational Condition: Protest Dynamics in an Entangled Europe,* ed. S. Teune. New York: Berghahn.

Fahlenbrach, K. 2002. *Protestinszenierungen: Visuelle Kommunikation und kollektive Identitäten in Neuen Sozialen Bewegungen.* Wiesbaden, Germany: Westdeutscher Verlag.

Gamson, W. A., and G. Wolfsfeld. 1993. "Movements and Media as Interacting Systems." *Annals of the American Academy of Political and Social Science* 528, no. 1: 114–27.

Gitlin, T. 1980. *The Whole World Is Watching: Mass Media in the Making and Unmaking of the Left.* Berkeley: University of California Press.

Kolb, F. 2005. "The Impact of Transnational Protest on Social Movement Organisations: Mass Media and the Making of ATTAC Germany." In *Transnational Movements and Global Activism,* ed. D. della Porta and S. Tarrow. Lanham, MD: Rowman & Littlefield.

Koopmans, R. 2004. "Movements and Media: Selection Processes and Evolutionary Dynamics in the Public Sphere." *Theory and Society* 33, nos. 3–4 (June): 367–91.

Koopmans, R., and S. Olzak. 2004. "Discursive Opportunities and the Evolution of Right-Wing Violence in Germany." *American Journal of Sociology* 110, no. 1 (July): 198–230.

Lee, J. 2004. *The European Social Forum at 3: Facing Old Challenges to Go Forward.* Centre for Applied Studies in International Negotiations, Geneva.

Lefébure, P., and E. Langneau. 2001. "Media Construction in the Dynamic of Europrotest." In *Contentious Europeans: Protest and Politics in an Emerging Polity,* ed. D. Imig and S. Tarrow. Lanham, MD: Rowman & Littlefield.

Lévêque, S. 2005. "Usages croisés d'un 'événement médiatique.'" In *Radiographie du Mouvement Altermondialiste,* ed. É. Agricolansky and I. Sommier. Paris: La Dispute.

Lipsky, M. 1968. "Protest as a Political Resource." *The American Political Science Review* 62, no. 4 (December): 1144–58.

McCarthy, J. D., C. McPhail, and J. Smith. 1996. "Images of Protest: Dimensions of Selection Bias in Media Coverage of Washington Demonstrations, 1982 and 1991." *American Sociological Review* 61, no. 3 (June): 478–99.

Mosca, L., D. Rucht, and S. Teune with the cooperation of S. Lopez Martin. 2009. "Communicating the European Social Forum." In *Another Europe: Conceptions and*

Practices of Democracy in the European Social Forums, ed. D. della Porta. London: Routledge.

Oliver, P. E., and D. J. Meyer. 1999. "How Events Enter the Public Sphere: Conflict, Location, and Sponsorship in Local Newspaper Coverage of Public Events." *American Journal of Sociology* 105, no. 1 (July): 38–87.

Papadimitriou, T., C. Saunders, and C. Rootes. 2007. *Democracy and the London European Social Forum.* Presented at ecpr Joint Sessions of Workshops, Helsinki, 7–12 May 2007.

Schönbach, K. 1977. *Trennung von Nachricht und Meinung: Empirische Untersuchung eines journalistischen Qualitätskriteriums.* Munich: Karl Alber.

Smith, J., S. C. Byrd, E. Reese, and E. Smythe, eds. 2011. *Handbook on World Social Forum Activism.* Boulder, CO: Paradigm Publishers.

Staab, J. F. 1990. *Nachrichtenwert-Theorie: Formale Struktur und empirischer Gehalt.* Munich: Alber.

Part IV

Protest in the Digital Age

Performing and Covering Protest on the Internet

.

Chapter 18

Global Protest in Online News
Øystein Pedersen Dahlen

In a very short time, online newspapers have become an important news channel, on a par with television, radio, and newspapers. Most online newspapers were established by newspapers or television stations and continue many journalistic traditions and tasks. Thus, in online newspapers, journalists still perform a gatekeeper function in their daily work, and news priorities have to be on the front pages as well as in the individual stories. Focus is still on the recent, dramatic events that are believed to be relevant to the audience. The pace of updating news has even been sped up in the online world. But by using the web as the platform for news dissemination, there is an unlimited space available to provide much information and room for a vast number of sources. Web news outlets can therefore open up a more democratic debate with more voices able to be heard, where different sources can give their views on current affairs and the audience can relate to different perspectives.

These new elements create new opportunities and challenges for both online journalists and their audiences and sources. The question nevertheless remains the same: How do social movements and ad hoc protest groups generate media attention? Does this media attention legitimize the movement's existence and broaden public acceptance?

The historical change in news dissemination with the establishment of web news outlets is primarily the melding of two important features or combined possibilities:

1. The receiver's constant access to a huge amount of material.
2. The sender's possibility to constantly update the same material.

These two possibilities have never before been seen in any one media or device. The first feature is possible due to electronic hyperlinks and hypertext. The idea of hypertext in news stories can be said to "lead readers to deeper context, illustrations, background information, related stories, and so on" (Zeng and Li 2006: 142). Even if the online news sites are dominated by episodic news (Sparks and Yilmaz 2005: 272), there should be a possibility to further explore news items "through a few clicks to other news sites" (Nguyen 2006: 81). This additional material can be accessed via hyperlinks, which can also be called *relation links*. These relation links indicate that there is more content on another page that is related to the first page visited (Fagerjord 2006: 272). The readers are thereby automatically given access to additional information, which can be linked from the primary text to another site (external links) or to material within the domain (internal links). Current events can thereby be put into context.

By giving users more choice and more control of their news intake, it is claimed that the web is an excellent means of providing in-depth and background information (Nguyen 2006: 81). The content's richness and depth has also been defined as one of the major advantages of online news (Nguyen 2006: 80). The expectations and hopes for the web news format have therefore been optimistic concerning the possibilities to put episodic news into a thematic context. Shanto Iyengar (1991: 2) points out that news disseminators frame their stories in two different ways: episodically and thematically. The episodic news frame is event oriented and focuses on particular cases. Thematically framed news, on the other hand, places political issues and events in a more general or abstract context. With their focus on the latest updates, most of the journalistic resources are used to produce articles within *episodic frames,* with a focus on *what, where, when,* and *who.* The articles within *thematic frames,* with a focus on *why* and the *consequences,* can therefore be scarce in news outlets. Thus, *relation links* can help to address two of the problems journalists routinely face:

1. How much of the previous day's events need to be recapped in today's story?
2. How many alternative points of view shall be included in the story?

Concerning the first question, Mark Tremayne (2006) suggests that online journalists can link to yesterday's news and dispense with a background paragraph in the new, updated story. The second problem can be solved by links to websites established by alternative groups or organizations (Tremayne 2006: 53), something that will be thoroughly investigated in this chapter. Research and studies on hyperlinks in web news outlets have so far only counted the number of hyperlinks, without going into a text analysis or content analysis of these interlinked texts (Engebretsen 2007; Greer and Mensing 2006; Li 2006; van der Wurff 2005). There is therefore a lack of understanding of the connection between the primary texts and the linked texts. The question of whether the linked texts give the reader more knowledge about the news by using these hyperlinks has not been explored thoroughly. Some studies have nevertheless shown that web outlets are unlikely to link to external news sources that could *potentially* increase their readers' understanding of a story (Tremayne 2006; Peng et al. 1999: 59; Dimitraova et al. 2003: 407), even if there is a clear tendency for more external links in more recent years (Dahlen 2010).

The possibility to constantly update the news has been present ever since the first radio transmissions, but the new element in this is the possibility for the reader to access all these directly transmitted messages. Web news outlets, as other news outlets, are expected to contain the latest information on the stories they convey to the public. Just as an audience expects the latest news when listening to a radio bulletin, the same audience expects the latest version whenever they access a specific web news outlet.

These two possibilities pull the web news outlets in two different directions. On the one hand, the receivers' constant access to the material indicates that the outlets should create thematic articles that can be linked up with episodic articles. On the other hand, the expectation of always finding the latest news indicates that the outlets should allocate more resources to creating episodic news. The pressure to produce news in a high tempo has in any case led to new working conditions, where journalists have made themselves dependent upon other online sources, and a few actors are dominating the international online news agenda. Chris Paterson's research "indicates that discourse on international events of consequence within the global public sphere is substantially determined by the production practices and institutional priorities of two information services—Reuters and the Associated Press" (2006: 19). Paterson claims that only four organizations carry out extensive international reporting: Reuters, Associated Press, Agence France-Presse, and the British Broadcasting Corporation (BBC). Paterson (2006: 17–18) states, however, that the BBC Online News uses news agency material without any editing in a lesser degree than others and that they have more sources for their foreign news than outlets based in the United States.

An investigation based on interviews with fourteen Norwegian journalists working with foreign news items indicates that online journalists do more research *online* than their colleagues working in other platforms, and that the online sources are dominated by the well-known British and North American web outlets like the BBC, the *Guardian,* the *New York Times,* and CNN.com (Piene 2008). Astrid Gynnild (2006) saw the same tendencies of limitations and standardization in her investigations into Norwegian online newsrooms. She states that individual creativity "may be reduced to handling and editing other media's news instead of shaping one's own" (Gynnild 2006: 171).

Research into media coverage on protests against the World Trade Organization (WTO) and other similar international organizations seems to reach the same negative conclusion regarding the depiction of the protesters and the ability of the protesters to share their arguments (Ackerman 2000; Solomon 2000; Fedorova 2007; Jha 2007). Several studies have been devoted the analysis of the media response to the so-called antiglobalization protests, many based on the WTO meeting in Seattle in 1999. Many of these analyses focus on the lack of room in the media for expressions and explanations of the reasons behind the protests (Ackerman 2000; Solomon 2000; Fedorova 2000; Jha 2007). The news coverage of social protest marginalizes challenging groups and depicts selection bias or description bias. Journalists "limit the comments of both the marginalized and social movements' activists to the experimental world they confront, relying on credentialed experts to provide an analytical understanding of the forces that shape this world" (Ryan et al. 2001). Sonora Jha saw the same tendency in her analysis of the US media's coverage of the WTO conference in 1999, focusing on the "use of protester sources or thematic versus episodic frames in story valence" (Jha 2007: 40). Jha argues that these thematic stories concerning the movements' arguments are presented as episodic news with a negative valence, citing "quote-worthy" protesters and "employing description of color, costumes, and mayhem" (Jha 2007: 50). There is, therefore, a demand for a broader understanding of the protests and a wider connection to the politics they are opposing, through what Shanto Iyengar (1991: 14) calls thematic news. The dramatic events are emphasized as they occur, and journalists are "using their own frames and filters to the detriment of the movement message" (Jha 2007: 50) and the rationale behind the movements' arguments. Novelty, polemics, confrontation, and controversy are thus the frames that attract attention for social movements and get movement spokespersons media access (Gamson and Meyer 1996: 288). The movements must become newsworthy "by conforming to journalistic notions" (Gitlin 2003: 3).

As with previous WTO ministerial conferences, the 2005 conference received worldwide media coverage in December 2005. International newspapers, TV and radio stations, and online outlets all covered both the negotiations inside the conference hall in Hong Kong and the protests outside extensively. Both the organizers and the media anticipated the protests. In a post-Seattle world, the violent protests had almost become a necessary ingredient in the media coverage of international conferences on international economics and trade.

The two most frequently consulted British web news outlets (the BBC and the *Guardian* online) and the three most frequently consulted Norwegian web news outlets (*VG Nett,* Dagbladet.no, and TV2 Nettavisen) are used as empirical material to study how the protesters were presented, the role they had in the media drama, and to what extent they had the chance to present their arguments in the debate. The two British outlets were at the forefront in making use of the possibilities inherent in new technology (Nguyen 2006: 94; Sparks and Yilmaz 2005: 265; van der Wurff 2005: 47–48). The British outlets were also chosen due to their central role in international news (Thurman 2007: 287), especially in connection to international events (Hall 2001: 17). The two British outlets are the most frequently used European outlets among Norwegian foreign news reporters (Piene 2008: 177), and according to numbers from the *Guardian,* their website has more readers in the United States that it has in the UK (Mayes 2004). The three Norwegian outlets are prominent examples of outlets from Scandinavia that have been regarded as "fertile and representative ground to identify emerging practices in the area of participatory mediamaking" (Deuze et al. 2007: 325), and have a high internet penetration (Karlsson 2009: 6). *VG Nett* has also attracted international attention and has been called "the star performer online" by journalist Bill Doskoch on CTV Toronto in 2009. On the Danish School of Journalism's website, *VG Nett* is called a role model for Scandinavian online newspapers:

> VG Nett is awarded repeatedly for their web-pages, and is in many ways a role-model for other Scandinavian newspapers on how to use the online-possibilities (Danish School of Journalism 2007).

VG Nett and Dagbladet.no have their origins in printed newspapers, and both the printed and online versions have a nationwide audience and represent the popular and tabloid form of journalism in a country where only these two papers are based on single copy sale and not on subscribers. Nevertheless, neither of the two titles are "tabloid in the sense of the British popular press" (Eide 1997: 174). The newspapers contain journalism that can be said to be "somewhere in the middle-ground between academic elitism and vulgar ignorance" (Eide 1997: 174). TV2 Nettavisen was originally established as a detached online service in 1996. TV2 bought the online service in 2003 and renamed it TV2 Nettavisen. The name was later changed back to simply Nettavisen in 2006. The news on the outlet can also be regarded as popular and tabloid, on the same level as the two other Norwegian outlets investigated here.

Two Separate Stories

All articles published between 1 December and 20 December 2005 dealing with the WTO's 2005 Ministerial Conference have been assessed and analyzed. The sites that are linked to the articles have also been analyzed. The actual ministerial meeting was held in Hong Kong on 14–18 December.

The media coverage in the five outlets was divided into two, almost separate main stories. One was about the negotiations inside the conference hall. The other story was about the (mostly) violent protests outside the conference hall, mainly depicted as fights between South Korean farmers and the police. The two main stories are connected, however, by the police, who helped the negotiators to fulfill their tasks without disturbance from the protesters. With the two dominating stories or frames in hand, the stories can be presented in a traditional, semantic actor-project model, as suggested by A. J. Greimas (1974: 287). If we look only at the front-page references as single stories, almost all the stories in the outlets are about negotiations between politicians and the police on the one hand, and the protesters on the other. The police wanted to help the negotiators with their project, while the protesters tried to obstruct this project. The negotiators' project was to agree on a new free trade deal, where the WTO is the benefactor. It is difficult to define clearly who the receivers are, but the national economy or nation-state, or even people living in the nation-state, could be a suggestion (see figure 18.1[1]). In other words, all the stories are framed as being either along the conflict axis or the project axis in figure 18.1, or both. In the conflict axis, there are fights between the protesters and the police, where the police try to keep the protesters from obstructing the negotiations. In the project axis, different arguments meet in the negotiators' struggle to complete a new trade deal. The reports from the official meeting depicted an atmosphere of rational communication and negotiation and differed markedly from the

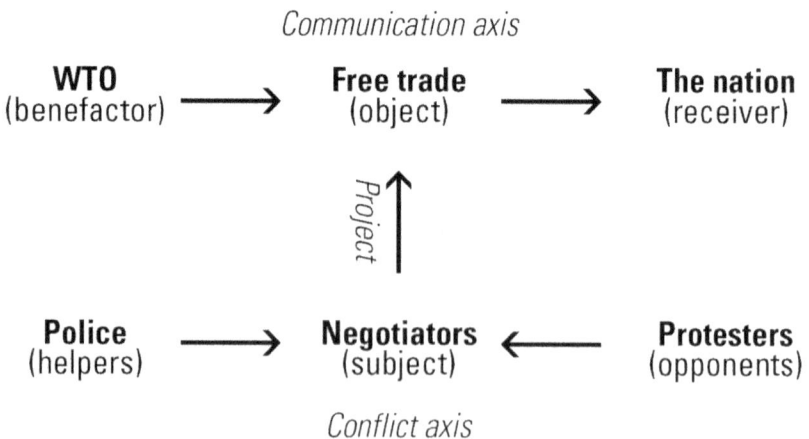

Communication axis

| **WTO** (benefactor) | ⟶ | **Free trade** (object) | ⟶ | **The nation** (receiver) |

Project ↑

| **Police** (helpers) | ⟶ | **Negotiators** (subject) | ⟵ | **Protesters** (opponents) |

Conflict axis

Figure 18.1. Actor-Project Model on the Coverage of the WTO Meeting in Hong Kong

reports from outside the official meeting, which were dominated by clashes between police and demonstrators.

The story on the WTO was established differently in the five outlets, but the violent protests were in focus during the dramatic peaks in all the outlets. All but the *Guardian* ended the story by saying that there was an agreement on export subsides, and called the conference a modest success. The *Guardian,* on the other hand, called the negotiations a failure and argued that the rich countries had betrayed the poor countries.

Parts of the two main stories were often included in the same article, but even then, it was hard to see the connection between the negotiations and the protests, apart from the underlying statements that the police were helping the negotiators to do their job inside the conference hall without disturbance from the protesters. The protests are in very few cases linked to the negotiations in a way that explains the reasons behind the anger and frustration among the protesters. Only half of the articles dealing with protesters or protests have any explanation at all on the reasons for there being protests and rallies in Hong Kong. In half of these explanations, there is only one sentence from the journalist to explain the background for the protests (see table 18.1), like this one in Dagbladet.no: "The protesters claim that the trade organization reinforces environment problems and impairs the development in poor countries"[2] (Dagbladet.no 2005). With only one general, simplistic sentence as an explanation, the protesters' array of views became, as Solomon (2000) concluded in his analysis of the 1999 conference, oversimplified.[3] The British outlets had a higher degree of quotations from the protesters, but most of these consisted of only a couple of sentences, like this one from the *Guardian:*

Free trade is destroying the lives of rice and corn growers" said Tri-Heru Wardoya, a Sumatran farmer. "People in my village earn just

Table 18.1. Explanation of the Protests in Articles on the Protests in the Five Outlets, As a Percentage

	VG Nett	TV2 Nettavisen	Dagbladet.no	BBC	*Guardian*	All Outlets
No explanation	44	69	(33)	33	48	49
Short explanation	56	31	(67)	66	48	50
Extensive explanation	0	0	0	0	5	2
Total	100	100	100	99	101	101
	n = 9	*n* = 13	*n* = 3	*n* = 9	*n* = 21	*N* = 55

$20 a month and use traditional methods ... How can they com-
pete with rich international businesses? (*Guardian* 2005)

Either representatives from social movements or people that were directly
connected to the protesters delivered these short quotes. The statements
from representatives from social movements were in some cases placed in
connection with the depiction of the protests, without stating directly that
these people are participating in the protest, like this one on the BBC:

> The Hong Kong government has mobilised its police force and
> spent weeks cementing up bricks in the pavement to prevent their
> use in riots. "Rich countries have the opportunity in Hong Kong to
> deliver on their promises to make trade work for the poor. Millions
> of farmers, campaigners and workers will be watching them," said
> Amy Barry, a spokeswoman for the charity Oxfam. (BBC 2005b)

In all of the material, there is only one occurrence of an extensive thematic
explanation of the reasons behind the protests. The *Guardian* has a page
with links to 10 two- to three-minute audio clips with representatives from
social movements, where three of the representatives are directly connected
to the demonstrations. In these presentations, those involved get the chance
to explain why they are in Hong Kong, why they think it is important to
be present, and what they think about the WTO and the negotiations. This
page is a clear exception in the analyzed material, but the two British outlets
still differ clearly from their Norwegian regarding the space allocated to explanations of the protests.

Only one of the twenty-six articles in the Norwegian online outlets had
a quote from a representative from the protesters giving an explanation for
why they were protesting. The only Norwegian example of such a quote is
found in TV2 Nettavisen, and is a statement from a representative from a
Norwegian organization in connection with a protest in Norway against the
Norwegian government (TV2 Nettavisen 2005b). All the other quotes in
the Norwegian material are protesters commenting on the protests as phenomena, without explaining the connection between the protests and the
negotiations, like this comment on *VG Nett*: "'If we break the police's limits
some think it is violence, but the point is that violence has different signifi-
cations,' says one of the farm leaders"[4] (*VG Nett* 2005). The outlets mostly
used authoritative sources who were mainly representatives from Western
governments and the WTO (see table 18.2). These sources had the chance
to elaborate their points of view, framed within a rational political debate.
Some names recurred frequently as official sources in all five outlets. These

Table 18.2. Sources in All the Articles on the WTO in the Five Outlets, As a Percentage

Sources From:	*VG Nett*	TV2 Nettavisen	Dagbladet.no	BBC	*Guardian*	All Outlets
Political institutions	66	74	83	67	55	63
Social movements and protesters	20	10	0	21	30	23
Interest groups	14	14	8	8	7	9
Others: researchers, consultants, private individuals, etc.	0	2	8	4	7	5
Total	100	100	99	100	99	100
	n = 35	*n* = 42	*n* = 12	*n* = 126	*n* = 141	*N* = 356

were the director-general of the WTO (Pascal Lamy), the US trade representative (Rob Portman), the European Union (EU) trade commissioner (Peter Mandelson), and two frequently named representatives from Southern governments: the Indian commerce minister (Kamal Nath) and Brazil's foreign minister (Celso Amorim). There were very few examples of discussions around the rules for negotiations and the WTO was mostly depicted as a neutral playing field for the negotiators from different countries. We have seen that the *Guardian* provided further information on the protests, but the official representatives dominate this outlet as well. The internal links to their own articles do not moderate this tendency, since these links take the readers to (mostly) already published news articles.

In contrast to the Norwegian outlets, the two British outlets had many hyperlinks to other websites, and half of these sites were set up by different social movements.[5] However, the problem here is also the relationship between the protests and the negotiations. There is no example of links that are connected to what is said about the protests or how they are depicted in any of the articles. Moreover, in the articles there is very little information related to the hyperlinks that highlights the connection between the protests and the negotiations. Furthermore, it is hard for the readers to know where to find useful information when only the headline or a name of an organization is used as the link, with no additional information. To find information about the protests, the readers have to try the links to the different organizations at random. The pages made by, for instance, World Development Movement and Christian Aid, which were linked up to both the *Guardian* and the BBC, had a lot of information on the negotiations and even connections to the protests. Christian Aid also provided different perspectives on the protests, other than the usual fights between South Korean farmers and the police in Hong Kong. One of the stories on the Christian Aid website states that "Bangladeshi Women Take to the Streets of Dhaka in Protest against WTO Negotiations Being Held in Hong Kong" (ChristianAid.org.uk 2005). The challenge is to know where to find this information when there is only a list of links to different organizations, without further information on what the pages contain.

Even if the protesters are not used frequently as sources, they still play an important role in the coverage of the WTO meeting in Hong Kong. An essential part of the stories on the conference is the images, which were often of protesters, who were frequently depicted in fights with the police. Of the 183 images, 53 percent of those (98 images) illustrate the protesters, and 21 percent (39 images) show the violent clashes between the police and protesters (see table 18.3). In 14 of the 145 articles (10 percent), there are images of protesters, even though the protesters are not even mentioned in the text (see table 18.4 and figures 18.2 and 18.3).

Table 18.3. Images in the Five Outlets, As a Percentage

Images	VG Nett	TV2 Nettavisen	Dagbladet.no	BBC	Guardian	All Outlets
Violent protests[6]	20	24	62	12	26	21
Peaceful protests[7]	40	40	8	24	50	32
Other pictures	40	36	31	65	24	48
Total pictures[8]	100	100	101	101	100	101
	$n = 21$	$n = 25$	$n = 13$	$n = 91$	$n = 33$	$N = 183$

Table 18.4. Images of Protesters when the Protesters Are Not Mentioned in the Article

	VG Nett	TV2 Nettavisen	Dagbladet.no	BBC	Guardian	All Outlets
Picture of protesters when protesters are not mentioned in the article	2	4	1	7	0	14
Total number of articles	18	22	8	42	53	143

The protests were even used as illustrations before the conference started on the BBC, although there was no information on the protests in the articles (see figures 18.2 and 18.3). In 10 percent of the articles, the protests are *not* mentioned, even if there are still images of protesters connected to these articles. This phenomenon clearly illustrates that the protests were expected to become an important part of the upcoming conference. This can therefore be called a preframing that obligated the press to include the protesters in their coverage of the upcoming conference.

Where the protesters are depicted, they are normally in a violent confrontation with the police. In 69 percent of the articles, the protesters are put in relation to violence, either in a description of a violent incident or as a potential disturbance (see table 18.5). There are no examples in the material of the combination of a depiction of violence linked to an explanation from the protesters as to why they are protesting.

The *Guardian* differs from the four other outlets in many respects. Whereas the other outlets show the protesters in a violent context in a total of 82 percent of their articles, that number for the *Guardian* is only 52 percent. There are no images of the protestors without mentioning the protests in the articles in the *Guardian,* but five of the eight main images do still illustrate the protests.

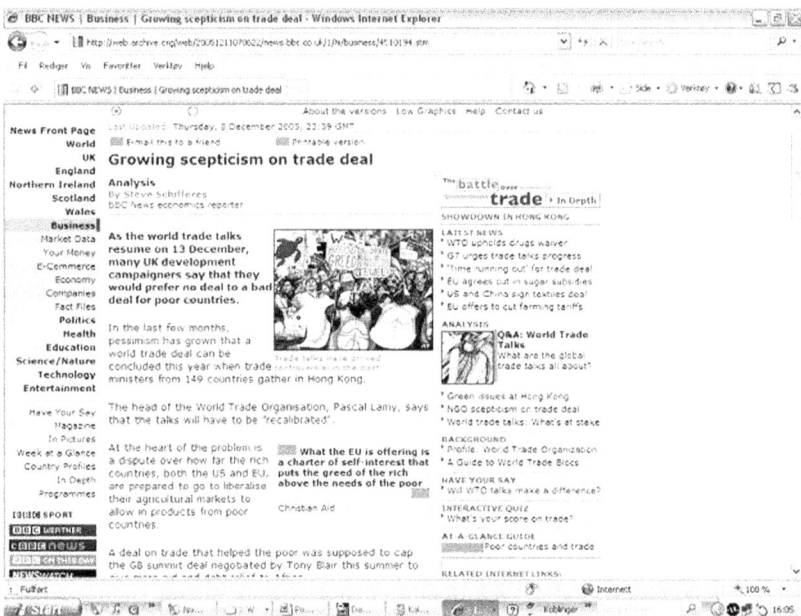

Figure 18.2. A BBC Article Prior to the Onset of the Conference Is Illustrated with an Image of a Protest from "the Past" (BBC 2005a).

Figure 18.3. This Article Contains Nothing About the Protests, Apart from the Text Below the Image of Protestors: "There have been violent clashes between the police and WTO opponents during the ministerial meeting in Hong Kong" (TV2 Nettavisen 2005a).

Almost half of the articles in the material can be assessed as (mostly) thematic (see table 18.6). There should therefore be room for the protesters to provide an explanation for why they are protesting. Nevertheless, the thematic articles are mostly used to give the readers background information on only one of the two stories, the negotiations inside the conference hall. There is not a high degree of thematic information on the events outside the

Table 18.5. Depiction of the Protesters in the Five Outlets, As a Percentage

	Percentage of Articles
Confrontation between police and protesters	53
Violent protests, without police involvement	11
Protesters as a potential disturbance problem	5
Peaceful protesters	30
Others	2
Total	100
	$n = 57$

Table 18.6. Generic Framing of the Articles on the WTO in the Five Outlets, As a Percentage

Generic Framing:	VG Nett	TV2 Nettavisen	Dagbladet.no	BBC	Guardian	All Outlets
Mostly thematic	26	23	57	58	55	48
Mainly episodic	74	77	43	42	44	52
Total	100	100	100	100	99	100
	n = 19	n = 22	n = 7	n = 43	n = 48	N = 145

Table 18.7. Generic Framing of the Articles on the WTO Protests in the Five Outlets, As a Percentage

Generic Framing:	VG Nett	TV2 Nettavisen	Dagbladet.no	BBC	Guardian	All Outlets
Mostly thematic	0	0	0	33	27	16
Mainly episodic	100	100	100	76	73	84
Total	100	100	100	100	100	100
	n = 7	n = 6	n = 2	n = 6	n = 11	N = 32

conference hall; coverage on these events consists mostly of the actual (episodic) happenings. Very few of the articles on the protesters can be said to be thematic. None of the articles on the protests in the Norwegian outlets is thematic. Moreover, just two articles in the BBC and three in the *Guardian* focusing on the protests are thematic articles (see table 18.7).

Some Conclusions

When the web news outlets are assessed to analyze how they created a broader political debate and if they showcased alternative voices via the case of the WTO, they are still seen as immature forms of media. The news stories are still written in a traditional manner, as though everything has to be told in every story. Every article contains the latest updates about different aspects of a story to provide readers with an understanding of the latest news, thus discouraging them from accessing external hyperlinks. In some cases, there are links to thematic articles on the WTO in general or comments/analyses on the ongoing negotiations. Nevertheless, the (episodic) news articles do not have any obviously useful hyperlinks where the reader can access adapted information that can increase their understanding of the current news. The hyperlinks are not developed in such a way that the reader can easily trace the connections between the stories on the outlets' domain and the arguments on other (alternative) sites. Most of the links provided are disconnected from the article, in that they do not sustain or support the basic arguments or the frame of the article they appear in. The episodic news stories are sometimes updated with the latest news, but they do not develop a broader perspective of the (thematic) reasons behind the development of the stories. This is a rather disappointing conclusion, when the content's richness and depth has been defined as one of the major advantages of online news (Nguyen 2006: 80).

The *Guardian* differs in some respects from these rather negative conclusions. This outlet gave more room for the protesters and the social movement to come forward with their arguments. The outlet did not use the protesters as illustrations without mentioning the protests in the same article. The BBC also provided some room for quotations from the protesters in articles on the protests, but it is also the outlet with the fewest articles on the protests relatively (23 percent of all the articles—see table 18.4). The number of protest and social movement sources is thus relatively low (see table 18.2).

The Norwegian outlets delivered very few explanations and quotations from the protesters themselves (see table 18.1). None of the Norwegian outlets had information explaining why the protesters were protesting, apart from one sentence, at most, in each article. The protesters were quoted in some of the articles, but these quotes were mainly about their actions, not about why they were opposing the negotiations and the WTO. It is therefore fair to say that at least the Norwegian web news outlets did not allow for a broader perspective on the protests, and the journalists did still undermine the rationale behind the movements' arguments. The protesters' voices were not heard through the mainstream web media, and web news outlets have not developed a suitable method for putting the episodic news into a broader (thematic) context. The impression the readers got from the five outlets was that the protesters were violent, yet it was hard to find explanations for why they were protesting.

Social movements and protesters have to be involved in dramatic scenes to gain attention, even in online news outlets, but their arguments do not receive much attention. It is therefore doubtful whether this media attention legitimizes the movement's existence and broadens public acceptance.

Notes

1. Most of the WTO stories on the front pages of the five outlets can be put into this figure. The negotiators want to agree on a free trade agreement, where the WTO is the facilitator for this agreement, which will be applied to the different member states. The protesters try to (violently) stop the negotiators, but the police secure the negotiators and their work.

2. "Demonstrantene mener handelsorganisasjonen forsterker miljøproblemer og svekker utviklingen i fattige land."
3. William S. Solomon (2000) examined fifty-seven articles on the protests against the WTO in 1999 in the *New York Times* and the *Los Angeles Times*.
4. "Hvis vi trår over politiets grenser mener noen det er vold, men poenget er at vold har ulike betydning, sier en av bondelederne."
5. 102 of the 200 external links to nonmedia sites took the readers to sites set up by social movements.
6. Including police preparing for protests.
7. Including injured protesters.
8. A collage of pictures is counted as one picture.

Bibliography

Ackerman, S. 2000. "Prattle in Seattle: Media Coverage Misrepresented Protests." In *Globalize This! The Battle Against the World Trade Organization and Corporate Rule*, ed. K. Danaher and R. Burbach. Monroe, ME: Common Courage Press.

BBC. 2005a. "Growing Scepticism on Trade Deal." 8 December. http://news.bbc.co.uk/2/hi/business/4510194.stm. (accessed 08.12.05)

———. 2005b. "Trade Talks Showdown in Hong Kong." 11 December. (accessed 11.12.05)

ChristianAid.org.uk. 2005. "Bangladeshi women say no to the WTO." www.christianaid.org.uk/news/stories/051215s.htm (last accessed 19.12.05).

Dagbladet.no. 2005. "Teargas, Pepper Spray, and Water Canons" [Tåregass, pepperspray og vannkanoner]. http://www.dagbladet.no/nyheter/2005/12/17/452506.html (accessed17.12.05)

Dahlen, Ø. P. 2010. "Nyheter i nettaviser: Muligheter og begrensninger" [News in online newspapers: Possibilities and limitations]. *Sosiologi i dag* 4 (2010): 32-54

Danish School of Journalism. 2007. "Cutting Edge in Scandinavia – VG Nett. " http://www.jourlab.com/2007/globaldialogue/2007/09/13/cutting-edge-in-scandinavia-vg-nett (last accessed 01.09.09)

Deuze, M., A. Bruns, and C. Neuberger. 2007. "Preparing for an Age of Participatory News." *Journalism Practice* 1, no. 3: 322–38.

Dimitraova, D., C. Connolly-Ahern, A. P. Williams, L. L. Kaid, and A. Reid. 2003. "Hyperlinking As Gatekeeping: Online Newspapers Coverage of the Execution of an American Terrorist." *Journalism Studies* 4, no. 3: 401–14.

Eide, M. 1997. "A New Kind of Newspaper?" *Media, Culture and Society* 19, no. 2 (April): 173–82.

Engebretsen, M. 2007. *Digitale diskurser: Nettavisen som kommunikativ flerbruksarena* [Digital discourses: Online newspapers as communicative multitask arena]. Kristiansand, Norway: Høyskoleforlaget.

Fagerjord, A. 2006. "Frihet: TV 2 på nett" [Freedom: TV 2 online]. In *Et hjem for oss—et hjem for deg? Analyser av TV 2* [A home for us—a home for you?], ed. G. S. Enli, T. Syvertsen, and S. Østby Sæther. 2nd ed. Kristiansand, Norway: IJ-forlaget.

Fedorova, E. 2007. "Global Political Response to Anti-Globalist Activities in the Early XXI Century." Conference presentation at "The Establishment Responds: The Institutional and Social Impact of Protest Movements During and After the Cold War," University of Heidelberg, Germany, 22–24 November 2007.

Gamson, W. A., and D. S. Meyer. 1996. "Framing Political Opportunity." In *Comparative Perspectives on Social Movements: Political Opportunities, Mobilizing Structures, and Cultural Framings*, ed. D. McAdam, J. McCarthy, and M. N. Zald. Cambridge: Cambridge University Press.

Gitlin, T. 2003. *The Whole World Is Watching: Mass Media in the Making and Unmaking of the New Left*. Berkeley: University of California Press.

Greer, J. D., and D. Mensing. 2006. "The Evolution of Online Newspapers: A Longitudinal Content Analysis, 1997–2003." In *Internet Newspapers: The Making of a Mainstream Medium*, ed. X. Li. Mahwah, NJ: Lawrence Erlbaum Associates. Publishers.

Greimas, A. J. 1974. *Structural Semantics: An Attempt at a Method*. Lincoln: University of Nebraska Press.

Guardian. 2005. "Korean Farmers Take Lemming-like Plunge into Hong Kong Harbour." http://business.guardian.co.uk/story/0,,1666609,00.html (accessed 14.12.05)

Gynnild, A. 2006. "Creative Cycling in the News Profession: A Grounded Theory." PhD diss., University of Bergen.

Hall, J. 2001. *Online Journalism: A Critical Primer*. London: Pluto Press.

Iyengar, S. 1991. *Is Anyone Responsible? How Television Frames Political Issues*. Chicago: University Press of Chicago.

Jha, S. 2007. "Exploring Internet Influence on the Coverage of Social Protests: Content Analysis Comparing Protests Coverage in 1967 and 1999." *Journalism & Mass Communication Quarterly* 84, no. 1: 40–57.

Karlsson, M. 2009. "Mapping the Liquidity of Online News Content: The Case of Sweden." Paper presented to the Nordmedia conference, Karlstad, Sweden, 13–15 August 2009.

Li, X. 2006. "Graphic Use and Interconnectedness of Internet Newspapers: A Many-to-Many Communication Model." In *Internet Newspapers: The Making of a Mainstream Medium*, ed. X. Li. London: Lawrence Erlbaum Associates.

Mayes, I. 2004. "A Girdle Round about the Earth." *Guardian*, 10 July, www.guardian .co.uk/news/2004/jul/10/commentanddebate.mainsection/print (accessed 20 August 2009).

Nguyen, A. D. 2006. "The Diffusion and Social Impact of Online News: Studying the Past and Present to Understand the Future of the Internet as a News Medium." PhD diss., University of Queensland.

Paterson, C. 2006. "News Agency Dominance in International News on the Internet." *Papers in International and Global Communication*, no. 1/06. Centre for International Communication Research, http://ics.leeds.ac.uk/papers/cicr/exhibits/42/cicrpaterson.pdf (accessed 17 June 2009).

Peng, F. Y., N. I. Tham, and H. Xiaoming. 1999. "Trends in Online Newspapers: A Look at the U.S. Web." *Newspaper Research Journal* 20, no. 2: 52–64.

Piene, B. D. 2008. "På nett med verden" [On the web of the world]. In *Journalistikk i en digital hverdag* [Journalism in digital surroundings], ed. R. Ottosen and A. Krumsvik. Kristiansand, Norway: IJ-forlaget.

Ryan, C., Kevin M. Carragee, and W. Meinhofer. 2001. "Theory into Practice: Framing, the News Media, and Collective Action." *Journal of Broadcasting and Electronic Media* 45, no. 1: 175–82.

Solomon, W. 2000. "More Form than Substance: Press Coverage of the WTO Protests in Seattle." *Monthly Review* 52, no. 1. www.monthlyreview.org/500solo.htm (accessed 10 September 2008).

Sparks, C., and A. Yilmaz. 2005. "United Kingdom: The Triumph of Quality." In *Print and Online Newspapers in Europe: A Comparative Analysis in 16 Countries,* ed. R. van der Wurff and E. Lauf. Amsterdam: Het Spinhuis.

Thurman, N. 2007. "The Globalization of Journalism Online: A Transatlantic Study of News Websites and their International Readers." *Journalism* 8, no. 3: 285–307.

Tremayne, M. 2006. "Applying Network Theory to the Use of External Links on News Web Sites." In *Internet Newspapers: The Making of a Mainstream Medium,* ed. X. L. Mahwah, NJ.: Lawrence Erlbaum Associates. Publishers. *TV2 Nettavisen.* 2005a. "Kirkens Nødhjelp refser ego-Norge" [Church Aid chastises egoistic Norway]. http://pub.tv2.no/nettavisen/verden/article514176.ece. (accessed 14.12.05)

———. 2005b. "Støre Wants to Reduce Agriculture" [Støre vil redusere landbruket]. http://pub.tv2.no/nettavisen/innenriks/politikk/article510646.ece (accessed 09.12.05).

Van der Wurff, R. 2005. "A Profile of Online and Print Newspapers in Europe." In *Print and Online Newspapers in Europe: A Comparative Analysis in 16 Countries,* ed. R. van der Wurff and E. Lauf. Amsterdam: Het Spinhuis.

VG Nett. 2005. "Tense WTO Start" [Spent WTO-start]. http://www.vg.no/nyheter/utenriks/artikkel.php?artid=110953 (accessed 13.12.05.)

Zeng, Q., and X. Li. 2006. "Factors Influencing Interactivity of Internet Newspapers: A Content Analysis of 106 U.S. Newspapers' Web Sites." In *Internet Newspapers: The Making of a Mainstream Medium,* ed. X. Li. Mahwah, NJ.: Lawrence Erlbaum Associates. Publishers.

Chapter 19

Cyberprotest
Protest in the Digital Age

Luca Rossi and Giovanni Boccia Artieri

Networked Public Spheres and Political Participation

In order to fully understand contemporary protest movements, it is necessary to frame them in the wider picture of how the relationship between media and society has changed during the digital age. In this communication-centered scenario, every aspect of how protest movements act today can be described as a consequence of (or as an opportunity offered by) the new media scene in which protest takes place.

Within this perspective communication practices have the power to impact on every social system and to contribute, together with many different social actors, to the continuous reflexive reshaping of them. This analytical framework is rooted in contemporary sociological theory, from Giddens's distinction between various social institutions (Giddens 1991) to Habermas's opposition between lifeworld, economic system, and political system (Habermas 1987), ending with Luhmann's social system theory (Luhmann 2000).

From a communicative point of view, protest movements have always acted within society in order to gain public attention from the social system or, at least, from a specific subsystem. The final goal of protest movements is to move a specific topic into the social agenda in order to push the social system toward an (desirable) action. These social forces have been described as a foundational connection between mass media and public opinion. This connection is observed through the concept of "public sphere." Using the concept of "public sphere" Jürgen Habermas introduces, in the classic *Strukturwandel der Öffentlichkeit* (Habermas 1987), a communication-based social space between the state and citizen society, embedded in the lifeworld (Habermas 1987, 1992).

So, the public sphere must be considered an abstraction of the public space in ancient civilizations (the Greek agora and Roman forum) creating a communication space independent of where the conversation actually takes place and of other social spheres, such as economy, finance, and law. The public sphere has the ability to connect different opinions, removing them from the specific region in which they were formed and allowing them to hold conversation in an abstract state. A new territory for collective and shared discussions could come into being, a place where society could reach a shared opinion on the most important matters. This idea of a "public sphere" rotates around a representational activity performed by the media system (earlier by the press, then by audiovisual media, with television as the most important mass media). We can say that the public sphere is the place where mass communication appears as a completely different and distinct reality (Boccia Artieri 2004), as an autonomous form of social communication. This chapter will describe how the contemporary change in forms and practices of political participation and communication technologies push those boundaries toward new and unexplored scenarios.

Today, for the first time, we are facing a radical transformation with great grassroots foundation. Individuals, single human beings, now have a potentially huge communication power, the ability to present their themes or indeed themselves to a wide, unknown audience using networked media affordances: users can go public. What we are facing today can be described in terms of a networked public culture (Varnelis 2008), which shows how individual and interpersonal cultural production can come out of their isolation to become a new public language once again able to mix and stimulate mass languages.

A new media environment is produced where forms of self- and heterorepresentation exist together, where the mass media languages that have shaped us as the audience and consumers becomes resonant with highly symbolic individual and collective practices, in which the macro system and the microindividual sense exist together in new ways. In this environment, the traditional public sphere changes into something new. In addition to what can now be described as the mass media–based public sphere, it is now possible that alternative public spheres also be represented. The traditional middle-class public sphere crushed differences within its boundaries and represented them with its languages and media products. Today we face a possible multitude of languages representing several spheres in the archipelago established by the internet.

It is the grassroots conversations that are gaining a voice. The public sphere becomes plural and this plurality becomes visible and searchable, despite of elitist theories. This is a change from a scenario where there was a single public sphere based on the mass media that was constructed by crushing together several differences to create a scenario where multiple public spheres seemed able to coexist, networked to each other. The "new" reality of networked public spheres no longer represents topics in society. Its task is no longer to produce an opportunity for self-observation, but rather to irritate society or social subsystems (Luhmann 2000) using networked microlives and new developing practices as starting points. The general challenge now is understanding if and how this grassroots way of creating and living in public spheres could be related to the traditional public sphere as we have known it during the modern age, and how protest movements and participation practices will deal with this change. This shift of theoretical framework is the necessary premise to reflect on new protest movements in the digital age. What we can see today are just preliminary drafts of what they will become in the near future. This change will be based on two pillars: the emergence of the multiple public spheres described above, and a new sense of position within the communication process.

The Sense of Position in Communication

With the introduction of new possibilities for communication and "mass personal" connection (blogs, social networks, etc.) via the internet, we are witnessing a qualitative and quantitative change. From a qualitative perspective, individuals feel that they are no longer the "object" (as the audience, user, elector, etc.) of a conversation, but that they could be the "subject" of it, at any level. Both individuals and organizations could leave behind their passive role in public communication and address a very widely networked unknown audience via their communication channels in a simple and personalized way. This is a fundamental step in order to change the general "audience" into a "networked publics" scenario. As a consequence of this, what will be communicated also changes. While there were still a limited number of major broadcasters and the public was perceived as an undefined subject, their choice of what to communicate was mostly centralized. Of course, there were many different decisional centers, but the number of them was structurally limited. When we move the scenario toward a networked space, each and every user has the opportunity to decide what he or she communicates to the world. Side-by-side with the classic topics of communication (politics, public issues, health, etc.), we can see now the rise of thousands of minor subjects, often related to the personal lives of people, which previously would have been defined as trivial but now can be shared globally. We are facing an accumulation of occasions in which individuals "play" with forms of self-representation. These are occasions where individuals have the opportunity to share something with other users, to share their own thoughts, their own beliefs, their own Weltanschauung. These changes are rooted in a wider sociotechnological evolution that can be summarized in three major points:

1. The spreading of production and reproduction technologies in daily life: From digital cameras to powerful editing software, the number of technological tools aimed at media production that are available in our daily life is growing daily, together with the practices of digital vernacular creativity (Burgess 2007).
2. The growth of systems for disintermediation and content sharing. From web platforms to social networking sites, from YouTube to Facebook and Flickr, there are a growing number of services that support media sharing and online publication. These services allow people to share their content by making the media content available and searchable online, thus making them relatively easy to find (Burgess and Green 2009).
3. Acknowledgment of the logic for the construction of content and languages similar to those of the mass media, but used in an environment where individuals are connected with each other. Especially among young people, the technical skills to create high-quality digital media products are often widespread and the so-called digital natives (Prensky 2006) can use these skills for personal expression and creativity.

These three elements are the sociotechnological starting point for digital protests and participation. People are generally aware that exposing their individuality to a general audience turns their living experience into a chance to communicate with other people, whose lives will then be connected to ours. This constitutes a shift in the position within the communication process. This position shifting, which is taking place in daily communication, results in an incredible strength and is clearly visible, even in environments that seem very far removed from each other: from political communication to advertising, from creative practices to protest movements.

Participative Cultures and Social Web

Given the scenario described above, how are participation and protest practices changing? What does it mean to participate in a protest movement in the networked context? Participation is inclined to assume semantics and meanings different from those produced in an environment characterized by mass communications with a unique and prevailing public sphere. Today, participation seems to be characterized by a logic that includes a semantic continuum rather than a binary opposition between involvement and avoidance. This logic considers different participation levels and gives different meanings to that sense of participation—from reader to leader (Preece and Shneiderman 2009).

The technological scenario just described is unquestionably the background of this participation continuum. Technological platforms feature several different "interaction" methods people can just read, but can also be more active, expressing a "like" for what they have just read. They can also share content, as well as commenting and answering posts by other users and becoming producers of original content or, as we will see below, coordinating offline actions. This whole set of possibilities is now significant because of the persistency and ability to search in digital technologies (boyd 2008). These actions happen in a networked space and, therefore, they are visible.

Think about what happens when you are on Facebook your homepage shows every action you perform, from accepting a friendship to subscribing to a group, from writing a note to tagging a photo or a movie. Selecting "like" on a page related to a public issue now becomes the first grade of participation. It is intended as a means of making a statement in a semipublic space, something that can be later counted, aggregated, and used for further actions. This leads to the emergence of several loosely connected networks of light participants (readers) and toward participation as an emergent reality made up of hundreds of thousands of different interactions. Participation and its visibility move along together in modern communication and social scenery. When participation, physical or digital, becomes visible, observable, and representable, it becomes recognizable by participants. Joining a cause or a contemporary movement, online and offline, through actions such as wearing red ribbons against AIDS or putting peace flags on balconies just before the second Gulf War could be considered a form of participation. Making things visible to acknowledge the shifted sense of position is extremely important in modern political and participative strategies. Thus, we are now facing a kind of participation that exists and reveals itself before the action happens. It shows itself as a potential communication bond, but also as a connection. A connection that is observable and representable day after day. This is the visual aspect of contemporary protest actions.

In addition, contemporary digital technologies offer a wide range of tools to coordinate and manage large groups of people—often spread throughout different countries—in an efficient way. Organizing mass protests, coordinating public action, deciding whether to boycott specific goods or brands, and spreading alternative information and unofficial news is easier today than it was twenty years ago. Nevertheless, describing the change that digital, networked technologies are introducing in protest movements only in terms of "a greater coordination power" would miss the systemic point. Digital technologies are affecting protest movements on three major levels:

1. Digital networked technologies and social media tools offer an incredible power to coordinate large and loosely structured crowds even when people are physically located in many different countries in the world.
2. The networked space becomes a stage where protest movements can show themselves in terms of numbers and participation. The network is now an additional "square" for protests to take place.
3. Social media practices offer a wide range of possibilities for action: from very low to very high levels of engagement—from reader to leader—protest movements today have to be described as a continuum instead as a binary opposition.

The mechanisms presented so far could appear with different participation levels in different physical or media environments. Not only in online contexts, but also, and above all, in hybrid forms capable of mixing online visibility and offline recognizability, online coordination and offline representation (or vice versa), and so on. In order to describe these, we will now analyze two different examples: the case of the Italian activist and blogger Beppe Grillo, the leader of a large protest movement against the current Italian political scene, which has been coordinated mainly through the social media; and the use of Twitter, a well-known microblogging platform, during the protest against the Iranian political election in 2009.

Intermediate Participation: Beppe Grillo

The example represented by the Italian blogger, actor, activist, and politician Beppe Grillo is particularly interesting from this point of view. Telling this character's story is a very difficult endeavor, because his actions have always been part of an interconnected and transmedia reality. Beppe Grillo's career as a stand-up comedian and actor started at the end of the 1970s. During the first half of the 1980s, he became a "real celebrity," after appearing in several TV shows as a guest and hosting popular comedy shows such as *Te la do io L'America* (1982), *Te lo do io il Brasile* (1984), and *Grillometro* (1985). This overwhelming success, always prized in terms of ratings, was interrupted suddenly in 1987 when he appeared on the popular Saturday night prime-time show *Fantastico 7* and attacked the Italian Socialist Party and the prime minister, Bettino Craxi, with a ferocious joke. This was related to Prime Minister Craxi's recent trip to the People's Republic of China and went along the lines of: "If Chinese people are all socialist, who do they steal from?" The attack referred not to the socialist Chinese dictatorship, but was a jab at the extremely corrupt Italian political system, embodied by the Socialist and Christian Democratic parties, who were the main political parties in Italy. Following this attack, Grillo was forbidden to appear on Italian television until 1993, when his new show was broadcast by RAI (an Italian public television broadcaster). Despite its incredible ratings (it was watched by an audience of sixteen million people), it produced a lot of backlash and controversies. This show marked Beppe Grillo's last appearance on Italian public television.

His disappearance from television allowed him to focus more on his career as a stand-up comedian. In recent years, Beppe Grillo has toured Italian theaters with his shows and continues to satirize politics and criticize Italian culture as a whole. Since the 1990s, a handful of the charges he leveled against politicians and Italian companies during his shows have been proven to be true. The Mani Pulite (Clean Hands) investigation revealed the huge scale of corruption within the whole Italian political system, especially affecting the Italian Socialist Party. He also attacked a popular Italian multinational food company, Parmalat, which suffered one of the greatest financial bankruptcies in history. Its financial crack had erased lots of people's savings, and he attacked the company after noticing huge deficiencies in its budgets and balances.

His activism has developed in parallel with the creation of his blog, www.beppegrillo.it, which became one of the top ten visited blogs in the world. Using his blog, Beppe Grillo continues his ethical and moral campaign attacking the political system, as well as many big companies, for their behavior or choices. Within Beppe Grillo's story, the blog has a very symbolic value: it is a place where visibility has been made possible. He, the comedian banned from public television, found a new free media space. As a "free space," his blog has progressively become the starting point for political mobilization and sensitization campaigns, mainly addressed against the political system, which have resulted in signature collections for a handful of popular initiative bills, with the objective of moralizing the Italian political system. His popularity reached a high on 8 September 2007, when Beppe Grillo organized the first "Vaffanculo Day" (Fuck Off Day) to collect signatures required for the popular initiative bill. The event, organized on 8 September, a very important and symbolic day for Italy that reminds when the Cassibile armistice was declared during WW II, was an enormous success, with more than 340,000 signatures collected. The number of participants who were more or less active can be estimated at several million. The first Vaffan-culo Day was followed, on 25 April 2008, by a second Vaffanculo Day, also known as V2 Day. If the first V Day was aimed directly against politics, V2 Day was focused on newspapers and traditional press. The objective was to collect signatures to organize referendums to abrogate laws on public financ-ing to newspapers. It was once again a great success in terms of collected signatures, and mobilized people in each of the many cities involved. The growing political participation in 2009 allowed the creation of a few civic lists referable to Beppe Grillo himself, whose political plans show particular attention to the issues related to the transparency of government processes and the morality of politicians and other people working in politics.

This is obviously just a short summary of Beppe Grillo's evolution and the battles he fought in his thirty years of public appearances. What is in-teresting, following the line of reasoning introduced at the beginning of this chapter, is not just the extraordinary nature of his political evolution, but also his ability to enter new digital communication spaces and create a po-litical community outside of classic mass media. Grillo's ostracism by tradi-tional mass media, especially TV, never ended. It has even amplified since V2 Day, when the comedian aimed his jokes towards the press system and its relationship with politics. From a more theoretical point of view, Beppe Grillo's communication strategies appear as something transitional, with two conflicting dynamics. On one hand, there are the groups of people known as Grillini, the name used to determine Beppe Grillo's supporters, whose phenomenon shows how the internet is capable of being a place for com-munication, reciprocal identification, and action coordination. On the other hand, the way Beppe Grillo handles his web activities and communication dynamics does not venture far from a unidirectional broadcasting logic. For a detailed analysis of this ambivalence, the transition stage could be seen as being between a broadcasting logic and a participative and conversational logic. The former is the most typical in traditional mass media, because it is their way of conceiving the audience position in communication processes; the latter is found in new media.

The communication space chosen by Beppe Grillo for his campaigns is the internet. His blog features a lot of digital content, taking advantage of the most popular modern 2.0 web services. Everything, from blog posts to videos hosted on YouTube, from important documents to investigations, is available online and can be read and watched by everyone. At the same time, users, who always start discussing the subjects of posts and videos, are able to comment on this content. Beppe Grillo never appeared in any of these debates. He did not want to take part in these and, furthermore, did not answer blog comments or write comment posts on other blogs and videos on

YouTube. He simply communicates in one direction, setting up the subject and giving free space, within certain boundaries, to his readers.

These dynamics could be considered a carrier of some kind of internal conflict. On one hand, this choice of giving freedom to usually silent readers, who can then comment and express their opinion, raises their participation level to a higher state. On the other hand, his choice to avoid taking part in discussions and only launch new subjects seems to create a fine line between who decides what to talk about and who can only express his opinions. Despite this lack of communication between the discussion themes' decision maker and the opinion givers, which is a stark reminder of broadcasting logics typical of traditional mass media, there is also something different. This is happening online, in a place where people act outside the realms of traditional media censorships and boundaries, offering them a self-observation possibility and making them aware of their role in communication processes. The audience with an active participation in Beppe Grillo's blog is aware of its role as an audience, but also of its communication capabilities. There is a shift from individual fruition to collective fruition, which itself is aware of being collective, even when there is no spatial and temporal synchronism.

Beppe Grillo's networked public is not those emerging from individual and self-aware interactions in social media. It is not an emerging reality, made up of several people who are independent communication producers. This is a hybrid reality, which, even facing a unidirectional communication source, gives some room to the audience, who are able to express their thoughts as an audience does (commenting, criticizing, etc.).

The perception of themselves as an audience is a core element of Beppe Grillo's audience. Thinking about "us" when we read Beppe Grillo's blog is the first step in being aware that there are other readers out there, people like "us" that we can perceive in the comments or trace on the related websites. It is this awareness of being "us" that is the feeling supporting all the actions proposed by Beppe Grillo and his staff. We are still talking about all the networked gathering forms, from a simple daily visit to the website to writing comments, from sharing news reported by Beppe Grillo to adding in readers' websites/blogs a banner for one of those promoted campaigns. Furthermore, for readers looking for a higher level of involvement, it is also possible to join offline groups, called Meetups, which are still organized through the internet and that represent the physical manifestation of the larger online participation process. It is the (physical) pinnacle of a large pyramid that is solidly based on the large online audience of Beppe Grillo.

So, if Beppe Grillo's communication methods could not be observed within a scattered and horizontal logic when compared to people connected to the internet, because they reflect a centralized model that is highly centered on the comedian's charismatic figure, then it is also true that his main audience is a networked public; an audience who is highly aware of being a networked public, but also of its size as an audience. This audience is also able to take part in communicative actions in several ways, making extremely clear each of the several tones in the participative continuum (Shneiderman and Preece 2009).

Twitter: Swarms of Networked Communication

Beppe Grillo's case, even with its strong political and media relevance against the Italian background, shows just a little of the transformation going on. When we observe what happens on Twitter, one of the most-used social networking tools, we can see that we are facing a phenomenon that is tremendously hard to explain following traditional thought patterns and thus requires a paradigm shift.

Twitter is a social network that offers a microblogging service. Posts in microblogging are very short, with Twitter's tweets having a maximum length of 140 characters. This feature, initially designed to make Twitter compatible with SMS updates, translates into an incredibly easy-to-use system, where there is no elaboration, writing, and reviewing time, as is typically required in a blog. You can update your Twitter status from any location, even with a mobile connection. Its user-friendly interface and immediateness has allowed Twitter to exponentially increase its user numbers day after day since its foundation in 2006. Today, several analysts consider it part of the top five most-used social networks, but also as the social network with the highest and most impressive growth rate. In 2009, its monthly growth in percentage was about 1,382 percent (McGiboney 2009).

Each Twitter user shares short text messages (called tweets) containing text clips, thoughts, news, or just moods with other users. On Twitter everything becomes communicable, lowering that threshold between what has traditionally been considered "worthy of public mention" and what was thought better to be kept private. Here, the mood of a dull Monday morning becomes a subject of communication in the same way as the latest political and financial news. In this communication stream, made up of millions of actors, innovative and unpredictable coordinative phenomena can emerge. On Twitter, people talk about their lives; those lives intertwine with other lives, generating coordinated narrations that are nothing other than streams made up of single micromessages, grouped by a previously chosen identification code.[1] These message swarms have no constant structure, so could derail in a very short time, when the generating event ends or for any other reason.

In this scenario, unlike in the Beppe Grillo example, subjects are not chosen by a central person. There are no differences between a central individual deciding on what to talk about and lots of less "important" users giving their opinions on the proposed subjects. Themes on Twitter come out progressively and become clear as an emergent phenomenon that cannot be linked to any of the single tweets. In this emergent dimension, we can observe some of the most important participative and protest phenomena in recent years. Among those, the protest movement born just after the 2009 Iranian presidential elections can be considered as one of the most interesting. Protests started on 13 June 2009, following the announcement of election results, with the victory of outgoing president Ahmadinejad challenged by protestors. The crowd reaction, especially for supporters of rival candidate Mousavi, was immediate and incredibly sound. Thousands of people gathered in the streets accusing the ruling administration of fraud and demanding the annulment of the election. In the days following 13 June, demonstrations continued, with several clashes between protestors and paramilitary groups working for the government. Protests lasted until July, when protestors, following the Guardian Council approval of the electoral result, agreed to start a "phase two," with less open demonstrations and a more pronounced continuous boycotting of the government. Regardless of the outcome of these protests, it is impossible to deny that between 13 June and the end of July, the world saw what could be considered an anticipation of protest and conflict styles that would occur in the future.

This movement, nicknamed the Green Revolution (following the line traced by colored revolutions born in Eastern Europe countries and embracing the color of Mousavi's electoral campaign) has also been labeled one of the first Twitter revolutions. The role played by the social networking site has been incredibly important, both within the protest movement, as a tool to coordinate activities and exchanging information, but also outside of the protest, as a tool that allowed world public opinion to follow events and support the people. In this case, more than in previous cases, observers were able to notice that participation forms were included in a strong continuum between active participation and emotional support, but also that simple communications by thousands of people had been able to produce highly complex coordinated processes.

The Twitter reports on what was happening in Iran were completely different from the information provided by the mass media. Images and stories from those witnessing events were not provided by major international TV networks, but by thousands of networked micromessages, hundreds of thousands of mobile phone photos, which were shared online, several amateur videos published on YouTube, and so on. On one hand, the strong Iranian government control of both Western and Arab traditional media favored this outcome; on the other hand, it shows a great change in the communication scenery, with single individuals having an increasing ability to enter the information arena as actors and not just as the audience, with completely new logics and production styles.

Using Twitter to report what was happening[2] allowed people to create a new reality, with features and functions that were impossible to find in typical press reports. Twitter coordinated protestors' actions, allowing them to exchange information useful for organizing demonstrations, even in a situation where the government had a strong grip on the media, especially on television. At the same time, Twitter was also somewhere where the protest was able to talk about itself through the progressive aggregation of hundreds of millions of tweets. On one hand, this made a self-observation of the protest and the existence of a movement going beyond the crowds gathered in the open possible; on the other hand, these reports reached global status and, therefore, were read all around the world. Twitter became the medium that was watched by the whole world, where people could not only read reports about the protest, but also give support to protestors via messages and other particular forms. In those days, millions of avatars—the images representing an online user—were replaced with a green image. This communicative connection between where the organization took place and where people talked about demonstrations and collected support displays produced a highly complex reality, able to easily generate a short circuit never seen before. Some observers claim that the communicative surplus produced by support messages written mainly by American or British users made this tool useless when it came to organizing demonstrative actions (Schectman 2009).

The huge communication stream could have cluttered up and, in specific cases, made it impossible to access information. It should be reminded that, on one hand, it gave a global visibility to the protest, putting it at the top of world agenda. This is illustrated by the request Twitter received from the US State Department, which asked Twitter to postpone its weekly scheduled maintenance (it cannot be used during this downtime) to avoid the interruption of the service for Iranian users. On the other hand, it allowed the emergence of collective participation and collaborative problem-solving phenomena, such as those collectively devised strategies to try to deceive Iranian administration firewalls.

So, even if a few analysts raised undeniable doubts about the real number of Iranian Twitter users and how this tool could be considered of central importance in connection to protest management, it should be observed, regardless of their actual number, that Iranian demonstrations found something important in Twitter and its grassroots communication system: This was a place where individual micronarrations could be posted and exposed on a global level, and it was also a place that permitted the showing of a possible format for modern protests and demonstrations.

Conclusion

What has been said up to now focused on some recent protest movements within a wider change, related to what we have called "sense of position" in communication processes. Social media and networked communication technologies allow, for the first time in history, the role of an individual in communication processes to be reversed. What happens in the described dynamics is not necessarily related to the idea of citizen journalism; here citizens or individuals do not necessarily claim the role of newsmaker. We are facing an ability deeply connected with the new modern communicative scenario. Now communication is possible even starting from conversational practices rooted into individuals' daily lives. Participation, from this point of view, redefines itself on a much more complex axis with lots of possible options, ranging from the communicative value of support to real and actual participation. People are aware of their new role in it and show a growing ability to use it strategically.

From this point of view, both of the examples illustrated above—the Italian movement born around Beppe Grillo and the relationship between Twitter and the demonstrations following the 2009 Iranian presidential elections—show some common points and a possible line of development, despite their several differences. In both cases, it is a question of movements that use social media, from blogs to content aggregation on Twitter, representing forms both with an internal and an external use. Social media sites allow these realities to observe themselves and feel that there are other users even outside the typical open gatherings and demonstrations. From this point of view, Beppe Grillo's campaign supporters, but also all those people tweeting in support of Iranian demonstrations, feel their presence where communication takes place. Their media presence goes beyond the typical mass media filter, because it is created by the supporters' actions.

So, if the feeling of a shifted position in communication processes is one of the shared elements between both reported examples, it should, however, be pointed out that in Beppe Grillo's case, communication logic must still be considered as a broadcasting logic. The comedian and activist does not take part in discussions; he simply suggests or, sometimes, imposes discussion subjects. On the other hand, conversations on Twitter find a shared starting point in people's daily experiences. These subjects can emerge as a single, shared public issue only when a large number of users have similar experiences or thoughts. There is no centrality on Twitter. No one is setting the agenda. It is just temporary aggregation logics around specific subjects without one-to-many logics available in broadcasting communications. Here, users do not express their opinions on proposed subjects. Users generate and create subjects in their communications, and these subjects would not exist without users.

Notes

1. On Twitter, conversations can be grouped by special tags called hashtags. Hashtags are created with the addition of a "#" to the message, followed by the word used as a tag. A hashtag has a double purpose: on one hand, it allows users to read all messages containing that specific hashtag; on the other hand, users can be sure that their messages will be grouped together with others sharing the same subject. With no centralized choice of hashtags, users often choose very few hashtags, sometimes only one. This is a very interesting example of a new phenomenon concerning the action coordination of individuals.

2. The hashtags mainly used were #iran, #iranelection, #neda, and #gr88. The first two don't need further explanation. #neda refers to Neda Agha-Soltan, a twenty-year-old girl killed during the demonstrations. The movie of her killing, accidentally shot by another person, was also aired by traditional mass media, making Neda one of the symbols of the entire protest. #gr88 is the contraction of "Green Revolution 1388," where 1388 is the year 2009 according to the Iranian calendar.

Bibliography

Boccia Artieri, G. 2004. *I media-mondo*. Rome: Meltemi Editore.

boyd, D. M. 2008. *Taken out of context: American teen sociality in networked publics*. Ann Arbor: ProQuest.

Burgess, J. 2007. "Vernacular Creativity and New Media." PhD diss., Queensland University of Technology.

Burgess, J., and J. Green. 2009. *YouTube: Online Video and Participatory Culture*. Cambridge: Polity.

Giddens, A. 1991. Modernity and Self-Identity: Self and Society in the Late Modern Age. Palo Alto, CA: Stanford University Press.

Habermas, J. 1987. Strukturwandel der Öffentlichkeit. Hamburg: Luchterhand.

———. 1992. Faktizität und Geltung. Berlin: Suhrkamp.

Luhmann, N. 2000. The Reality of the Mass Media. Palo Alto, CA: Stanford University Press.

McGiboney, M. 2009. "Twitter's Tweet Smell of Success." http://blog.nielsen.com/nielsen wire/online_mobile/twitters-tweet-smell-of-success/ (accessed 1 February 2011).

Preece, J. and Shneiderman, B. 2009. "The Reader to Leader Framework: Motivating Technology-mediated Social Participation," AIS Transactions on Human-Computer Interaction (1) 1, pp. 13–32.

Prensky, M. 2006. Don't Bother Me Mom—I'm Learning! St. Paul, MI: Paragon House.

Schectman, J. 2009. "Iran's Twitter Revolution? Maybe Not Yet." Business Week. http://www.businessweek.com/technology/content/jun2009/tc20090617_803990.htm (accessed 1 February 2011).

Shneiderman, B., and J. Preece 2009. "The Reader-to-Leader Framework: Motivating Technology-Mediated Social Participation." AIS Transactions on Human-Computer Interaction 1, no. 1: 13–32.

Varnelis K., ed. 2008. Networked Publics. Cambridge, MA: MIT Press.

Chapter 20

Insurgency in the Age of the Internet
The Case of the Zapatistas

Roy Krøvel

The Zapatista uprising began in January 1994, as use of the internet started to spread in Mexico. Mexico was still ruled by the often authoritarian Partido Revolucionario Institucional (PRI), and the media was far from free. The first communiqué from the Ejército Zapatista de Liberación Nacional (EZLN) placed the movement solidly within a Latin American tradition of guerrilla organizations. Numerous Mexican guerrillas had been formed after the brutal repression of student demonstrations in 1968. In 1994, the Zapatistas demanded land for landless peasants and called for a national revolution to roll back liberal economic reforms and the North American Free Trade Agreement (NAFTA). But nowhere in the first communiqué was any reference to indigenous rights to be found. Nevertheless, journalists and solidarity activists travelling to Chiapas in hordes found a movement different from that of other Latin American guerrillas; they saw, first and foremost, a conflict between oppressed indigenous peoples, fighting for dignity and cultural and political autonomy, and a brutal regime. Reports were sent back home and a version of the movement was constructed that underlined identity politics and the multicultural dimensions of the conflict.

A number of studies have concluded that the Zapatistas' clever use of the internet and other new communication technologies played an important role in breaking the regime's authoritarian grip on the media. Some, therefore, called the Zapatistas the world's first postmodern guerrilla movement. Others saw it as the introduction of a new time or a new society (Burbach 1994; Castells 1996; Castells and Ince 2003; Cleaver 1998; Cleaver1998b). Still others have studied how activists used the internet to support the Zapatistas (Krøvel 2006; Olesen 2004a, 2004b, 2005a, 2005b).

In Subcomandante Marcos, the military commander of the Zapatistas, Manuel Castells saw a kind of "prophet," perfectly suited to form the way we think in the age of the "network society" (Castells 1997). The think tank

RAND Corporation warned that a swarm of millions of flies could overrun even the strongest government (Arquilla and Ronfeldt 2001: 190). While many have underlined the importance of the internet and "information warfare," others have noted that such claims are overstating the case. The term "postmodern" is not suited to describe an organization consisting largely of poor indigenous peasants. The danger is "romanticizing" the Zapatistas, according to Berger—seeing what one wants to see in the uprising of indigenous peasants, rather than the reality of Chiapas (M. T. Berger 2001).

This chapter tracks meetings between the Zapatistas and prominent supporters. It deals with the "information strategy" of the Zapatistas and asks how it can be understood in relation to the experience of other Latin American guerrilla organizations. Did the Zapatistas have an "information strategy"? What role did visiting intellectuals play in the media framing of the Zapatistas and the conflict in Chiapas? The chapter focuses on the solidarity movement and media sympathetic toward the Zapatistas and the solidarity movement.

Methodology

This chapter is partly based on investigations undertaken for my PhD dissertation in history on guerrilla organizations and indigenous movements in Mexico and Central America (Krøvel 2006). I have interviewed current and former leaders of guerrillas in Colombia, Nicaragua, Guatemala, El Salvador, Mexico, and other countries, in addition to civilian leaders, "ordinary" citizens, refugees, and members of numerous nongovernmental organizations (NGOs). The interviews include a large number of Zapatistas, both civilians and armed members. I have also interviewed leading members of La Neta, the organization that provided internet services in San Cristobal de las Casas, and members and leaders of NGOs in Chiapas who have been working closely with the Zapatistas, often helping them to disseminate information.

The investigation of written sources for this chapter followed two steps. First, a large number of texts from diverse sources were consulted. These include all EZLN communiqués since 1993. Since 2005, the Zapatistas themselves have run a webpage at www.ezln.org.mx, and this was also studied. The body of texts also includes reports from solidarity organizations, such as the Irish Mexico Group and the online newslist Chiapas-L. In addition, homepages of NGOs cooperating with the Zapatistas were studied. The NGOs include the Fray Bartolomé de las Casas Center for Human Rights, Enlace, Centro de Análisis Político e Investigaciones Sociales y Económicas A.C., and Centro de Investigaciones Económicas y Políticas de Acción Comunitaria. The list of newspapers and magazines included in the study include *La Jornada* (Mexico), *Cuarto Poder* (Chiapas Mexico), *Newsweek* (USA), *Time* (USA), *Radio Havanna* (Cuba), *Reuters* (UK), *Associated Press* (USA), and others. All relevant texts from two periods on the Zapatistas and the conflict were studied. The first period runs from February to March 1995, and covers a last military offensive by the Mexican army against the Zapatistas. The second period begins in February 2001 and ends in April of the same year. This period encompasses events related to a Zapatista caravan from Chiapas to Mexico City and a debate in the Mexican Congress on a proposed peace agreement with the Zapatistas. A full list of all sources can be found in my dissertation (Krøvel 2006).

Second, based on the study of the larger body of texts presented above, I assembled a selection of particularly interesting reports from Chiapas for closer qualitative study. These texts were selected because they were deemed to be particularly influential in view of their authors or the publication, but also because they were included in an anthology on the Zapatistas, thereby forming part of something reminiscent of a canon on the Zapatistas (Hayden 2002). Numerous other texts could also have been included, but these stand out, in my view, because they all stimulated intense discussion on webpages, lists, and elsewhere where activists in the global solidarity movement communicated with each other. These texts were all published in newspapers or magazines with a much wider audience than most reports from Chiapas. They are not seen here as separate from the media discourse on the Zapatistas and the conflict in Chiapas, but as particularly influential articulations of the various and sometimes conflicting media frames available for the conflict.

The texts, in chronological order, are: Paco Ignacio Taibo II, "Zapatistas! The Phoenix Rises," *Nation,* 28 March 1994; Octavio Paz, "The Media Spectacle Comes to Mexico," *New Perspectives Quarterly,* volume 59 (Spring 1994); Régis Debray, "Talking to the Zapatistas," *New Left Review,* July/August 1996; Eduardo Galeano, "Chiapas Chronicle," *La Jornada,* 7 August 1996; John Berger, "Against the Great Defeat of the World," *Race and Class,* October 1998–March 1999; Manuel Vázquez Montalbán, *Marcos: El Señor de los Espejos* (Madrid, 1999); José Saramago, "Moral Force versus the State: Chiapas, Land of Hope and Sorrow," *Le Monde Diplomatique,* English version, March 1999; Naomi Klein, "The Unknown Icon," *Guardian,* 3 March 2001; Carlos Monsiváis, "El indígena visible (movimiento por los derechos civiles de pueblos indígenas en México)," *El Proceso,* 4 March 2001; Saul Landau, "The Zapatista Army of National Liberation: Part of the Latin American Tradition—But Also Very Different," *The Zapatista Reader,* edited by Tom Hayden (New York, 2002); and Gabriel García Márquez, "Habla Marcos," *Cambio,* 24 March 2001. The texts will be read and analyzed from a constructivist perspective in relation to the way they deal with the terms "revolution," "guerrilla," and "indigenous peoples."

The Historical Context

The EZLN has many roots, but arguably one of the most important takes us back to Ernesto "Che" Guevara, Fidel Castro, and the Cuban Revolution of 1959. Castro's was by no means the first Latin American guerrilla organization, but what surprised many, including the Cuban leadership, was the speed with which the regime fell apart. It took only three years from the time Castro, Guevara, and a few guerrilleros landed on the Cuban shores until the final victory. This inspired Guevara to formulate a theory on revolution in Latin America (Guevara 1972, 1997; Guevara and Deutschmann 2003). Where Marxist-Leninists saw the Communist Party as the organizing force of the revolution, Guevara reserved that role for the guerrilla organization. A small group of dedicated men and women (the *foco*) could make the situation ripe for revolution by military means. This was due to what Guevara saw as a special situation in Latin America, where many countries were run by authoritarian and often isolated regimes or dictators, ripe for social revolt. By attacking the regime and resisting repression, the *foco* would prove that the regime was not invincible, according to Guevara, thereby unleashing the full potential of the farmers, workers, and other revolutionary forces.

The first wave of Cuba-inspired guerrillas that hit Latin America in the 1960s, culminating with the capture and subsequent killing of Guevara in Bolivia in 1967, did not succeed in defeating governments anywhere. Only in a few countries did the guerrillas evade total annihilation, making reorganization possible. A second wave of guerrillas in the late 1970s and early 1980s scored some notable successes, including the victory of the Sandinistas in Nicaragua and the strength of the Farabundo Marti para la Liberación Nacional (FMLN) in El Salvador and other places. Guerrillas and regime agreed on peace agreements, including democratization in Guatemala (1996) and El Salvador (1991), while several smaller armed organizations in Colombia agreed to disarm without initially making much of a difference to the escalating civil war.

The ideologies of the various armed organizations in Latin America developed notably over the years, but most continued to see disseminating information as an integral part of the armed struggle. Only by publicizing their perceived victories could they hope to stimulate the resistance to the regime they sought. Castro and Guevara thus had several journalists reporting from Sierra Maestra during their Cuban campaign, while the Sandinistas (Frente

Sandinista de Liberación Nacional) in Nicaragua and the FMLN in the late 1970s and 1980s used international media to resist or limit US meddling in the civil wars. Central American guerrillas effectively provided information to Europe and North America in the 1980s, successfully collecting large sums of money from supporters overseas. In the El Salvadorian case, at least 80 percent of FMLN's funding came from Europe or North America (Kruijt 2008: 85).

Latin American guerrillas succeeded in building international alliances and establishing networks in North America and Europe. Renowned writers like Harold Pinter and Noam Chomsky became vocal supporters of the Sandinista government in Nicaragua, while the punk band The Clash released a triple LP in 1980 called "Sandinistas" and several Hollywood productions constructed versions of the conflicts in Central America that were not unsympathetic to the guerrillas—most notably *Under Fire* (1983), with Nick Nolte, Gene Hackman, and Ed Harris in leading roles. A number of NGOs also supported the armed opposition in their struggle to overthrow Latin American regimes; in Norway the Sandinistas found support in what became Latin-Amerikagruppene i Norge and Studentene og Akademikernes Internasjonale Hjelpefond, among others.

Less well-known is the guerrilla organizations' own capacity for producing and disseminating information. The FMLN, for instance, ran a network of radio stations from their rural strongholds; the documentary *Las mil y una historias de Radio Venceremos* later became a national best seller (Lopez Vigil 1991). Elsewhere, the guerrillas used radio and print media to spread their version of the conflicts—often successfully, because of the many excellent writers and orators in the guerrilla groups. The Sandinistas had *guerrillero* and prizewinning novelist Omar Cabezas and priest Ernesto Cardenal to tell stories of the revolution (Cabezas 1986; Cardenal 1976, 1980, 1982). In El Salvador, no one could express the feelings of the guerrillas like the poet Roque Dalton (Castillo 1975; Dalton 1969, 1970, 2002, 2004). Dalton was executed by his fellow *guerrilleros* in 1975 after what turned out to be false accusations of trying to divide the guerrilla organization. In Guatemala, Mario Payeras published the horrible but wonderfully written story of the failed urban uprising (Payeras 1987, 1989). At risk of becoming one more victim of the internal violence of the guerrilla organizations, Payeras finally left the guerrilla for fear of being executed (Castañeda 1994). In Gaspar Ilom, the Guatemalan Unidad Revolucionaria Nacional Guatemalteca (URNG) tried to create a real version of the Latin American poetic "magical realism." Gaspar Ilom was the nom de guerre of one of the commanders of the URNG. His real name was Rodrigo Asturias Amado, the first-born son of Nobel Prize–winning author Miguel Ángel Asturias. He chose Gaspar Ilom from a character in *Hombres de maíz,* one of his father's novels (Asturias 1972). (It is probably not necessary to say that Gaspar Ilom knew how to handle the media.)

This short background note about Latin American guerrillas, writing, and the media is not meant to be exhaustive—Brazilian, Colombian, Argentinean, Uruguayan, and other cases could have also been mentioned. But here I want to stress only the fact that Latin American guerrillas valued information or propaganda for many reasons, including reasons of ideology. The very idea of the *foco* rested on the guerrilla being able to awake the masses through information or propaganda.

The Internet and Guerrillas in Chiapas

The Zapatistas attacked spectacularly on 1 January 1994, but it did not take long before the army had forced the rebels to go on the run, so the EZLN retreated deep into the jungle and up into the mountains.

The Mexican regime tried to control the information seeping out from the war zone, but soon realized that this was not possible. Information kept coming from the jungle, distributed on the internet, which had only recently been introduced in Chiapas. Global networks of organizations and activists began arranging activities supporting the EZLN, using newslists and, later, homepages to mobilize support. A number of studies have highlighted the importance of the internet and information for an understanding of the development of the war in Chiapas. The Zapatistas have been seen by some as the world's first postmodern guerrilla, and by others as heralding a new time or a new society (Burbach 1994; Castells 1996; Castells and Ince 2003; Cleaver 1998; Cleaver 1998b). Nobel laureate Octavio Paz lamented the fact that political disagreement now seemed to be decided by feelings, not arguments (Paz 1994). Others have studied the way in which activists used the internet to support the Zapatistas (Olesen 2004a, 2005a). Many of these studies point to the fact that the audience now had many alternatives to traditional journalism, sometimes, as with the Zapatistas, even the opportunity to communicate directly with the sources of information. This could potentially be a serious challenge for journalism. These perceived changes were to a large extent seen to have their roots in technological developments, especially new communications technology. The underlying assumption in many cases was a development toward a society where the media and journalists, or in the words of Octavio Paz, "the Media Spectacle," play an increasingly dominant role, so that appealing to feelings becomes more important than reasoning.

I have elsewhere underlined the real and important effects of the new communications technology for the conflict in Chiapas (Krøvel 2006). In particular, the introduction of the internet to Chiapas in 1993 enabled activists and NGOs to out-maneuver the Mexican system of official and nonofficial control over the media, according to some of the activists. But a closer look at the empirical evidence shows that this had little to do with the Zapatistas having a strategy for information warfare (Ronfeldt and Fuller 1998) or being a postmodern guerrilla organization (Burbach 1994).

The first attack of the Zapatistas was, of course, a formidable media event, but was in itself more of a continuation of Latin American guerrilla strategy than something new. It was reminiscent of Comandante Zero's spectacular attack on the parliament in Managua, Nicaragua, and the Colombian M-19's siege of the high court in Bogota. The first declaration from the EZLN, in fact, placed the organization firmly within the framework of Cuban-inspired guerrilla movements. It talked of peasants, workers, revolution, and social justice, but did not mention indigenous peoples and their collective rights, as later declarations did. In fact, there was little evidence of a media strategy; on the contrary, as the EZLN's military leader, Subcomandante Marcos, explained to me and other journalists a few months later, the Zapatistas were actually surprised to survive the first days of fighting. With good reason: the second *subcomandante* was killed only a few hours after the fighting began. It is reasonable to assume that many more would have perished had the Mexican government not ordered the army, after only twelve days, not to push further into the Lacandon jungle.

Still, the Zapatistas, and especially Subcomandante Marcos, had the intelligence and willingness to improvise when the occasion demanded it. Over the next twelve months, the Zapatistas received, and handled with great skill, hordes of journalists travelling to Chiapas from every corner of the world. By accident, the Zapatistas had reached out to people of almost all nations. As information warriors, though, they could hardly measure up to other guerrilla organizations of that period, as far as I can judge from my experience as a journalist. The Liberation Tigers of Tamil Eelam (LTTE) in Sri Lanka, for instance, had professional "war correspondents" covering their every move, and presented us with videos and photos from the front line when we (photographer Håvard Houen and I) visited them the following year. Kurdish groups connected to the Partîya Karkeren Kurdîstan (PKK) operated a TV station transmitting via satellite to exiled Kurds all over the world. And in El Salvador hundreds of thousands had tuned in every night to listen to the FMLN's radio stations. The EZLN had some equipment in their training camps, as it turned out. In a mountainous area called Corralchen, the Mexican army found a television and video player in an abandoned camp, probably used by the EZLN for educational purposes. Rumors had it that Subcomandante Marcos wrote his poetic essays on a laptop and, as it turned out to be at least half-true, this also fuelled the mythology of the "net war." Again, the truth behind the rumors was rather more modest. The first activists providing internet services in Chiapas, La Neta, later told how they had to ask Subcomandante Marcos again and again to send the essay on a disc. For a long time, though, he continued to send only print on paper, making the activists in La Neta type the whole thing into their computers (Krøvel 2004).

Framing the Zapatistas in the Global Solidarity Movement

Nevertheless, the Zapatistas undoubtedly hit a nerve with a global audience. Thousands of activists travelled to Chiapas to support them, often sending home reports on the internet or published in newspapers. This process reveals a lot about what was really new in the conflict in Chiapas.

Many of those visiting the Zapatistas were famous writers and able to reach a wide audience. In my view, these authors played an important role in constructing a specific understanding of the conflict in Chiapas, an understanding that, over the years, has restricted the Mexican government's range of options for repression or military action in Chiapas. They were also important in defining the media discourse on the conflict and the Zapatistas, especially in the media sympathetic toward the Zapatistas and the global solidarity movement. I will, therefore, use examples from these writers to describe the dominating frames among solidarity activists in the following.

The Democratic Indigenous Society

The stories told by Taibo, Saramago, and Klein all deal with poverty, repression, and the fight for justice (Klein 2001; Saramago 1999; Taibo II 1994). The combination of racism and poverty is the real reason for the conflict, according to these writers. But Saramago, Klein, García Márquez, Mosiváis, and Vázquez Montalbán (García Márquez 2001; Monsiváis 2001; Vázquez Montalbán 1999) ask for more before accepting the armed rebellion. A justified rebellion must also present a viable alternative to existing injustice, and they want an alternative project of rebellion, based on democratic participation. In these stories the arguments of democracy and participation are linked to an image of indigenous societies and indigenous politics: democratic participation means something deeper and more meaningful in these societies than in Western society, according to the authors.

Different from other Revolutionary Movements

Many of the articles go on to compare the EZLN with other Latin American guerrilla organizations trying to encourage indigenous peoples to rebel. Debray is particularly interesting because he had such a profound effect on the revolutionary Left in Latin America and Europe after he published his accounts of the Cuban Revolution (Debray 1967, 1973). He also joined Che Guevara's fatal insurgency in Bolivia, but survived. His article was initially printed in *Le Monde* in 1996, and later reprinted elsewhere (Debray 1996). Much of the article tells the story of his meeting with Subcomandante Marcos in the village of La Realidad. Debray constructs an image of a romantic revolutionary "Indian"—his indigenous peoples are oppressed, but proud, free, and democratic by nature. The EZLN is said to be built on the Indian communities' nature, where power flows "from below." The Zapatistas are therefore the opposite of, and the perfect antidote to, the Shining Path of Peru.

Debray's article is in many ways typical of the reporting from Chiapas. It is a story of disillusion; not disillusion because of the fall of the communist regimes of Eastern Europe, but disillusion with the revolutionary movements of Latin America. Guerrilla organizations like Shining Path and the Fuerzas Armadas Revolucionarias de Colombia (FARC) were isolated, were loathed by workers and intellectuals, depended on criminal activity to survive, and were responsible for massive violations of human rights. The EZLN is presented as an alternative, which demonstrates the possibility of being revolutionary while not supporting authoritarian movements.

Indigenous and Revolutionary

The selected articles also construct the Zapatistas as a movement in contrast to other indigenous movements in Latin America, as clearly seen in the article by Eduardo Galeano (Galeano 1996). Galeano received instant fame when he published *The Open Veins of Latin America* (Galeano 1973). He did not see himself as a neutral observer, but felt part of a community of activists and Zapatistas. The EZLN has many dimensions in Galeano's story, but the identity as indigenous is particularly important. The imagined community of the indigenous peoples is born from "500 years" of cruelty. This oppression of indigenous peoples justifies the armed insurgency in Galeano's account. While both Galeano and Debray see a democratic political practice as a natural part of indigenous tradition in Chiapas, Naomi Klein and Saul Landau develop this argument further, using Zapatista slogans to build an argument for antiauthoritarian revolutionary movements.

These articles present an organization, the EZLN, which is indigenous, in contrast to those Latin American guerrilla organizations that claimed to fight on behalf of indigenous peoples, and failed miserably in most cases. According to these articles, it was the identity as indigenous that transformed the Zapatistas into a democratic movement, which underlines the difference between the EZLN and other Latin American guerrilla organizations.

Against Authoritarian Modernization

All these authors seem to support the EZLN for at least three reasons: because it is revolutionary, but still democratic, and because it is indigenous. John Berger brings these three together elegantly to form a new and surprising argument against neoliberalism (J. Berger 2006): free trade and the free markets may have celebrated victories all over the world, but if the supposedly rational competition to maximize profits wins everywhere, the world will become poorer. Neoliberalism must be fought because it has become such a success. José Saramago, Carlos Monsiváis, and John Holloway also follow this line of thought (Holloway and Peláez 1998; Holloway 2005; Monsiváis Aceves, 2001). The Zapatistas are fighting for the right to be different from the rational profit-maximizing ideal. Which is a fight for us all, according to the authors.

These media frames are not necessarily mutually exclusive. Many reports from Chiapas display elements from several of these media frames. This is to be expected, since the dominating frames all revolve around a few related key issues, like *revolution, democracy,* and imaginations of indigenous identities. As we have already seen, the Zapatistas themselves did not refer to any indigenous identity when they first entered the stage in 1994. They presented themselves as peasants, revolutionaries, and Mexicans. The outsiders seem to have seen something else: they saw indigenous peoples, not peasants. Nonetheless, being indigenous increasingly became more important when the Zapatistas communicated with the outside world. Thus, being *seen* and *framed* by outsiders was one of the causes that set in motion a process of reconstruction of local identity and understandings of "community."

The Public Sphere of the Movement

In contrast to the hype of a "postmodern" movement engaged in "information warfare," the reality of Chiapas was somewhat different. The public sphere of the indigenous communities that joined the EZLN was characterized by oral tradition and oral communication. Almost all communication on issues of interest between members of a community or between communities was made orally, preferably in meetings where the relevant members of the communities could have face-to-face dialogues. Very little was and still is *mediated*.

The Zapatistas draw support from indigenous communities where illiteracy has been a serious problem for generations. This is particularly true for the many settlements in the Lacandon jungle, which formed the backbone of the EZLN in the early years. In many of these settlements, more than 70 percent of the population was illiterate. This should not be taken as an indication of a weak public sphere. On the contrary, anthropological studies have shown a rich and lively public debate in a variety of arenas in these villages. The indigenous communities are typically organized according to local understandings of "tradition" in a complex web of committees and delegations, each responsible for specific tasks in the social and political life of the community. All adults are expected to participate, and positions in committees and delegations are supposed to rotate between the members of the community. One study found that more than half of the adult population at any given time would serve in a committee or a commission (Leyva Solano and Ascencio Franco 1996). Decision making is based on consensus. The emphasis on oral communication and consensus has led some analysts to use the term "premodern" to describe the political organization (Nugent 1995).

After 1994, the EZLN continued to emphasize dialogue in face-to-face settings both on a regional, national, and global scale. This was particularly evident in 2001 and 2006, as the Zapatistas sent delegations to all corners of Mexico to dialogue with interested groups. Nonetheless, more recent developments hint at increasing Zapatista interest in other forms of communication. First, the Zapatista launched Radio Insurgente in 2002, communicating first directly with base communities in Chiapas, and later with solidarity activists globally through their webpage. The webpage www.ezln. org was originally run by activists from the global solidarity movement, but from 2006 came directly under control of the Zapatistas themselves, and is now found at www.ezln.org.mx. Here new spaces of communication have opened up as activists globally use forums to communicate directly with Major Moises and Subcomandante Marcos.

Conclusion

It is not my intention here to say that the Zapatistas are not indigenous, democratic, or revolutionary, or that the authors of the articles discussed earlier were wrong. The Zapatistas were indeed indigenous, or to be more precise, they were Tzeltal, Tzotzil, Tojolobal, Chol, and more. Some even wore traditional costumes. All had experienced discrimination because of their ethnicity. But what unified the Zapatistas in one organization was their common interests as peasants and Mexicans, and this is why the first declaration talks of land for the landless and of revolution in Mexico. It was from the outside that they were seen as indigenous peoples. And maybe they needed to be seen as indigenous from the outside to discover the many similarities between their own experiences and those of the Aymaras of Bolivia, Miskitos of Nicaragua, and Sami of Norway. There are also several reasons to support the claim that the Zapatistas were more democratic than other revolutionary movements. The very decision to go to war, for instance, was made at a conference somewhere in Lacandon a year before the war actually began. It seems to have been made after a long debate followed by a popular vote among the representatives of hundreds of villages (Tello Diaz 2001). Many Cuban-inspired urban members of the organization left the EZLN in protest after a majority of indigenous peasants won the vote. As far as I know, this is the only time a Latin American guerrilla organization, at least in modern times, has taken a more or less popular vote on whether or not to go to war. This model of governing seems deeply rooted in the isolated communities of the Lacandon, where consensus on all important issues is highly valued as an ideal.

So, does this support the far-reaching claims of Castells, Cleaver, and others? According to Castells, information has become the most important resource in the "network society": "hierarchical and rigid forms of organization" will in the future be no match for flexible networks organized around symbols of identity. Castells felt that a few "prophets," like Subcomandante Marcos, were the protagonists in this process (1997). Harry M. Cleaver said: "Today those networks are providing the nerve system of increasingly global challenges to the dominant economic policies of this period" (Cleaver 1998a: 621). The "fabric of politics … is being rewoven" and is challenging the "existing political, social and economic order" (Cleaver 1998a: 637).

In my view, there is little evidence to suggest that the Zapatistas had any information strategy, except for the fact that the war itself was supposed to attract attention to their cause, just like it had previously elsewhere in Central America. There is even less evidence to support the claim that the Zapatistas exploited the internet to wage war against the Mexican government, as it took at least ten years from when the war broke out until the Zapatistas themselves began to connect to the internet. Such claims are exaggerated. In reality, the Zapatistas had been planning for a different war, a war for times long gone. They were inspired by the Cuban Revolution, but met a Mexico that was very different from Cuba in the late 1950s. In Mexico and elsewhere, there were thousands of activists ready to exploit the internet in support of the Zapatistas, making them icons of the "age of the networks."

Twenty years after the rebellion in Chiapas, it is worthwhile to reflect on the results. Indigenous groups in a number of countries, for instance, Brazil, Panama, Colombia, and Nicaragua, have won far-reaching collective rights to territories and the natural resources they contain. Many Latin American countries, including neighboring Guatemala, have ratified the International Labour Organization's (ILO) Convention 169 on indigenous rights. In spite of the massive "media spectacle," the activists, the international protests, the internet, the reweaving of the "fabric of politics," and the continued poetic essays from the "prophet's" hands, Mexico has resisted calls for the full adoption of the ILO's Convention 169.

In my view, claims of "new society," "net warfare," and new forms of power were premature. The Zapatistas did not win the war because of a clever information strategy—they probably did not even have such a strategy. But what we saw was the Western media reframing or reconstructing the Zapatistas as an indigenous movement. Seen as an indigenous movement, the Zapatistas could see their struggle in a much larger context of oppressed indigenous peoples. Being indigenous was a cause for discrimination, but became something to be proud of—important in itself, but hardly a new world.

Bibliography

Arquilla, J., and D. Ronfeldt. 2001. *Networks and Netwars: The Future of Terror, Crime, and Militancy.* Santa Monica, CA: Rand.

Asturias, M. A. 1972. *Hombres de maíz.* Madrid: Alianza Editorial.

Berger, J. 2006. "Against the Great Defeat of the World." *Race and Class* 40, nos. 2–3 (October 1998–March 1999): 1–4.

Berger, M. T. 2001. "Romancing the Zapatistas: International Intellectuals and the Chiapas Rebellion." *Latin American Perspectives* 28, no. 2 (March): 149–70.

Burbach, R. (1994a). "Roots of Postmodern Rebellion in Chiapas." *New Left Review* 1, no. 205 (May/June): 113–14.

Cabezas, O. 1986. *Fire from the Mountain: The Making of a Sandinista.* New York: New American Library.

Cardenal, E. 1976. *Poesía cubana de la revolución.* 1st ed. México: Extemporáneos.

———. 1980. *La Batalla de Nicaragua.* Mexican edition. México: Bruguera Mexicana de Ediciones.

———. 1982. *La democratización de la cultura: Exposición hecha ante la Unesco, Paris, 23 de abril de 1982.* 1st ed. Managua: Ministerio de Cultura.

Castañeda, J. G. 1994. *La Utopia Desarmada.* Bogota: Tercer Mundo.

Castells, M. 1996. *The Rise of the Network Society.* Cambridge, MA: Blackwell Publishers.

———. 1997. *The Power of Identity*. Oxford: Blackwell

Castells, M., and M. Ince. 2003. *Conversations with Manuel Castells*. Oxford: Polity.

Castillo, O. R. 1975. *Informe de una injusticia: Antología poética*. 1st ed. San José, Costa Rica: Editorial Universitaria Centroamericana.

Cleaver, H. 1998. "The Zapatista Effect: The Internet and the Rise of an Alternative Political Fabric." *Journal of International Affairs* 51, no. 2: 621–40.

———. 1998. "The Zapatistas and the Electronic Fabric of the Struggle." In *Zapatista! Reinventing Revolution in Mexico*, ed. J. Holloway and E. Peláez. London: Pluto Press.

Dalton, R. 1969. *El Intelectual y la Sociedad*. 1st ed. Mexico City: Siglo Veintiuno Editores.

———. 1970. *Revolucion en la revolucion y la crítica de derecha*. Havana: Casa de las americas.

———. 2002. *El Salvador*. 13th ed., San Salvador: UCA Editores.

———. 2004. *Las historias prohibidas del Pulgarcito*. San Salvador: UCA Editores.

Debray, R. 1967. *Revolution in the Revolution? Armed Struggle and Political Struggle in Latin America*. New York: Grove Press.

———. 1973. *Prison Writings*. London: Allen Lane.

———. 1996. "Talking to the Zapatistas." *New Left Review* 1, no. 218 (July/August): 128–37.

Galeano, E. 1973. *Open Veins of Latin America: Five Centuries of the Pillage of a Continent*. New York: Monthly Review Press.

———. 1996. Chiapas Chronicle. *La Jornada*. 7 August.

García Márquez, G. 2001, "Habla Marcos," *Cambio*, 24 March.

Guevara, E. 1972. *Escritos y discursos*. Havana: Editorial de ciencias sociales.

———. 1997. *Guerrilla warfare*. Wilmington, Del.: Scholarly Resources Inc.

Guevara, E., and D. Deutschmann. 2003. *Che Guevara Reader*. Melbourne: Ocean Press.

Hayden, T. 2002. *The Zapatista Reader*. New York: Basic Books.

Holloway, J. 2005. *Change the World without Taking Power*. London: Pluto Press.

Holloway, J., and E. Peláez. 1998. *Zapatista! Reinventing Revolution in Mexico*. London: Pluto Press.

Klein, N. 2001. "The Unknown Icon." *Guardian*. 3 March.

Kruijt, D. 2008. *Guerrillas: War and Peace in Central America*. New York: Zed Books.

Krøvel, R. 2004. *Carlos Eugenio Rodriguez*. San Cristobal de las Casas, Mexico: stifter av La Neta.

———. 2006. "Fra gerilja til globale solidaritetsnettverk i Chiapas, Mexico." Phd diss., Norges teknisk-naturvitenskapelige universitet, Det historisk-filosofiske fakultet, Institutt for historie og klassiske fag, Trondheim.

Leyva Solano, X., and G. Ascencio Franco. 1996. *Lacandonia al filo del agua*. Mexico: Fondo de Cultura Eonomica.

Lopez Vigil, J. I.,. 1991. *Rebel Radio: The Story of El Salvadors Radio Venceremos*. San Salvador: UCA Editors.

Monsiváis, C. (2001) *"El indígena visible." Proceso*, Mexico, March 4, 10–13 3 April.

Nugent, D. 1995. "Northern Intellectuals and the EZLN." *Monthly Review* 47 (June/August): 124–38.

Olesen, T. 2004a. "Globalising the Zapatistas: From Third World Solidarity to Global Solidarity?" *Third World Quarterly* 25, no. 1 (February): 255–67.

————. 2004b. "The Transnational Zapatista Solidarity Network: An Infrastructure Analysis." *Global Networks* 4, no. 1 (January): 89–107.

————. 2005a. *International Zapatismo: The Construction of Solidarity in the Age of Globalization.* London: Zed Books.

————. 2005b. "Transnational Publics: New Spaces of Social Movement Activism and the Problem of Global Long-Sightedness." *Current Sociology* 53, no. 3 (May): 419–40.

Payeras, M. 1987. *El trueno en la ciudad.* Mexico City: Juan Pablos Editor, S. A.

————. 1989. *Los dias de la selva.* Mexico City: Editorial Universitaria Centroamericana.

Paz, O. 1994. "The Media Spectacle Comes to Mexico." *New Perspectives Quarterly* 59, no. 2: 59–61.

Ronfeldt, A., and F. Fuller. 1998. *The Zapatista "Social Netwar" in Mexico.* Santa Monica, CA: RAND Corporation.

Saramago, J. 1999. "Moral Force versus the State: Chiapas, Land of Hope and Sorrow." *Le Monde Diplomatique,* English version. March.

Taibo II, P. I. 1994. "Zapatistas: The Phoenix Rises." *Nation.* 28 March.

Tello Diaz, C. 2001. *La Rebelion de las Cañadas.* Mexico City: Cal y Arena.

Vázquez Montalbán, M. (1999). *Marcos: El Señor de los Espejos.* Madrid: Aguilar.

Chapter 21

Punks, Hackers, and Unruly Technology
Countercultures in the Communication Society

Hendrik Storstein Spilker

Do-It-Yourself in the Communication Society

This article will explore how the punk movement has appropriated the internet and other digital technologies as part of its cultural and political repertoire. Traditionally, the punk movement has rejected the use of mass media for tactical measures. It has instead focused on the construction of alternative communication and distribution channels based on the principles of do-it-yourself (DIY). Initially, we expect that some of the supposed capabilities of the internet offer new possibilities for DIY-based action. Our research therefore revolves around the question of whether the internet and other digital technologies have been taken up and utilized as an opportunity to strengthen and renew the cultural and political practices of the punk movement. As part of this questioning, we will also explore the relationship between the punk movement and the hacker movement.

The punk movement is interesting for several reasons. It is a music counterculture with an overt and potent political agenda. It has also—perhaps paradoxically—managed to remain meaningful and to renew itself through the years, making it a lasting element of the underground music scenes for three decades. Certainly, there exist opposing narratives regarding the history of punk. According to one popular version created basically by mass media (and some of the punk pioneers themselves), punk was a short-lived phenomenon that collapsed in an orgy of blood, drugs, and violence in 1979. However, following Gosling's (2004) "revisionist" history, after the outburst years of 1977–79, the punk movement managed to transform itself from an "anticulture" into a counterculture.

Historically, the most important part of the movement's transformation consisted of the establishment of an alternative institutional network centered around self-governed youth houses or "autonomous zones" in urban areas throughout Europe and South and North America. Arguably, this institutional network is an important part of the reason why the punk movement has managed to remain more consistent and enduring than, for example, the hippie movement (see further discussion later on). Also, while punk through the years has experienced the development of a lot of offshoots—hardcore, third wave ska, emo, riot grrrl, queer core, straight-edge—the scene has not undergone the same splintering and fragmentation that occurred, for example, in the rave scene (see Gulla 2006).

But has the existence of the internet caused any difference in this picture? We will examine this question with an analysis of the appropriation of information and communication technologies (ICTs) by the Norwegian punk scene. More specifically, we have conducted a case study of the activities at UFFA,[1] the self-governed youth house in Trondheim, one of two such houses in Norway.[2]

Our starting point is that new technology brings the potential to change existing practices and formations. However, human appropriation of technologies is a complex matter. Theoretically, these activities may be conceptualized as *domestication* (Silverstone and Hirsch 1992; Lie and Sørensen 1996; Berker et al. 2005; Levold and Spilker 2007). The domestication perspective takes as its point of departure how people construct their "own" technologies by integrating them into networks of meanings and practices in everyday life. Domestication of new technology is rarely a simple matter, thus triggering possibilities and challenges that may often lead to conflicting situations. Appropriation requires changing existing practices. Practices must be framed again (Callon 1999; Callon et al. 2004).

A central premise in domestication theory is that technology appropriation must be understood as a two-way process (Oudshoorn and Pinch 2003; Jasanoff 2004. On the one hand, new technology may change existing social practices and formations. Haraway (1991) points out how new technology may appear as a disruptive element in social contexts. The introduction of new technology may bring uncertainty and instability into existing cultural networks. However, it is equally important to be aware that its introduction in new settings can transform technology, its fields of application, and its meaning content. Looking at it from this perspective, studies of countercultures and alternative cultures become particularly important. The punk counterculture is a potential field of tension in the communication society.

Our interest in punk counterculture is connected to the expectation that the appropriation by counterculture of new ICTs will assume forms that will rattle and threaten more habitual ideas of the importance and use of these technologies. We will study this on two levels. In general, we will examine how new ICTs, with their communication opportunities, have—or have not—been absorbed in and been made part of the countercultural repertoire. We will, moreover, focus on how the punk scene deals with digital distribution of music. Music is a defining element for the punk counterculture, while the controversies linked to file sharing and copyright protection have long been perhaps the most heated conflict area in the development of the internet. It is therefore interesting to examine the type of viewpoints a political activist community with many performing musicians has adopted in this context. What is the morally correct way of dealing with ICTs in the counterculture, and how is it distinguished from a more "average" way of dealing with digital technologies? How has the introduction of digital technology transformed the counterculture, and how have the moral codes of the punk movement influenced the uptake of the technology?

The analysis is based on qualitative in-depth interviews with active or previously active actors at UFFA, the house for free youth activities in Trondheim. Interviews with five contacts between nineteen and twenty-six years of age represent today's active UFFA members. We also interviewed five people who were active during the consolidation of UFFA in the 1980s, who at the time of the interviews were between thirty-eight and forty-two years of age. In all interviews, we focused on the contacts' understanding of technologically related change processes and countercultural strategies in the encounter with new ICTs. Our data collection also consisted of a total of eight supplementary interviews, including interviews with performers from other music communities such as hip-hop and electronic music, local and internet radio actors from Trondheim Underground Radio (TUR) and the Student Radio in Trondheim, as well as an interview with a representative of the network activists called Electronic Frontier Norway (EFN). We have also studied fanzines, magazines, netzines, network forums, band websites, and other media from the 1980s until today.

The Quest for the Hacker Punk

We have formulated our expectations concerning the counterculture's appropriation of new ICTs more specifically as a quest to find a projected character we have called the *hacker punk*. We can start in this context by envisioning a person who is involved in countercultural activism with some type of political commitment, someone who is eager to express himself musically and is fascinated with the opportunities afforded by information and communication technologies.

Let us outline a historical backdrop for these expectations. An important inspiration for this case study was a passage in Manuel Castells's book *Internet Galaxy*, where he states that there was "an interesting connection between some of the social subcultures of the post-1960s period and the hacker culture" (2001: 51). The connection between the hippie movement and the hacker movement in the 1960s and 1970s was later documented in John Markoff's *What the Dormouse Said: How the Sixties Counterculture Shaped the Personal Computer Industry* (2005) and Fred Turner's *From Counterculture to Cyberculture: Stewart Brand, the Whole Earth Network, and the Rise of Digital Utopianism* (2006). These studies describe how a significant overlap and exchange existed between the music and computer countercultures of the 1960s and 1970s, both in terms of the people and the ideas involved.

"Hacking" is a term that was initially used by students who were members of computer clubs at MIT and Stanford to describe the activities undertaken by these clubs. Ceruzzi defines the original meaning of hacking as "not to do a programming job specified by one's employer" (2000: 215). Hackers thus came to represent a sophisticated form of playful and exploratory ways of using computers. Many descriptions of the hacker phenomenon also attach importance to the development of an ideological rationale for the activity, linked to an understanding of ICTs as liberating and antiauthoritarian tools, which indicates the ties to the hippie movement. This ideological rationale has become known as the *hackers' ethos:* "[H]ackers were defined by their adherence to an ethic, a code of beliefs that was predicted on access to computers, freedom of information, the mistrust of authority, and the belief that computers could be used for constructive social change" (Thomas 2000: 204).

We cannot review the genealogy of the development of the hacker movement here, as Taylor (1999) does when identifying five generations of hackers. What is important is that the hacker movement has continued to be the reference point of computer countercultures in various forms up to contemporary times. Ross, for example, offers the following enthusiastic description of the importance of hacking: "[H]acking, as guerrilla know-how, is essential to the task of maintaining fronts of cultural resistance and stocks of oppositional knowledge as a hedge against a technofascist future" (2000: 255). Today, we must situate the practice of hackerlike countercultural activity in movements like the open source movement and organizations like Electronic Frontier Foundation (EFF) (and its Norwegian counterpart, Electronic Frontier Norway [EFN]).

Our research questions are thus connected to the ties between this type of computer counterculture and the punk movement. In a certain sense one might claim that our quest for the hacker punk was anticipated as early as in 1984, when William Gibson presented the *cyberpunk* in his novel *Neuromancer*. Gibson created the cyberpunk metaphor based on the force and appeal that the punk counterculture had for contemporary youth. In *Neuromancer*, a picture is drawn of a computer-mediated future where tribal groups dominate urban life through their ability to integrate "the hyperefficient structures of high technology with the anarchy of street cultures" (Cavallero 2000: xi). Others also found inspiration in the punk movement when attempting to describe how computer networks would change social formations, such as Hakim Bey's (1991) idea of computer networks as tools in the construction of "temporary autonomous zones."

Cyberpunk is above all a literary science fiction genre that had its heyday in the 1980s, and that used elements from contemporary youth culture and technological development to construe its fictional universe (see Bell et al. 2004). To some extent this fictional universe then served as inspiration for the formation of new subcultural identities, such as the community around the periodical *Mondo 2000* and their "New Edge". Arguments against cyberpunk literature (and against subcultures such as the one surrounding *Mondo 2000*) have, however, also been heard, where it is claimed that cyberpunk only has marginal ties to punk—as McKay (1999) claims in his article with the appropriately worded subtitle, "The Punk in Cyberpunk." His argument is that cyberpunk only borrows the aesthetic from punk—that is, the provocative use of cultural artifacts—while the political agenda of the punk movement is left out. In the words of Gosling's (2004) history of the movement, we can say that cyberpunk embeds the exhibitionist phase of punk in 1977–79, but it does not incorporate the reconstruction and new consolidation of the punk movement that occurred from 1979 onward.

A further reason for avoiding the use of the cyberpunk term is that cyberpunk has to be seen as having little to do with music and music countercultures. Our projection, the hacker punk, is conversely a character that has a firm base in a particular music counterculture, where music continues to be a constituting element in the practice of the countercultural elements, and where the counterculture elements are countercultural beyond the use of provocative aesthetic expressions, that is, with a more explicit political agenda. We thus expect these elements to be combined with a fascination and critical involvement in new ICTs and their possibilities.

The use of the internet and other digital technologies in the development of new forms of political resistance is a well-researched area with comprehensive literature (see Hill and Hughes 1998; Meikle 2002; McCaughey and Ayers 2003; van de Donk et al. 2004). The most commonly used examples are connected to how different social movements and countercultural activists exploited digital technology to organize protests in connection with the WTO summit meetings in Seattle and Prague around the turn of the century. This literature is generally enthusiastic about the internet and the potential of other digital communication technologies for the renewal of grassroots activism, and tends to praise the possibilities it gives for participation in a creative application of digital protest.

These works do not, however, tell us much about the importance of music and music countercultures in connection with these new forms of activism. Nevertheless, one particularly interesting study in this context is St. John's (2003) study of rave music communities in Australia at the end of the 1990s. St. John finds that the rave culture he studied cannot be described as exclusively nihilistic, Dionysian, nomadic, and unstable, the way other commentators previously described the house and rave culture (see Maffesoli 1995). He describes how the Australian rave scene has developed new types of protest in addition to partying, and often at the same time. Actions/festivals such as "Reclaim the Streets" and "Ohms Not Bombs" are examples of what is designated as "carnivals of protest" and "political partying." A central element here is the innovative utilization of the new digital surroundings to increase the tactical repertoire and organizational capacity of the counterculture. In this context, St. John draws attention to how "the repurposing of technology for countercultural ends has a lineage in early ham radio enthusiasts, personal computer hackers, independent radical desk-top publishers, audio and video scratchers" (2003: 72).

In the same vein as the literature about social movements on the internet, St. John is enthusiastic on behalf of the ability of the rave scene to exploit digital technologies to transform cultural expressions, mobilize new participants, and expand in time and space. Other studies, however, draw a more trivial picture of what happens in the encounter between music subcultures and digital technologies. Hodkinson (2003, 2004) argues that new communication technology primarily creates social spaces in the extension of established social patterns. Based on an observation of the presence of the Goth movement on the internet, he asserts that it is used to maintain the external dividing lines and the internal sense of identity in a subcultural youth formation. Hodkinson describes Goths as a "self-sufficient and self-contained" group, where the adoption of digital technologies makes little difference when it comes to recruitment to or the practice of the music subculture.

St. John and Hodkinson have studied two different types of music scenes, one presented as expressive, outgoing, and with a stated political agenda, the other closed, introverted, and apparently apolitical. Therefore, it is not surprising that they find two different approaches to digital technologies. We call the appropriation of the rave movement a *transformation strategy*, and the appropriation of the Goth movement a *trivialization strategy*. Based on our hypothesis on the hacker punk, it is clear that we expect that the domestication strategy of the punk movement will be closer to that of the Australian rave scene. Is this the case?

Furthermore, a striking feature of the analyses undertaken both by St. John and Hodkinson is the absence of turbulence, conflict, or resistance in connection with the appropriation of technology. It does not appear that the selection of appropriation strategy has been subjected to controversies in these communities. Does appropriation really occur so painlessly?

What Is So Punk about Punk?

When on 10 November 1981 young people in Trondheim occupied an abandoned house and founded UFFA (the Norwegian abbreviation for Youth for Free Activity), this occupation was part of a wave running through Europe. While the punk movement in earlier years had been responsible for random riots, such as those on the night before 1 May (in Oslo) and 17 May (in Trondheim), these actions were now focused on a demand for self-governed arenas for youth activities. Gosling (2004) asserts that the punk movement in this period went through a transformation from being an anticulture to a counterculture. The punk communities developed a new agenda around 1980, focusing on the development of alternatives to the mainstream culture/general society. This self-searching came to form the underpinning of a viable counterculture, which continues to attract new generations of young people.

We would like to point out five elements that have come to characterize the punk movement:

1. *The DIY ethos.* In connection with the redefinition of the punk movement, the DIY ethos was a key element. The aim was generally to establish as many independent arenas and channels as possible for music performance and other activities as alternatives to the established cultural industry and general society. The DIY culture has come to include a whole "value chain" of bands, fans, dealers, studios, promoters, media, and other resources.

2. *Link between politics and music.* The focus on the establishment of independent arenas and channels did not lead to a depoliticization of the punk movement. It did not drop out of society as many other "self-reliant" groups have done. Comments on, criticism of, and protests against the authorities and capitalist organizations have always

been an important feature of the activities. The movement has thus always been about more than just music. It has developed in the fusion or overlap between music and politics.

3. *"Autonomous zones."* An important banner issue for the punk movement in Europe in the 1980s was the establishment of self-governed youth houses, or "autonomous zones," as they eventually came to be called. These were acquired through a wave of house occupations. Blitz in Oslo and UFFA in Trondheim are the Norwegian examples of this (see Maat 1983; Johansen 1988). The squatted houses have doubtlessly functioned as identity anchor points, continuity carriers, and recruitment arenas.

4. *Urbanity.* The punk movement has always been primarily oriented toward urban spaces, which is another way in which it differs from the hippie movement. On the aesthetic level, the movement has idolized what we may call an "aesthetics of concrete," which has dominated clothing styles and musical expressions. Politically, the city has also served as the central arena for resistance, expressed in slogans such "the street is ours." The idea has been to open new niches and spaces in the metropolis.

5. *Innovative protest forms.* The final element we will point out here concerns the ability of the punk movement to renew the expressions and forms of political protest through creative utilization of technology, artistic techniques, and the opportunities of urban space. In this context, we can mention examples such as house occupations, street concerts, carnival-like protest street parades, fanzines and poster art, and political tagging. Punks have also demonstrated the ability to expand their repertoire in recent years, demonstrated, for example, by the phenomenon of adbusting (see Haugdahl 2005).

These five elements are vital to the understanding of the remarkable survival ability of the punk scene and its continued appeal.

The vitality of the UFFA milieu is a good example in this respect. UFFA is an autonomous youth house with the weekly general meeting as the supreme decision-making body. The general meeting is in principle open to all, but an implicit requirement is that you must be a user of the house and involved in the community if your vote is to count. The form of government may perhaps most appropriately be called a "do-ocracy." UFFA has housed and houses a number of activities, such as café operations, a book café, music rehearsal rooms, a music studio, concert premises, fanzine and magazine production, local radio, and various action groups. The punk community based at the UFFA house has had substantial offshoots over the years, highly visible in the nearby neighborhood of Svartlamoen, with relatively self-governed housing areas, cafés, secondhand shops, studios, musical practice studios, and day care center operations (see Johansen 1988; Haugdahl 2005).

Our premise is thus that the punk movement has constituted a creative force that has helped transform physical and social urban spaces through the establishment of alternative arenas and channels for activity, and by appearing as a disturbing element in its relations to the general society. The UFFA entrepreneurs spoke about how at the start of the 1980s, there were no places for young people in Trondheim to hang out. They feel the situation today is different, and punk is ascribed much of the honor for this: "This need for a place to hang out, that's different now, really. People hang out all over the place."

We do not problematize this premise, instead asking: Has the punk movement carried this creative force over to its dealings with the new ICTs? Does punk transform digital spaces in the same way as physical spaces have been transformed? Has the DIY ethos been renewed to also include an agenda for the use and production of ICTs?

The Digitalized Underground

Digital technology, spearheaded by the internet, has obviously made its mark in relation to the punk counterculture, as it has in most other aspects of society. Concerning music-related activities, the contacts generally pointed out that the internet was quite important. Bands at UFFA today use different web services, such as Trondheim Underground Radio and urørt.no, to promote their activities to the audience, concert arrangers, record companies, and other stakeholders. It is common to post songs and videos on these websites, which visitors can then stream or download. The internet is used actively in booking and in communication between artists and concert arrangers via email, websites, or web forums.

One special underground phenomenon has been the distribution of music via "distros." Music enthusiasts have acted as go-betweens for artists and fans and acquired and distributed music via distribution lists, preferably made available via fanzines or bulletin boards. This activity has found its electronic extension, and the tools are now email lists, websites, and discussion forums. Many of the contacts mentioned that they find much of the music they are attracted to by using specially dedicated file-sharing networks. Swedish and Dutch-based networks for punk and hardcore music were mentioned in particular.

Some bands also use the internet to download free software to establish home studios and produce music. A few also use the internet more directly and interactively in processes with music production, for example, by sending unfinished material to be processed by a studio or to receive tracks from musicians who live far away, without depending on playing together at the same time in the same studio (see Théberge 2004; Moen 2007).

The internet is thus used extensively as the medium of distribution, communication, and, in part, production of music. Where underground bands in the 1980s distributed their music on cassettes through the postal system, digitalized formats distributed via the internet have enabled more rapid and immediate distribution. The internet has increased the mobility of the underground music further by, on the one hand, making existing networks more efficient and, on the other hand, making them more all-encompassing.

However, even if making oneself visible to a broader audience now also takes on virtual forms, concerts and releasing records continue to be core activities for the underground community. Trading and selling physical records—both CDs and vinyl—continue to be surprisingly common, and also function as a vital "glue" connecting bands and fans. It appears that in the punk culture, the idea of exchanging music on a physical medium is a part of the culture that should be preserved.

In the 1980s, fanzines and eventually also local radio were crucial channels for the exchange of information and opinions. Today, new idealist web services have in part taken over the functions of fanzines and local radio. Net forums have become an important arena where people can stay updated and exchange opinions. Many bands and private individuals have created websites with forums that have been popular for some time. In Trondheim, Trondheim Hardcore[3] and the UFFA house website[4] have been particularly key elements.

Trondheim Hardcore was established in 2001 by members of central hardcore bands in the city with connections to UFFA. The idea was to write and inform about a music genre the press in general hardly covered. The aim was also to reach beyond the core UFFA community. Trondheim Hardcore was popular as a netzine and net forum until the spring of 2004, but then something happened with the forum. After some years, the community fragmented and the initiators gave up. At the end of 2006, the website stated the following:

> Trondheim Hardcore has been laid to rest. Much has happened since a group of enthusiasts came together in Jarleveien in Trondheim in the autumn of 2001 to create an alternative channel to disseminate our enthusiasm for the genre. Much good came of this, and as the case should be in a radical community, several factions arose, and things were watered down … Much has also been said

about a forum which at times was quite heated by the typical internet discussions of the time. (http://www.trondheimhardcore.com 16 November 2006)

The UFFA house website experienced some of the same problems. UFFA's website has been operated and moderated by persons who are involved in the community on assignment from the general meeting. The website has maintained an overview of events arranged at UFFA, and provided the history of the center, picture galleries, information about the café menu, and book café offers and so on. A discussion forum has also been attempted. The UFFA forum was established in 2003. Some discussions were political. The problem with putting these on the web was that outsiders, such as members of "Unge Høyre" (the youth association of the Norwegian Conservative Party), would log on and create an unpleasant discussion climate. Eventually this led to the forum being closed down due to the bickering and publication of in-house discussions.

In addition to connecting like-minded people, web forums enable the observation of countercultural discussions for outsiders. This was not always easy to handle. On the one hand, web services with forums such as Trondheim Hardcore and uffahus.org have contributed to extending the exchange range of countercultural opinion and information. On the other hand, the experience with such services is that they might launch processes over which the counterculture has no control. The contacts experience much "noise" and "lack of seriousness" in discussion forums. Therefore, they have been seen as less appropriate, particularly in relation to the political aspects of their activities.

Because of the internet, more people probably know about UFFA and the punk environment today than previously, and subsequently more people establish more peripheral and loose ties to the community than previously. One might claim that the periphery of the UFFA community has become more densely populated. There is, however, nothing to indicate that the active core at UFFA has grown. The most important decisions connected to the community activity continue to be made through face-to-face contact—at the general meeting or in "the corridors" and "on the street" among those who are in the house or in its neighborhood on a day-to-day basis.

In Search of the Hacker Punk

In our interviews, we also wished to determine whether the punk movement had developed its own ICT morals and ICT policy—a renewal of the DIY ethos that comprises an agenda for the use and production of ICTs. Furthermore, we wanted to examine the kind of link that existed between the music counterculture and computer counterculture, such as the open source movement.

According to UFFA veterans, discussions on new technological artifacts for UFFA have traditionally focused mostly on practical or financial matters. But purchases were rarely made without some political debate. The appropriation of a Xerox copier, for example, led to discussions about buying a photocopier from a multinational company and the consumption of electricity. Political debates could arise on many levels and in most contexts. Kristin, one of the veterans, tells about the criticism that arose when the use of Letraset in fanzine production was substituted with typewriting. This was a selling out!

Today UFFA has two computers in the house, both running Windows XP Pro as the operative system. UFFA has installed a wireless network, which users with portable computers can use anywhere in the house. Most active UFFA activists also have PCs with internet connections at home. PCs running Windows dominate.

The UFFA activists find it totally acceptable to run software from, for example, Microsoft, without having the proper license. What about using free open-source software as an alternative to Microsoft's software? One of our contacts outside UFFA itself—Anders, the founder of the web service Trondheim Undergrunnsradio (TUR)[5]—believes it is a paradox that people from the political music underground do not get more involved in open and democratic structures on the internet and in the software market. He bases his TUR operation on General Public License (GPL) software with open-source code. A degree of competence is required to operate these, but Anders feels it is nevertheless strange that so few in the punk movement bother to understand this issue. When using Microsoft software, you are basically distributing goods you are actually against, he argued, and you are also strengthening the hegemony of an industry that is working against you.

There is a dawning recognition of this issue internally in the UFFA community, as expressed by Thomas:

> There is free software, for both this and the other thing. I have friends who keep telling me I should use such things, since I'm dabbling in political involvement and am against some big companies, so I really shouldn't have been using Microsoft products and things like that.

In spite of this, the typical UFFA punks are not active users of licensed open-source software. Nor is UFFA an active institution when it comes to hacking or other digital action forms. Several of the activists believe that hacking may well have a political activist function, but they feel that hacking is primarily about personal adrenalin kicks to achieve status or to commit financial fraud. None stated that they knew hackers or that they had heard of something of that sort in connection with UFFA and the punk/hardcore community. Kristin, the veteran, is nevertheless certain that hackers exist in the punk counterculture: "Hackers in our community, I'm sure they exist. I'm dead certain about this, people who … Or … Well, like people who make viruses and stuff like that, I believe so." Kristin envisions that hackers and people from the punk movement may have common political goals and interests. Therefore, it is "logical" that someone with a background from a political punk/hardcore community might start hacking and committing computer sabotage. It is, however, striking that our contacts do not claim to have any specific connections to political hacker communities in spite of the opportunities technological innovations in combination with the DIY spirit to make statements might lead us to expect. Hacking is something other people do.

When it comes to downloading music, the UFFA youths see a political-moral dilemma in the they in principle support free distribution of music, but they also want to support small bands and record companies that want to distribute music but also survive financially. The UFFA youths feel there is a difference between downloading music from big rock stars versus small, unknown bands. Small record companies may have a problem with a lack of revenues, but they feel no pity for bands such as Metallica and Coldplay or the record companies Universal and EMI. Several of these youths also expressed worry about a future where one would have to pay for all use of intellectual property.

There may be a political statement in the way they are aware of whom they are "cheating." Their conscience does not bother them when they pirate large commercial actors. This also applies to not paying license fees for using Microsoft products. A Robin Hood attitude may be looming here that chimes well with punk's fundamental anarchist attitudes. It is, however, a stretch to only consider the file sharing of UFFA youths as a countercultural political strategy. Pirate copying and file sharing are practiced by a wide range of young people, regardless of such background variables as income, gender, and countercultural belonging. Marksten (2005) explains this by saying that access to free music is easy, while confusion in relation to the actual legislation in the field of file sharing makes those who download files unafraid of the legal consequences. UFFA youths are undoubtedly more politically involved than the average youth, but it does not appear that their political involvement can easily be linked to downloading habits, even if they like to "defend" their actions by referring to anticapitalist principles.

There are few developed or stated attitudes to copyright and general access to music. Following the success of the open-source movement internationally, initiatives have been made to offer alternatives to the traditional copyright legislation for music and other cultural products, the most prominent of these being the "creative commons" licenses.[6] In the interviews with musicians affiliated with UFFA, however, nobody mentioned creative commons licenses as a possible strategy for managing their music digitally across prevailing administrative structures.

The traditional response to capitalist structures in the cultural industry from the punk movement is DIY: create your own industry. It appears that this continues to be the strategy that will ensure a sustainable underground scene. However, the DIY ethos does not appear to have been significantly reformulated due to the introduction of ICTs in the music counterculture.

The overriding impression is that today's UFFA activists generally use the internet in the same way as most other young people. Their activities in general revolve around checking email, surfing, playing online games, chatting, discussing, and downloading music. Apparently, they do not connect their use of the internet to their involvement in the punk counterculture. In this chapter, we introduced the expectation of finding established interfaces between music counterculture and ICT counterculture, a countercultural cooperation, which on paper appears to be opportune for both parties. What is blocking such a connection?

The punk culture is known for developing creative ways of demonstrating resistance and independence. In recent years, adbusting is an example of this. As a music counterculture, it is based on the ability of the participants to manage an underground-based industry outside the established structures of the mass culture. Our hypothesis about a countercultural demonstration that would be seen through the technological solutions the punk movement links up with cannot, however, be proven. What is it that makes it so difficult for punkers to let their creativity loose in the digital field?

The Gap between Near and Binary Things

While companies such as Statoil and Coca-Cola are the targets of political activism and countercultural campaigns, there is apparently very little computer activism in the punk culture. An explanation the UFFA youths give for this absence of a clearer political stance with respect to ICTs is that there are limitations on how much attention one can devote to the political aspects of all conditions in life. Even punkers have to deal with the world they are living in, even if they may not be fully comfortable with the way things happen. UFFA youths clearly feel that the internet is dominated by the same political structures they basically oppose. The lack of active resistance against this is defended by the argument that you cannot boycott absolutely everything—as Eirik aptly puts it:

> That's really a very interesting topic you have there, as in how punk is it to join this internet thing. How punk is it to buy Converse shoes which have been bought up by Nike, how punk is it to drink Coca-Cola … I think we should be aware of what we consume and which channels we use, through the internet and everything. But it mustn't be a goal to be 100 percent politically correct in everything; that would only make your life fucking tiresome.

The UFFA youths also feel that competence is required to develop an updated music policy resistance strategy in the day-to-day digital world. Thomas, for example, believed that "the problem with such open source code things is that it's too complicated, at least a lot of the time, you know, if you don't have the adequate technological competence." As a community, UFFA has moved from being at the cutting edge of ICT competence development to now being in the middle of the pack. At the end of the 1980s it could reasonably be argued that UFFA was very advanced, due in large part to the enthusiasm and competence developed in the production of various fanzines. This competence was further enhanced through UFFA's flagship, the *Folk & Røvere* (Folk & Robbers) magazine. The activities at the time were propelled by creative missionaries in the community.

Today there seems to be a lack of this type of enterprising project. Even if hacker visions of open structures in cyberspace may appear attractive, the community today lacks proactive entrepreneurs who can create interesting projects where the punk/hardcore culture's DIY ethos can be adapted and developed in digital surroundings. Some of the UFFA youths also state that they understand hackers and proponents of open-source code as a closed culture with little ability to communicate principles and competence to the external world.

Several of the interviewees mentioned that it might be easier to take political standpoints in relation to things felt, in some sense, to be nearer. The punk counterculture has competence when it comes to more traditional political issues such as resistance against American cultural or political imperialism, suppression of women, and police violence. Cyber activism is not part of this established political repertoire. One could then claim that the UFFA punk culture stands for an orientation toward the near rather than binary things. Creative new forms of action take the form of initiatives such as adbusting and dealing with urban space, instead of, for example, so-called DoS attacks (blocking network services), which might have been the digital space counterpart.[7] In this context, it is important to bear in mind that UFFA draws on a tradition linked to visibility in the physical urban landscape. Adbusting is a relatively new action form that can be added to this tradition.

The networks of physical locations and social relations in the punk culture today seem to have more of a preserving rather than an innovative function. In UFFA's case, this has proven to be a strength in terms of cultural continuity and recruitment. In the eager endeavor to preserve original ideals, some of the ability to face political challenges with creativity seems to disappear from the punk movement. In this way, the domestication process is influenced in a direction that prevents the possibility of a constructive update of the countercultural DIY repertoire in the digital domain.

The Unruliness of Technology

Previously in this chapter we referred to the comprehensive literature that is strongly optimistic in relation to the possibilities for utilizing the internet and other digital technologies to develop new forms of political resistance. St. John's (2003) study of the Australian rave scene, and its innovative exploitation of the new digital sphere, was given as an example of the countercultural renewal of the link between politics and music. We expected that it would also be in the interest of the punk counterculture—here represented by UFFA—to appear as an element of unrest in the ICT policy landscape.

Our findings suggest, however, that the realities are somewhat more trivial, while the difficulties and challenges of countercultural appropriation of ICTs are greater than the optimism found in the literature we mentioned. A process of appropriation has been going on, and is still going on, when it comes to new ICTs in the punk movement, but this only negligibly refers to hacker counterculture ideals. The link between music and politics is important for UFFA, but no link appears to have arisen between politics and the digital reality where much of today's music activity occurs. The DIY ethos has not been renewed to include ICT policy issues. This means that apparently no new underground policy has been produced at UFFA in the wake of the internet. Even if ICTs act as an enrolled resource in the tool chest of the counterculture, the UFFA community so far does not truly take to heart the political aspect of the new technological spheres. UFFA thus reveals an ambivalent and in part unresolved relation to new ICTs. The culture lacks a creative strategy in relation to influencing or opposing today's distribution regimes.

In our study, we were hunting for the "hacker punk" at UFFA—a hunt inspired by such works as Markoff (2005) and Turner (2006) and their uncovering of the links between hippies and hackers in the 1960s and 1970s. However, the study showed that few or no links existed between the local music counterculture at UFFA and computer countercultures. Even though punk counterculture and computer counterculture should, "on paper," have much in common, they appear to be two different projects.

To our knowledge, no other inquiries into the relationship between the punk movement and the hacker movement have been conducted. Therefore, Kristin's assertion that there probably are "hackers in our community" remains a question for further research. Actually, few studies have explored the use of ICTs in the punk counterculture. Haenfler's (2006) ethnography of straight-edge punkers in the United States includes some considerations of the role of internet in the community and reveals contradictions and mixed emotions in line with what we have observed. Citing one of Haenfler's contacts, the internet has "really taken a lot of fun out of hardcore" (2006: 179).

Even if our picture is somewhat more nuanced, for UFFA the appropriation of ICTs contributes to making the music counterculture deal with a more unruly hybrid collective of technology, competence, and social relations. This new order does not simply mean a plethora of new ways of approaching countercultural activities, but also offers a new type of challenge with respect to social control.

The lack of a clarified policy and strategy for ICT issues may be considered a symptom of the ambiguous value ascribed to ICTs in the punk movement. When it comes to music policy, this may be interpreted as a paradox, as the music counterculture lacks a creative strategy against the ICT policy of the commercial music industry. Where the punk/hardcore culture had DIY as its strategy to avoid intervention from commercial actors in the early 1980s, no corresponding creative strategy exists to match the digital surroundings through which much of today's music life is mediated.

We believe that this may stem from the fact that being countercultural is a job demanding competence. We have seen that the activists at UFFA today lack the insight and will to get involved in the political challenges of ICTs. Domestication may for the music counterculture be seen as a way of defining order and disorder (Green 2001). As a counterculture it is basically dependent on retaining some disorder as part of a survival project. It is, however, hard and demanding to always stand for alternative ways of doing things. Moreover, the expanded distribution of politics and music may be a threat to social control. It becomes more difficult to control what is kept inside the community and what is "leaked" to the outside world. Thus, the music counterculture does not necessarily have the same political interests as the computer counterculture. It appears that for the time being we should forget the hacker punk.

UFFA's ambivalent relation to ICTs reveals that the appropriation process has not occurred as painlessly as Hodkinson (2003, 2004) and St. John (2003) found in their studies. Our study has showed how internet use has been embedded in the punk scene and contributed to creating new space for niche activities. The fact that the internet has been taken into use by the music counterculture does not necessarily mean that the counterculture determines the conditions for that use. It rather appears that ICTs function as a disruptive element that the music counterculture does not have full control over. At any rate, in this picture, the punk is not the source for the unruliness.

Notes

1. UFFA stands for Ungdom for fri aktivitet (Youth for Free Activities). Trondheim is the third biggest city in Norway.
2. The other is Blitz in Oslo, the capital.
3. http://www.trondheimhardcore.com.
4. http://www.uffahus.org.
5. http://www.turmusic.no.
6. See http://www.creativecommons.org.
7. DoS: denial of service.

Bibliography

Bell, D., B. D. Loader, N. Pleace, and D. Schuler. 2004. *Cyberculture: The Key Concepts*. London: Routledge.

Berker, T., M. Hartmann, Y. Punie, and K. Ward. 2005. *Domestication of Media and Technology*. Maidenhead, UK: Open University Press.

Bey, H. 1991. *The Temporary Autonomous Zone: Ontological Anarchy, Poetic Terrorism*. http://www.hermetic.com/bey/taz_cont.html. (accessed 12 August 2013)

Callon, M., ed.1999. *The Laws of the Market*. Oxford: Blackwell.

Callon, M., C. Meadel, and V. Rabeharisoa. 2004. "The Economy of Qualities." In *The Technological Economy*, ed. A. Barry and D. Slater. London: Routledge.

Castells, M. 2001. *The Internet Galaxy: Reflections on the Internet, Business and Society*. New York: Oxford University Press.

Cavallero, D. 2000. *Cyberpunk and Cyberculture: Science Fiction and the Work of William Gibson*. New Jersey: Athlone Press.

Ceruzzi, P. 2000. *A History of Modern Computing*. Cambridge, MA: MIT Press.

Gibson, W. 2004. *Neuromancer*. New York: Ace Books.

Gosling, T. 2004. "Not for Sale: The Underground Network of Anarcho-Punk." In *Music Scenes: Local Translocal and Virtual*, ed. A. Bennett and R. A. Peterson. Nashville: Vanderbilt University Press.

Green, L. 2001. *Communication, Technology and Society.* London: Sage.

Gulla, B. 2006. *The Greenwood Encyclopedia of Rock History,* Vol. 6, *The Grunge and Post-Grunge Years, 1991–2005.* London: Greenwood Press

Haenfler, R. 2006. *Straight Edge: Clean-Living Youth, Hardcore Punk, and Social Change.* New Brunswick, NJ: Rutgers University Press.

Haraway, D. 1991. "A Cyborg Manifesto." In *Simians, Cyborgs and Women: The Reinvention of Nature,* ed. D. Haraway. London: Routledge.

Haugdahl, M. 2005. "Jakten på en kjerne: Adbusters. Domestisering av et fenomen i grenselandet motkultur og mainstream."*Master thesis.* Trondheim: Institutt for tverrfaglige kulturstudier, NTNU.

———. 2006. *UFFA 1981–2006: Alternativ ungdomskultur i Trondheim.* Trondheim: Tapir Akademisk Forlag.

Hill, K., and J. Hughes. 1998. *Cyberpolitics: Citizen Activism in the Age of the Internet.* Oxford: Rowman & Littlefield.

Hodkinson, P. 2003. "'Net.Goth': Internet Communication and (Sub-)Cultural Boundaries." In *The Post-Subcultures Reader,* ed. D. Muggleton and R. Weinzierl. Oxford: Berg Publishers.

———. 2004. "Translocal Connections in the Goth Scene." In *Music Scenes: Local, Translocal, and Virtual,* ed. A. Bennett and R. A. Peterson. Nashville: Vanderbilt University Press.

Jasanoff, S., ed. 2004. *States of Knowledge: The Co-production of Science and Social Order.* London: Routledge.

Johansen, S. E. 1988. *24-timers mennesker: Om livet hinsides arbeid blant motkulturell ungdom i Trondhjem.* Master thesis. Sosialantropologisk institutt, Universitetet i Trondheim.

Levold, N., and H. S. Spilker, eds. 2007. *Kommunikasjonssamfunnet: Moral, praksis og digital teknologi.* Oslo: Universitetsforlaget.

Lie, M., and K. H. Sørensen, eds. 1996. *Making Technology Our Own.* Oslo: Universitetsforlaget.

Maat, B. 1983. "Fra slumstormergruppe til social bevægelse: BZ vesteuropa 1969–1982." *Skriftserie fra Roskilde universitetsbibliotek* 13. Roskilde, Denmark: Roskilde universitetsbibliotek.

Maffesoli, M. 1995. *The Time of the Tribes: The Decline of Individualism in Mass Society.* London: Sage.

Markoff, J. 2005. *What the Dormouse Said: How the Sixties Counterculture Shaped the Personal Computer Industry.* New York: Viking.

Marksten, O. M. 2005. "Musikkdistribusjon på Internett: Tar fildeling livet av musikkindustrien?" *Master thesis.* Institutt for medier og kommunikasjon: Universitetet i Oslo.

McCaughey, M., and A. D. Ayers. 2003. *Cyberactivism: Online Activism in Theory and Practice.* London: Routledge.

McKay, G. 1999. "I'm So Bored with the USA: The Punk in Cyberpunk." In *Punk Rock: So What? The Cultural Legacy of Punk,* ed. R. Sabin. London: Routledge.

Meikle, G. 2002. *Future Active: Media Activism and the Internet.* New York: Routledge.

Moen, K. 2007. "Musikkens mobilisering: Hvordan det digitale hjemmestudioet forandrer musikken." *Master thesis.* Trondheim: Institute for sociology and political science, NTNU.

Oudshoorn, N., and T. Pinch, eds. 2003. *How Users Matter: The Co-construction of Users and Technology.* Cambridge, MA: The MIT Press.

Ross, A. 2000. "Hacking Away at the Counterculture." In *The Cybercultures Reader,* ed. D. Bell and B. Kennedy. London: Routledge.

Silverstone, R., and E. Hirsch, eds. 1992. *Consuming Technologies: Media and Information in Domestic Spaces.* London: Routledge.

St. John, G. 2003. "Post-Rave Technotribalism and the Carnival of Protest." In *The Post-Subcultures Reader,* ed. D. Muggleton and R. Weinzierl. Oxford: Berg Publishers.

Taylor, P. 1999. *Hackers: Crime in the Digital Sublime.* London: Routledge.

Théberge, P. 2004. "The Network Studio: Historical and Technological Paths to a New Ideal in Music Making." *Social Studies of Science* 34, no. 5 (October): 759–81.

Thomas, D. 2000. "New Ways to Break the Law: Cybercrime and the Politics of Hacking." In *Web Studies: Rewiring Media Studies for the Digital Age,* ed. D. Gauntlett. Oxford: Oxford University Press.

Turner, F. 2006. *From Counterculture to Cyberculture: Stewart Brand, the Whole Earth Network, and the Rise of Digital Utopianism.* Chicago: University of Chicago Press.

Van de Donk, W., B. D. Loader, P. G. Nixon, and D. Rucht. 2004. *Cyberprotest: New Media, Citizens and Social Movements.* New York: Routledge.

Chapter 22

Public Spaces and Alternative Media Practices in Europe

The Case of the EuroMayDay Parade against Precarity

Nicole Doerr and Alice Mattoni

This chapter deals with the role of emerging transnational public spaces for communication and collective identification in contemporary social movement groups in different European countries and at the transnational level of European Union (EU) politics. Related to globalization, European integration, and the increasing use of internet communication technologies (ICTs) by activists, national public spaces in the twenty-seven member states of the EU pass through a process of transformation that might deeply redefine democratic and participation practices. In this chapter, we discuss the emergence of a loose critical Europeanist collective identity[1] revolving around the political concept of "precarity" and linked to the organization of a transnational protest campaign, the EuroMayDay Parade (EMP), against precarious and insecure work.[2] In particular, we focus on how collective identification processes were discursively constructed in the protest campaign through the elaboration of alternative media practices toward the transnational European level. Activists constructed "parallel discursive arenas" (Fraser 1992: 123) in which the feeling of being European precarious workers found a potential space of expression and consolidation. Though these arenas were and still are fragile and temporary, they show how important alternative media practices and the resulting independent spaces of communication are for the emergence of critical Europeanist collective identities. In doing this, we offer important insights related to the existence of the so-called public deficit of the European Union, including the lack of truly European mainstream media. We also suggest that scholars interested in the emergence of European public spheres might look not only at the mainstream media, but also at more grassroots forms of mediation and communication.

This chapter is structured as follows. The first section presents the broad theoretical framework that supported the analysis. The second section introduces the methods employed to construct and analyze data, and the third section presents the case study. The fourth section investigates how collective identification processes took place in the EMP, focusing on alternative media practices. The fifth section discusses the challenges that the construction of critical Europeanist collective identities implied for activists. The conclusion sums up the most interesting points that the analysis raised.

Theoretical Framework and Concepts

In literature about the democratic deficit, the so-called public deficit of the European Union, analysts diagnose the lack of citizen participation in an idealized European mainstream media public. We propose another perspective. Starting from the ongoing debate on the existence of a European public sphere, we explore a field that up to now has received less attention: the development of transnational alternative activist media practices by citizens and activists that we believe may foster the emergence of European collective identities through communicative interaction.[3] To focus on alternative activist media practices at the transnational level not only helps assess the existence (or not) of transnational social movements at the European level, but also helps scholars investigating the emergence (or not) of European public spheres (della Porta and Caiani 2005; Doerr 2010; Feron 2007).

The debate about the possible existence of a European public sphere has led to diverse definitions of the concept of the public sphere (Bozzini and Bee 2010; Van de Steeg 2002), based on normative as well as empirical approaches (Karpinnen 2009). Scholars of social movements argue that most empirical studies about the Europeanization of the public sphere restrict their analysis to mainstream media texts, institutional political actors, and a national focus (Olesen 2005; Doerr 2010). In this chapter, we start from a definition of the public sphere as "an open field of communicative exchange" that is "made up of communication flows and discourses that allow for the diffusion of intersubjective meaning and understanding" (Trenz 2009: 37).

When considering the macro level of mass media in public spheres, it is worth noticing that media environments also have a multilayered structure shaped by multiple flows of information and communication (Mattoni 2012a; Couldry 2006). Along this line, Cottle argues that today's media ecology is complex and comprises "different and overlapping media formations, horizontal and vertical communications flows and new interactional capabilities, offering unprecedented opportunities for the wider dissemination of political protest and dissent" (2008: 855). Starting from this perspective, the critiques that social movement scholars make about the democratic deficit in Europe seem even more relevant. When assuming the existence of a multilayered media environment, it is easier to include other types of media than mainstream ones in the definition of the public sphere. Activists who have no direct access to mainstream media can communicate across national boundaries by establishing their own alternative activist media practices. Certainly, mainstream media play a crucial role in the public arena of politics in contemporary societies and, sometimes, also in the making of a European public sphere (Van de Steeg 2002). Mainstream media, however, are just one specific set of media outlets in the media environments.

Thanks to the recent development of ICTs, computer-mediated communication (CMC) and internet applications play an important role for citizens, and among them activists (Cammaerts et al. 2012; Van de Donk et al. 2004; Loader 2008), who try to overcome mainstream media, frequently biased and difficult to access (Smith et al. 2001). Cyberspace could function as a radical layer of the media environment, where bloggers, alternative informational websites, and independent journalists spread a mass of information that might also push toward a process of "cross-national diffusion" of mobilization (Soule 2004).

Departing from this theoretical framework, we will focus on the role of social movement actors employing ICTs at the transnational European level in the creation of new "fields of communicative exchange" (see Trenz 2009). Based on qualitative cross-national comparative data, we will investigate alternative activist media practices that provide temporary spaces of mediation and communication crossing national boundaries, involve activists in ongoing discussion about contentious issues that are no longer merely national but have become more and more European, and establish the basis for the emergence of radical "discursive arenas" (Fraser 1992: 123) that might be seen as an example of a fragile and temporary European public sphere. In doing this, we also aim to add an empirical contribution to the limited amount of literature dealing with processes of Europeanization occurring at the meso level of civil society actors (see, e.g., Imig and Tarrow 2001; della Porta and Caiani 2005). We will also present findings that show how activists' cultural familiarity and experiences from local protests become an all the more important resource to foster the development and use of *visuals in alternative media practices*. As will be shown, visual images circulated in alternative media practices facilitate the diffusion of activists' claims from one particular domestic context up to the European level. Visual media practices also facilitate the recontextualization of claims into culturally distinct and disparate national and localized settings and contexts (see Soule 2004).

A Short Note on Methods

We investigate the role of alternative media in the construction of transnational collective identification processes through a case study that focuses in particular on collective action frames and organizational patterns. Taking a diachronic perspective, we studied the EMP protest campaign from 2001 (when it started as a local/national protest event) to 2006 (when it had grown into a national/transnational protest campaign). This diachronic perspective allows us to trace the development of collective identity toward the transnational level. Unlike most studies on collective identification and citizen participation in transnational European public debates, our interdisciplinary approach has the advantage of relying on several primary sources, including ethnographic as well as discursive analysis. First, we engaged in participant observation within the transnational EMP preparatory meetings, by which we explore the practice of transnational communication, campaign organization, and diffusion by activists. We studied these transnational meetings, as well as local EMP activist groups in Italy (Milan) and Germany (Berlin), working with diachronic process analysis. Second, we gathered semistructured in-depth interviews with activists involved in the EMP campaign to explore cross-diffusion processes related to the precarity political concept as well as alternative media practices developed by the EMP network. We collected thirty in-depth interviews lasting about forty-five minutes each. In particular, semistructured in-depth interviews collected during preparatory meetings focused on transnational communication and diffusion processes, while semistructured in-depth interviews collected after the EuroMayDay Parade in 2006 were mainly centered on alternative activist media practices. Finally, we also used secondary sources, such as leaflets, official declarations, press releases, and media texts produced by activists. These sources are investigated through qualitative content analysis, which is applied by taking into account all those moments and passages in which social movements' dynamics of diffusion, as well as communication processes, are visible and openly mentioned by activists themselves.

The EuroMayDay Parade against Precarity

The EMP began as a local protest event in Italy against precarious work[4] and hence related to precarity. It first took place in Milan on 1 May 2001 under the name "MayDay Parade." The MayDay Parade in Milan was initiated by three activist groups: a group of self-organized casual workers, the Chainworkers Crew (CW),[5] activists belonging to the social center Deposito

Bulk,[6] and the local section of the RdB-CUB,[7] a radical trade union. These three activist groups established linkages with other political and social actors rooted at the local level. As a multiorganizational network, in 2002, the MayDay Parade had already undergone a shift from the local to the regional level and, in 2003, it established a national network organized through national preparatory meetings and a common mailing list to plan the protest campaign, thus encouraging various political and social actors from a number of Italian cities to participate in the parade organization and meet in Milan on the afternoon of 1 May. The increasing involvement of activist groups made the parade grow exponentially. According to the organizers, protest participants in Milan, which were about five thousand in 2001, became about one hundred thousand five years later in 2006.[8]

In 2004, the parade changed its name to the EMP. Spanish activist groups organized it in Barcelona, while smaller protest events also occurred in Dublin, Helsinki, and Palermo. Furthermore, in 2004, a transnational meeting of European activist groups against precarity took place during the so-called Beyond the ESF forum, a counter–European Social Forum organized at Middlesex University by the Wombles (Doerr 2008; Juris 2005). In the following years, there was a proliferation of preparatory meetings and assemblies, both national and transnational: in 2005, the EMP took place in nineteen European cities, extending to twenty-two in 2006.[9] This fluid transnational network also extended to include other activist groups based in non-European countries, such as in Tokyo, Japan, in 2008 and Toronto, Canada, in 2010.

Both at the level of organizational patterns and collective action frames, there is evidence for a process construction of a collective European identification in the EMP facilitated through transnational alternative media practices (Mattoni 2008a). With regard to the first dimension (organizational patterns), our data shows that "direct relational ties" (McAdam and Rucht 1993) stimulated the transnational participation of a high number of activists in the EMP and the diffusion of the precarity discourse from the Italian to the European level. Importantly, the communicative role of a network of relations, in which activists exchanged mutual ideas and knowledge, also triggered the creation of a shared political struggle and familiarity with the concept of precarity, and thus a "cultural proximity" (Passy 2003: 41), among activist groups across different and previously separate national movement communities. With regard to the second dimension (collective action frames), the loose and dispersed (transnational and local) network of relations sustaining the EMP also had the task of defining shared political frames. The challenge was, indeed, to assess and bring together in a political meaning some traits that might be collectively shared by people experiencing the precarity condition, who were usually characterized by a variety of working and living conditions. This was evident especially in the call for actions, official declarations, and other materials linked to the EMP, in which collective action frames pointed out that precarity was a European social problem, precarious workers were millions of people all over Europe, and the demands were new social rights at the European level (see EuroMayDay Network 2004; MayDay Network 2001, 2002, 2003).

The transnationalization toward the European level brought with it an increasing thematic focus on Europe within collective action frames, which was also reflected in organizational patterns. Despite the apparent successful "upward scale shift" (Tilly and Tarrow 2007), interviews with activists underlined the existence of a translation problem concerning the very concepts of precarity and precarious workers. In this vein, Carlo,[10] an Italian activist, mentioned some of the concrete difficulties in building a transnational network of activist groups:

> To coordinate an international network of people who want to organize contemporaneous protest events is very stimulating and may have a very strong impact. It may lead to a very strong mechanism of imagery construction. But this is really not easy. There are different kinds of limits: the linguistic one, the cultural one, and even the social movement history in a specific place.

While commenting on the strong potential in the construction of a common collective identity, Carlo also stressed the need to overcome some important barriers. To deal with the need of linguistic translation, the transnational social movement network mainly worked together in English as the common language, something that was at times contested (Doerr 2008). Other challenges of translation activists confronted were linked more to the political level of collective identification processes and the translation of concepts such as "precarity" and "precarious workers": not only at a linguistic level, but also and above all concerning the entire system of meaning attached to them. Another activist, Marco, remembered that this was not an easy task to accomplish:

> I remember a debate in London, during the Social Forum, about the flexible labor theme. There was a discussion about the terms to be used with the English activists. An activity of ... let's say, a translation activity was needed because the term precarity was not clear to them.

Transnationalization thus brought with it the challenging task of creating a common system of meanings sustained by a shared language on precarity beyond national differences in terms of welfare state, labor flexibility, and the status of precarious workers and people. While similar political translation problems had already been an issue at the national level in Italy, the interviews with activists show that the "upward scale shift" process of the protest campaign rendered them even more complex and thus visible within the transnational social movement network.

ICTs and Alternative Media Practices in the Transnational Media Environment

The analysis of the three data sets shows that the "upward scale shift" that occurred in the EMP revolved around three specific sets of alternative media practices, in which the online and offline level often intertwined, creating "multi-modal communication" (Gillan et al. 2008: 177–78).

Radical Magazines, Independent Journals

The first set of alternative activist media practices concerned the use of already existing channels of communication: independent underground magazines based in countries other than Italy and targeting transnational audiences. Among others, the Dutch magazine *Green Pepper* was crucial, as Sara[11] recounted:

> The *Green Pepper* magazine was published at the European level thanks to the collaboration with fellows from Amsterdam. We did a special issue of twenty pages devoted to precarity, with articles written by us, the Italians. We presented it during the European Social Forum in London and the parallel event which was named Beyond the ESF … We brought the magazine there and you found people, not Italian people, who began to be interested in it and they asked us "what precarity is" … sometimes strange terms came out.

The magazine was used as a medium to prepare the terrain for further, face-to-face debates about the concept of precarity, which began to be part of the social movement language in different European countries, where it was translated according to its Italian origins. As the years went by, the contentious issue slowly continued to spread in a number of countries, due to radical academic journals and independent publications, such as *Mute* and *Fibreculture* in Australia, *Republicart* in Austria, *Adbusters* in the United States, and *Fuse* in Canada.

The concept of precarity, therefore, went beyond the fluid boundaries of the social movement milieu and entered the field of radical academia through political translation and recontextualization. Articles published in these journals were written by Italian researchers and academics, but also activists, who often lived abroad but continued to maintain linkages with Italian social movements.[12] Precarity and the alternative system of meaning attached to this term seemed to travel across Europe and beyond the borders of the EU due to the presence of an underground, informal network of activists and researchers who introduced the concept in various social, theoretical, political, and professional contexts. Activists' combined use of traditional media like journals as well as ICTs was key to facilitating the diffusion of a new political language linked to the issue of precarity beyond the national boundaries of Italy.

Icons, Symbols, and Other Visual Tools

While academic and radical journals in particular focus on written language, there were other cultural and political devices that engendered the diffusion of the precarity discourse relying on a "visual language." The common EMP website clearly reflects this tendency. The EMP homepage did, in fact, have a strong visual feature based on pictures and images more than written texts. An example of this was a virtual parade of precarious workers invented by the Italian Molleindustria project in 2004 and 2005 and eventually added to the website of the EMP. The visual side of the net parade was strongly stressed by its call for action, spread in a variety of mailing lists and social movement websites: "Why don't you give your pictorial contribution to this multicolored parade, and reclaim that visibility that mainstream media, unions, parties are denying us? Make yourself heard! Voice your anger and/or irony!"[13] The inventors of the net parade asked for a "pictorial contribution" to overcome the lack of visibility within the mainstream media. The goal was also to impart new visual representations of precarious workers. In this vein, Michele[14] pointed out the need for a new aesthetic related to precarious workers: "To some extent, it was necessary to give visibility to this novel identity, to this novel class which is not a class. The virtual parade was intended to be a collective representation, a multicolored mosaic, which give back also an aesthetic visibility." As Michele stressed, the net parade, with the possibility of having personalized avatars, attempted to represent precarious workers as a "multitude" of individuals, rather than an undistinguishable mass of people or a homogeneous class of workers. In 2004 and 2005, thousands of net protestors joined the virtual parade and claimed slogans in more than five languages. The result was a composite visual representation of precarious workers, since each of them was able to create his or her virtual avatar, claiming their own slogans. Besides colorful avatars, activist groups involved in the protest campaign also invented a number of icons and symbols to speak about precarity and represent precarious workers. The most famous among them was icon of "San Precario," the protector saint of all precarious workers, who came into being in Milan on 29 February 2004, and was invented by the Chainworkers Crew (Tarì and Vanni 2005; Mattoni 2008b). As underlined by Guido, there was a need for creating a "common imagery" related to precarity that could be recognized not only in Italy, but also in other countries:

> Actually, it was not a matter of identification, but of recognition and imagery construction. Then, the first creation was San Precario, who was born by chance to some extent. And then it really exploded, in the sense after 15 days there were people from Canada who asked for the small holy pictures.

The icon of San Precario was diffused to countries other than Italy and to contexts other than the social movement milieu. With regard to the strengthening of the collective identification process, this was important because it represented the common traits of diverse struggles against precarity, different from the EMP: activist groups, but also precarious workers in general, recognized in San Precario an icon able to represent their struggles in a rather flexible way. Similar to what happened with the very term precarity, which was translated from Italian into several languages, the icon of San Precario was also absorbed and "translated" into new icons in other countries where the parade took place: activist groups created "Nuestra Señora de la Precariedad" in Spain and "Alice au pays de précaries" in France.[15] In Germany, press magazines associated with large traditional trade unions, such as the official member magazine of the German Böckler Foundation, showed the San Precario icon on their title page (Doerr 2010).

In 2005, the Chainworkers Crew, based in Milan, together with a temporary network of other activists groups mobilized against precarity at a local level, invented the Imbattibili.[16] These were nineteen sticker cards representing superhero precarious workers able to face daily problems due to the precarity condition. Apart from San Precario, other characters like "Piger Man" or "Super-Flex" were designed with a common graphic style to speak about precarity in an innovative way.[17] In 2005, activists distributed the Imbattibili sticker cards during the parade in Milan and then also during transnational preparatory meetings for the next parade in 2006. Activists from other countries connected with these visual tools and sometimes reinterpreted them at their own local level. For instance, the Imbattibili characters were used during a direct action in a supermarket in Hamburg at the end of April 2006, which was covered by the German national press and, quite surprisingly due to the relatively small protest event at stake, by some foreign newspapers.[18] Through cross-national diffusion, the visual protest heroes were "translated" by German local activists into a guerrilla theater and a direct action within a German supermarket. Indeed, the posters designed by Hamburg-based EuroMayDay organizers aimed at creating visual images of precarious subjectivities that break with the stereotype of workers as men, often used in visual representation of (traditional) left iconographies of May Day protests in Germany. Hans, an activist from an EMP activist group in Hamburg said:

> We controversially discussed [our] EuroMayDay poster [designed by Hamburg-based activists in 2005]. Actually, the poster we designed also has queer elements: the person it shows is based on two photos, one of a man another of a woman. It was designed by some friends of our network some of whom are graphic designers and others photographers.[19]

The use of a shared visual iconography, transformed and readapted at the local level of activist groups mobilized against precarity in countries other than Italy, was important to create a sense of common belonging to the same transnational network of activists groups. Without abandoning the work of translation at the textual and verbal level, images, semantically more open for interpretation than the other two means of expression, played an important role in sustaining collective identification processes related to the EMP. The use of shared images, in fact, was also facilitated through the EMP website, where posters, postcards, and other illustrative materials might be downloaded, printed, and then used by every activist group involved in the organization of the parade.

Live Broadcasting and Web Radio

Activist groups engaged in yet another set of alternative media practices, aimed at representing the parade in the media environment. They broadcast the parade live through traditional radios, satellite radios, and web radios and independent informational websites. In this way, activist groups constructed direct and lively narratives about the EMP, which especially reinforced the original collective action frame as it was presented in calls for action and official declarations: the parade was to some extent filled with sounds, voices, and images that, all together, made the existence of the transnational network of activist groups and those who included themselves in the "precarious worker" category visible. Alternative media practices, in fact, seemed to impart shared meanings linked to precarity, but also to elaborate, diffuse, and exchange stories about the variety of local parades occurring in different European cities.

In 2004 and 2005, activists involved in the independent informational website Global Project prepared and carried out live broadcasts of the parade in Milan and other European cities.[20] In doing so, they connected with the same mediated and "temporary space" activist groups participating in the transnational network that sustained the EMP used. Francesco,[21] who participated in the live broadcasts from Milan, explained how it happened:

> We were within the EMP as Global Radio and we constructed these two days through a website and a satellite radio, which was used not only by ourselves, but also by the varied European groups. … And we have this broad radio program, whose direction was made in Milan. Moreover, there were a lot of forays which crossed each other from other European cities: from Spain, France, Germany, Great Britain, Norway, and even from Finland.

The combined use of different technological supports, satellite radio and the web, allowed a multimedia text to be constructed, which changed while the parade was going on, and in which a variety of narrations from all over Europe imparted a composite and multifaceted picture of the EMP. The following live broadcast extract renders it easier to understand how two different parades, one in Milan and the other in Barcelona, connected:

> May Day Milan calling May Day Barcelona. So, how are the preparations for the May Day going?
> Hi, here it is all going well, there are much more people than we expected, the most numerous group are the migrants, with different banners. One of them reminds us that we are all migrants. Then there are various groups of precarious workers, different one from another, but finding a common path in the May Day.[22]

In this media environment, constructed from alternative media practices that activist groups developed, various subjective narrations about the parades intertwined and underlined both common features and differences concerning the elaboration of collective action frames, which were developed according to the local context. According to Marinella,[23] the creation of such a media environment was extremely useful, since:

> you are no more inserted in a local dimension. Everyone speaks about globalization, but the next step is to unite the globalized struggles. … In my opinion, the role of movement media is to link [different struggles to each other]. And the MayDay has the potential to construct European relationships of struggle, not only from the territorial point of view, but also from a much broader one.

The live broadcasting of the parade put into practice and rendered more tangible for activists themselves the elaboration of common struggles beyond national borders. Though necessary for the reinforcement of collective identification processes, live broadcasting at the transnational level of the parade also had some limits. First, it was temporary and linked to a specific day of action. The second limit was linked to the activist groups who organized the live broadcasting. Instead of being conceived and then carried out by the whole transnational network of activist groups sustaining the EMP, the live broadcasting was managed by a set of activist groups engaged in an already existing communication project, the independent website Global Project, which is strictly linked to one particular activist network, the (ex-) Disobbedienti. This sort of role specialization did not assure continuity over the years of the live broadcasting. In 2006, in fact, it did not occur: the (ex-) Disobbedienti where not in Milan taking care of the live broadcasting, since they decided instead to take part in the anti-CPE[24] demonstrations in France and the parade in Paris.

Cultural Familiarity and Local Experiences in Digital Media Environments: Translating Local Protest Cultures

A problem that needs further consideration is the existence of different "languages of the political" at the European level, which is key to building joint collective action in the pluralist EMP network. Apart from linguistic communication problems (Doerr 2008), our participant observation shows a basic political problem of translation in transnational EuroMayDay network meetings. In interviews, activists continuously mention the challenge of dealing with an (in)translatability related to the creation of a shared language on precarity beyond national differences, in terms of the welfare state, labor flexibility, and the status of precarious workers and people. In joint EMP preparatory meetings, activists would explain to each other specific national policies and legislations on the welfare state. In this kind of interactive learning by narration, the dense exchange of information and listening further stimulated collective action in the EMP network, and concrete initiatives were taken to institutionalize mutual learning. One proposal was a project to build a homepage on EU politics hosted by NGO activists in Brussels with in-depth expertise on EU legislation. It would inform activists in advance of specific policy initiatives by the European Commission, EU member states, or the European Parliament. Another was the creation of a European ring of militant research by precarious activist-researchers on the subject of precarity as a form of self-empowerment.[25]

In this context, the potential relevance of various distinct types of cultural experiences[26] and informational resources can be noted that could facilitate communication and collective action beyond the nation-state. For example, the organizers of the EMP lacked material resources, equally related to their choice of a decentralized organization and their focus on a single issue. EMP organizers had a cultural and experiential familiarity with organizing protest creatively without institutional actors and, even more importantly, with developing DIY practices of communication in alternative media in their local environment. Activists' cultural and experiential familiarity (and knowledge) of different ICT applications in professional work (Mattoni 2012a), and their local and transnational experiences with multilingual networking in previous European protest summits and local immigrant mobilization (Doerr 2008), facilitated the building of transnational collective action. We would even suspect that the importance of such culturally distinct experiences gain a higher relevance for a successful upward shift of resource-poor networks like EuroMayDay, given that these actors, in comparison to more institutionalized transnational activist public spaces like the ESF, rely on fewer logistics and material organizational resources (Andretta and Reiter 2009).

What makes activists' experiences and familiarity with transnational contexts from previous collective action interesting is that they help build joint collective action at a European level, building on *informal* networks fostered by friendship ties and "affective solidarity" (Juris 2008) born within international summits of the global justice movement, as Claudio from Italy explains:

> We, Italian activists had met some of the European activists before. … Not all of them, but some of them are those we met during the "no global cycle of struggle." I'm thinking of English, some Germans, French, and Spanish. They were all people who we had met before and then met once again during the international meetings to organize the May Day.[27]

In particular, the demonstrations in Genoa during the G8 meeting in 2001 seem to have had a crucial importance in connecting Italian activists with social movement groups based in other countries. For instance, the following interview abstract shows that the first EuroMayDay, organized in Barcelona as well as Milan, sprang from informal meetings during the anti-G8 mobilization in Genoa. More interviews confirm that it was personal networks together with geographic proximity and exchange that conditioned and constrained the patterns of transmission. In particular, informal personal networks provide an *important precondition for transnationalization* and are not related or connected to (creating) formal political alliances with representatives of unions or parties from other countries. As an immaterial type of resource, they gain all the more significance because of the little public attention the EuroMayDay received in the mainstream media. An interview with a EuroMayDay activist from Slovenia illustrates this:

> We from Maribor got involved in the EuroMayDay process because Slovenian activists participated in [the protest against the G8 summit in] Genoa and some of us had friends in the Italian EuroMayDay network. … I think that for the EuroMayDay process it is good that, despite all the different groups from different countries, we all have in common that we struggle locally. Locally, we fight with the same problems, and then we make common demands at the European level. … Our problem is that we are too closed within the national context and that we need a transnational space, otherwise we are locked up in identity politics.[28]

Furthermore, as this interview abstract shows, what holds the EuroMayDay activists together despite the aforementioned *national differences* is not a specific shared ideology, but their shared *experience of participation* in the protest summits within the global justice movement together with their direct engagement in local grassroots activism. The European level in this framing gets a common space for exchange, in which protest strategies from the local or national level get *diffused* to the transnational level or are *readopted and adapted* back to the local level. For activists from all the different local groups, the transnational level represents a *new window of opportunity* to leave behind the national context with its limited significance and its perceived closed and divided context of "identity politics" and build alliances beyond the nation-state.

Conclusion

In this chapter we have shown that alternative media practices played an important role in transnational collective organizing and identification processes. Alternative media practices, in fact, created spaces and moments of communication in which activists exchanged meanings related to precarity and, in doing so, redefined the concept at a translocal level. We illustrated, however, the difficulties of the work required in terms of translation, readaptation, and transformation when a protest campaign turns transnational and European. We also demonstrated the fragility of "discursive arenas": they were temporary, linked to one specific protest campaign and contentious issue, and dependent on specific activist groups. Despite these limits, this chapter shows that social movements, involving thousands of European citizens in transnational meetings and protest events, could be a promising ground for the construction of radical European identities, which are neither anti-European nor pro-European as such, but revolve more pragmatically around the claims for a radical left-wing, cosmopolitan Europe (see della Porta and Caiani 2005). It is the activists' double discourse on "another" globalization and "another" radical democratic Europe that scholars have conceptualized in notions describing activists' collective identifications as "critical Europeanists," reaching both beyond the conventional status-quo oriented pro-Europeanist discourses and populist nationalism or Euroskepticism (della Porta and Caiani 2005).

Furthermore, this chapter especially argues that collective identification processes became transnational through alternative *participatory* media practices rather than through representative mainstream media channels. Activists created their own spaces of mediation and communication that seemed to be particularly relevant for the ongoing debates about the European public sphere(s). Due to the extensive use of ICTs, often combined with the creation of distinct images, citizens bypassed mainstream media in the creation of spaces for discussion, exchange, and debate at the transnational, European level. When comparing the EMP to the European Social Forum and traditional leftist May Day iconographies, our analysis of the EMP shows that young protesters use media cultures beyond the traditional text-based public sphere by drawing on culture jamming (Schober 2009), as well as on locally distinct postreligious visual cultures and global manga and comic icons that are recognizable transnationally. This evolution must be seen in relation to an ongoing development within the public sphere in which the political impact of visual representation becomes relevant on a global scale and has been theorized as the so-called visual turn of the transcultural reality of everyday life and the political public sphere (Doerr et al. 2013). Future research should explore the limits, as well as the consequences, of alternative media practices that transcend the national level to create new imaginaries, narratives, and collective identifications through transnational diffusion and readaptation in movement publics. Theorists of democracy and transnational media may find it interesting that alterative cultural practices of communication in public spaces created by social movement groups work visually as well as verbally, challenging conventional conceptualizations of the democratic public sphere in Europe as a text-based arena of national newspapers.

Acknowledgments

The authors thank activists who shared their experiences and narratives related to the EuroMayDay Parade with them. Both authors contributed equally to this work. However, in compliance with Italian academic norms, the authors acknowledge that Nicole Doerr wrote sections 2, 4.2, and 5, as well as the conclusion. Alice Mattoni wrote the introduction and sections 1, 3, 4.1, and 4.3.

Notes

1. We consider collective identity as an ongoing process of negotiations and interactions that occur within a network of social actors (Diani and Bison 2004; Melucci 1996). Throughout the chapter, therefore, we will use the expressions "collective identity" and "collective identification process" as synonyms.

2. The political concept of "precarity" as developed in the EMP refers to the proliferation of short-term contracts due to the introduction a high degree of labor market flexibility, beginning in Italy in the early 1990s (Gallino 2007). However, precarity was also linked to the private sphere: the lack of permanent employment and income protection is seen as the main cause of the impossibility of making long-term life plans and, therefore, precarity of work frequently becomes "existential precarity" (Fumagalli 2007: 29). In this chapter, we use the term "precarity" as framed in the context of activist discourses developed in the social movement network that sustains the EMP, which is in dialogue with scholarly discourses and knowledge production on precarious work (Andall and Puwar 2007).

3. For a definition of activist media practices see Mattoni (2012 and 2013). When speaking about alternative layers of the media environment, we draw on Atton, who broadly defines alternative media as those media that are produced outside mainstream media institutions and networks (2002).

4. For a discussion about the spread of precarious work in Western societies and a definition of the term, see Mattoni (2012a) and Choi and Mattoni (2010).

5. The CW, founded in 1999, immediately created its own webzine in order to promote "media and mall activism for awareness-building and unionization of precarious workers" (Chainworkers Crew n.d.). For a more detailed history of the CW and its approach to political struggles against economic precarity, see Chainworkers Crew (2001).

6. The Deposito Bulk was a social center in Milan from 1997 to 2006. Social centers, *centri sociali* in Italian, are abandoned buildings, frequently owned by the state, that are occupied by groups of people in order to have a space to promote underground

cultures and offer autonomously organized services to the neighborhood where they are located. In some cases, social centers are also spaces in which activists live.

7. The national confederation RdB-CUB, founded in 1992 after a coalition of the rank-and-file union RdB, founded in 1987 and rooted in workers' struggles during the 1970s, and a group of workers formerly belonging to the FILM-CGIL. The Rdb-CUB was inspired by the tradition of local workers' councils and, as with other radical leftist trade unions, is based on the direct participation of workers.

8. See www.chainworkers.org and the EuroMayDay mailing list at www.euromaday .org.

9. More precisely, in 2005 it took place in Amsterdam, Barcelona, Copenhagen, Hamburg, Helsinki, L'Aquila, Liège, Ljubljana, London, Maribor, Marseille, Milan, Naples, Palermo, Paris, Seville, Stockholm, and Vienna. In 2006, it took place in Amsterdam, Barcelona, Berlin, Copenhagen, Hamburg, Helsinki, L'Aquila, Leon, Liège, Limoges, London, Maribor, Marseille, Milan, Naples, Palermo, Paris, Seville, Stockholm, Tornio, Turin, and Vienna. Except for Slovenia, Eastern European countries were not involved in the EuroMayDay network (Curcio 2006).

10. All the names of the interviewees are fictional to protect their confidentiality. Carlo is an Italian activist in the Chainworkers Crew, from Milan. The interview took place in his home on 22 December 2006.

11. Sara is an activist in the Chainworkers Crew in Milan. The interview took place in a café on 21 December 2006.

12. The concept of precarity continues its journey in more established academic journals today. In 2008, volume 25 (nos. 7–8) of *Theory, Culture and Society* was entirely devoted to this concept and mobilizations related to it, both in Italy and abroad.

13. See www.euromayday.org/netparade, accessed 1 March 2007.

14. Michele is an activist of the Molleindustria project, based in Milan. The interview took place in his home in Milan on 18 December 2006.

15. The French icon is inspired by the famous novel *Alice in Wonderland* by Lewis Carroll, whose title is transformed into "Alice in the Precarious Land" by French activists.

16. The same activist groups translated the term "Imbattibili" as "Unbeatable" in English.

17. In this chapter, "San Precario" and the "Imbattibili" are presented taking into account their visual level as well as their cross-national diffusion. The Chainworkers Crew, however, considered these icons political tools (Tarì and Vanni 2005; Vanni 2007; Mattoni 2008b).

18. See the EuroMayDay mailing list at www.euromayday.org.

19. Hans is an activist of the EuroMayday network in Germany. The interview took place in Hamburg on 14 February 2006.

20. Global Project is a communication project mainly based on a website that combines text, audio, and video materials created by media activists.

21. Francesco is an activist of the Global Project group in Milan. The interview took place in the Cantiere social centre on 27 December 2006.

22. www.globalproject.info, accessed 1 May 2005.

23. Marinella is an activist of the Global Project group in Padua. The interview took place in her home in Padua on 12 November 2006.

24. CPE stands for Contrat Première Embauche, that would be First Employment Contract in English.
25. See www.precarity-map.net.
26. We assume that activists' experiences and cultural familiarity made in distinct local contexts of daily life and protest may facilitate as well as constrain new forms of collective action innovating traditional structures of organizing and protest, circulating through transnational networks (cf. Polletta 2008).
27. Claudio is an Italian activist linked to the Global Project group. The interview took place in his home in Marghera on 13 November 2006.
28. Interview with a member of Nietwork Maribor, Milan, February 2006.

Bibliography

Andall, J., and N. Puwar. 2007. "Editorial." In "Italian Feminisms," special issue, *Feminist Review* 87, no. 1 (December): 1–2.

Andretta, M., and H. Reiter. 2009. "Parties, Unions and Movements: The European Left and the ESF." In *Another Europe: Conceptions and Practices of Democracy in the European Social Forums,* ed. D. della Porta. New York: Routledge.

Atton, C. 2002. *Alternative Media.* London: Sage publications.

Bozzini, E., and C. Bee. 2010. *Mapping the European Public Sphere: Institutions, Media and Civil Society.* London: Ashgate.

Cammaerts, B, A. Mattoni, and P. McCurdy, eds. 2012. *Mediation and Protest Movements.* London: Intellect.

Chainworkers Crew. 2001. *ChainWorkers. Lavorare Nelle Cattedrali Del Consumo.* Roma: DeriveApprodi.

Chainworkers Crew. n.d. "Chi Siamo." http://www.chainworkers.org/faq. Last Accessed August 2013.

Choi, H., and A. Mattoni. 2010. "The Contentious Field of Precarious Work in Italy: Political Actors, Strategies and Coalitions." *WorkingUSA: The Journal of Labor and Society* 13, no. 2 (June): 213–43.

Cottle, S. 2008. "Reporting Demonstrations: The Changing Media Politics of Dissent." *Media Culture & Society* 30, no. 6 (November): 853–72.

Couldry, N. 2006. *Listening Beyond the Echoes: Media, Ethics, and Agency in an Uncertain World.* London: Paradigm.

Curcio, A. 2006. "The New Labour Actors Around Europe: The Contentious Politics and the Dealing with the Representative Politics Institutions." Paper presented at the conference Alternative Futures and Popular Protest, Manchester.

della Porta, D., and M. Caiani. 2005. *Quale Europa? Europeanizzazione, identità e conflitti.* Rome: Il Mulino.

Diani, M., and I. Bison. 2004. "Organizations, Coalitions and Movements." *Theory and Society* 33, no. 3–4 (June): 281–309.

Doerr, N. 2008. "Deliberative Discussion, Language, and Efficiency in the World Social Forum Process." *Mobilization: An International Quarterly* 13, no. 4 (December): 395–410.

————. 2010. "Politicizing Precarity, Producing Visual Dialogues on Migration: Transnational Public Spaces in Social Movement." *Forum Qualitative Social Research* 11, no. 2 (May): art. 30.

Doerr, N., A. Mattoni, and S. Teune. 2013. "Toward a Visual Analysis of Social Movements, Conflict, and Political Mobilization." *Research on Social Movements, Conflict, and Change* Vol. 35: xi–xxvi.

EuroMayDay Network 2004. "EuroMayDay 2004." http://www.euromayday.org/mayday004/lang_eng.html (accessed 8 February 2011).

Feron, E. 2007. "The Anti-Globalization Movement and the European Agenda." In *Democracy in the European Union: Towards the Emergence of a Public Sphere,* ed. L. Giorgi, I. Von Homeyer, and W. Parsons. London: Routledge.

Fraser, N. 1992. "Rethinking the Public Sphere: A Contribution to the Critique of Actually Existing Democracy." In *Habermas and the Public Sphere,* ed. C. Calhoun. Cambridge, MA: MIT Press.

Fumagalli, A.. 2007. "Precarietà." *Parole di una nuova politica: Transform! Italia.* Rome: XL Edizioni.

Gallino, L. 2007. *Il Lavoro Non è Una Merce. Contro La Flessibilità.* Roma: Laterza.

Gillan, K., J. Pickerill, and F. Webster. 2008. *Anti-War Activism: New Media and Protest in the Information Age.* New York: Palgrave MacMillan.

Imig, D. R., and S. Tarrow, eds. 2001. *Contentious Europeans: Protest and Politics in an Emerging Polity.* Lanham, MD: Rowman Littlefield.

Juris, J. S. 2005. "Social Forums and Their Margins: Networking Logics and the Cultural Politics of Autonomous Space." *Ephemera* 5, no. 2: 253–72.

————. 2008. "Performing Politics: Image, Embodiment, and Affective Solidarity during Anti-Corporate Globalization Protests." *Ethnography* 9, no. 1 (March): 61–97.

Loader, B. D. 2008. "Social Movements and New Media." *Sociological Compass* 2, no. 6: 1920–33.

Karpinnen, Kari. 2009. "European Public Spheres and the Challenge of Radical Pluralism." In *Manufacturing Europe. Spaces of Democracy, Diversity and Communication,* ed. I. Salovaara-Moring. Göteborg: NORDICOM.

Mattoni, A. 2008a. "Organisation, Mobilisation and Identity: National and Transnational Grassroots Campaigns between Face-to-Face and Computer-Mediated Communication." In *Political Campaigning on the Web,* ed. S. Baringhorst, V. Kneip, and J. Niesyto. Bielefeld: transcript.

————. 2008b. "Serpica Naro and the Others. The Social Media Experience in the Italian Precarious Workers Struggles." *Portal: Journal of Multidisciplinary International Studies* 5, no. 2.

Mattoni, A. 2012. *Media Practices and Protest Politics: How Precarious Workers Mobilise.* Burlington, VT: Ashgate.

Mattoni, A. 2013. "Repertoires of Communication in Social Movement Processes." In *Mediation and Protest Movements,* ed. B. Cammaerts, A. Mattoni, and P. McCurdy. Bristol, UK: Intellect.

MayDay Network. 2001. "Mayday 2001." http://www.ecn.org/chainworkers/chainw/mayday/mayday.html (accessed 8 February 2011).

————. 2002. "Mayday 2002." http://www.ecn.org/chainworkers/chainw/md2002/index.htm (accessed 8 February 2011).

————. 2003. "Mayday003." http://www.ecn.org/chainworkers/chainw/mayday003/autonomo_anglo.htm (accessed 8 February 2011).

McAdam, D. and D. Rucht. 1993. "The Cross-National Diffusion of Movement Ideas." *Annals of the American Academy of Political and Social Science* 528: 56–74.

Melucci, A. 1996. *Challenging Code: Collective Action in the Information Age.* Cambridge, UK: Cambridge University Press.

Olesen, T. 2005. "Transnational Publics: New Spaces of Social Movement Activism and the Problem of Global Long-Sightedness." *Current Sociology* 53, no. 3 (May): 419–40.

Passy, F. 2003. "Social Networks Matter: But How?" In *Social Movements and Networks. Relational Approaches to Collective Action,* ed. M. Diani and D. McAdam. Oxford: Oxford University Press.

Schober, A. 2009. *Ironie, Montage, Verfremdung: Ästhetische Taktiken und die politische Gestalt der Demokratie.* Munich: Wilhelm Fink.

Smith, J., J. D. McCarthy, C. McPhail and A. Boguslaw. 2001. "From Protest to Agenda Building: Description Bias in Media Coverage of Protest Events in Washington, D.C." *Social Forces* 79, no. 4 (June): 1397–1423.

Soule, Sarah A. (2004). "Diffusion processes within and across movements." In: David A. Snow, Sarah A. Soule, and Hanspeter Kriesi. *The Blackwell companion to social movements.* Pp. 294–310.

Tarì, M., and I. Vanni. 2005. "On the Life and Deeds of San Precario, Patron Saint of Precarious Workers and Lives." *Fibreculture* 5 (December).

Tilly, C., and S. G. Tarrow. 2007. *Contentious Politics.* Boulder, CO: Paradigm Publishers.

Trenz, H.-J. 2009. "In Search of a European Public Sphere: Between Normative Over-stretch and Empirical Dis-enchantment." In *Manufacturing Europe: Spaces of Democracy, Diversity and Communication,* ed. I. S. Moring. Gothenburg, Sweden: Nordicom.

Van de Donk, W. B., B. D. Loader, P. G. Nixon, and D. Rucht. 2004. "Introduction: Social Movements and ICTs." In *Cyberprotest: New Media, Citizens, and Social Movements,* ed. W. B. Van de Donk, B. D. Loader, P. G. Nixon, and D. Rucht. London: Routledge.

Van de Steeg, M. 2002. "Rethinking the Conditions for a Public Sphere in the European Union." *European Journal of Social Theory* 5, no. 4 (November): 499–519.

Vanni, I. 2007. "How to Do Things with Words and Images: Gli Imbattibili." In *Images and Communities. The Visual Construction of the Social,* ed. M. Stocchetti and J. Sumalia-Sappanen. Helsinki: University of Helsinki Press.

Contributors

Sigurd Allern is professor of Journalism Studies at the Department of Media and Communication, University of Oslo, Norway, and guest professor at the Department of Media Studies, Stockholm University, Sweden. He is project leader of the Nordic Research Network in Journalism Studies. His publications include books and articles on news values, the relations between PR and journalism, political scandals, political communication in television, and the political economy of news production.

Hanno Balz is a visiting assistant professor in German and European History at Johns Hopkins University, Baltimore. His fields of research are the history of social movements, media and discourse history, Cold War studies, history of anticommunism, and the Shoah and Nazi rule. Selected publications include: (edited with Jan-Henrik Friedrichs) *Europäische Protestbewegungen der 1980er Jahre* [European protest movements of the 1980s] (Dietz Verlag, 2012); and *Von Terroristen, Sympathisanten und dem starken Staat: Die öffentliche Debatte über die RAF in den 70er Jahren* [On terrorists, sympathizers and the strong state:. The public debate on the Red Army Fraction in the 70s] (Campus Verlag, 2008).

Giovanni Boccia Artieri is professor of Sociology of New Media at the Department of Communication Studies of the University of Urbino "Carlo Bo." His main research interests are online identity and participatory culture. Recent publications include: "Generational 'We Sense' in the Networked Space in Colombo," in *Broadband Society and Generational Changes Series: Participation in Broadband Society,* edited by Fausto and Fortunati (Peter Lang, 2011).

David Carter is associate professor of History at Auburn University, Alabama. His research interests are in the history of the civil rights movement, post-1945 US history, and race and ideology in the American South since the Civil War. Carter is the author of *The Music Has Gone Out of the Movement: Civil Rights and the Johnson Administration, 1965–1968* (University of North Carolina Press, 2009) and coeditor—with Kent Germany—of *Mississippi Burning and the Passage of the Civil Rights Act: The Presidential Recordings, Lyndon B. Johnson* (Norton, 2011).

Øystein Pedersen Dahlen is associate professor at the Oslo School of Management, where he is also head of the Department of Social Sciences and Communication and in charge of the bachelor degree program in PR and Communications. Recent publications include: "Nyheter i nettaviser: muligheter og begrensninger" [News in online newspapers: Possibilities and limitations] in *Sosiologi i dag* and "Full tilgang og flytende produksjon" [Total access and liquid production] in *Norsk medietidsskrift*. He received the Best Paper Award at the European Public Relation Education and Research Association Conference 2012 with the paper "Communication Managers as Strategists: Are They Making the Grade Yet? A View of How Other Leaders View Communication Managers and Communication in Norwegian Private and Public Sector Organizations," together with Peggy Brønn.

Nicole Doerr is assistant professor of International Relations and Transnational Social Movement Studies at Mount Holyoke College, South Hadley, Massachusetts. Her work concerns translation as a model for democracy in social movements and mainstream deliberation. Doerr has published contributions in the *European Political Science Review, Forum Qualitative Social Research, Mobilization, Social Movement Studies, Feminist Review,* and the *Journal of International Women's Studies.*

Stefan Eichinger studied film and philosophy at the Free University in Berlin and is completing a master's degree in logic at the University of Amsterdam. His research interests include formal semantics of natural language (especially the semantics of conditionals) and the relation between social movements and mass media, notably cinema.

Kathrin Fahlenbrach is professor of Media and Communication Studies at Hamburg University, Germany. One of her main research topics is the interrelation between mass media and protest movements, especially focusing on the level of imagery. She is author of a book on visual protest performances in mass media and collective identities, using the example of the student movement around 1968 (*Protestinszenierungen: Visuelle Kommunikation und kollektive Identitäten in Protestbewegungen,* Westdeutscher Verlag, 2002). Together with Martin Klimke and Joachim Scharloth, she is editor of the book series Protest, Culture, and Society, published by Berghahn Books.

Todd Michael Goehle is a PhD candidate in the Department of History at the State University of New York (SUNY) at Binghamton and he teaches in the department of history at SUNY Geneseo. His research interests include contemporary German history, especially media history, collective memory studies, and theories about violence. He has contributed to the edited volume *1968: Societies in Crisis: A Global Perspective,* Presses de L'Université Laval, 2010) and is finalizing his dissertation, "Visualizing 1968: Media, Memory, and Social Change in West Germany."

Stuart Hilwig[†] was professor of History at Adams State College in Colorado. His research interest was in European history, especially in the history of modern Italy and Germany, as well as in social movements of post-1945 Europe. A major focus of his work was the student movements of the 1960s. Publications include several articles on Italian, German, and European history and his landmark study *Italy and 1968: Youthful Unrest and Democratic Culture* (Palgrave Macmillan, 2009).

Bert Klandermans is professor of Applied Social Psychology at the VU University, Amsterdam. His lifelong research interest concerns participation in social movements. Recent publications include "Embeddedness and Grievances: Collective Action Participation among Immigrants" in *American Sociological Review,* 2008 (with van de Toorn and van Stekelenburg), and *Identity and Participation in Cultural Diverse Societies,* with Azzi, Chryssochoou, and Simon (Blackwell Wiley, 2010).

Naoko Koda is a doctoral student in the Department of History, New York University. Her areas of interest are the twentieth-century US Left, the Cold War, and postwar Japanese history. She is currently working on the transnational networks between US and Japanese New Left movements and the US Cold War foreign policy.

Roy Krøvel is professor in Journalism at Oslo University College in Norway. In his dissertation he studied the relationship between the media and guerrilla organizations and indigenous peoples in Mexico and Central America. He is also a civil engineer specializing in the environment and risk analysis. Outside academia, he has published several books on journalism and conflict.

Alice Mattoni is a research fellow at the Centre for Social Movement Studies (COSMOS) at the European University Institute in Italy. She is also co-convenor of the ECPR standing group "Participation and Mobilization" and coeditor of *Interface: A Journal for and about Social Movements.* Recent publications include: *Mediation and Protest Movements,* coedited with Bart Cammaerts and Patrick McCurdy (Intellect, 2013); and *Media Practices and Protest Politics: How Precarious Workers Mobilise* (Ashgate, 2012).

Antigoni Memou is a lecturer in the history and theory of art at the University of East London. Her research focuses on the interrelation of photography and social movements, and more generally on the cultural aspects of political struggles. She has published in the journals *Third Text, Photographies* and *Philosophy of Photography*. Her book *Photography and Social Movements: From the Globalisation of the Movement (1968) to the Movement Against Globalisation* will be published by Manchester University Press in 2013.

Ralph Negrine is professor of Political Communication, University of Sheffield. Major research interests include the communication of politics, and communications policy. Recent publications include *The Transformation of Political Communication* (Palgrave, 2008) and *European Media* (Polity, 2012; with S. Papathanassopoulos).

Craig J. Peariso is assistant professor of the history of art and visual culture at Boise State University. His work, which deals with the representation of politics and the politics of representation, has been featured in the journal *Third Text,* and in edited volumes including *The Scandal of Susan Sontag* (Columbia University Press, 2009). He is currently completing a book-length study of the performance of stereotypes in late 1960s American protest.

Juliane Riese is associate professor at the Faculty of Business, Languages, and Social Sciences at Østfold University College, Halden, Norway. She volunteered for Greenpeace Nordic in Stockholm for one year after finishing school. She received her PhD in the social sciences from the University of Bremen. Her dissertation, which seeks to contribute to systems theory as founded by Niklas Luhmann, includes a systems-theoretic case study of Greenpeace's antiwhaling campaign in Norway.

Luca Rossi is assistant professor at IT University of Copenhagen. His research interest is focused on internet studies particularly in the field of internet culture, games studies and social network studies. He is currently working on social network analysis methods applied to the online propagation of information and cultural phenomena. Recent articles include: "The Role of Emotional Stability in Twitter Conversations" in *Proceedings of Workshop on Semantic Analysis in Social Media* (Springer, 2012) and "The Open Laboratory: Limits and Possibilities of Using Facebook, Twitter, and YouTube as a Research Data Source" in the *Journal of Technology in Human Services* (Taylor & Francis, 2012).

Dieter Rucht is retired professor of Sociology at the Free University of Berlin. He was codirector of the research group "Civil Society, Citizenship and Political Mobilization in Europe" at the Social Science Research Center Berlin. His research interests include political participation, social movements, political protest, and public discourse. Among his recent books in English are: (coedited with Stefaan Walgrave) *The World Says No to War: Demonstrations against the War on Iraq* (University of Minnesota Press, 2010); and (coedited with Donatella della Porte) *Meeting Democracy: Power and Deliberation in Global Justice Movements* (Cambridge University Press, 2013).

Erling Sivertsen is associate professor at the Faculty of Media and Journalism, Volda University College, Norway. He teaches media studies and photojournalism. Sivertsen is a sociologist who has published several studies on the media and politicians, media and banks, and on photography and mobile communication in journalism. For several years he was member of the editorial board of and editor of *Norsk medietidsskrift* (Norwegian Journal of Media Studies), and member of the Norwegian National Board of Media Studies.

Hendrik Sorstein Spilker is associate professor in Media Sociology at the Institute for Sociology and Political Science, NTNU, Trondheim, Norway. His research interests are the culture and politics of the internet, media development and change, and subculture studies. His major publications are: *Kommunikasjonssamfunnet: Moral, praksis og digital teknologi* [The communication society: Moral, practice and digital technology], edited with Nora Levold (Oslo University Press, 2007). In recent years, he has published several articles on changes in the field of digital music distribution.

Simon Teune works at the Social Science Research Center, Berlin. His research interests are social movements, protest, and culture. As a fellow of the Hans-Böckler-Stiftung he is preparing a PhD dissertation that deals with the choice of action repertoires during the anti-G8 protests in Germany in 2007. He is coeditor of *Nur Clowns und Chaoten?* (Campus, 2008), a book that unpacks the media event of the Heiligendamm protests, and editor of *The Transnational Condition: Protest in an Entangled Europe* (Berghahn Books, 2010).

Baldwin Van Gorp is assistant professor at the Institute for Media Studies at KU Leuven, Belgium, where he teaches journalism and organizational communication. His research interests include the framing approach, news production, and crisis communication. Recent publications include a study on the framing of sustainable agriculture (with Margot van der Goot in *Communication, Culture & Critique*), and studies on the framing of Alzheimer's disease (with Tom Vercruysse in *Social Science & Medicine,* and with Tom Vercruysse and Jan Van den Bulck in *American Journal of Alzheimer's Disease and Other Dementias*).

Rolf Werenskjold is associate professor at the Faculty of Media and Journalism, Volda University College, Norway. He teaches media studies and media history. He is a historian and media scholar who has published several studies on the media and 1968, modern American history and Norwegian foreign news journalism during the Cold War. His dissertation examines protests and the media in 1968. He is currently project leader of a Norwegian and Nordic research network on the Media and the Second Cold War as part of the international project on the Nuclear Crisis: Cold War Cultures and the Politics of Peace and Security, 1975–90.

Index

www.ingramcontent.com/pod-product-compliance
Lightning Source LLC
Chambersburg PA
CBHW060019030426
42334CB00019B/2103